Talent.
Success.

You're about to go on a fascinating journey.
Eighteen in-depth conversations on what it takes
to make it in the challenging, fast-paced world of advertising.
Whether you're in the middle of your career or
in a bit of a muddle, on the outside looking to get in,
you'll find each and every conversation full of
good advice, amazing examples, and practical lessons
on how to be truly exceptional.

Norm Grey of the Creative Circus added this observation...

I couldn't help but notice how these famous, talented, successful people are willing to reveal their failures, which they accepted as great lessons for their success.

Bottom line: most creative people in advertising are among the nicest, most generous people in the world. They're not afraid to share.

It starts with Laurence Minsky. And it includes everyone he interviewed for this terrific "nonfiction novel." Each chapter reads like one.

Whether you're a beginner or a pro, these life stories are easy to read—and hard to put down.

— Norm Grey, Founder & Creative Director, Creative Circus

SECOND EDITION : COMPLETELY REVISED AND EXPANDED

HOW TO
SUCCEED
IN
ADVERTISING
WHEN ALL YOU HAVE IS TALENT

BEST
—of—
SHOW

Foreword by MAXINE PAETRO
Introduction by LUKE SULLIVAN

BY LAURENCE MINSKY

HOW TO SUCCEED IN ADVERTISING
WHEN ALL YOU HAVE IS TALENT
2ND EDITION

by Laurence Minsky

©2007 THE COPY WORKSHOP

ISBN-13: 978-1-887229-20-3 (paper)
ISBN-10: 1-887229-20-5 (paper)

ISBN-13: 978-1-887229-31-9 (cloth)
ISBN-10: 1-887229-31-0 (cloth)

Cover Design: Mark Ingraham

THE COPY WORKSHOP
2144 N. Hudson • Chicago, IL 60614
V: 773.871.1179 • F: 773.281.4643
www.adbuzz.com • thecopyworkshop@aol.com

For Rhonda and Jorie

Contents

BUILDING A BOOK BASED ON BERNBACH & BEYOND

CREATING BETTER WORK—SOME INITIAL STRATEGIES

FOREVER MORE: STRATEGIES TO KEEP YOUR CAREER GOING… AND GOING… AND GOING

Foreword
By Maxine Paetro

WHEN I WROTE *How to Put Your Book Together and Get a Job in Advertising*, sometime during the previous century, I ended my book with a section called "A Little Help from Some Friends."

It contained good advice from some of the top creative people in advertising. And each of those people added a useful dimension to the basic principles in *How to Put Your Book Together*.

When I read *How to Succeed* it felt to me as though Laurence Minsky had continued the work my friends and I had started. He's brought together words and wisdom from more top creative talents, and expanded these profiles with examples of their classic, award-winning advertising.

Right now, you hold in your hands the experience and good advice of some truly remarkable and creative people.

I know some of them personally, and it was good to spend time with them again. Of those I haven't met, I now feel that I've come to know them a little bit as well, and I appreciate why they have had great success in this exciting but difficult business.

Most important, from your perspective, you get to know them all.

You get to read how they did it. You get to see some examples of the ads that helped them break through, and read the stories behind the ads. And, when you're done, maybe you will have found a few more role models for your own career.

In case after case, you'll find that the talented professionals you'll meet in this book learned from someone else who helped them get to that next level.

Because if there's one piece of good advice that this book represents it's this—work with good people and learn as much from them as you can.

I had such an experience myself.

When I was the creative department manager of several top agencies, the part of my job that I found most rewarding was hiring creative talent.

Among the 25,000 copywriters, art directors, and television producers I interviewed, was a talented young man with a junior copywriter portfolio that I critiqued.

Over the course of time, this junior writer became the Worldwide Creative Director of J. Walter Thompson, a huge advertising agency that was winning awards for Kodak, Burger King, Ford, and other first-class clients.

His name was James Patterson.

In addition to supervising two hundred creative people and writing much of Thompson's award-winning work, Jim Patterson wrote killer-thrillers in his spare time and developed an adrenalin-charged style that really connected with the reading public. His novels rocketed to the top of the best sellers lists every time.

Years passed. I had written a few novels and had left advertising to write full time. One day, I called Jim Patterson and asked if I could use an office at Thompson. I told him that I missed the advertising business, particularly the camaraderie. "I feel a little isolated in my cold apartment with my computer and my cat," I said.

Without hesitation, Jim said, "Come on over. Bring your cat." So, for five years in the mid-1990s I went to work at JWT where I wrote magazine adventure stories, a biography of a rock 'n' roll star, and I helped JWT recruit creative talent at the same time.

And, Jim Patterson, a guy whose junior portfolio I'd once critiqued, began critiquing my writing and became not only a good friend, but a source of encouragement and good advice. He taught me how to take a good story and turn it into one the reader can't put down.

Then, one day, Jim invited me to help him with one of his books. And then another—and last year, a novel I co-wrote with James Patterson was #1 on the *New York Times* best seller list!

What better proof could I give you that it's good to work with and learn from talented people?

Laurence Minsky has produced a treasure trove for you in *How to Succeed in Advertising When All You Have Is Talent*. It's full of great stories and smart advice from exceptional creative people.

Take their advice to heart. And use these lessons on your own road to success— wherever that may lead you. And when you do get your first job, learn from everyone, because the people you work with will all know more about the real world of advertising than you do.

I've made lifelong friends, had enriching experiences, and an altogether rewarding career in advertising.

I wish the same good luck to all of you.

—Maxine Paetro
How to Put Your Book Together and Get a Job in Advertising
New York, NY

Introduction

By Luke Sullivan

THERE WAS A TIME when every commercial and every advertisement in America was corny, boring, horrible, and sad—the 1950s.

Actually, come to think of it, during the '50s everything was corny, boring, horrible, and sad.

Anacin cured headaches "Fast! Fast! Fast!" Pepsi was "Ever so smart. So Debonair." And Chevrolet, with a straight face, ran an ad headlined "The sweet, smooth, and sassy '57 Chevrolet likes to flex those big new muscles!"

Advertising may have been a new industry growing up right alongside television, but it was up to the task of filling those first 5-inch black-and-white screens with the most banal clutter imaginable.

In fact, the more grating, offensive, and pedestrian an idea was, the more certain the "ad men" seemed of its effectiveness. They could even "prove it."

Because these people had charts, overhead projectors, and everything.

It was as if all the agencies were run by purse-lipped nuns from some Catholic school. But instead of whacking students with rulers, these Madison Avenue school marms whacked creatives with rolled-up research reports like Burke scores, Starch readership numbers, and a whole bunch of other useless right-brain crap.

Humorless, number crunchers they were, and cynical, too. Cynical because from the looks of their work, they didn't believe in the intelligence of the average person and they held no hope that things could be any better, smarter, prettier, or cooler than they were.

The people making the ads were simply ex-research people who'd traded in their clipboards for storyboards and began making commercials that worked mostly because they paid to air the damned things over and over.

Then a guy named William Bernbach opened an agency, did an ad which didn't suck and, lo and behold, it made the client some money.

The entire industry looked up from its Burke results and Starch scores and went, "What?!? We don't *have* to suck?!?"

Nobody could believe it. The men in gray flannel suits had always said that showing two moms in a kitchen was smart.

And now this Bernbach fella was saying, no, being smart is smart. Being interesting is smart.

Treating people like they're intelligent is smart.

It was indeed a revolution.

But Bill didn't do it all himself. He was the trailblazer, yes, but even he feared losing the battle to the calculator-bearers; and he did, occasionally.

But just when it seemed the suits were going to win the war, Bernbach's flag was picked up by new waves of true believers—true believers like the people in this book.

People who continued to believe, as Bernbach did, that customers aren't idiots, that ads aren't lectures, and that money can be made by saying something relevant in a distinctive and memorable way.

In this updated and thoroughly revised edition, these true believers speak their minds on a wide variety of topics.

You'll see some of their work and hear the thinking that went on behind it.

The voices are strong ones, and disparate, too; advertising is full of bright minds solving problems from about a million divergent directions.

This is good strong stuff.

And if you're considering joining the ranks of advertising, I urge you to spend some time reading their words.

Remember, these are people who've done a lot of spade work on your behalf, fighting the good fight.

Before they got here, all that was on TV was Whipple squeezing toilet paper, Madge with her fingers "soaking in it," and "Don't hate me because I'm beautiful."

Oh, do we owe them.

—Luke Sullivan
GSD&M, Austin, TX
Author: *Hey, Whipple, Squeeze This!* (AdWeek Books)

Preface: My Take on My Book

WELCOME TO THE SECOND EDITION of *How to Succeed in Advertising When All You Have Is Talent*. If you're familiar with the first edition, you will find that all of the chapters have been updated and expanded, and you will find new chapters.

If you're new to *How to Succeed in Advertising When All You Have Is Talent*, you will find what I believe is the first virtual hyper-textual book on advertising.

You can read it in any order and still get something out of it.

I also have to warn you that you'll find that some advice in this book contradicts other advice. Also very "post-postmodern." My hope is that you pick and choose among the suggestions, strategies, stories, and comments, and find those that are right for you. And, feel free to combine ideas and change them to fit your unique situation. The point of this book is to give you ideas on how you can create your own path, not to teach you to follow the step-by-step paths to success taken by these individuals.

With that in mind, I hope that you're inspired by the stories of these exceptional individuals and their work. The goal for this book is to focus on the creative leaders and learn from their work, their advice, and their stories.

There's very little about me in this book (a change from most books on advertising, I guess). But if it helps, I will give you a bit of history. When Emily Calvo and I wrote the first edition in 1994, we were both struggling to develop our own portfolios. We'd read most of the then-current books on advertising and felt that they were too prescriptive. They gave formulas for the number and type of ads, made it seem like everyone was in agreement of what characterized a good ad, and did not capture the competitiveness of the industry and the need to continually reinvent it. We felt that by learning about the formative years of the top people in the field, we'd gain some career strategies and insights into creating better portfolios and finding a faster road to success.

Leading up to this point, both of us had made every possible mistake. We had created reams of meaningless pun ads and shown tons of business-to-business work that had been published, but was really pretty ordinary. The big reason for this was that neither of us had started our careers with strong mentors in the creative field.

Then, as part of my early job search, I had a chance to meet Joel Hochberg, who was then president of DDB Needham/Chicago. The highlight of that interview was not the critique of my portfolio. Hochberg graciously avoided that. Instead, he talked about his early days writing catalog copy for Spiegel and how hard it was for him to throw everything away to create a spec portfolio that would get him a job in an ad agency.

Since my portfolio was mostly filled with ads targeted to elementary educators—valid, but inappropriate—I was inspired by Hochberg's story and wanted to find out more about what the creative leaders of the day had discovered, how they overcame their struggles, what they sought in a spec book, and what they included in their beginning portfolios. I knew that other beginners and people early in their ad careers would benefit from this information. Since no book like that existed, I decided to write it.

Wanting to produce the book, I again postponed creating my spec portfolio and took a job at a small outpost of a large trade show promoter. Admittedly, it wasn't what I wanted to do, but at least it gave me the opportunity to string words together. Sometimes the punctuation even fell in the right places.

Meanwhile, Emily was on the fence about the direction in which to take her career. She had spent more than a year working in a design firm as an account executive and marketing director. But she didn't realize how important it was for her to express herself creatively until she began to have opportunities to develop communications materials, and then she decided to pursue copywriting.

When I told Emily about my idea—in addition to my full-time work, I had landed a small freelance copywriting assignment at the design firm where she was working—we kicked around these issues, put together a proposal for this book, and won a contract.

Around that time I also met Phil Gayter, then a creative director at Leo Burnett, and finally had an opportunity to gather some guidance and feedback on my work—as well as get the reassurance I needed that perhaps I did have something to offer the ad industry. Coupled with ideas I gained from the initial stages of researching the first edition, I put together a book of sample ads that helped me find a job at a consumer-oriented agency. And, since then, I have returned to the book for advice and inspiration, helping me build a career that enabled me to work with such top brands as Frito-Lay, McDonald's, Motorola, and United Airlines.

Emily, meanwhile, also built her career. Today she provides design, art direction, and copywriting services to a number of healthcare institutions and consumer-oriented firms.

While the first edition was written for aspiring copywriters and art directors, I discovered that people from all levels of the industry read the book. When I started on this updated and completely revised edition—Emily had decided not to work on this one—I kept this expanded audience in mind and decided to keep the original 13 copywriters and art directors from the first edition and then include an additional five ad leaders.

Perhaps driven by my desire to continue to develop my career in the industry and my dilemma of where to take the next steps, I wanted to better capture the career arc of the original 13 and complete their professional stories; I wanted to see where they took their careers, if their advice had changed—it remained pretty constant—and if they had any new thoughts to share (the answer is yes). While some of the 13 have retired, two have died, and the rest are continuing to produce great work, all of those still with us have provided additional insights, advice, and inspiration. And with this expanded line up, you can now compare the perspectives of some of the key creative leaders from the 1960s, '70s, '80s, '90s, and today.

With this in mind, I recognize that advertising is a quickly changing field. Ideas and strategies that succeeded in the past may never work again. Yet these same ideas and strategies may help lead to a new solution somewhere in the future. I know that they have helped shape my outlook on my creative work and my career.

And, while you will encounter a wide range of ideas in my book, I want to leave you with three consistent, important themes from it. They are ideas that all of the 18 creative leaders seemed to have followed:

1) **Remember to keep your portfolio fresh:** This is especially important when returning to an agency for a second or third interview. Even if a spec ad is new and truly great, because it has been seen before, it won't seem fresh the second time around.

2) **Keep working:** It is important to remember that you're never done. There's no perfect job, client, boss, or product. So you must keep working on your portfolio even after you have a position. You never know when you'll need to show it again.

3) **Pay attention to your gut:** After reading this book, you might be feeling confused at the often conflicting advice these ad legends offer. Good. You're right where you need to be to plot your next move. Just take directions from those feelings.

I also want you to do one more thing when you read this book. Please sit back, relax, and enjoy. Advertising is an exhilarating profession. I truly hope my book captures that excitement.

—Laurence Minsky

THE BASIC INGREDIENTS OF SUCCESS

Alex Bogusky

"I was not considered a very artistic child by my family."

Both of Alex's parents were graphic designers. "It's the family business. It's what we Boguskys do." His father ran a twenty-employee design studio called Brothers Bogusky in Miami. And, his mother was an art director for a variety of trade magazines. He grew up with copies of *CA* on the coffee table. This background helped Alex and his partners create one of the nation's hottest ad agencies, Crispin Porter + Bogusky (CP+B).

During the last few years, they have developed breakthrough campaigns for Burger King, Ikea, American Legacy (Truth), the Mini, and others. They're recognized for their record of innovation and for producing integrated, nontraditional solutions. While many agencies speak about the importance of going beyond the traditional media options of TV, radio, outdoor, magazines, and newspapers, CP+B practices what they preach.

Because of its work, CP+B has won virtually every major industry award and was named Agency of the Year by *Creativity* in 2000, 2002, and again in 2004. (The runner up in 2004 was Fallon, the significance of which will become apparent later in this chapter.)

While Crispin Advertising has roots that go back to the early '60s, it wasn't until the late 1990s that Chuck Porter and Bogusky joined the agency and turned it into a "hot" agency with a national reputation. "I'm one of the oldest guys here," says Bogusky, now in his early forties.

"For me, a lot of this business has been luck," he says "I've been fortunate to be around good people, get in the right position, and do the kind of work that I really love to do."

THE FREELANCE ATTITUDE THAT HELPED BUILD A BIG-TIME AGENCY

As people working in artistic professions, Alex's parents were considered "hippie" types and had a skewed point of view. During Christmas, for instance, Bogusky's parents used to get a bush to plant and decorate as the family Christmas tree. "Their attitude was that a tree is a tree," he says.

Then, one day at school, his class was asked to draw Christmas trees and put them on the blackboard. "I looked down the line," he says, "and they were all triangles. Mine was round. All of the kids laughed. It was traumatic. I came home choking back the tears and asked, 'Mom, can we have a pointy Christmas tree this year?' I believed my parents that not all Christmas trees were pointy. They told me that. But I thought, 'Let me just get the pointy one this year.' They liked that kind of skewed point of view." Bogusky now believes that this skewed viewpoint is helpful for people who work in any kind of creative endeavor.

His parents also approached design and art direction from a trade perspective—that it's more of a craft than a profession—and trained him in the production of "mechanicals." "My mom taught it to me as a fallback. She told me that if I knew how to do them, I'd always have a job."

"That's when I decided to quit school."

But Bogusky's real career goal was to become a professional motocross racer. And he started attending community college. But when he needed money, he became a freelance designer. "It was what I fell back on," he says. This put him at odds with the instructor of a graphics course he was taking. "The assignment was to create a brochure. I asked if I could use the same brochure that I was working on as a freelancer and I was told no. I thought, 'Well, I can make money at this and actually do it or I can pay somebody else.' That was when I decided to quit school."

After he dropped out, he continued as a freelance illustrator and mechanical production artist. And he set out to achieve his new goal: to become a professional windsurfer.

"I went to Hawaii," he recalls. "I called my dad and said, 'Send all my stuff.' He wanted me to come back." His father made some calls to help him find a job. When he returned to Miami, he got an interview at an agency called Ryder and Schield.

At this point, he had more of a designer and illustrator portfolio. In the interview, he was asked, "Do you want to be an art director or a designer?" He answered, "Yes." "I didn't understand the distinction," he says. "There never was a distinction in my family."

Bogusky was offered a job and was told that the agency had just gotten a new jewelry store account. "Dick Schield, my boss-to-be said, 'When you show up, we'll start working on that.' I spent the whole weekend sketching jewelry layouts and concepting jewelry ads. When I got there, it was like, 'Here's the key to the stat room.' I kind of slid my pad under some things on the desk."

Bogusky spent all day in the stat room. Working in a position that no longer exists, other employees would slide the job under the door of the darkened room, and he'd make stats. "I remember my first goal," he says. "I sat between two other mechanical artists. People would come in all day and ask them what they thought of this or that. No one ever asked me what I thought of anything. That became my first goal in advertising: To have someone ask my opinion."

Did he have them? "Sure, I was cocky," he says. "But I wasn't turning my head to look. I was trying to do my thing."

"Wow, advertising can be that!"

While working in the stat room, he realized that he was more interested in art direction than design. "With advertising, I realized that feedback would be so quick and clear, as to the job I was doing. I loved that."

Two campaigns cemented his interest: Wieden+Kennedy's Honda Scooter campaign featuring Lou Reed and a Pizza Hut campaign from Chiat/Day. "Before I was in the business, I didn't think much about advertising," he says. "But when I saw these campaigns, I thought, 'Wow, advertising can be that!' They helped me realize that advertising could be interesting. At the time, they were extremely unusual."

His reaction, however, comes with an observation that shows how quickly advertising wears out: "When I look at them today, they don't feel unusual."

He also paid attention to the work coming out of Fallon McElligott Rice (see chapters 6 and 13), who were then exploding on the scene with low-budget and simply designed print. "It was a charge, because budgets always seemed like a problem," he says. "They blew that away. Everybody was trying to emulate them. I thought, 'Gosh, here are some people who aren't in New York, L.A., or another big city and look at the stuff they're doing.' It was so good."

Bogusky was hooked. "I just have an addictive personality," he says. "What I find myself into, I get way into."

"There's always too much to do in advertising."

So what got him out of the stat room? He acted on a truism of advertising: "There's always too much to do in advertising," he says. "If you're willing to do anything that somebody asks, you're going to wind up getting opportunities. And if you don't mess up, they'll give you more. That basically was my process. People would pawn off stuff on me, and I'd do the best I could. Pretty soon, I became art director."

At the time, Ryder and Schield was considered a good but small south Florida agency. He worked on Mayer's Jewelers and Admiral Cruise Lines, among others, as an art director. "I don't think I did anything very good at all," he says, noting that he worked at this agency at the end of its era. "Dick Schield was starting to get out of the business," says Bogusky. "He was working on his retirement home." Bogusky helped design it.

But Bogusky also considers Schield one of his mentors. "My father, Bill Bogusky, was also a big influence," he says. "When I think of them, the two go hand in hand, my father and Dick. They were friends and, for a long time, they worked together. I'm sure Dick just did my dad a favor to hire me. But he did hire me."

Hundreds and Hundreds of Layouts

Bogusky remembers that Dick Shield did all of his thinking on paper. "My dad does most of his thinking in his head," says Bogusky, "and then he throws something down, 95 percent complete. But Dick would make you do all your thinking on paper too. So I did hundreds and hundreds of layouts for an ad. This is before computers and I had to draw them over and over and over. This forced me to see the differences and learn how to control those differences. I also learned the importance of 'hierarchy'—that you want people to look at things in your communication in a certain order—and if you don't pay attention to the steps, you may lay out ads counter to that order."

The Importance of Finding the Right Partner

After about two years as an art director at Ryder and Shield, Bogusky started trying to create more "conceptual work." "I'd spend the weekends doing ads for things we were pitching. I'd bring them in, and these guys would explain what was wrong with them," he says. "At first, I thought, 'I'll never be smart enough to do advertising.' Everything they said was very convincing." But then he ran into a longtime Miami-based freelancer named Chuck Porter, and he showed him some of the ads that he'd been doing. Porter, who had an extensive list of creative awards to his name, thought they were great.

Around this time, Bogusky also went to his first advertising seminar. "I asked my boss if I could go to it, and he said, 'Yeah.' I then asked if he could pay for it, and he said, 'Never be afraid to invest in yourself,' a very nice way of saying no, but still good advice. I decided to pay for it myself."

At this seminar, they were talking about the end of print. "I don't know why there's a self-loathing in the industry, but ever since I've been in advertising, practitioners have been predicting its demise," he says. "It wasn't the Internet or computers or anything. It was video magazines. The concept was that you would watch videotapes instead of read magazines. That was the big thing. Do you even remember video magazines? I was like, 'I really need to learn about video. There's not going to be print.' All I knew was print."

But this inspired Bogusky to expand his horizons. "All of the reasons I do things are stupid," he says. "But I have learned from making dumb decisions for dumb reasons that while decisions are the things we agonize over—they're always such split seconds in our lives—it's what you do in the time in between those decisions that really matters." He decided to leave Ryder and Schield.

Another speech at the seminar gave him the confidence to stay in the industry. "There were all these agency people presenting their work, and each person was more dramatic about the fact that they were tough with clients," he says. "It was like, 'If the client doesn't buy it, we fire them.' The next guy came up, showed his work, and said, 'Not only that, but we changed their logo. And if they didn't buy that, we'd fire them.' I was just into this business and thinking that I did not have the intestinal fortitude to do what these people said they did. I couldn't see myself arguing with people that much."

Earlier in the morning, Bogusky saw a tall man in the lobby wearing flip-flops and shorts. "He looked like an old-school surfer. That was my thing too," says Bogusky. "I like to surf. I'm just watching this guy all day in the morning. Then during the speeches, they call Lee Clow. Although I had heard the name, I'd never seen a picture of him. And that guy walks up. I thought, how cool is that? Here he is, obviously a legend, but embodying the things that matter to me. He didn't lose himself in it all."

Clow went on to say that Chiat/Day probably had more good work in the trash can than most agencies do all year—that they just do more work until the client buys something or gets sick of seeing them and fires them. Says Bogusky, "That was such a big deal to me, because I remember thinking, 'I could do that. I could work my ass off.' Before this speech, I was convinced that I was going to have to get out of the business because I could not fire a client. I either thank him or blame him for the fact that I'm still in it." (Ironically, while Bogusky has now had a chance to meet most of the industry icons, he has not yet met Clow face to face.)

Bogusky & Son

After resigning from Ryder and Schield, Bogusky went into a freelance business with his father, and Porter became their freelance writer. "Freelance was agonizing for me," says Bogusky. "As a freelancer, you're either unbelievably busy or there's nothing going on. I could never enjoy the part when nothing was going on. I didn't believe there would be another job, ever. It was miserable. When I was in it,

I was always trying to get away from freelance. But Chuck really liked that lifestyle. As a freelancer, with a very small nut to cover, you don't suffer fools."

Crispin + Porter

Then Chuck Porter, at the ripe old age of 45, took a job as creative director of Crispin Advertising, an agency that had been around since the sixties.

The owner, Sam Crispin, was retiring and Crispin's son became president. The new leader wanted to enhance the creative reputation of the agency by bringing in Porter, and it was renamed Crispin & Porter. At the time, it was considered to be the third-best agency in Miami.

Bogusky continued to freelance. "But I wanted to get back into an agency because of the end of print that was about to happen," he says. "I thought that, as a designer, I'm really going to be screwed."

Staying in touch with Porter, he joined Crispin about nine months later. "When I went from being an owner of a freelance agency to staff over here, I really liked the idea," says Bogusky. "I'm a bit of a worrier. But we have such a good team—and I now have such great partners—I believe in them. With freelance, you can only believe in yourself."

+ Bogusky

Over time, Bogusky became a partner, and then Porter and Bogusky bought out Crispin. "Sam still keeps an office here," says Bogusky. "He's not involved financially, but it's nice to have that link."

Early in his career, there was another link that intrigued Bogusky: Porter had gone to high school with Pat Fallon. "I don't think that they both decided to go into advertising in high school, but they both wound up in it," he says. "Since he knew Fallon, and Fallon was like the Holy Grail, Chuck was a bit of a rock star in my mind. While he never worked with them as a freelancer, he was able to say, 'I was just over at Fallon's.' The very early naïve notion of the agency was 'Let's do what Fallon did.' That was the mission. But wanting to be Fallon was not the kind of thing we brought up. It felt embarrassing."

This changed when they hired Jeff Hicks to run business development. "He's as into the work as any creative person," says Bogusky. "He helped us realize that unless the people in the agency who make thousands of little decisions every day base those decisions on some mission, we're not going to achieve the things we want to achieve."

+ a Mission Statement

The team crafted a mission statement declaring their goal of becoming one of the most creative agencies in the country and then shared it with the rest of the agency. "I said that maybe people are going to laugh, but I'm going to risk it, because it wouldn't happen unless we told them and everyone worked toward the same goal."

+ a Strategy

Then, once they crafted their mission, they outlined a strategy to achieve it, deciding to be a small national agency known for good work. They believed this was key because small and large *national* accounts have the same issues, while *local* accounts have different issues. "For years and years, we did really great local work, but it wasn't creating interest beyond Miami," he says. "We decided to get out of this market, develop a national base, and then get bigger national accounts. Our criteria was almost, 'If you're not in Miami, you're more interesting to us.' The strategy worked, and we wound up with small clients all over the country. The nice thing is that we were able to work in more interesting categories."

How do they decide who to pitch? "One of the partners has to be passionate about it. It could be for anything, except money," he says. "You could be passionate about it because you love the client or because you like the color of their logo." They also check to see if what they do can help them. "The answer is not always yes. Sometimes what they truly need may be different from what we do. If we're not the right thing for them, that's not going to be a good situation. And then there's the chemistry."

"Production is like Pavlov's bell."

Today, he usually works on his own and if he has any ideas, he offers them to a team to see if they want them. "I believe a creative director should never compete against others in the agency," he says. "I'm usually most involved in the very early stages of a campaign, trying to position the client. I don't write a lot of headlines once we have an account. Not for any other reason than it's established and people know where to go."

How does he maintain creative standards? "Production is like Pavlov's bell," he says. "As a creative director, you have to be careful about the level you ring that bell. No matter how much you might preach the importance of doing good work, it doesn't matter if you put average work into production. Creatives look at the level of the work going into production and shoot for that. They don't do it consciously. It just happens."

Bogusky believes every creative director's job is to keep raising the bar. "It doesn't go anywhere," he says, "but pushing on it at least keeps it from falling down."

And, even though CP+B has been winning buckets of awards as of late, he downplays their importance. "Awards are more important for recruiting and keeping people happy," he says. "Creatives like to win them and they like to go to shows." But he believes that they don't help CP+B build new business.

Outside of work, he bikes, skis, and snowboards. "I've taken up motocross again," he says. "I have a lake house. I've got a boat there, a wakeboard. I'm kind of a toy junky." But, as a husband and father, his success comes with a price: the loss of free time. "Your work is your baby. You steal from it to give to your family. And you steal from your family to give to work. So you're always stealing from something. And you just don't do anything for yourself. If you want to work out, forget it. That's gone."

CP+B PROOF POINTS: SELECTIONS FROM THEIR PORTFOLIO

—— COMPASS BANK ——

People don't like banks, says Bogusky, "so we try to separate ourselves from the category." To help, CP+B focuses on creating what they call "proof points." "It's proving who you are instead of saying who you are," he says. "Rather than saying we're cool, just do something cool."

Bogusky believes that good advertising does that too.

"One of my favorite things is that we took the chains off the pens," he says. Instead of having pens chained to the counter, the bank now has a cup of pens and a sign that says, "We took the chain off the pens, because we're not like other banks. We trust you." The sign also indicates that since they value the customer's business, go ahead and take a pen if you need one. The pen then becomes a promotional piece. "It is such a silly thing that banks do. But we took what really pisses off customers, tweaked it a little, and it became marketing," he says. "We're continuing to look for things like that."

It's sick. It's wrong. It's sick and wrong. Especially when it's your money. But switch to Compass, and you can forget about paying ATM fees. Forever. We'll even reimburse you for the ATM charges all those other banks hit you with. Well...O.K.

Compass Bank

Compass Bank also offers free ATM usage, not only for their machines, but also for other sites. "Why it's free was what we worked on," he says. "It's free because while other banks still charge, we pay those fees. The idea that we're paying the charges when other banks hit you with fees was much more motivating than just saying free. It makes you feel like they're on your side. That's a great proof point in adverting."

—— Truth ——

This campaign represented a turning point in CP+B's billings—and creative approach. "When Florida went into review with this anti-tobacco campaign, we looked at it and we debated if we should throw our hat in the ring," says Bogusky. "Having a free-spirited, freelance mentality, we were afraid of doing government work. But we decided the issue was important, and we thought we could do a good job on it."

But CP+B was surprised that they kept making it through each cut—and they went into a panic when they realized what they were up against. "If we were the tobacco companies, we'd settle too," says Bogusky. "Any money spent on telling kids not to do something is going to result in the opposite. If we did this in a traditional PSA form, it was going to backfire. Ineffective seemed best, and actually backfiring seemed more likely."

Out of that panic grew the strategy for Truth: Use the natural teenage rebellion that's creating the desire for tobacco and turn it against tobacco companies. "If you want to rebel, smoking tobacco is an effective way," says Bogusky. "If we were going to take away that channel of rebellion, we'd have to replace it with something else."

CP+B struggled to find a solution. "At first, it felt impossible because we were thinking in traditional commercial terms." Then they hit on an answer: the first Florida spots featured kids making phone calls to the tobacco industry. "It was like a Jerky Boys or Michael Moore kind of thing," says Bogusky. "After we did the phone calls, it was easy to do body bags. And it became easier to do some of the other campaigns."

The spots became very popular. "Kids in Florida could recite the entire spot. Within a year, it became the most effective youth campaign against tobacco. The numbers went down 50 percent in middle schools and 20-some percent in high schools." Today, CP+B shares the national Truth campaign with Arnold Worldwide.

In addition, the Truth campaign has influenced CP+B's thinking on their other work. "We had to change behavior with this campaign, and to change behavior, we had to tweak the youth culture," says Bogusky. "When we now come to a problem, we rarely say to our clients, 'Here's what the world wants, and here's how you need to change to be that.' Now we work to figure out what we need to tweak in the world or culture so that it works better for our client. We wouldn't look at things that way if it weren't for Truth, because, in general, people don't believe that they can change culture, especially with an advertising budget. But we found that if the seeds are there and the right catalyst, culture wants to change. That's a lot of what our advertising has become over the last few years."

—— IKEA ——

The insight behind CP+B's work for Ikea, an account they resigned in 2004, was that, on average, Americans have more spouses in a lifetime than they have dining room tables or coffee tables. "Almost everything else has become a fashion category—phones, televisions, cars, stereos," he says. "Something as expensive as a car is a fashion category because leasing enables you to make short-term decisions about it."

Bogusky believes that the U.S. does not treat furniture as a fashion category. "The American furniture buying culture says, 'Till death do us part. I'm going to get this thing and I'm going to have it forever.' Because of that kind of hard goods mentality, we tend to be more conservative and go toward reproductions of older styles. You don't see a lot of Americans looking at contemporary furnishings because it's too risky."

Ikea's Swedish design furnishings, however, are typically more modern and cleaner. "They have some traditional things, but if you look at their range, it's a little more progressive," he says. "And while their furniture is beautiful and well-made, it's probably not going to last two hundred years or even a hundred years."

Like Truth, this campaign was about working to change the culture to better fit a product rather than changing the product to fit the culture. "When we look at how and what we buy, it seems right," he says. "Other cultures, like in the Bahamas, refresh their furniture once a year. It's a seasonal thing. They'll go through their homes and change all the colors of the pillows or get rid of a couch and get a new one. The first time you hear that, you may think it's ridiculous. But why? Because we've become so accepting of our way that we think it's the only right way?"

For Ikea, CP+B presented the idea that furniture is fashion. "People will buy a pair of $110 shoes without blinking an eye, knowing that they won't last long. But the decision to buy a $9 lamp is much tougher. Buy the lamp and, when you don't like it anymore, give it to somebody else or Good Will and move it along the circle of life. Our job was to give Americans permission to think that way about furnishings."

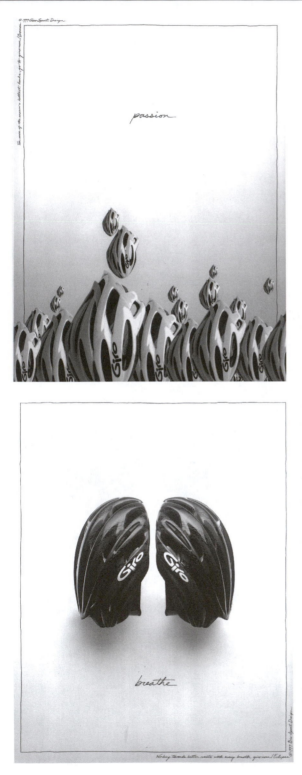

passion

breathe

——— GIRO ———

How do you sell something when its positioning is unacceptable to its target audience? That's the challenge CP+B faces with Giro. "We do these ads every year," says Bogusky; "They're really hard because, basically, Giro is about design. These helmets look better than any other. But we're selling to mountain bikers who, if you ever uttered the word, they would be disgusted. Mountain biking is a tough sport. So you can't mention design. But if that's our position, let's stick to it and figure out ways to say design without ever saying it."

——— Checkers ———

Long before CP+B landed Burger King and invented the Subservient Chicken and had office workers arguing over "have it your way," they had Checkers/Rally as a client. The campaign they developed for this drive-thru chain demonstrates their innovative thinking.

"McDonald's and Burger King, with their toys, rule the really young kid segment. And they rule their parents as well," says Bogusky. "We found that the real opportunity was to break people off at about 12 years old when they're starting to wonder whether they should be getting a Happy Meal or Kids Meal. They start to question McDonald's, because it's so ingrained with being a kid. The notion of the campaign was to go in with something much cooler and very honest. A lot of young people said, 'It's just to keep you going. I use it like fuel.' We thought that was a usable idea—human fuel."

CP+B settled on the Japanese animation style because they found it was popular with the target group. "The whole car vibe came from the fact that Checkers/Rallys are actually double drive thrus," he says. "They're more connected to car culture than McDonald's or Burger King." CP+B developed everything from TV spots to outdoor and bag graphics.

Most of CP+B's ideas for Checkers/Rally never got produced. "We invented a straw that was twice as long as a regular one," says Bogusky. "You could keep your drink in your lap and sip from it without taking your hands off the wheel. We also created special dash-mounted ketchup dispensers." What happened? A new CEO at the client was hired about two months after the campaign launched and he hated it. "He wanted the heroine to get married, have kids, and drive a minivan, which I think would have ruined it."

—— GT BICYCLES ——

This is an example of a campaign where CP+B spent more time focusing on figuring out the "hierarchy" of the communication. "Sometimes it's obvious," says Bogusky: "An ad may have a tagline style headline, a caption style headline, or more of a traditional headline. With this campaign, we weren't sure where the line should go. I have some explorations where the line is big across the top."

Bogusky believes that many art directors don't understand the concept of hierarchy. "The training just isn't really there," he says. "Ad schools are not graphic design schools. You may get a certain amount of graphic design training, but you could certainly go all the way through most ad schools and never have anyone talk to you about hierarchy. The new teaching is all about concepts. The old teaching was about typography, hierarchy, and layout. You need a balance. So when people get here, hierarchy is something that comes up pretty quickly. They might have something, and I'd be like, 'This is completely wrong, because you definitely don't want people to read this before they see that, do you?' This training doesn't take long if they're smart."

——— Mini ———

The Mini is an icon in Europe. In launching the car in America, CP+B's planners worked to identify the audience who would be interested in the car—the smallest-sized car in America—and then talked to those people. "We found that they were people who are a little more forward thinking, a little more aggressive with their lives, and more concerned with design," he says. "These people felt that they could determine what they liked and that they didn't need to look to the rest of the world to tell them what to like."

CP+B then set out to define the experience of driving the car. "We knew that it was going to be different than driving in general and made up all these rules about it. We thought that a book was a better way than TV to distribute these rules, and it served as the foundation of the launch."

The description of the experience also helped them develop the "motoring" theme. "We originally called it 'going.' That was terrible because it sounded like you're using the restroom. And nearly every car company has got 'drive' in their tag line: 'the Ultimate Driving Machine,' 'What to Drive,' 'Drivers Wanted.' But we eventually realized that there is an archaic term for driving—motoring—and liked the notion. And we liked it even more as just 'motor.' It sounds backwards, but that was the last part of the campaign."

Here's another example of the use of "proof points." In creating the campaign, CP+B wrote a television spot where viewers see a guy drive along and a voiceover announces, "You want to get away from it all." The imagery and voiceover style make it seem like it is a spot for an SUV. We see the guy through the window of the unidentified vehicle when he stops and goes into reverse. We realize that he's in a Mini and he's backing it off the racks of his SUV. He then tears down a twisting road in the Mini. The message: SUVs aren't really fun to drive on the road. Everything that's fun—such as bikes, skis, or snowboards—is put on the roof of an SUV.

"We thought that it was a cool script," says Bogusky, "but it's much cooler to go do it. Advertisers and advertising tend to say things, but rarely prove things. We try to use the media to add proof to what we're saying. Being untraditional is part of the Mini brand. If we did a spot saying, 'We're the untraditional automotive choice,' it would not be very convincing. But if we do something that other car companies aren't doing, we are adding proof that we're untraditional."

The Mini launch was one of the most integrated campaigns ever. "One of the things that we do is go for stuff that's none of our business," says Bogusky. "For instance, we asked for a lease that doesn't penalize you for driving too many miles, because that's very anti-motoring. Motoring is about putting on miles." The result: Mini devised a plan that lets people drive as much as they want without having to pay more and named it a "Motoring Lease." "We tell clients that we'll get into stuff that's none of our business and apologize up front. We acknowledge that we don't know what we're talking about when we throw out these ideas, but that we're going to offer them anyway."

Now that the launch was a success, CP+B is going to maintain its direction. "The brand is known for untraditional print work. To walk away from what we've built isn't smart," Bogusky says. "At the same time, I'd like to see it in more mainstream media, on TV really, to get more impressions. I think that would be the right thing for it, but we can't do both with our budget." Bogusky also recognizes a challenge. "It's such a good-looking small car, it can easily become feminine. We're going to have to work hard to keep that from happening." This piece is part of that attempt. "People want the Mini to come to life. There is a strange anthropomorphizing attribute to it."

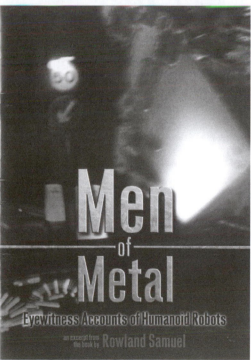

MOLSON

Here's another example of CP+B stepping outside of typical ad boundaries. "Most beer advertising is about trying to imbibe the label with meaning so that guys in bars can hold it and have it say something about them," says Bogusky. "Since we couldn't afford to do much advertising, we thought we'd cheat by adding another label on the other side of the bottle. They say bizarre things like, 'I'm not wearing any underwear.' We've created 190 of these labels so far." The result: Since the launch of the campaign, Molson has become one of the fastest growing import beers.

CREATIVE ADVICE ABOUT FITTING INTO A CREATIVE ENVIRONMENT

Bogusky believes that CP+B is the worst place to start because it really isn't an environment where a junior can place ideas in the pile. "There's going to be a day in the not-so-distant future when the only thing between us completely failing is you," says Bogusky. "That's a lot of pressure for a beginner. You need time to develop."

He also believes that he's not the best person to look at portfolios.

"I find so little in them," he says. "It's more of a conversation piece. There's got to be something that feels creative. I cannot explain what it is. It may not be what other people think of as creative or even as a nice campaign, but it's a spark that I must see."

Then it just comes down to the individual. "Do I feel that you've talked enough, or do I want to keep talking to this person," he asks, echoing remarks by Koelker and Richards.

If you think you can pass those screens, here's some advice to help you show your spark, keep the conversation going, and create more effective advertising:

Identify agencies that share your style: In this industry, one person may love an ad and think it's the greatest in the world, and someone else may hate it and wonder how it got produced. "Neither is right," says Bogusky. "There's a certain genius to those screamer ads where people yell on the radio. I know people that do a lot of that stuff, and they believe in them—that it's the best way for the client to get a point across. Since they believe in that style, they're able to do them far better than I could ever do them, because I just don't believe in them."

Find a place where you fit: Bogusky believes it's the individual's "fit" with the agency that's truly important. "There are so many talented people in this business," he says. "A person who may not be very celebrated at one agency may be a star in the right environment." He points to himself as an example. "I did the exact same thing in two different places. At one place it was all wrong, and at the other place I was a genius."

Be prepared for team hiring situations: When interviewing people, Bogusky believes, "It's everybody's decision. It's not fair for me to interview somebody and say, 'This is the one.' Here, everybody meets the candidate."

Show your resiliency: This is probably one of the most important abilities, according to Bogusky. "Every day in this business is a kick in the nuts—even if you're a good agency who cares about the work and has an environment that supports it—because ideas die. They die here. But we know that we're going to keep coming back. There are some who are naturally tenacious.

"There are others who are very talented, but more fragile. You can help them through it. You can assure them that if they believe in themselves, it will work out.

"But, in the end, they have to be able to get up and do it again."

Let go of your ideas: "Some people become afraid their idea might be their last good one. So they become overprotective parents of it. They almost smother it with their own love. Then, if it dies, they find that they can't get back up because they don't know if they're going to have another idea," says Bogusky. "The people who do very well are those who have faith in the process and realize they'll get another idea."

Put your hobbies on your resume: This is key, according to Bogusky. "Most people here have hobbies," he says. "I have no time, but I have a ton of them.

"When I interview people, I tell them that the only thing I go by is their hobbies. It says something about them. Some tell me that they like to listen to music or read. But those don't count. It must be something more involving."

Understand the difference between art and design: When Bogusky started, he didn't know the difference between the two. He now believes the difference, while subtle, is important: "With pure design, you almost exclusively use implicit communication to give people a feeling or elicit a mood. When people looked at my designs, I asked them, 'Does it seem like this or like that?' And they all had different feelings looking at it. With art direction, you want to communicate something specific, so you use different amounts of design and different kinds of design to help you convey the message.

"You either move people exactly how you want them to be moved or you don't. If it hinders the communication, no matter how beautiful it might be, it's not good art direction. On the other side, there are well-known art directors who aren't very good designers. Sometimes, they'll get help with the design."

Give yourself a breather when going from art direction to design: At CP+B, people switch back and forth between art direction and design. "We always laugh because it usually takes a couple of days before you can shift into one from the other," he says. "This decompression period has to happen."

Work hard at everything: "Even when you're laying out a grocery store ad and you're trying to figure out where to put all the meats and how to make the selection of poultry look good, do the best you can," says Bogusky. "That's where I started, and I never thought, 'Man, I deserve to get out of that world.'

"Give it your all. The rest is luck."

Talk in plain English: "We have all this terminology in advertising—and each term means something different at each agency—and people are constantly adding more," says Bogusky. "But we try to avoid any of the ad-speak and have any CP+B process, circle C, registered.

"Sometimes clients are like, 'Is that the brand strategy or the launch strategy,' or, 'Is that an implicit strategy or an explicit strategy?' I'm honest. I tell them that I don't know, but I can do this stuff called advertising if you want me to do it."

Make sure the agency takes it to a client: "It's ridiculous, the amount of amazing thinking in this industry," says Bogusky. "You can go to just about any art director's office right now in most agencies and find stuff on the wall, on the floor, or in a drawer that's really cool or really smart. The big difference is in creating or finding an environment where that stuff actually gets to your client."

Look beyond traditional media: "People and things within our culture are constantly becoming famous without the use of advertising," says Bogusky.

"Most famous things get that way without the use of advertising.

"There are a lot of ways to generate fame and awareness outside of 30- and 60-second television, magazine advertising, and newspaper advertising. Those are awesome forms of distribution, yet, for some reason, people in the industry tend to think that those are all we have. But, here, we try to remind ourselves that there are lots of other opportunities out there. And because we've become successful at it, I don't even have to ask for it anymore, and often that's where people now start.

"It's become part of the DNA of the agency. It is our identity now."

Keep up with the styles of advertising: Bogusky believes that age doesn't matter when interviewing. "It's purely the work," he says. "What happens, though, is styles change. There's quality and there's style. There is quality work in different schools.

"You can often tell when somebody went to college by what they wear on the weekends. When they hang out, people kind of stick in the style that was popular during their college years. The same is true in advertising. At a certain point, one may find a comfortable place and not be open to moving to someplace else."

Be a fan of popular culture: Bogusky believes this is key to your continued development. "It's really easy to say, 'I don't like rap music.' You might not understand it. You maybe haven't spent the time to learn about it and listen to enough of it. You stop developing when you no longer stay involved. And probably the best way to stay involved is by just asking people, 'Hey, why is this going on,' because people want to share all of that stuff."

Understand the hierarchy of your message: As mentioned earlier, this is something that creatives in CP+B always try to keep it in mind. "When somebody is new and fresh out of school, he or she most likely has not thought a lot about it. There is not a lot of teachers who deal with it," says Bogusky. "But some headlines are more traditional headlines, and others are actually more like captions.

"In some cases, you want the headline to be read after you see the visual, and other times you want it to be read before the visual. So you need to play with the size and placement of the type on the page and the size and placement of the visual on the page to get them in the right order."

Become a planner: One thing different about CP+B is that when a job comes in all departments work on it at the same time. "You don't have a handoff from account service to planning and from planning to creative," says Bogusky. "Planning may develop a brief, but creative is working on it with them and adjacent to them while they're doing it. Account service never bails on the process either. Everyone's involved all of the time."

Find the realities of the situation: Get as far away from the problem as possible and separate yourself from the things that our culture accepts, Bogusky advises. "Behavior is not necessarily rational, and it's not necessarily based on the things we believe it's based on," he says. "It's telling that a lot of good creatives grew up on army bases outside of the United States, but followed U.S. culture. If you look at culture from within, it's a lot harder to see what people are really doing and why they are doing them, because we're so blinded by the acceptance of it. But once you free yourself from the cultural rules, you start to find really interesting answers. That's the first step. But it's not easy to do."

Check for proof points: As mentioned earlier, CP+B tries to create "proof points" with their advertising. "When it's being created, it's probably more intuitive," says Bogusky. "The notion of using media to prove your proposition—instead of saying we're an interesting, fun car, we're proving we're an interesting, fun car by what we do—that is not something we think about before we do it. But when we're analyzing what actually worked, that seems to be at the root of the successes."

Weed out the wrong clients: "The funny thing about this business is that your success can lead to failure if the wrong people hire you for the wrong reasons," says Bogusky. "Every now and then you may go all the way through the pitch process, or more often you may skip the pitch process, and wind up in not a great situation with a client that didn't really believe that you meant what you were saying. You try not to fail anyway. But with our agency brochure, we try to weed out the wrong clients beforehand."

Write a story: "I write down everything," Bogusky says about his process of developing concepts. "And I write fictional sketches about the past, the company, and what it's going to be like in the future."

Find inspiration in everything you read: Bogusky reads books on philosophy and marketing. "Whatever I'm reading inspires me," he says. "I think it's an illusion, but it seems like the answers for whatever problems I have are in what I've decided to pick up."

Surround yourself with great ad people: "There are ad people, and then there are those who aren't really ad people," says Bogusky. "In the creative department, there are those who are really ad people and others who, while extremely talented, became art directors because they get to make little films and they like everything about their films except the part that sells product. The very best are the ad people. They love the process and the product. They don't love the part of the product that's not advertising. The great account people—the ones who get the good stuff sold— are in it for the product and not for the relationships or the golf."

Postscript 1:

A NEW BRAND DAY IN PORTFOLIO DEVELOPMENT

CP+B is known for creating innovative, nontraditional advertising.

To get them started in this process, CP+B employs an activity that they developed called a "brand day."

Bogusky believes that juniors could use the techniques from a brand day to help them develop their portfolio. "You could definitely perform a brand day from the outside," he says. "And they're kind of fun."

Here's what he says about the process:

"It's basically a brand intervention. It's for when you have a dysfunctional brand and maybe a dysfunctional corporate family behind it. We ask for the very top people, the CEO and the president, for some mid-level people, including people from marketing, and for a couple of their smartest very junior people. We go into a room, lock the door, and don't come out until people are aligned.

"The notion is that anybody can say anything in the room. We find that senior people are a bit disconnected from the brand, that middle managers have pretty good jobs and don't want to say anything that will get them fired, and that most of the great stuff comes from those junior people who have crap jobs that don't pay.

"They get in the face of the CEO.

"It could get really ugly, but in the end, it's pretty good.

"We go in with a bunch of exercises, worksheets, games, basic things, complicated things. A lot of the little exercises are things that we've read here and there. Things like, 'If tomorrow you could no longer make X, what would this company make?' Forget the machinery, but based on who you are and what you care about, what would you make? Or: 'If it were an animal, what kind of animal would it be?' We also developed some proprietary exercises.

"We also analyze all of the competitors. We develop a complete, pretty robust personality for each competitor based on people's opinions in the room. Each competitor is out there trying to stand for something. Their communications are public. So you know when you've hit the bull's-eye.

"We usually try to get to one sentence about each one.

"Sometimes we try to develop a positioning statement and one mission statement or brand statement—their core and the wrapper. How far you get depends on how much time you want to spend.

"It helps them realize who they are at the core. At first, clients are like, 'This is dumb,' because a lot of the questions are dumb. Then they see that it's actually working. You wind up with some pretty clear direction. When you get back with the work, they're expecting it because they were there.

"The biggest fundamental difference between our approach and the approaches that are in vogue now is that we start with the realities of a company and then find the alignment between that and what consumers are saying they want. The other approaches try to find out what consumers say they want and then to try to position the product or sell the product in a way that feels like it answers what the customer wants. But customers don't know what they really want. So our preference is usually to tweak the alignment on the consumer side, not on the company side.

"This helps the client get on board and gives us direction.

"You create insights about the brand that you bring back to your communication. Usually, we go in with some kind of an idea, but it's pretty rough. It can't be a game where we're trying to lead you somewhere."

Postscript 2:

MORE THOUGHTS ON THE
IMPORTANCE OF STAYING OPEN

Earlier, Bogusky talked about the importance of staying current. In their attempt to stay current, CP+B developed a new way for the agency to conduct brainstorm sessions, and Bogusky gained some insights into culture and himself.

Here are his comments about it:

"A couple people conducted brainstorm sessions using instant messaging. They were really pumped up the next day, and some neat stuff came out of it. People just started going. In most brainstorming sessions, there are always those silences, but there were none in this session, probably because it was nonthreatening. You can't see the person's reaction to your comment. No one bothers typing in, 'That's dumb.' They just went on to the next thing.

"If you've ever done those chats, you notice that it isn't really linear. Someone will be answering something that's three questions behind, and other people are chiming in about something else. It creates connections between two ideas that don't necessarily connect, and yet visually they connect because they're adjacent to each other. I think that that's probably one of the reasons why the brainstorm just keeps building on itself.

"I was also a little surprised by something else—the generational shift between people in their 30s and those in their 20s. We're all computer savvy. We pretty much run our entire lives on computers, but at about 27, maybe 25, there's this incredible break where the younger people use it just in such an advanced way.

"A guy was in my office, and he was telling this story about how he and his girlfriend met. It was classic. He told this story in such a way that if you missed the part that it all happened online, you wouldn't have noticed because he said, 'I was in this room with about 30 people there. And there was just something about her. We started talking, and I invited her to a smaller room. A bunch of us broke off and went into a smaller room, and she came along.'

"I wonder how many stories are out there exactly like that one. How different is that from what I would consider a traditional way of meeting somebody? It's going to become a traditional way. You're either going to be okay with it or not. You either find delight in it or you don't.

"I think you just have to be open to the fact that people are delightful and doing delightful things, even when you can't understand it. Even when you look at it and go, 'That's terrible,' you're probably wrong if you really look into it a little bit more. I would hope that I could live my whole life with a level of openness, but it remains to be seen."

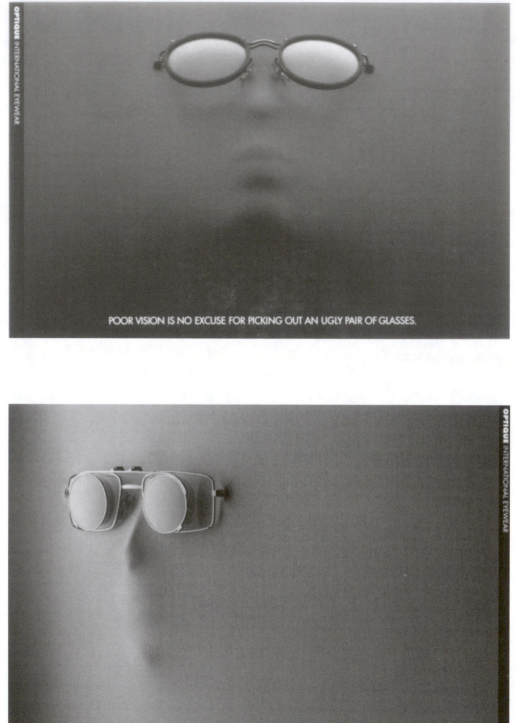

Stan Richards

"I think people who go into advertising should do so because they absolutely love it."

"These people watch television at night, paying little attention to the show, but perk up when a commercial comes on. They're so vitally interested in the way people communicate that they see it as a life's work," observes Stan Richards, founder and leader of The Richards Group in Dallas, Texas.

Richards is someone who truly made a life's work out of studying communications—from his days as an art student, to founding a leading Dallas design studio (some call him the dean of Texas design), to turning that studio into one of the largest privately held full-service agencies in America—one that is consistently considered among the best in the world.

His organization creates work that is consistently recognized as among the best in the country—by *Adweek*, the *New York Times*, and New York Art Directors Club—working for such clients as Chick-fil-A, Corona Beer, Fruit of the Loom, Motel 6, Hyundai, and The Home Depot, among many others. He has also served a number of nonprofit organizations on a volunteer basis, including Junior Achievement, United Way, and the Salvation Army.

Richards is the author of *The Peaceable Kingdom*, which describes how he structured The Richards Group, built its culture, and maintains it today.

Richards' early years were spent in Philadelphia and Atlantic City. He settled in Dallas after graduating from Pratt in the mid-1950s. Today, he balances his business and personal responsibilities by setting aside evening hours for his family.

He leaves the office every night by six o'clock. If he has four hours of extra work he returns at four o'clock the next morning. Richards has been married for 49 years and has two sons. One is a partner in his own ad agency in San Francisco and the other is a Ph.D. in clinical psychology. He also has two grandchildren. An avid jogger, he's logged over 43,000 miles.

DRAWN TO DESIGN

What makes someone successful in one creative area and not in another? Nature or nurture? Whatever instills talent, Richards firmly believes environment is what leads an individual to manifest one or another. "A designer is a designer in any medium," he says. "I'm convinced that if a great designer were taught the tools of musical composition instead, he or she could write a pretty nifty piece of music. The judgments are essentially the same. Designers just don't have the facility to use the particular tools that a composer uses. I believe the same talents apply to playwriting, sculpture, all the arts."

In this section, we're going to explore this concept—as well as see how this idea developed. Richards started his arts exploration very young. Even at ten years old, he was one of those children who could draw better than anyone else in the class. (In fact, his mother was convinced that not only could he draw better than any kid in the class, he could draw better than every kid in America.) "That led me to believe that I was going to do something in art," says Richards.

Then, in high school, he learned from a teacher that he could actually make a living as a commercial artist. On a recommendation from this teacher, he went on to Pratt in New York. He chose that design school because it was the only one with a basketball team, an important consideration for him at the time.

The school consistently turned out students with great potential in advertising and design. Richards credits Herschel Levit, one of his teachers at Pratt, with greatly influencing him, as well as a group of two- or three-dozen other art students.

Along with Richards, these people went on to have outstanding careers in advertising or design.

Levit helped Richards understand what graphic design was all about.

"In the very first session," says Richards, "he marched us all down to the school auditorium, sat at the piano and explained, in great detail, Arnold Schoenberg's 12-tone row system for composition. He explained how Schoenberg built his compositions and the wonderful symmetry involved without explaining its relevance to the class. At the end of this class session, we were dismissed and it was never mentioned again."

This taught Richards his greatest lesson. Here was a group of people who planned to work their entire lives without having to ever write a piece of music. As he reflected on it over the course of his studies, he realized that Levit was saying that to be a great designer, everything you know is relevant.

"Every time I went to class, I never knew where the discussion was going to go. We could critique our work and then the conversation would move off into very interesting discussions of architecture or dance," recalls Richards. "All of us gained tremendously from those discussions."

Heading West

Richards graduated from Pratt in 1953 and got some job offers in New York. But he noticed that some talented designers who worked in New York improved when they moved on to Los Angeles. "So I thought Los Angeles was the place for me," he says.

He headed out for Los Angeles, but took a detour to Dallas because he had seen terrific work being done by Neiman Marcus. The exclusive Dallas retailer's advertising design was ahead of the industry and very well regarded. "It was brilliant," he says. "It was always great fun and had a nice light touch." He applied there, but, although he received encouragement, he did not get a job.

This frustrated him. "I was this 20-year-old kid out of one of the best art schools in America," Richards says. "Maybe I wasn't the very best kid in my graduating class, but there were a few of us who dominated the class. I was coming to a city that was not much more than a frontier town. It had a very sedentary, quiet, unexciting advertising industry."

Richards' portfolio consisted of a dozen highly experimental pieces from school. "I sat down and talked with a creative director who headed the biggest agency in Dallas at the time. He looked at my work and got very excited. He offered what turned out to be extraordinary counsel."

He told Richards that nobody in Dallas would hire him because his work was too advanced. But Dallas was going to grow and flourish. "He said if I could stick it out through the lean years, I'd be in a position to dominate the market. Because I'd be responsible for all the good stuff."

The creative director's prediction made Richards' detour well worthwhile. He took this advice and started a freelance design and advertising practice. He won local advertising awards over the next couple of years. Then, in 1955, the head of the Bloom Agency, the second biggest agency in Dallas, called and asked if he'd be interested in working as a creative director there.

A Career Blooms

"I took the job thinking I'd enjoy heading up the creative efforts for a big agency," says Richards. "But I hated it. It was all the classic things you hear about advertising agencies. It was bureaucratic, hierarchical—a stultifying environment. It was one in which the account managers said, 'No, that's not what my client is looking for and so I won't show it.' Then we battled over it. I left a year to the day after starting and reestablished my freelance practice."

Richards had to struggle very hard to reestablish himself. He had virtually no income for several months, but soon his business began to flourish. Business from Dallas-area companies and agencies came first, then from around Texas, and soon from the rest of the country. Eventually he built up a 20-person staff.

His organization developed relationships with advertising agencies based on print work. Sometimes a television assignment would come up, and the studio would be asked to work on it. Richards would conceive it, write it, and storyboard it—and on some occasions produce it. "I always felt that it was the most natural thing in the world to do both advertising and design," he says. "I might sit down in the morning and work on a logo and in the afternoon, work on an advertising campaign." Over the next 20 years, his organization grew into an important creative resource for advertising agencies.

An Ad Agency Is Born

Then, in 1976, when his design firm was firmly established, the CEO of a major Dallas bank asked him if he'd be interested in handling their account as a full-service agency. "It was an interesting moment," recalls Richards, "because if we became an advertising agency, we'd say good-bye to all of our clients. So I thought long and hard about that one, and decided it was time to make the transition."

When The Richards Group became a full-service ad agency, his design group was kept intact and moved a few blocks from the agency. Eventually, the business grew to also include groups that specialize in direct marketing, interactive communications, public relations, sales promotion, and employee brand training.

Different by Design

As an advertising agency, several factors set The Richards Group apart from other organizations. He was one of the first to eliminate seating departmental groups together. Even early on, art directors are just as likely to be next to account executives or researchers as another creative at The Richards Group. "That way, they'll see that the others care just as much about their side of the business. That's enormously helpful in avoiding confrontations," observes Richards. "I don't tolerate barriers that make it difficult to do great advertising. I want to remove those barriers and have all the decisions based on the merits of the work."

Another Important Difference

Richards doesn't pattern his organization after current trends or the traditional practices of other agencies. He maintained his agency's independence in a period of buyouts and consolidation.

"If you're part of a holding company agency, your mission from the moment you walk into the office in the morning to the time you walk out in the evening is to enhance the wealth of the shareholders," says Richards. "Here, we don't have to do that. We also don't borrow money," he adds. "So we don't have to concern ourselves with bankers. It means that all of us, all day, every day, can focus on the only thing that counts, and that is the work. At the very top of our priority list is, how good is the work and how good can we make it? If that is fundamental, it changes the way you look at your job."

This independence also enabled him to avoid deep cuts in his staff during the severe industry downturn. So while his competitors were laying off 100, 200, 300 people, and the agency business as a whole lost nearly 19,000 jobs—a high number for such a small industry—The Richards Group maintained its staff (except for a few they lost through attrition and a handful of others).

"It was a choice that I made," says Richards. "It meant accepting a dramatically reduced level of profitability. But I'm in a position to do that because of our lack of shareholders, partners, and investors. I didn't have to concern myself with anyone else's welfare, except for the welfare of the people who are part of the company."

"The business is cyclical. It always has been and it always will be. And I felt that it was much more important to maintain our strength during a down period than to maintain profitability."

As part of his unique culture, Richards prefers that his employees spend time with their families and avoid late hours. "It's a business that requires considerably more than nine hours a day on a fairly regular basis," he says. "So I learned early in my career to set aside my evening hours for my family. If I have extra work to do, I just come in early. Nobody at my house cared whether I was gone at 4:00 a.m., but they cared a lot if I wasn't home at 7:00 in the evening."

In addition, Richards expects all his creative staffers to present their own work. "We don't shield any of them from our clients," he notes. However, this does not demand exceptional presentation skills. Richard believes, "Good work speaks for itself. You can be absolutely silent and put five ads on the table and a person sitting on the other side is going to find it pretty easy to pick the best one."

But individual work styles are respected, too. Richards prefers to work alone, but recognizes that others may need a partner to be productive. So most of his creative teams work in partnership, while others choose to work by themselves.

His unique take on the business also extends to what he looks for in a client. "Avoid working for clients in multi-layered organizations where the work travels through an endless series of approvals," he suggests. "At each level of approval, reviews make the work weaker and weaker. That's frustrating for a creative."

Four Client Questions

In deciding whether to take on a new client, he asks four questions:

"The first question to ask is can we do great work?" says Richards. "Is the client open to great creative? Do they trust fresh ideas? And are they willing to provide enough input to get it?"

The second question focuses on getting results. "Can we measure how the advertising works or are we going to have to be satisfied that the client's spouse thinks it's nice?" he asks. "It's important to measure results. Being able to look at sales and determine whether the advertising did the job is important to effective campaigns in the future."

Remuneration is the third question. "Can we make a profit?" asks Richards. "The client has to understand that we both assume the responsibility of helping each other profit in the relationship."

And the final question looks at the personal relationship with a potential client. "Can we have fun?" he asks. "That's the human side. Do we like the people? Do they like us? When we show up for a meeting are we going to be treated with respect? Will we enjoy the experience?"

He asks these questions because he believes the client is one of the greatest determining factors in producing great work, which reflects on his view of the industry overall.

A Look Back

Looking back on his more than 50 years in communications, he says, "There is no business that is as emotionally rewarding as the one I'm in—with the exception of being a performer. And the only reason is that with a performance, you get to hear the applause. We don't. We have to assume that there is applause. You legitimately want to please.

"In dealing with clients, you want very much for them to sit across the table from you, listen to your presentation, and when you're finished say, 'That's wonderful.' That's the applause I'm talking about."

And clearly, Richards has gotten lots of applause over the years.

"I'd do this whether anybody paid me or not," he says.

"I work with very, very bright people who care about their craft. We spend our days trying to figure out how to create something wonderful. What more could anyone ask for? Every morning I get up and I'm excited about coming to the office. And, I'm overpaid for doing it!"

Today, Richards feels that his biggest challenge is maintaining the kind of electricity and vitality at his agency that it had when it was a much smaller firm.

"We've managed to do that," he says, because of its culture, philosophy, and business structure. "It is still the same place today as it was ten years ago, 20 years ago. And we now have 662 people."

A BEAUTIFULLY DESIGNED PORTFOLIO

—— Mercantile Bank ——

Mercantile Bank's business had stagnated for years while other Dallas banks were growing dramatically. The bank brought in a new CEO, who decided they were not being served well by their current agency.

He wanted to project a more aggressive image. He wanted to communicate a willingness to take prudent risks—not to be regarded as the bank that easily rejects new ideas.

The Richards Group won the account on their credentials without even presenting a campaign. The agency found the bank's stuffy, stodgy, old-fashioned image was hurting them. "Our first assignment was to develop a new graphic identity and apply it to all of the business papers, signs—everything," Richards says. When he finished presenting the mark, the CEO said he liked the work because "it captured a feeling of momentum." The CEO then asked if a campaign could be built using the word "momentum."

Richards went back to his office and wrote a couple of TV scripts and print ads. A week later he presented the line, "Never underestimate the power of momentum."

Wanting to attract the Dallas business community—which, at the time, was almost 100 percent male—the campaign presented analogies between business and sports. The results were phenomenal. The bank grew from $900 million in assets to more than $23 billion over the 12-year period this campaign was used.

Richards is also proud that the CEO offered the direction and the agency respected his idea. Says Richards, "Most agency people are so arrogant that if an idea comes from a client, it is automatically put aside as not having any merit."

—— Memorex Audio ——

The Richards Group represented Memorex for two years. "We were a convenient hire for Memorex," says Richards. "They are headquartered in Fort Worth, but were dealing with Weiden+Kennedy, a fine agency in Oregon. They were experiencing the problems that often occur when an agency and client are a significant distance from each other."

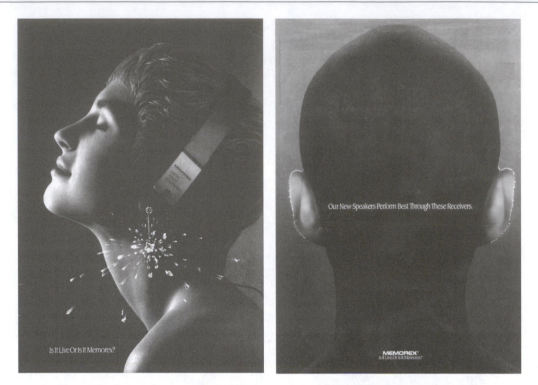

Our New Speakers Perform Best Through These Receivers.

Is It Live Or Is It Memorex?

MEMOREX
Is It Live Or Is It Memorex?

When they won the account, The Richards Group inherited the tagline "Is it live or is it Memorex?" which was originally written by Leo Burnett. They recognized the line's value and great heritage. It was meaningful to people of all ages. So there was never a question of replacing it. But the new ads were visually very different from those done by Weiden+Kennedy, who had used rock stars. Richards chose not to do that, but has still created arresting and provocative work. "Once we decided on that photograph, there was only one way to lay out that ad," says Richards.

—— Motel 6 ——

To some, the most prominent campaign The Richards Group has created—and the most successful in the marketplace—is the one for Motel 6. It has been running for more than 17 years now.

In the early '80s, Motel 6 was only using outdoor advertising. They asked The Richards Group to help them expand into other media. "It was a big opportunity for us," he says. "We were asked to work for this terrific organization that was preparing to spend several million dollars in advertising. After looking at the research, however, the first advice we gave was not to advertise. The product needed to be fixed. At that time, there were no phones in the Motel 6 rooms. Guests were expected to go down the hall to make a telephone call. If guests wanted to watch television, they had to pay an extra dollar and a half. And there was no reservation system.

"Without telephones, televisions, and a reservation system, we felt their advertising dollars would be wasted," says Richards. "The advertising could entice consumers to try Motel 6, but disappointed guests would never come back again."

Motel 6 management took Richards' advice and made an enormous financial commitment to upgrade their product. Just installing the telephones resulted in the biggest order AT&T had ever received at that time—40,000 telephones in all.

Then The Richards Group developed the concept for the advertising. "This came directly from what we learned from qualitative research," says Richards. "Focus groups consisting of ten or 12 people who had stayed at Motel 6 were recruited. The participants thought they were only there to talk about lodging. The moderator began by talking about where they stayed when traveling. The participants said they normally stayed at Marriott, Hilton, Holiday Inn, and about 20 other hotel chains. Nobody was willing to admit they had stayed in a Motel 6.

"When the moderator pressed harder, one person admitted it. And, once one person in the room admitted it, others followed. They justified their stay by saying that it helped them save money to buy an extra tank of gas or eat steak instead of

---

:60 Radio – "Fiscal Responsibility"

Hi. Tom Bodett for Motel 6 with a few thoughts about fiscal responsibility. You know this bein' an election year and all, I got a suggestion. If you're runnin' for office and you're out there on the campaign trail, why not stay at Motel 6 and save a few bucks. What with money bein' too tight to mention and government tools costin' millions, it'll be refreshing to get a clean, comfortable room for the lowest prices of any national chain. And while stayin' at Motel 6 may not win you the election, it'll sure make you popular with us regular folks. And don't forget, with the free local phone calls you can rally support from some of those local constituents right from the comfort of your room. And with the free color TV, you can sit back, watch the headlines, and see how you're doin' in the polls. Well give it some thought. For the rest of you not runnin' for office, well, Motel 6 is still a heck of a deal, and who knows, you just might run into your next elected official. I'm Tom Bodett for Motel 6 with America's future on my mind.

---

hamburger. Suddenly, people responded with enormous pride in being frugal and deciding to stay in a Motel 6."

Richards sat behind the glass and watched this great welling-up of pride. It became relatively easy for him to decide that the creative strategy should be to point out that Motel 6 was a smart choice for the frugal traveler. With this strategy in place, the execution was simple.

Two years earlier, one of Richards' writers had come into his office saying he'd heard an interesting voice on National Public Radio. It was Tom Bodett. They agreed that Bodett's voice and personal style could be very interesting, and kept him in mind for a future opportunity. When Motel 6 came along, they remembered him and wrote the series of commercials for him. Because of the longevity of the campaign, Richards says, "We've made him a very wealthy man."

—— THE HOME DEPOT ——

Richards believes "advertising should be endearing, rewarding and relevant. It should make the reader enjoy the experience of viewing the ad."

This work for The Home Depot is a good example.

It is based on common experiences and attitudes. And, while product-oriented, the headline communicates the message in a simple, endearing, personable manner.

"I want the viewers to go through an intellectual process," he says. "I want them to say to themselves, 'I like what you said. I like the way you said it. I therefore like you. And if I like you, I find it easy to do business with you.' It's not terribly different from the way you would sell something across the counter."

The Gift Registry

Okay, it's not as traditional as china or silver. But for practical gifts you'll actually use for years to come, nothing beats Home Depot's Gift Registry. Tools, gas grills, lawn mowers. If you need it, your local Home Depot makes it easy for friends and family across the entire country to purchase it for you. In fact, it's a piece of cake.

Richards looks for some endearing way to communicate the message in broadcast as well as print. This endearing quality distinguishes Richards' work from some of the advertising in today's annuals, which he often describes as the "in-your-face" school of advertising. "In-your-face advertising is confrontational and highly provocative," Richards says, "and can gain an enormous amount of attention. But it's really pretty easy to do—and rarely endearing."

—— Butch Cassidy and the Sundance Kid ——

While this example is out of date, there's a strong message behind its story: That you must be prepared to work on unusual things—things that you can never anticipate.

While still a design studio, The Richards Group was assigned the advertising campaign for a new movie. Richards received the script and thought it was brilliant. "I knew this movie was going to be a smash hit," he recalls. "So I did the ad campaign, sent it to California, and got a call from the director a couple of days later. He loved what we did in the ad campaign, and asked if we would be interested in designing the main title sequence. He said he was having trouble with that. I told him I'd be delighted."

His work was approved and became part of the movie *Butch Cassidy and the Sundance Kid*. "It's our only credential in the movie business," says Richards, "but it won an Oscar for best picture. So I have a great track record with the Academy Awards."

—— Chick-fil-A ——

When The Richards Group won Chick-fil-A, they had three significant barriers to overcome: 1) They were being outspent 20 to 1 by each of its hamburger competitors in every one of its markets; 2) Chick-fil-A doesn't discount; 3) They're closed on Sundays. Points 2 and 3 were tenets of the company founder and were not going to change.

"As a matter of fact, McDonald's spends more in a week than Chick-fil-A does in a year," notes Richards. "And you can't drive past a fast-food hamburger place that doesn't have a 99¢ banner out front."

The solution? A direct hit against burgers with renegade cows that, in enlightened self-interest, advise people to eat more chicken. "All of our executions are as if they were done by cows," says Richards. "We invented this kind of extraordinary campaign where cows are talking to people. They don't spell very well, and they can't write very well, but it's a campaign that really has resonated."

How did they come up with the talking cows? "We have a highly disciplined branding process that always gets us to a simple answer," says Richards (see Postscript 1 for details).

"The simple answer in this case was to recognize that the competitor is the hamburger, so how could we gain share from it. Then it was just a matter of the creative process to bring us to the use of cows, the source of hamburger meat."

THE RICHARDS GROUP CREATIVE BRIEF

Warning: People don't like ads. People don't trust ads. People don't remember ads. How do we make sure this one will be different?

Why are we advertising?

To position the Chick-fil-A chicken sandwich as the best alternative to other fast food sandwiches and remind people how much they like them.

Who are we talking to?

Adults, 18-49, who are infrequent or nonusers of Chick-fil-A. They are primarily women, college graduates, in white collar jobs. They associate chicken with a healthy lifestyle and believe that quality food is better for you and worth the money.

What do they currently think?

"Unless I'm in the mall, I just don't think of Chick-fil-A. I guess they're pretty good, but I haven't been there in a long time."

What would we like them to think?

"I'd rather have a chicken sandwich than a hamburger. And Chick-fil-A makes the best one."

What is the single most persuasive idea we can convey?

Every other sandwich is second-rate.

Why should they believe it?

Chick-fil-A is simple, wholesome and doesn't take itself too seriously.

Are there any creative guidelines?

14x48 outdoor.

HOW TO ENDEAR YOURSELF TO A POTENTIAL EMPLOYER

Richards has an unusually honest approach in making his hiring decisions. "I hire people I like. That may sound stupid," says Richards, "but personality counts. Integrity counts. It's an intuitive process. I get a feeling for the beginner, not just for the work in the portfolio."

When he interviews, Richards wants to find out what the beginner is like. "I try to draw that person out—beginning with high school years," says Richards. "I want to find out if he or she played sports, was involved in politics, or what his or her folks do. I try to understand what kind of person he or she is. I want to be satisfied that, when I expose this person to my client, he or she will represent both himself or herself and our organization very well. And if I hire people I like, there's a pretty good chance they'll like each other, too."

In the portfolio, Richards looks for two or three pieces that are so brilliant he could expect to see them in the annuals. Says Richards, "If a beginner is capable of doing that, I'd hire him or her." Here is some advice that can help you get to that level.

Review the annuals: Richards believes this helps you develop your instincts and abilities to make sound judgments. "Spend time reviewing *CA*, the *One Show* annuals, *New York Art Director's Annual*, and *Graphis*," says Richards. "Those books help you to recognize what is possible in advertising. While it's important to look at current ones, it's also useful to look at older editions to understand where advertising came from, why things are done the way they are done—and how we got here. If you only read this week's *Time*, whose ads are 90 percent garbage, you won't ever develop a sense for really terrific work. Emulate the best work that's being done in the field."

Stir up your creative juices: To come up with ideas, Richards tells us that anything can trigger a stream of consciousness. "I can pick up a magazine, the annuals, or the Yellow Pages and make some sort of word association that starts a thought process. Something might trigger a whole string of thoughts and lead me to a place I wouldn't come to otherwise," he says. "Also, I'm a runner and when I'm running alone, I find that helps me to solve advertising problems."

Understand the customer's position: Advertising's primary mission is to sell a product or service. That's simple. But to do that means identifying the potential customer's point of view. Ideally, research will tell us that. "We need to understand what information will change a potential customer's point of view," says Richards, "and what information will motivate them to do business with the client."

Use familiar products for a spec book...: Your portfolio should have ads for products anybody can understand. Says Richards, "If somebody comes in with an ad for some highly sophisticated software program, an ad that only he and an engineer understand, it's very difficult to evaluate the work. The simpler the product, the better it is. Also avoid fictional products. Presenting real products, with real marketing considerations, has more impact."

... With obvious marketing considerations: "Suppose a beginner chooses WD-40. You don't have to be a genius to figure out that most households in America have a can of WD-40 sitting on a shelf. And it could last a lifetime. Therefore, the marketing strategy should be to motivate people to use it up. That's simple."

Include radio in a copy portfolio: Richards sees very little radio work in spec portfolios. However, he feels this is an important component of advertising. So he is always encouraged when a beginner presents some terrific radio. Richards recognizes that beginners should also include TV because some employers want to see it, but he believes TV is difficult to evaluate. "It's a collaborative medium. It involves many people. In a television spot, there can be ten people who played a major part in the process," he says.

Be prepared to talk about anything: Richards wants to work with people who will be able to work with his clients. "I ask applicants to talk about subjects they are unprepared to talk about," he says. "I prefer to hear about their parents, brothers and sisters, and what they like to do for fun, rather than the details of their last position."

Don't worry about the packaging of your portfolio: "I never even reflect on the outside packaging of a portfolio," says Richards. "All I care about is what they've tried. I want to sit across the table from them and get a sense of what they're like as people, but the packaging of the portfolio is inconsequential."

Evaluate the agency: In the same way that a beginner needs to look at the walls of the agency to evaluate the work during a job interview, you need to evaluate the culture. "If it is not a place that exudes energy and electricity, then it may be the wrong place for you," says Richards. "It's important that the people around you have as much fire in their bellies as you do. If you're surrounded by a bunch of functionaries, then sooner or later you'll become functionary."

Be a grown-up: Richards particularly wants to avoid hiring people who seem arrogant. "I don't believe in artistic temperaments. I think that's often an excuse for infantile behavior. In my own organization, I simply will not accept that. I won't accept arrogance, and I won't accept temper tantrums," he says. "We want to present the work. We want the client to respond. And we want to be able to respond to the client's comments and then make the changes that satisfy all of the concerns. That's hard to do with people who are arrogant or cocky."

Always question your work: When you finish an ad, Richards suggests asking yourself questions about its effectiveness. "Does the ad make a point? And does it make that point clearly? Does it make the point without the body copy? If it's an outdoor board, can it be read at 70 mph? All of those questions are important," says Richards.

Include only about a dozen pieces: "You can have a few more," says Richards. "But not many. Secondly, they ought to be the very best you've ever done."

Attend an art school: "I hire a lot of kids out of art schools," says Richards. "They do a marvelous job of preparing people to enter the business. They're, for the most part, highly competitive. Those who distinguish themselves in an exceedingly demanding environment are going to be successful in business. So it's about as predictable as anything can be."

Invite client participation (once on the job): "We go into every client/agency relationship understanding that we'll never know our client's business as well as he knows it," says Richards. "But we'll know his customer better than he ever can. And we'll know advertising better than he ever can. But we will never know his business as well as he does because he has ways of casually picking up information that will never come to us. We want to take full advantage of that. So we want our client to be a participant in the process. Consequently, if he or she has reservations about an ad, we want to understand why. That insight will help us reach the best answer."

POSTSCRIPT 1:

A BRANDING PROCESS FOR BUILDING YOUR BOOK

Throughout this book, we hear a lot about brands. Here's The Richards Group take on brands and the branding process, which they call Spherical® Branding. While you can't use it on the same level as The Richards Group because you don't have the same level of resources to put against it, you can apply the thinking behind their process to help you put together your portfolio.

"I have a very simple definition for a brand," says Richards. "A brand is a promise. That brand needs to deliver on its promise at every point of contact over an extended period of time. That's how a brand is built. That's why some brands are strong and some are weak.

"Our branding process is to provide, at the end of it, the consistency that every brand needs over every point of contact.

"Our system demands that there be conviction behind that brand promise, and that it has to be held at the highest levels of management in the company. If we can develop the conviction about the brand promise, if we can then assure consistency at every point of contact, then we can build a strong brand.

"The process itself begins with qualitative and quantitative research to understand the characteristics of the brand. We go through that very diligently. It also involves an extensive series of management interviews to talk with the people who have the responsibility of managing the brand and understand their point of view. How they feel about the way that brand presents itself to the consumer.

"After that, we hold a workshop for one or two days (occasionally it's even three days), where our key people are in a room with their key management people—there could be as many as 15 people—and we begin to define the characteristics of the brand that are going to dictate where we head for the next several years.

"We begin with the development of a brand vision statement, which is the highest calling of the brand. This is not a mission statement. As an example—this is not one of ours—the Disney company in defining its brand vision could talk about animated films, cruise ships, resorts, but instead their brand vision is 'keeping the magic of childhood alive.' We try to find a brand vision statement that is as lofty as that.

"Then we go through a positioning exercise. This is not terribly different from conventional wisdom: we define the target audience, the category in which we compete, and identify the brand's most compelling benefit.

"So, we wind up writing a sentence that says, for example: 'To frugal people, Motel 6 is the brand of comfortable places to stay, and is the lowest price of any national chain.' That's pretty close to our positioning statement for Motel 6.

"Once we've defined a positioning statement—that's really the intellectual positioning—we need to look at the emotional side of why the brand is selected. So we do a personality statement, which is usually not more than five or six words to describe the personality of the brand. And then we do something that few other people do, and that is an affiliation statement.

"That is, what club do I join when I buy into this brand? Let's say it's a retail store like The Home Depot. Somebody sees me opening the trunk of my car and taking out a Home Depot bag. I've just shopped at Home Depot, what do they think of me? What club am I a member of?

"Those are important issues we're dealing with today in our new Hyundai relationship, because the Hyundai is a remarkably good car at a remarkably good price, but it doesn't enjoy, at this point, the benefits of having a strong affiliation. And, certainly they should not be proceeding as a car that's purchased because one doesn't have the means to buy a better car. Rather, it's a car that you purchase if you have your head on straight, and you recognize what's important in life. You don't want to spend a ton of money for a badge on a car. What you want is a really good car that'll do everything you want it to do. So the affiliation statement for Hyundai is people who are winners at life."

POSTSCRIPT 2:

FINDING YOUR PLACE IN ADVERTISING OR DESIGN

Where do you best fit: in an ad agency or a design organization? While many art directors and even writers may be able to fit into both, the beginner who knows where his or her strengths are has an advantage.

Let's have Richards shed some light on this topic.

"The basic difference between the design organization and the ad agency is that design work is done on a project basis," he says. "Even if the organization designed an annual report for a client for 20 consecutive years, it's still a project. We do his annual report and at the end of it, he gets a great annual report, we send a bill, and that's the end of it.

"With an ad agency, it's a total relationship where concerns go beyond the advertising. The agency works to help improve the sales organization. Or understand the products and services enough to recommend enhancements. That way, creative people can have a profound influence on a client's business.

"I think designers are pretty much the way they always have been with the exception of the fact that they all have had to learn to deal with the graphic world. Obviously designers in the design organization need superb design skills. Most good designers have a sense of how to string words together to support an idea.

"In the case of writers, someone who can write an annual report, slide presentation, or a film may not necessarily have the skills to write an ad. It's a matter of style. It's always been a lot easier for me to write ten pages than to entertain, excite, and explain in a seven-word headline. Consequently, a writer in our design organization may be excellent in writing long assignments, but may never have written a headline in his or her life.

"This person who is likely to wind up writing annual reports is more interested in journalism or in writing the great American novel. He or she may love to read English prose or enjoy writing three-page letters to erudite friends.

"Within the advertising agency, I look for great conceptual skills. A successful art director needs the right combination of verbal/visual skills. They have to be able to write headlines as well as conceive an ad or TV spot visually. The people I hire in my design organization will have superior design skills, but won't necessarily be able to sit down and write a headline. Several of our people are able to work in both areas comfortably.

"With everybody working in teams now in advertising, which wasn't the case 15, 20 years ago, it is very difficult to determine who came up with the concept. Did it come from the art directors or did it come from the writer? Or was it somehow magically born from both of them?

"One of the interesting things that happens in advertising is that once you've been in the industry for a while, you cease to be either art director or writer. You become both. In advertising, if you're an art director, you're as comfortable writing as a writer. If you're a writer, you're as comfortable with art direction. Both people are usually on a shoot, so they both have a high degree of television experience. A lot has blurred between a writer and an art director although both hold a different title, so there's something separating the two. The further in the development of the business the people are, the more blurred the demarcation becomes."

What's on your PowerBook?

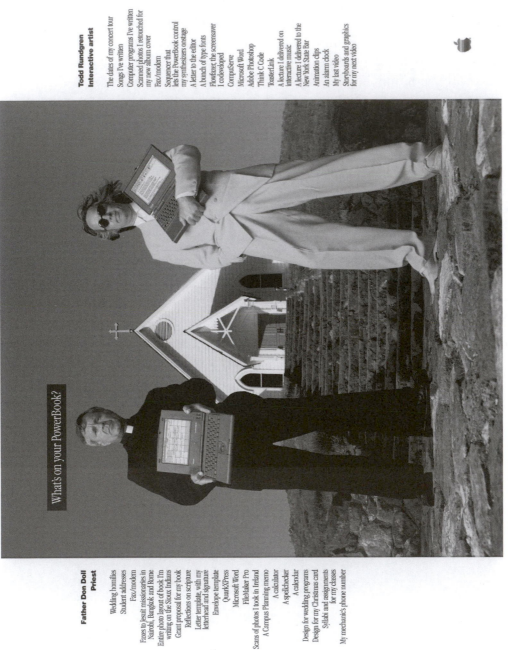

Father Don Doll
Priest

Wedding homilies
Student addresses
Fax/modem
Faxes to Jesuit missionaries in
Nairobi, Bangkok and Rome
Entire photo layout of book I'm
writing on the Sioux Indians
Grant proposal for my book
Reflections on scripture
Letter template, with my
letterhead and signature
Envelope template
QuarkXPress
Microsoft Word
FileMaker Pro
Scans of photos I took in Ireland
A Campus Planning memo
A calculator
A spellchecker
A calendar
Design for wedding programs
Design for my Christmas card
Syllabi and assignments
for my classes
My mechanic's phone number

Todd Rundgren
Interactive artist

The dates of my concert tour
Songs I've written
Computer programs I've written
Scanned photos I retouched for
my new album cover
Fax/modem
Sequencer that
lets the PowerBook control
my synthesizers onstage
A letter to the editor
A bunch of type fonts
Flowfazer, the screensaver
I codeveloped
CompuServe
Microsoft Word
Adobe Photoshop
Think C Code
ToasterLink
A lecture I delivered on
interactive music
A lecture I delivered to the
New York State Bar
Animation clips
An alarm clock
My last video
Storyboards and graphics
for my next video

Steve Hayden

"I think all advertising people come from dysfunctional families."

Steve Hayden, Vice Chairman of Ogilvy & Mather Worldwide, believes creative people have an ingrained need to receive extra attention and to please people—traits that are often developed as a result of an unhealthy family environment.

"I probably had them very early on," he observes.

A similar observation is voiced in Susan Gillette's chapter. In Tom McElligott's chapter, we will hear his theory about why children of dysfunctional families make great creative people. In this chapter, we will see the results of someone who grew up in a dysfunctional family and went on to create some of America's most memorable advertising.

Over the course of his career, Hayden has worked on top accounts such as Apple Computer, IBM, Porsche, Pizza Hut, Nike, Kodak, SAP, Motorola, and American Express. He has received some of advertising's most prestigious awards, including the Cannes Gold Lion award, the One Show award, the Clio award, the British D&AD award, and the New York Art Directors Club award.

Hayden attributes much of his success to his collaborative nature. He believes that it's better to own 20 percent of a great idea than 100 percent of a so-so idea.

FROM MUSIC TO ENGLISH TO ADVERTISING

If there's a lesson to be learned by looking at Steve Hayden's career, it's that while goals might shift and change, you can still come out on top. Hayden originally wanted to become a professional musician. He then became a writer, went back and forth between big and small agencies, and even explored the option of writing for television. It wasn't until almost ten years into his advertising career that he decided to dedicate himself to advertising as a lifelong profession.

Hayden's career shifts may at first seem to have served no purpose. But his later success was a direct result of his varied background. Studying his career transitions may also help you along.

A budding cellist, Hayden enrolled in the University of Southern California in Los Angeles to study with Gregor Piatigorsky. He claims he was the worst cellist in the class. "Out of a class of twelve," says Hayden, "ten went to Moscow—four of whom placed first through fourth in the Tchaikovsky Competition." He was left behind playing bar mitzvahs.

At the same time, Hayden started writing. His work came to the attention of USC's English Department; they asked him to join an experimental honors program. The reward for joining: straight As and a limited number of hours in class.

This was more than enough of an incentive to get him to become an English major. He kept music as a minor and went on to publish a "hippie humor magazine" at USC, which was his first semi-commercial writing experience.

After college, Hayden married and moved to Michigan, where his wife was working on her master's degree. He initially tried to support himself playing cello. But when his money ran out, he began looking for full-time work. His reasoning for applying for jobs in advertising: "It sounded like more fun than being a Xerox sales trainee."

To have something to show during job interviews, Hayden created a spec portfolio using the Campbell-Ewald Creative Test. In the test, he was asked to solve a series of advertising problems.

For instance, he developed a campaign for oatmeal and another one for a coffee maker. His book was more rudimentary than those developed today. He had stick figure illustrations and handwritten headlines.

Hayden's portfolio—as he readily admits—might not be strong enough to land him a job today, but back in the sixties it did the trick. MacManus, Johns & Adams/ Bloomfield Hills hired him as a junior copywriter to work on industrial accounts, a position that helped change his attitude toward the morality of advertising.

Says Hayden, "I went into advertising with this sixties sensibility that all advertising was a manipulation and that it was created by horrible, criminal people who put property rights above human rights—and that all of them probably should be killed—but I was going to do this anyway, just to make a few dollars."

By working on industrial accounts, Hayden learned that a copywriter really couldn't lie. In industrial advertising, you are writing to engineers and other people who know a great deal more about vitrified grinding wheels or centrifugal vacuum pumps than you do. So if you lie, you will eventually be found out.

Industrial advertising gave Hayden the foundation for later success for two fundamental reasons. First, he was forced to produce a high volume of work. Profit margins are typically much lower in industrial advertising, so the amount of work creative people need to produce is higher than with larger consumer accounts.

Second, he had to cope with vast amounts of source material and to delve into technical areas he didn't know anything about. This taught him how to be a "quick study" and to learn new areas rapidly.

As we've seen in earlier chapters, careers are sometimes shaped by events outside of an individual's control or professional life. We find this here, too.

Despite his initial success, Hayden quit his job and moved back to Los Angeles. His parents had become ill, and they asked him to live closer to them.

Back home with a portfolio of published industrial work and some unpublished samples for Pontiac, a client of his former employer, Hayden started looking for work. He was well received at DDB, but they didn't have an immediate opening, so he took a job at a small industrial shop.

Hayden worked at a series of small shops before the next major twist in his career, a position with Clinton E. Frank. At that time, Clinton E. Frank was one of the largest and most creative agencies in Los Angeles. They'd won the Belding Award two years in a row, and had Toyota as one of their major accounts. "Going from working at a little industrial agency to working for Clinton E. Frank was a big jump," says Hayden. There, he worked as a liaison between the account and creative areas, doing strategic planning for Toyota.

Satisfied at being allowed to write at least some ads along with his strategy papers, Hayden continued to work as a liaison until he was asked to become an account executive. But Hayden wanted to stay on the creative side of advertising. Says Hayden, "While the strategy side is very interesting, it's a much colder endeavor. It's more removed from people. It doesn't allow you to be quite as silly. It seemed like a choice between working for an insurance company or a film company. I'd much rather work for a film company."

Since he didn't want the promotion, Hayden went to the creative director and asked for a shot at staying in the creative department. With this simple request, Hayden became a full-time copywriter.

Within a year and a half, he was promoted again, this time to group supervisor on Toyota. Then in 1975, two major events changed Hayden's career. First, his father passed away, prompting him to reevaluate his life and career goals. Second, Toyota fired Clinton E. Frank.

"The firing was ironic," recalls Hayden. "Three months before, Toyota had thrown a big party for us because they'd passed Volkswagen in sales for the first time. They said they were on their way to becoming a dominant force in the world automotive industry and thanked us for our contribution. When Toyota fired us, they said we were too small for them now that they were bigger than Volkswagen."

In response to the firing, Clinton E. Frank laid off more than 100 employees. Fewer than 20 people remained at the agency. Says Hayden, "I thought, advertising certainly is a horrible, disreputable way to make a living because these things can happen to you and there's absolutely no security."

To revive the agency, they tried bringing in new clients, but without success. Their last hope was getting the Kawasaki motorcycle account. For the pitch, they brought up motorcycles in the elevator and put them in their lobby. And they were confident about showing their reel of award-winning spots. Unfortunately, when the prospective client came in for a tour of the offices, someone opened a door off the conference room and exposed a long hallway of empty offices. "It was unbelievable," says Hayden. "All we needed was tumbleweed blowing through." Of course, they did not win the Kawasaki account and a few months later the office closed.

A Break from Commercials

Luckily, Hayden wasn't out in the cold. He'd decided to write for television and had just sold a script to *Welcome Back, Kotter*, a popular show at the time. Since the script was produced and aired, he thought he was on his way to having a successful second career. He wrote for other television shows. He discovered that writing episodic television was not that much different from writing commercials since it's a collaborative effort. The producer is, in effect, the creative director. And it's much more of a commercial form than an art form. Many formulas have to be followed. The difference? Hayden found the people in advertising to be more pleasant.

Since he still needed a way to pay the rent while launching his TV-writing career, Hayden accepted a part-time freelance job at yet another small industrial agency. He planned to work only four hours a day. While at the agency, Hayden wrote several ads that attracted a lot of attention within the advertising community and brought assignments from major advertisers, including *Time* magazine and Universal Pictures. Consequently the agency grew and his role expanded.

One of the ads he wrote even won a Belding Award (see the ad for KFAC in the portfolio section). Suddenly, he was attracting the attention of senior creatives and was being recognized as somebody who had enormous creative potential.

So he decided to give up television writing and get serious about advertising. He felt he needed to work for a larger agency where he could get the training and experience to develop his skills.

Hayden first took a writing position at Foote, Cone & Belding. He got the job because he had worked on Toyota and they wanted him to work on Mazda. But he wasn't getting the training he needed, so Hayden stayed for only three months.

Chiat/Day and the Apple-Go-Round

Jay Chiat also noticed the KFAC ad and subsequently hired Hayden. "For my first five months, I thought I was going to get fired every day," says Hayden. "The level of competition was so intense, and the people so hip-swanking cool. It was a very intimidating environment to be in."

But Hayden had a solid reputation. He was known as someone who could produce good long-copy ads—a rarity in the early eighties.

After a little over a year at Chiat/Day, Hayden was asked to help Jay Chiat open a New York office. However, New York was not the only city targeted in Chiat's expansion plans. Eight months after opening New York, Chiat bought Regis McKenna Advertising in San Francisco, which had the Apple Computer account. Since Hayden had a technical/industrial background, Chiat had him write on Apple while the San Francisco office was being assembled. But Chiat wanted to keep Hayden's contribution a secret because he didn't want him to leave New York.

When Chiat/Day acquired Regis McKenna Advertising, they also acquired Dick Cavett as Apple's spokesperson. Hayden's task was to figure out how best to use him.

He wrote some spots where Cavett interviewed the computer. Hayden claims these spots were very simple-minded and not very good. But they were noticed. Consequently, Hayden was kept as Apple's copywriter and eventually moved to San Francisco.

The success of Apple is legendary; it changed the composition of the entire computer industry and, more importantly, increased the accessibility of computers. Hayden believes much of this success was due to the personalities involved with Apple.

According to legend, Jay Chiat was constantly dissatisfied with the work and the people. "He was like General Patton," says Hayden. "Every couple of weeks, he'd fly into town, fire the creative director, and put someone else into place."

Apple boss Steve Jobs was also very demanding. Jobs didn't just want the best advertising in the computer category. He wanted the best advertising ever.

Since Chiat felt that the San Francisco office wasn't working well enough and since Jobs felt that he needed more from the agency, the Apple account, along with Hayden, was moved to the main office in Los Angeles in 1982. This enabled Chiat/Day to draw from a bigger creative department. It also enabled Lee Clow, creative director at Chiat/Day's L.A. office (see Chapter 18), to get involved.

Apple was going through many changes, says Hayden. "Every week we'd have somebody new to deal with. Our working environment was abusive, threatening, and impossible."

Finally, the creative group was so fed up that in 1983 they asked Jay Chiat to resign the account. Chiat's advice was to be patient and to "hang in there." In retrospect, this paid off. "Subsequently, all of us got ground-breaking work in our portfolios," says Hayden. "But it took a lot of endurance."

When the environment is bad but the work is good, you too may want to "hang in there." It could pay off in an improved portfolio of published work. For Hayden, one result was the revolutionary "1984" spot that ran during the Super Bowl. We'll tell you about it in the portfolio section. Needless to say, not all Hayden's creative efforts were slam dunks.

In the fall of 1984, nine months after "1984," Apple sales had stalled-out completely. Jobs wanted to introduce a whole new suite of office products to enhance work-group productivity. Hayden came up with a name for it, the "Macintosh Office."

"But one little problem came up," says Hayden. "A lot of the things that were to make up the Macintosh Office didn't exist or wouldn't be ready for a long time.

"At that point, I came up with the phrases, 'Don't bite the karmic weenie,' which means if you lie in advertising, people have a way of finding out, and 'Never write a check with your advertising that your product can't cash.' Some people hold that against you, especially if you're a very high-profile company."

This directly relates to Hayden's experience as a writer on industrial accounts.

Because of his beliefs, Hayden got into a number of more or less public arguments with the Macintosh group around the time of "Lemmings" (see portfolio section), a spot that aired during the next Super Bowl. "I think the people at Chiat/Day felt I was not being a team player," says Hayden. "The agency position was that we wanted to run 'Lemmings' and other ads about the Macintosh Office. My position was that the Macintosh Office didn't exist, and we'd probably get in trouble advertising it."

Hayden believed that Macintosh sales should go up gradually as the product was able to deliver more functionality. He thought that Apple should keep putting resources toward the Apple II family, which was still the cash cow of the company. "I was kind of vocal about this at a couple of meetings and I used the phrase, 'The caboose is trying to blow up the locomotive,'" says Hayden. "In other words, Macintosh was being dragged along by the Apple II, yet we were trying everything possible to destroy Apple II sales."

As a result of his public arguments, Hayden was asked off the Macintosh portion of the account. Normally, that would have been enough of a blow to get anybody to quit. But Hayden didn't. He stuck around and wrote more commercials for the Apple II.

Tracy-Locke & Tacos

Then a huge offer came in for Hayden from Tracy-Locke. They wanted him to start their Los Angeles office and run the $50 million Taco Bell account. They promised to double his salary. "Being essentially unhappy—I felt I had made a contribution to Macintosh and that I was unfairly banished—I took the offer," says Hayden.

Hayden claims he developed one of L.A.'s best creative departments in only a month, thanks to a number of Chiat/Day creatives who followed him to Tracy-Locke. "We'd won the Princess Cruises account, and it looked like we were going to have a very successful new agency," says Hayden. "But I was not the kind of guy to get along with Tracy-Locke's culture."

Selling tacos was also new to Hayden. He didn't know how to make taco meat look good. Strategically, he thought Taco Bell was an alternative to McDonald's and Burger King. So he developed a theme line, "Burgers? We don't want no stinking burgers!" and got Cheech Marin to be their spokesperson. Says Hayden, "The object of the game was to get every ten-year-old in America to say this line whenever they were asked to go to McDonald's or Burger King."

When Hayden presented the campaign to Taco Bell's marketing people, they were horrified. "At Chiat/Day, you'd be forgiven if the client was horrified but you believed in the campaign," says Hayden. "But, with Tracy-Locke, the agency was more horrified than the client."

Consequently, the relationship between Hayden's creative department and the rest of Tracy-Locke began to deteriorate. "The body had rejected the transplant," says Hayden. "They came to me with 19 demands on how the creative department and I had to change our behavior." Instead of trying to meet these demands, Hayden and his staff quit. "Subsequently, most went on to freelance, and I was home for a few days," says Hayden.

Back on the Apple-Go-Round...

Meanwhile, Chiat/Day was having some bad luck with Apple Computer, and the account went into review.

"Here's where the story gets rather kinky," says Hayden. "They were going to have a two-agency review between BBDO and Chiat/Day. I was at home after Tracy-Locke. BBDO contacted me and wanted to hire me. Apple Computer called up—they were speaking in some weird diplomatic code—but were essentially saying, 'We're not so sure you should go to Chiat/Day. If we were you, we wouldn't go to work for Chiat/Day.'"

But Hayden did go back to Chiat/Day. He met with Jay Chiat and Lee Clow, the two people who taught him the most about how to make great advertising. At the same time, he claims to have had a semi-abusive relationship with them. Says Hayden, "It's like if you went to a strict boarding school where they made you take cold showers every morning and beat you with paddles, but if the school were to burn down, it would still break your heart."

Chiat and Clow made Hayden the creative director of the Los Angeles office. But it didn't work out. Says Hayden, "As a rule, never ride into an ad agency on a white horse because people will throw mud on you right away. I ended up being blamed for the loss of Apple by Chiat/Day."

One of the things that got Hayden into trouble was that he came back with the creative director title. "It was apparent to everybody who had stayed with Chiat/ Day that this was a ploy to get a guy with a relationship with an important account back into the agency," says Hayden. "I think a lot of the hostility came from that phenomenon. People felt I didn't really earn the title. You need at least a couple of senior teams to agree that you're in the right position."

Even though Hayden returned to Chiat/Day, BBDO New York kept trying to recruit him to work on Apple now that they'd taken it over. "I didn't want to change agencies again," he says. "I wanted to be at the same place for a while and be able to stay there. And being creative director of Chiat/Day, even under the worst of circumstances, is still one of the best jobs in Los Angeles. It was very hard to walk away."

But, finally, in August of 1986, Hayden did walk. He hired two former Chiat/ Day staffers and within two weeks developed an entire year's print campaign for Apple. Although Hayden worked in Los Angeles, he was not made part of BBDO West, both to allow his small team to focus entirely on Apple and to keep them more closely tied to the mother ship, BBDO New York.

However, the presence of another agency in Los Angeles named BBDO caused the original one to disintegrate. According to Hayden, there was all sorts of jealousy and dissension. To put an end to this strife, Hayden was asked to take over all of the Los Angeles and San Francisco operations.

Hayden approached the merger with a little more humility than he had with Tracy-Locke. He wanted to integrate the agencies without making it an "us against them" situation. To do so, Hayden worked on some of the more difficult accounts and spent hours meeting with clients. For instance, with Sizzler, he learned their market system and the type of creative they needed for their business.

"This time I wasn't going to be this creative firebrand who is not going to tolerate any deviation from the highest possible standard," says Hayden. "Because there are different standards. One is, how many dinners did you sell last night?"

Part of Hayden's mission was to support his staff. Rather than managing through intimidation and tearing up storyboards, his goal was to create a collegial, respectful atmosphere.

For example, Hayden had a very talented senior art director—someone who'd been in *Communications Arts* many times—who came up with an ad that Hayden didn't think looked right. They worked back and forth on it. The art director did it Hayden's way, and he did it his own way. Hayden preferred it his way, but gave the art director the choice by saying, "We pay you a lot of money for your talent and expertise. I want you to go away and think about it and tell me if that's what you want to do." Of course, the art director wanted to run it his way. And Hayden was willing to live with that.

Around this time, however, Apple Computer's fortunes started to decline.

John Sculley, who had been CEO, left (Steve Jobs was already gone). Among the reasons, the Board of Directors thought Sculley was spending too much time with the Clintons and not enough time running the company. "He was probably the last person there who actually understood the value of the Apple brand," says Hayden. "From being an idealistic company, we suddenly had a bunch of leaders who wore diamond-encrusted Rolexes and Tony Soprano pinky rings—who had no conception of the Apple brand, Apple values, or Apple culture. Apple is a great brand, and seeing it put in the charge of people who didn't understand it, or even the promise of personal technology, was one of the most heartbreaking experiences of my life."

Consequently, the engineers, designers, and other creative people who had made Apple a great company started leaving. Sales were sinking. And their advertising process had become even more difficult. "I warned BBDO management of an impending disaster," he says, "that unless Steve Jobs came back, Apple would be finished as a company."

Hayden was also growing increasingly frustrated because BBDO West, due to conflicts with other offices in the network, was unable to pitch some major West Coast accounts. "One of the problems with working for a big agency is that there are conflicts all over the place," says Hayden. "So without being able to win a car account or a phone company, we simply couldn't grow."

...To Big Blue

Meanwhile, Ogilvy & Mather (O&M), with extensive technology experience because of their work for Microsoft and Compaq, was awarded the worldwide IBM business in May 1994. Nearly 70 agencies were fired in the consolidation. (Reportedly, BBDO had an opportunity to pitch the IBM account, but decided to stick with Apple.) Once O&M got the account, they discovered that they needed someone in a senior role to oversee the whole thing and started trying to recruit Hayden in July of that year. "I really didn't want to leave BBDO," says Hayden. "I actually don't like changing jobs all that much."

After a lot of soul-searching, however, Hayden decided to make the switch. He asked himself: "Do I want to be known just for Apple Computer or am I young enough to take another run at making a little history?"

He also wanted to see if he had the wherewithal to work in a major New York agency. When he'd worked in New York for Chiat/Day in 1980, it was a small shop. And while BBDO New York was a large, respected agency, Hayden felt that its "killer culture" wasn't quite right for him. O&M felt like a better cultural match. And he loved the senior IBM clients he met during the interview process. "Abby Kohnstamm is amazing and was willing to build a team in partnership with Ogilvy to do this massive job of brand revitalization. There was no comparison with the people driving Apple into the ground."

He started at Ogilvy in November of 1994 as President, Worldwide Brand Services–IBM. In making the move, he was asked to make up a title for himself that was big enough to justify his job change but wouldn't offend anybody who was already there. "So I made up this title, which remains to this day meaningless within Ogilvy," says Hayden. "Still, about five people had to become 'presidents' as soon as I arrived because I had made the mistake of putting the p-word in my title. Everybody wanted to be president of something. I've always wanted a title like 'Mystic Knight of the Five Rings' or 'Keeper of the Royal Works'—but I don't doubt someone else would want to become 'Mystic Knight of the *Six* Rings' as soon as I got my business cards."

He found that O&M's culture was perfect for his personality. "Part of David Ogilvy's written canon was that we hire people our clients wouldn't dream of hiring," says Hayden. "We're looking for talent in whatever form it takes. But we do demand that people treat each other civilly and with respect. I think the enforcement of that policy has made communication between departments, offices, and countries much easier than at any other place I've been."

In his new position, he was head of the entire worldwide IBM account. He found the transition to be much smoother than in the past. Work for IBM was already moving ahead. Hayden's job was to build a worldwide team, figure out the processes to use, solidify the client relationship, and make the Ogilvy network work with the speed and efficiency that was required. "We didn't even have worldwide e-mail when I got here," says Hayden. "So I got involved in a lot of non-creative activities. I think I was welcomed warmly because they needed all the help they could get."

In addition, the supportive attitude he projected helped with his transition: "It was not, 'I am the big boss and you're going to do what I say from now on,' but 'How can I help you?'" says Hayden. "You're doing an amazing thing. How can we pull this together?"

The unique culture of Ogilvy also helped Hayden succeed in his worldwide role. "There is bit more politeness in the system than you find elsewhere, and it really does help us to act as one company," he says. "At BBDO, because it was a federation of creative agencies, when you brought teams together from different offices they tended to fight with each other and be very suspicious. And Chiat/Day has been trying to move their culture out to other offices for a long, long time. But there's something about David Ogilvy's foundation for this company that makes this place work better internationally."

Drawing on his experience with Apple, where he learned the power of experiential marketing, Hayden set about the task of integrating advertising, sales promotion, direct marketing, design, packaging, and sales events.

"Apple Creative Services worked very closely with Chiat/Day," he notes, "and we put on tremendous MacWorld events and sales meetings that were totally integrated. But IBM and Ogilvy weren't working in that way."

He had two main challenges.

First, Ogilvy Direct, the agency's direct marketing arm, wasn't set up to do work unless they had a purchase order. OgilvyInteractive, after a brilliant beginning under the legendary interactive pioneer Martin Nisenholtz, was adrift and no longer even part of the main agency. Secondly, IBM's budgets were fragmented into silos and, therefore, they weren't structured to pay for integrated programs.

To overcome these internal challenges, Hayden built a separate organization called Team Blue, which was dedicated to providing integrated marketing solutions for IBM. He also brought OgilvyInteractive back into the fold, stating, "If direct is the future of advertising, certainly interactive is the future of direct."

Then, for about 18 months, Hayden pitched the idea of "360 degree branding" on every project. Once IBM started adjusting its budgets, the integrated approach began to take hold.

"IBM helped Ogilvy achieve leadership in 360 branding," says Hayden. "It was a commonsense move that allowed us to make the most of IBM's budgets."

Once IBM was solidified, Hayden started working on other accounts. "It wasn't until the summer of '95," recalls Hayden. The first big presentation was to Kodak. John Sculley was consulting for Kodak's CMO, Carl Gustin, and they invited Ogilvy to pitch the account. "It was a tremendous effort against BBDO, and a wonderful pulling together of Ogilvy's resources. We noticed that the Kodak media plan hadn't changed in 25 years. So reimagining media played a very important role in winning. We also did environmental design and packaging."

Having taken on an increased role within the organization, Hayden was named Vice Chairman in January 2001. Ogilvy Worldwide is divided into four regions (North America, Latin America, Asia Pacific, and EAME, which includes Europe, Africa, and the Middle East), with nearly 16,000 employees in more than 400 offices. Hayden likens his position to "the ghost in the machine," as he oversees creativity in this vast organization.

"I go where I'm needed," says Hayden. "I still work very much on IBM, Kodak, Dove, Motorola, SAP, and American Express. But I'm covering the world. Unfortunately, my ex-wives have taken most of my frequent-flyer miles."

Some Final Thoughts on Apple

As for the return of Apple to financial health, even though it's an IBM competitor, Hayden is thrilled.

"It is just phenomenal," he says. "Steve Jobs came back in the nick of time." Once Jobs returned to Apple, he moved the account back to Chiat/Day.

"The first thing Chiat/Day recommended was a campaign to reassert the value of the Apple brand, which is instructive for companies that think branding is a waste of money," notes Hayden. "That's where 'Think Different' came from. It was an absolutely brilliant piece of work, because the only product Apple had worth selling at that time was a PowerBook that tended to catch fire. The management preceding Jobs had done everything possible to make Apple computers as ugly as possible. But Jobs managed to reassure and reenergize the faithful, and buy enough time to get the iMac launched."

Hayden reports that he enjoys living in New York, although he recognizes that it's not as healthy as California. As for his resiliency and being able to thrive in such a competitive industry, Hayden says he relies on "functional Alzheimer's." "Part of my formula," says Hayden, "is to forget the past and move on."

A LOOK AT HAYDEN'S HISTORY-MAKING PORTFOLIO

—— BENDIX ELECTRONICS ——

Where else can you get this kind of choice in high-vacuum pumps?

Where else but Bendix, makers of the largest line of high-vacuum pumps available from a single source.

Bendix offers you 23 standard metal oil vapor pumps, more than anyone else. A dynamic line incorporating the latest advances such as the new WHITE HAT, an oleophobic polymer-coated cap, which significantly reduces back-streaming of BlueLine diffusion pumps. A broad range of metal, mercury and glass oil pumps. Sizes to suit every conceivable research and industrial application.

Bendix completes its line with the latest in ion and sublimation pumps, and a series of mechanical pumps.

The size and variety of the Bendix line allows spot comparisons, makes your final choice easier. Make it easy on yourself by finding out more about Bendix pumps. Start by checking the performance range chart. And write: The Bendix Corporation, Vacuum Division, 1775 Mt. Read Blvd., Rochester, New York 14603.

Bendix Electronics

Hayden claims he probably wouldn't have hired himself. "In my early years, I wasn't really trying to reach people," says Hayden. Today, he looks for creative people who can reach people in an emotional way, not just intellectually.

This ad is from his early years working on industrial products. It was effective but not exceptional—unless, of course, you were shopping for high-vacuum pumps. "My first headline was 'We've got plenty of nothing,' which would've been quite a bit better. I learned early the value of good account people and the cost of bad ones."

Although he claims that this piece does not show the humanity he would later express, this period did enable him to develop his style. Says Hayden, "It seemed to me that if I did something that, at its core, was rational and plausible but made it look irrational, I'd attract more attention."

What prompted Hayden to come to this discovery?

Basically, he says, it came from his need to keep things interesting and from the freedom of small budgets. Says Hayden, "I often find that you get your best work from accounts that are too small for anybody else to screw up. Some of the worst work comes out of the biggest budgets. If it's really important, it's almost guaranteed to be bad. It's kind of a backwards thing, but there's just too much resting on it."

—— KFAC ——

This is one of Hayden's first ads to gain recognition. "The ad was very, very successful," recalls Hayden. "Classical stations all over the country reprinted it. And it got a tremendous amount of attention in town. All these studios and advertising agencies noticed it, and it wound up pinned up over many desks."

A classical music listener himself, Hayden wrote the ad based on his knowledge of typical listeners as opposed to typical advertising for classical music stations.

"The ads that I'd seen usually had a violin with a rose next to it or a French horn with a glass of wine or something like that, but classical music listeners don't particularly think of themselves that way."

Hayden believed there must be a different way to attract attention. "Radio stations are not very interesting to advertise. However, it doesn't cost the reader anything to sample the product. It's totally free."

Based on that thinking, it occurred to Hayden to do something similar to a direct response ad. "I thought of it as something like an ad for, oh, a Dale Carnegie course or some kind of a snake oil. I took that approach and made it humorous and somewhat absurd. Obviously the man in the 'before' picture is not the same as in

BEFORE
*This is me before I started listening to
KFAC. Overweight, poor, unhappy and alone.*

AFTER
*This is I after 16 short years as a
KFAC listener. Rich, trim and sexy.*

How classical music changed my life.

The other day at Ma Maison, as I was waiting for the attendant to retrieve my chocolate brown 450 SLC, the Saudi prince I'd been noshing with said, "Say, Bill, how did an unassuming guy like yourself come to be so rich, so trim, so...sexy?"

My eyes grew misty. "It wasn't always this way, Ahmed, old buddy..."

My mind raced back to the Bad Time, before the investment tips, the real estate empire, before Dino bought my screenplay and I bought my Columbia 50...

Once I was a lot like you.

Working at a nowhere job, hitting the singles bars, watching situation comedies in my free time. I tipped the scales at a hefty 232, but my bank balance couldn't have tipped the bus boy at the Midnight Mission.

Finally, I hit bottom...picked up by the Castaic police for barreling my old heap the wrong way over some parking lot spikes.

My last friend in this lonely world, Hardy Gustavsen, set me straight while he was driving me back to L.A.

"Bill, get hold of yourself! Start listening to KFAC!"

"Gosh, Hardy, don't they play classical music? I'm not sure I cotton to that high brow stuff!"

Aside from a couple of summers at Tanglewood and Aspen, and one semester in Casals' Master Class...

I knew absolutely nothing about classical music.

"Bill, who would be wrong if you got better?"

Looking into his steely blue eyes, I realized Hardy was right. I resolved to give KFAC a shot.

At first, it was quite painful. Listening to all those 100-piece groups was confusing—I was used to having the drums on the right and the bass on the left and the singer in the middle. All those semidemihemiquavers made my head spin.

But I started to feel the beneficial effects of classical music listening in just one short week.

In no time, I was using napkins with every meal, I switched from Bourbon to an unpretentious Montrachet and I became able to hear sirens even with my car windows rolled up.

Soon I was spending every night with KFAC and a good book, like Aquinas' *Summa Theologica.*

I realized that some of the wealthiest, most famous people in this world listened to classical music—Napoleon, Bismark, George Washington, Beethoven...and many others who are yet alive today.

Then I met Marlene. The first girl who knew there was more to *Also Sprach Zarathustra* than the theme from *2001.* And I fell in love.

Today, I'm on top of the world with a wonderful wife, close friends in high places and a promising career in foreign currency manipulation.

Can classical music do for you what it did for me?

A few years back, scientific studies showed that when dairy cows are played classical music the quantity and quality of their milk dramatically

improves.

Now if it can do that for plain old moo cows, imagine what it can do for you!

You might use it to control disgusting personal habits and make fun new friends. The possibilities are endless!

Can you afford KFAC?

Is lox kosher?

Even though marketing surveys show that KFAC's audience is the most affluent assemblage of nice people in Southern California, yes, you *can* afford KFAC! Thanks to their Special Introductory Offer, you can listen FREE OF CHARGE for *as many hours as you like* without obligation!

Begin the KFAC habit today.

Remember, the longest journey begins by getting dressed. Don't let this opportunity slip through your fingers. Tune to KFAC right NOW, while you're thinking about it.

And get ready for a spectacular improvement in your life.

Warn your family and friends that you may start dressing for dinner.

You may lose your taste for beer nuts.

And the next time you're on the freeway thinking about playing with your nose, you'll find yourself asking:

"Really. Would a KFAC listener do this?"

the 'after' picture. I then had the copy come out of that—it's pretty funny, if I do say so myself.

"It rattles on in a very L.A. style. And it ends with a free offer. You can try the station with absolutely no obligation whatsoever."

Hayden says of the ad's appeal, "Rationally, classical music is not going to change you from being a fat slob into a rich, trim, and sexy person. But in terms of how classical music people feel about themselves and their relationship to the music—and as a broader statement of their cultural wardrobe—it gets at that. There is a kernel of truth under the irrational presentation."

—— Apple ——

This is one of the first ads Hayden "ghost wrote" for Apple while still stationed in Chiat/Day's New York office. It was produced by Chiat/Day San Francisco under Hy Yablonka's supervision.

Early in 1983, both Hayden and Apple moved to Chiat/Day Los Angeles. "Lee Clow literally saved my life. He was the only one who could talk both Jay Chiat and Steve Jobs off the ledge.

"We were caught in a meat grinder between these very extreme personalities. But the work got better and better under this pressure."

Baked Apple.

Last Thanksgiving, a designer from Lynn/Ohio Corporation took one of the company's Apple Personal Computers home for the holidays.

While he was out eating turkey, it got baked.

His cat, perhaps miffed at being left alone, knocked over a lamp which started a fire which, among other unpleasantries, melted his TV set all over his computer. He thought his goose was cooked.

But when he took the Apple to Cincinnati Computer Store, *mirabile dictu*, it still worked.

A new case and keyboard made it as good as new.

Nearly 1,000 Apple dealers have complete service centers that can quickly fix just about anything that might go wrong, no matter how bizarre.

So if you're looking for a personal computer that solves problems instead of creating them, look to your authorized Apple dealer.

You'll find everything well-done.

The personal computer. apple

Welcome, IBM.

Seriously.

Welcome to the most exciting and important marketplace since the computer revolution began 35 years ago.

And congratulations on your first personal computer.

Putting real computer power in the hands of the individual is already improving the way people work, think, learn, communicate and spend their leisure hours.

Computer literacy is fast becoming as fundamental a skill as reading or writing.

When we invented the first personal computer system, we estimated that over 140,000,000 people worldwide could justify the purchase of one, if only they understood its benefits.

Next year alone, we project that well over 1,000,000 will come to that understanding. Over the next decade, the growth of the personal computer will continue in logarithmic leaps.

We look forward to responsible competition in the massive effort to distribute this American technology to the world. And we appreciate the magnitude of your commitment.

Because what we are doing is increasing social capital by enhancing individual productivity.

Welcome to the task. **apple**

"Then, John Sculley came in from Pepsi to take over Apple. And that was yet another personality, one who was much more used to disciplined advertising and less to the kind of piratical craziness of Jobs and company.

"I can't emphasize enough how painful this period was, because Jay would beat everybody up and he'd leave the room. Then Jobs would come in and he'd do the same. And this continued.

"Every three months—or maybe every two months—Jobs would threaten to fire the agency. 'You guys aren't keeping up with us,' he'd say. Yet, under those circumstances, we kept getting better."

"Most copy," according to Hayden, "chases readers away. Clients can drive copywriters to a grinding level of dullness by editing out whatever they notice, which is to say whatever is actually interesting.

"To get around this, you need stamina, resilience, and an almost pitiable sense of optimism. Research demonstrates that you get better readership with ads that have some personality—that have some surprises and rewards for the reader."

To launch Macintosh, the first personal computer with a graphical user interface, Jobs said he wanted an ad that would "stop the world in its tracks." According to many critics, Hayden achieved that feat with the commercial shown at the top of the next page. It is one of the most remembered commercials in advertising history.

Although "1984" looks elaborate because of its sophisticated production, the thinking behind it is very simple. "To me, the secret of advertising is to make an irrational presentation of a rational argument," says Hayden. "The rational argument is that we're making computers accessible to everyone. So, theoretically, you should show a farmer with a computer, a fireman with a computer, a nurse with a computer, or a little kid with a computer. Indeed, commercials like that have been done. But why not try to come at it in an irrational way, creating something that's interesting and yet still gets to the idea that we're democratizing technology?"

Hayden clearly found a way with the "1984" commercial.

While "1984" received a lot of praise, "Lemmings" (1985), according to Hayden, "was totally reviled." Part of the problem, says Hayden, was the lack of redemption. "It had a threatening ending, as opposed to a hopeful one. We were showing customers walking off a cliff.

"It's interesting though. 'Lemmings' was played at the MacWorld convention a few years later and it received a standing ovation. And it was the most remembered commercial of 1985... but then the Hindenburg was the most remembered event of 1937."

On January 24th, Apple Computer will introduce Macintosh. And you'll see why 1984 won't be like "1984"

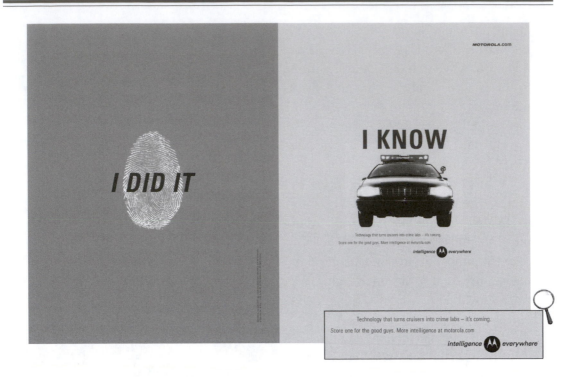

—— Motorola ——

Hayden says that Ogilvy's Motorola pitch was one of the agency's finest moments because it was an example of 360 marketing that extended into every aspect of the client's business on a global scale. "It was one of those magical times when everything came together, including thunder, lightning, and the threat of a tornado outside as we began to give our presentation," he recalls. "We just nailed it. I think it just blew them away."

It was also one of the first times that Ogilvy used the Web to pull everything together for the pitch, including photography and creative ideas from offices around the world. As for the 360 marketing, Ogilvy identified employees as a key audience. "We pulled together a manifesto that explained to all of the many divisions of Motorola the overarching strategy of the company," he says.

The television was based on the song "If I Only Had a Brain" from the *Wizard of Oz*, and it featured malfunctioning machines in the home, on the road, and even on the football field that Motorola's wireless intelligence could set to rights.

One of the print campaigns in the presentation was based on the insight from Ogilvy Hong Kong that young people called their Motorola handsets "Motos." This idea was the beginning of the MOTOCODE campaign crafted by Dan Burrier and Bill Oberlander that ran for the next five years in more than 38 countries. It literally created a language that Motorola could own.

"In the very first briefing," Hayden explained, "hearing about Motorola's vision and aspirations, I jotted down 'intelligence everywhere'—which seemed as much a business strategy as a tagline, and a pretty good promise for the future. When we were finishing the first TV spots, something seemed to be missing. So I ad-libbed 'Hello, Moto' into the studio mike just as a demo. Ultimately, the client liked my demo better than the pros we brought in later, so they used my voice on all the spots for years. They even turned it into a ring tone that wound up on millions of phones. Sadly, I forgot to get paid."

After being seen for years as a dowdy Midwestern engineering firm, Motorola actually became cool again, as it launched one hit product after another with Ogilvy's worldwide campaigns.

—— IBM ——

Look at awards books today and most of the awards are given for print ads that are essentially posters with no copy. But Hayden thinks the ability to produce long copy is still vital. "As more and more people communicate by e-mail and seek product information when they're going through their shopping process, long copy is going to come roaring back," predicts Hayden.

THE BOOK OF @ BUSINESS

@ business infrastructure

Nice facade. Bad infrastructure.

INFRASTRUCTURE:

SOONER OR LATER, IT MATTERS.

INFRASTRUCTURE. The physical foundation of any thriving enterprise. In the world of technology, infrastructure means integrating the servers, software and storage systems of an e-business into one finely tuned and solidly reinforced machine.

To put it simply: as goes infrastructure, so goes the enterprise. All the ingenious products, brilliant marketing and champion deal closers won't amount to much if your supply chain is buggy, the network crashes or the databases fail (and all you can say is, "Sorry, but the computers are down; can you call us back sometime tomorrow?").

Infrastructure is about hard questions: What platforms should I use? How do I plan for the unexpected? Will it grow when we grow? Will it work with new technology in the future? Will it build upon my current systems? Can I link it to my customers' and suppliers' systems? I've heard all about open standards, but what exactly can they do for my business? What about outsourcing? And how am I going to finance all of this?

The people of IBM, together with our Business Partners, help literally thousands of companies with questions like these every day. And then solve them with open, flexible technologies, like Linux-enabled servers and storage systems that scale on a simple, pay-as-you-grow basis. And using innovative IBM software tools like Tivoli, DB2 and WebSphere, IBM specialists are helping real businesses everywhere build solid, flexible infrastructures.

So, unless you can turn your botched infrastructure attempts into fabulously profitable tourist attractions, give us a call at 800 426 7080 (ask for infrastructure) or visit ibm.com/e-business for our latest white paper on e-business infrastructure.

The sooner, of course, the better.

"The Internet is a text-driven medium. E-mail is text driven. So I think that powerful writing is going to have more of a role in the future, not less."

He feels that we've coaxed ourselves into believing that a compelling visual is enough and that nobody reads the body copy anymore. "But people do read copy," says Hayden. "With IBM we're continuing to do long copy because we have complex arguments. And people do read every word."

Hayden believes people want information. "Something like 85 percent of people who are looking for a new car go online before they go to the dealership," he observes. "And one of the complaints we've heard from consumers is that they can see the cars, the pictures, the specs, but nobody's telling them the whole story. When it comes to life's big decisions, I think it's almost impossible to give people too much information."

While the Internet boom of the late '90s is over, Hayden maintains that the Internet is going to continue changing the field of advertising. "Just because we're no longer selling electric virility belts doesn't mean we're not interested in electricity," says Hayden. "You can't do business without the Internet. The number of people online continues to go up every week. So it's going to remain a central phenomenon. The Web is changing the world."

Hayden believes that the Internet is providing all sorts of new marketing opportunities. "We had a couple of interesting experiments for IBM early on and won a

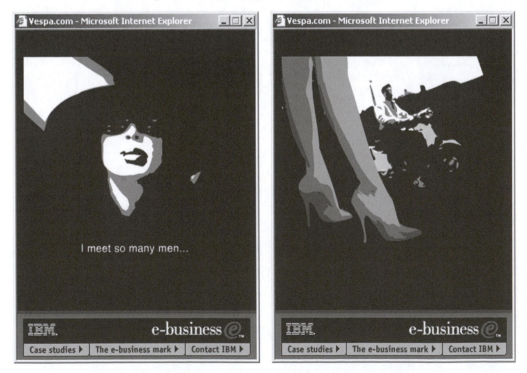

lot of awards at Cannes because the Internet stuff we were doing sort of looked like TV commercials," says Hayden, "so all the judges voted for it."

But that's not enough anymore. "The kind of marketing opportunity I'm talking about is coming up with an idea like BMW films," says Hayden referring to a campaign created by a competing agency. "I think that BMW films was a brilliant use of the Web. The indexing of BMW customers for Web usage is close to 100 percent. Everybody who buys a BMW is online." The result: BMW's sales went up at the peak of a recession. "They've had their two best sales years ever."

Hayden thinks this is only the beginning. "People are going to have the power to filter out communications they don't want," he says, "which means that your communications had better be desirable."

—— SAP ——

Like IBM, SAP had many agencies in many countries working for them when Ogilvy pitched the account. "They're in a really complex space," says Hayden. "Chris Wall and Susan Westre pulled it together in a global campaign with a simple black-

and-white execution that explained to their employees, even more than their customers, exactly what business SAP was in."

The result: "They were, I think, the only tech company whose brand value increased 3 percent on the Interbrand survey in 2001."

Again, this campaign is an example of reaching people emotionally as well as taking complicated stories and making them understandable.

"That's the problem we run up against all the time in technology," Hayden says. He notes that agencies often make the mistake of taking a relatively simple story for products like soft drinks and making it as complex as possible. "Ogilvy's attempt has been to keep it simple no matter what."

——— American Express ———

Ogilvy has had the American Express account for more than 40 years. "The American Express campaign is primarily a back-to-the-future reassertion of their brand values," says Hayden. "We got them to do a brand campaign that said they were more than a card. We took all the components of the American Express brand (Travelers' Cheques, travelers' services, the cards themselves, financial advisors) and put them together in corporate messaging that reminded the employees, first of all, of the important global scale and quality of the company."

"American Express has been a wild ride," says Hayden. "It is a brand that exists through advertising and needs a lot of it. It's been intriguing and exciting to work with this company."

A lot of brands spend a vast amount of money on sponsorships, and unless you go to Madison Square Garden or the NBA, you're not aware of it. "But if we're going to spend money to sponsor something like the NBA, rather than just having a couple of logos around the court, let's make a campaign out of it, and try to get more out of the investment," says Hayden. "So we try to throw a wrapper around everything having to do with sponsorships."

The solution: the "Official Card Of" campaign. "I think the issue was tying the role of the brand to the celebrities that they were sponsoring," says Hayden.

"The fact is, every NBA player has an American Express card and nobody mentioned that before." Working under David Apicella, the Ogilvy team of Chris Mitton and Terry Finley has also developed executions for their other sponsorships, including the U.S. Open. "What American Express wants to do is figure out how every dollar they spend fits into the marketing mix," says Hayden. "They want to understand the overall architecture."

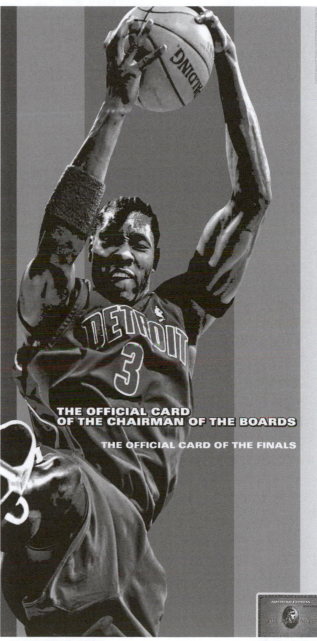

THE OFFICIAL CARD
OF THE CHAIRMAN OF THE BOARDS

THE OFFICIAL CARD OF THE FINALS

WWW.AMERICANEXPRESS.COM/NBA

MAKE LIFE REWARDING®

THE 'WELL-EXPRESSED' ADVICE AND OBSERVATIONS OF STEVE HAYDEN

What turns Steve Hayden on about advertising? He says it all boils down to the old Alexander Pope saying, "True wit is nature to advantage dressed, is often thought but ne'er so well expressed."

Hayden explains, "When there is a commercial concept that shows up on TV that seems so absolutely natural and yet riveting that it causes a reaction of delight and intrigue—and on top of that, everything works—that's what I find exciting."

Advertising that "makes life seem truly interesting" also excites Hayden. "Anything that hints that we're not a brain-dead culture makes me happy," he observes. "I think that most people are in kind of a rut, just muddling through. You look through a magazine and all the ads are pretty much expected and you're watching a sitcom and you've heard a version of all the jokes before.

"Life is grinding along. And you're just living somewhere. Then, all of a sudden, something strikes you as delightful. And you think, 'Maybe life is not so bad; maybe life is interesting after all.'

"What I love is when we can all come together and say, 'God. That's great. That's great stuff'—whatever quality 'that' may be. It can be as simple as a prune commercial that says, 'Today the pits, tomorrow the wrinkles,' and leaves you with a smile. Or it can be as elaborate as the Nike 'Move' commercial.

"Personally, Doyle Dane Bernbach's Volkswagen ads really turned me on. I thought there was something cool there. It showed that human beings do have a sense of humor, that they can be outrageous, that there's a never-ending flow of originality. I love the Fallon McElligott stuff, from their Episcopal Church ads to their Citibank campaign. I love Crispin's stuff for Mini and Wieden's stuff for Honda and just about everything Lee Clow ever touched."

To help you along in creating your portfolio and launching a successful career, Steve Hayden has the following suggestions.

Be aware of your natural tendency to filter: "I think that the measure of a great creative idea is when you laugh out loud at the thought. And yet, it's not necessarily funny, it's just the idea may have such power that you take delight in it.

"If you experience a spontaneous reaction of joy, then you know you're on to something. We are so self-critical and self-filtering that we often walk away from ideas that make us laugh, thinking we can never possibly get away with them. And yet some of the best things we've done are precisely those ideas brought to life."

Give your copy some personality: "I look for body copy that's written with care, copy that strikes the imagination. I look for phrases like, 'Most people come back from vacation with little more to show for it than tiny bars of stolen soap.' How did *that* get into the ad?

"It's that occasional application of wit that lets you know you're still alive. I look for surprises that say there's a human being behind this, as opposed to a corporation. And I look for that ability to project a human quality. To communicate one on one."

Study the advertising that strikes you: "The annuals are a great place to start. Emulate or even imitate what you admire—learn by doing that. Many times I've written down a headline by somebody else and tried to figure out what gives it power."

Attach yourself to a mentor…: "I've had very little mentoring in my career, which I feel in some ways has been a handicap. I know a number of people who were taught early on a certain way of doing things. A way of problem solving.

"By not having a mentor early on, I had to work in a series of small shops. I had to struggle. I did a lot of retail advertising. I spent a lot of time writing 'Boat Oxfords, $2.99' and 'Peel 'n' Eat Shrimp for the Holidays.'"

On the positive side, Hayden feels his lack of mentorship helped him evolve a unique style—it forced him to discover what works.

… especially if you're an art director: "Just in terms of the technical skills, there are a lot of things you have to learn about art direction that you're not going to get out of a book or a class." Apprentice yourself to someone experienced to help you develop the skills you need.

Play up your gift: "Every person I've met in advertising has a particular kind of gift. Some people are great at writing dialogue. Some copywriters are masters of strategic thought. Others are masters of a clever phrase. Some art directors are great at shooting objects. Others are great at shooting people.

"My style, if there is one, is the long-copy argument that combines a certain amount of technical information with a certain amount of emotional appeal. Figure out what your gift is and work from there."

Stay in touch with people who mean a lot to you in your career: Hayden reminds us that "jobs can be short but careers are long." As Apple worked its way into the ground, Hayden was able to hire two of his key players from his BBDO West days, Susan Westre and Chris Wall. "We've all stayed in touch throughout our adventures," says Hayden. This enabled him to know about their desire to switch jobs and enabled Westre and Wall to learn about opportunities at Ogilvy. (You'll read more about them in the postscript.)

Learn to work better in a partnership: "It's amazing just how few people it takes to transform an entire organization, and just how impossible it is for individuals, no matter how talented, to change an organization on their own.

"There's something special about the troika of Susan, Chris, and myself, where we provide wonderful inspiration for each other, as well as checks and balances. The weaknesses of one are compensated for by the strengths of the others. Find a great partner or two, and stick with them."

Be as multilingual as you possibly can: "The fundamental models of marketing and communication are changing and shifting. Your challenge is no longer confined to the printed page and how much power you can put into that.

"It's almost a return to a hundred years ago when the event was as important as the ad. The show, the store, the launch. Taking over the park for a concert. Creating entertainment that's advertising and vice versa. All the points of communication.

"So study design. Study store environments. Study the written word. Figure out the difference between a good e-mail and a bad e-mail. All of these skills are going to be important going forward, especially as we enter the era of the DVR and all media becomes individually addressable.

"I have a theory that we'd better learn how to do outdoor really well, because that will be about the only medium that won't be refusable ten years from now. Consumers will route around advertising the way the Net routes around damage."

Work where there is work, but strive: Hayden believes there's nothing wrong with working for a department store or a small agency or a radio station as long as you're able to keep striving. "Every time you're given an opportunity to do something good, do it," says Hayden. "Ogilvy's most successful team was hired away from an industrial agency in Los Angeles."

Make sure your portfolio is your own: Honesty is the best policy. If you steal ads, chances are you'll get caught. "Once I interviewed someone who had some of my work in his book," says Hayden. "He came to interview with me at Chiat/Day and he showed me these terrible ads I had done at another shop.

"He never dreamed that I had worked at the very agency he was attempting to escape. He didn't know that I'm actually a small-agency scrapper." So remember, you never know the background of the person reviewing your portfolio.

Seek an agency culture suited to your personality: "No matter how much money they give you, if you don't fit into the agency's culture, it's not going to work out.

"The other side is: you can't make an uncreative agency creative by hanging a couple of good reputations on it. It's like putting ornaments on a barren tree."

Stay close to billings…: "All power comes out of the barrel of the client. If you have big billings, a big title is fine. If you have a big title and no billings, then the next time there are layoffs, your name will appear on the list. It's that simple.

"It's the harsh side of capitalism. It's purely, 'What have you produced?'

"That's the core of this business: making advertising, making campaigns, working with creative people, and working directly with clients. Even with a multilayered agency, it still comes down to doing work for clients.

"You never want to have a title like Integration Manager or Director of Creative Services, or even Worldwide Creative Director if you don't have billings.

"Director of Client Services is one of the worst titles you can have. Nobody should have that title. When it comes to the big, global companies, there is a need for people who make the organization work. But, sadly, when an agency gets into economic difficulties, the highest salaries that are not paid for by actual work are the first to go."

...and don't get caught up in it: Politics. Meetings. All the things that can use up a day without much getting done. "The larger the organization, the more there's a danger of losing sight of the fact that it all starts with somebody and a piece of paper. At Ogilvy, we're absolutely clear about that, because it's the ideas that count. The structure, the technology, the training, the worldwide meetings are really for making communication frictionless, rather than creating a formula for global branding."

POSTSCRIPT 1:

OVERCOMING PRECONCEPTIONS ABOUT IN-HOUSE, DIRECT, AND INDUSTRIAL ADVERTISING

There's a preconception among many creative directors that once you've spent some time in an in-house or industrial agency, you're washed up. But, as Hayden proved, you can move from low-budget industrial work to big-budget consumer work.

Here's what Hayden has to say on the topic:

"There are many people who are fortunate to start their careers at prosperous agencies or big agencies or creative agencies and they motor on happily from there. When you're working hand-to-mouth at poor, small agencies, you feel like you're a second-class citizen... that you could not hope to aspire to work for one of these great, creative agencies... that it's just so far above what you're doing.

"Where I came from, we felt we were ahead of the game if we didn't run the coupons in reverse.

"I suppose there's a point to the argument that if you haven't gotten out of that environment there's cause for concern—people generally work themselves out and go on to something new—but I wouldn't say you're completely finished if you don't.

"But you must also be lucky enough to come across a creative director who recognizes your ability. I guess I was lucky.

"Similarly, Chris Wall and Susan Westre work here and, earlier, worked at BBDO West. Most creative directors in the city wouldn't give them the time of day before they landed at BBDO because they were from a small industrial agency that had crummy accounts. Creatives are dazzled when they see the right set of logos in a book. Usually, they're the same logos that have appeared in award books recently.

"One of the fortunate things for me is that Chris and Susan evolved into stars at BBDO, and now these same creative directors are calling them and begging for interviews. But since Chris and Susan weren't given a chance in the first place, they're not going to go over now, which is the good news.

"I suppose in an art director's book, I do look at the execution. The value of an art director is unsurpassed: an art director can make so-so headlines award winners, while the brightest copywriter in the world cannot survive bad art direction. I look for taste levels, and I want to get a feeling from the ads. I think that I could look at an art director's roughs and get a feeling of how his or her ad is going to look.

"I also look for the quality of ideas, the ability to turn a phrase and to take the unexpected approach. I'm looking for someone who does something arresting, but not just for shock value.

"In evaluating work from in-house and from industrial agencies, I probably have an internal point system, the same way you'd judge award shows. The lowest level is that the work is not embarrassing; the next level is it's pretty good; and the highest level is, 'Gee, I wish I'd done that. I wonder if I can steal it?'

"Overcoming people's perceptions is contingent upon the quality of your work. If all your headlines say '.0035 perimeters in a z-spec thurester,' you're not going to get many offers. On the other hand, if you get people reading about stuff they don't want to know—or care—about, then you're on to something.

"You can be doing things for the weirdest, oddest product and have a certain mind bent or put a certain power in your communication. Take that and apply it to something else and good things happen.

"And while it depends on the gifts of the individual, I do think that a great creative person can work on just about anything. Lee Clow, for example, can work on anything that he wants and good things will happen. There are people who do emotion more credibly. There are people who do dialogue a little better. There are people who are wonderful at consumer marketing who will never understand technology or the issues you have to sort through to get a good tech message.

"Perhaps I'm biased, but I think it's easier to take a tech person and put them on soft drinks than vice versa.

"I also think that people can jump back and forth between direct mail, promotions, and advertising. One of our most successful art/creative directors started off as a typographer. And some of our most successful teams have come out of the direct company; everything in direct is focused on changing behavior, and I think that understanding is central to all advertising.

"As for promotions and environmental design, there's a lot that can be applied to advertising. It's communication by other means.

"It's not simply adapting the ad campaign to a trade show. It's getting people to feel—and help them navigate a space in the real world. Ogilvy's Brand Integration Group (BIG), which Rick Boyko built, is perfectly capable of doing advertising, as well as doing design and creating retail environments and trade show booths. I have a tremendous amount of respect for Brian Collins and his entire team at BIG.

"Actually, Steve Jobs at Apple is one of the great design mavens and mentors of our time. One of the first things I did at Ogilvy was meet with the group within IBM responsible for product design and corporate identity. They knew the brand inside and out—literally.

"So, I would say you are free to experiment. Often times, advertising CDs have a lot of trouble hiring people who have a design-specific book or looking at a direct marketing portfolio and saying, yes, you can be in the general agency.

"To get over it, look for an enlightened boss. And look for a situation—and I'm going to use a cliché here—where the systems haven't become so sclerotic that you're locked in your box."

Postscript 2:

A BRIEF LOOK AT HOW TO WORK WITH A PLANNER

Throughout this book, we hear about strategic planning. But what is the most effective way to work with a planner? Steve Hayden has some thoughts on the subject:

"All good creative people are planners by instinct. They have to be. But a great planner can give you insights you didn't have before.

"Every once in a while you'll come across a planner who actually makes creative leaps. When you start working on the strategy that they've given you, things begin to happen. These people are rare and precious. Treasure them when you find them.

"What's tough about planning is that it can take time out of the creative process. Creative guys always complain that they need better creative briefs. You know, the brief is no good, therefore, the work is no good, therefore we're kicking the brief back to you.

"But rarely do you come up with something like the Visa brief at BBDO, where the brief was so good that you could envision the advertising ("It's everywhere you want to be"). The fact is, most of the time, the best briefs are the ones written after the advertising is finished.

"The way that I believe a creative team should work with a planner is through daily, or almost daily, contact as you're kicking ideas around. In other words, make your planner part of the creative process—assuming, of course, you get along.

"The other bit of advice is: even if things shift and change during the process of creating the brief, let the creative people start thinking about it at the same time the planners are thinking about it.

"What tends to happen, however, is that the account people and the planners take four or five months working on a brief to make sure they've got the perfect brief. The creative people then have three or four days to come up with a major campaign. I disagree.

"I tell people that as soon as you are done with the client meeting, call the creative team and give them an idea of what's going on."

8

BUILDING A BOOK BASED ON BERNBACH & BEYOND

Father's Day 1974

Father's Day 1974

Father's Day 1976

Father's Day 1977

Father's Day 1978

Father's Day 1979

Father's Day 1980

Father's Day 1981

Patience does have its rewards.

Ted Bell

"There are two kinds of people in this business... There are those who get it. And there are those who don't."

Theodore Bell, who served stints as Vice Chairman, President and Chief Creative Officer for Leo Burnett USA, and Worldwide Creative Director for Young & Rubicam, obviously "gets it."

In this chapter, we'll examine basic ideas for putting together a portfolio, as well as explore what it means to "get it." Ted Bell's career demonstrates how creative talent alone can foster a successful career in advertising—no matter what types of clients, products, or organizational politics may exist.

During his career, he has created spots for Chivas Regal, Dewars, Memorex, McDonald's, Volkswagen, and many others. And along the way, he has earned numerous awards including golds at both the One Show and Cannes.

Bell retired in 2000 to move to Florida and become a full-time novelist. He has since published five novels, *Nick of Time*, *Hawke*, *Assassin*, *Pirate*, and the most recent, *Spy*, which released in August of 2006. These days he spends his mornings working on his fiction. His primary interest outside of work—both when he was in advertising and today—is reading historical biographies and fiction, evidence of his lifelong romance with words and literature. In addition, he enjoys boating and shooting. He remarried in 2000 and has a daughter in college.

THRIVING IN THE BEST OF BOTH WORLDS—
AND CREATING A THIRD

Do you have what it takes to succeed? As the title of this book implies, you can make it in creative advertising—and make it big—if you have one thing. Talent. But what is talent? And what else needs to be learned to make the most of that talent? Perhaps a look at how Ted Bell's career developed can shed some light for you.

Bell didn't always display his talent for advertising. While attending Randolph-Macon College, he expected to earn a degree in English in order to teach English literature. But during his senior year he realized that he would have to learn more than Shakespeare's sonnets to survive in the academic environment; he discovered that faculty rivalries and tenure squabbles were as much a part of the job as were literary pursuits. Recalls Bell, "I thought I'd be better off in the real world than involved with the isolation and politics of academic life. At least that was my 21-year-old perception."

Off to Write His First Novel

With this new perspective—and financial support from his grandmother—Bell decided to move to Europe and try his hand at completing a novel he'd started in college. He settled in a tiny town in Switzerland where the sheep population seemed to outnumber the two-legged residents.

The location had the solitude a budding novelist needed, but lacked the stimulation a young man exploring Europe craved. Consequently, he drove every weekend to Milan to visit with a Swedish friend of his—a friend who led a glamorous life as one of Europe's hottest fashion photographers. As a result, he was soon introduced to Milan's leading advertising people. His interest in the industry was born. It was a creative and, luckily, remunerative field.

But considering the language difference, he knew it was probably a bad idea to start his career in Milan. Although he could have learned Italian, he knew that he would have trouble writing with enough idiomatic familiarity to create effective advertising. So he decided that perhaps England would be a better place to start.

Unfortunately, Britain in the early '70s was in recession, and to ensure that jobs didn't go to foreigners, visits of non-nationals were limited to only six weeks. Bell decided to make good use of his time, and during those weeks he sent three-page letters to London's agency directors to try to land a position.

"They weren't straightforward business letters," recalls Bell. "I talked about myself, my background in creative writing and English literature, and communicated how strongly I believed my creative energy could be channeled into something I could do, namely advertising. Also, I tried to make them funny."

Bell's letters detailed his background, his experiences, his passion for advertising in an interesting way—which managed to cut through the clutter. To his delight, a few of the creative directors took enough of an interest in him that they agreed to meet, and offered him encouragement. They were looking for good writers. They wanted fresh ideas. And they were always interested in new talent.

Off to Pursue His First Ads

A creative director at DDB's London office was particularly helpful. He instructed Bell to buy the *London Times*, sit in the park, look at the ads and try to improve them. Which Bell did.

He rewrote ads for heating equipment, credit cards, socks, watches—anything. Then he returned to his new friend, spread the ads on the table, and listened to a critique of his work. His friend offered advice on how to improve the ads—and there was plenty of room for improvement.

"I remember one terrible ad I did," recalls Bell. "It was an ad for socks and the headline read, 'Socks Appeal.' I thought it was clever. It had some socks on a clothesline. This guy, rightfully, hated it. He told me it was a cheap pun. He said I wasn't saying anything about the socks—why they're good, what they're made of.

"Anybody can be clever. Advertising is about much more than being able to come up with a cute turn of a phrase. Or a play on words. It's about finding truly new and fresh ways to make a sale."

The ads he created under his friend's direction became the basis for his first portfolio. He didn't present sophisticated renderings—or even the standard three campaigns with three ads each. Instead, his book consisted of very rough drawings, with press type for headlines—all displayed in a green plastic binder. "It was bad presentation!" says Bell. "I was starting from scratch and didn't know what I was doing."

Somehow, Bell's talent transcended his rough presentations. Feedback from the creative directors was positive. He was told he had the talent to be a copywriter, but that England's economy was squeezing the job market. And the final bit of feedback—his visa was running out.

On to His First Job

Unable to take a UK position, he returned to the United States. But now he had set goals and a tested portfolio, Bell was soon hired as a copywriter by a small agency in Hartford, Connecticut. To Bell, this was a stepping-stone to New York, where talented new creatives were changing the style of advertising.

Within two years, he was writing ads at Tinker Dodge & Delano in New York for Smirnoff and British Airways.

But he kept his eye on landing a position at the agency that was leading the creative revolution, DDB, and eventually he secured an interview with Bob

Levenson, probably one of the greatest advertising writers ever, who was then running DDB's creative department.

And Then to DDB

Bell was hired as a junior copywriter on the Volkswagen account. Of DDB, Bell says, "This was Mecca as far as I was concerned."

The environment at Doyle Dane Bernbach was energetic and filled with creative talent. Helmut Krone, Bob Gage, Bob Levenson, and Roy Grace (see Chapter 9) created an environment where everyone learned something every day.

The agency operated on the basis of "creative anarchy" with the creatives carrying the standard.

Bell recalls one lesson he learned while writing a VW ad.

Levenson didn't like a sentence and questioned it. Bell rewrote it and brought it back in to Levenson's office. But, again, Levenson didn't like it. So Bell tried it again and again. Finally, Levenson said, "Ted, just because you run over a snake in the road doesn't mean you have to replace it." Bell eliminated the offending sentence. And it's been an editing suggestion that he's followed ever since. Says Bell, "I got a year's education in one afternoon."

Bill Bernbach also had a tremendous influence on Bell. "He taught us all to start with the concept. The one thing you want people to take away from the communication. DDB was about ideas, not execution. Ideas that sold something!"

Bernbach also taught Bell to respect the audience. "Give them some credit for intelligence," explains Bell. "You don't have to pound them over the head with inane or repetitious copy slogans. There can be warmth, humor, wit, and style.

"That was Bill's battle cry. That there should be some charm and emotion and humanity in advertising. I like to think of it as 'relevant' charm."

The environment at DDB fostered Bell's talents and he soon rose to the level of Vice President, Copy Supervisor.

"Getting It" at Leo Burnett

But, after nearly ten years there, he was itching for a change. In 1982 he moved to Chicago to join Leo Burnett as an Associate Creative Director. It was a step down the corporate ladder, but Burnett wanted new energy in their creative department and Bell recognized this opportunity.

At first, Bell found it difficult to adjust to Burnett's culture.

At DDB the energy orbited around the creatives. Creative teams were guided by gut instinct, not market research. At Burnett, however, Bell found that the disciplines were expected to function as a team. The researchers, copywriters, art directors, and account teams all worked as a cohesive, balanced group. Market research, as well as post-production research, was considered valuable in directing a campaign.

For Bell, that took some getting used to. But he quickly learned that the intrinsic strengths of the Burnett system far outweighed any negative early perceptions. Indeed, at Burnett the idea that "none of us is as smart as all of us" has paid off in some of the biggest, most enduring ideas in advertising history; the Marlboro Man and the Green Giant are just two examples.

One of Bell's first tasks at Burnett was to build his own creative group.

He wanted a team of kindred spirits, people who thought the same way he did. So instead of building a group of seasoned veterans, he hired kids right out of school. "I was looking for punks," says Bell. "I wanted kids who had no experience in the business, who didn't have a clue how to create ads. Kids who didn't know the rules and just wanted to do great ads. They had to have talent, excitement, and raw energy about them. And a complete love of great advertising."

They also had to believe that nothing else mattered—except doing great advertising. Bell didn't care about politics. He didn't care who liked whom. If the person came up with great ideas he or she was in his group. If not, that person was out. That was his philosophy: the "get it" factor was key.

Bell's efforts paid off. He was soon promoted to Creative Director and then again to Group Creative Director. In 1986, he became President and Chief Executive Officer. Bell attributes much of his success to his mentors for instilling in him a sense of confidence. Says Bell, "I don't know if I'm right or wrong, but I make a gut decision to do something. This is what I think it should be. Not what I think is current, or hip, or politically correct. You may like it or not like it later, but you do it. And, eventually, your career is the sum of those decisions. You are what you make. Bernbach and Burnett helped me figure it out."

After awhile, Bell decided to start looking around for a new challenge.

He talked with Charlotte Beers, who had just been named chairman of Ogilvy & Mather Worldwide, and she asked him to become her partner as Worldwide Creative Director. Bell's friends at Y&R had heard that he was talking to Charlotte and invited him to talk to them. This left Bell with two opportunities.

Teaching Y&R to "Get It"

"I ultimately decided on Y&R because I thought that they needed more help," he says. Several factors helped guide his decision: First, Y&R gave him the chance to move back to London, a place where he'd enjoyed living. Second, he recognized that Ogilvy already had a strong creative culture, because of David Ogilvy's philosophy, giving him little opportunity to shape the department.

Says Bell, "I figured Y&R was a better canvas for me to work on." His title was Vice Chairman, Worldwide Creative Director for the entire Y&R network. His mission was to improve their creative product on a worldwide level.

Shortly after Bell took over the creative leadership of Y&R's worldwide network, their New York office took a nosedive. "They were losing a lot of clients and needed help," recalls Bell. "I basically spent most of my time putting out fires and commuting from London to New York every week to work on saving clients."

To save clients, Bell's strategy was to show them his own personal work and let them know that he was going to be directly involved in their business. He invited clients to go straight to him. And he promised to make things better.

He found the commute to be hard on him and moved back to New York after about a year. He teamed up with a guy named Ed Vick who had just been brought in from Landor and made Chairman. "We were a great team together because we both had the same vision of fixing the creative product," says Bell.

They succeeded. Two years after they started, *AdWeek* named them agency of the year. "I give him just as much credit," says Bell. "He backed me up no matter what. We told the account executives that having 'good meetings' was no longer a way to feel secure in your job—that you had to sell great advertising. We also fired a lot of creative people and brought in a lot of great creative people."

To transform the creative department, Bell's strategy was the same one he used when he built his team at Burnett. "Basically, I brought in a lot of young people," says Bell. "And I identified the good people who were already there and empowered them. The people who weren't very good went bye-bye."

As part of the agency transformation, Bell held a four-day retreat at an old estate on the Hudson River. "I gave every creative director an hour or so to stand up and show the work of his group, and then say, in his opinion, whether it was good or bad, and why," says Bell. "It was definitely an audition. I just sat there for four days and watched them all talk, and then made some decisions based on that."

Of course, he'd already begun forming impressions about his team's work through his day-to-day interactions with them. Says Bell, "If somebody walks into your office and shows you a horrible commercial, and does it a few times, you say, 'You know what, this guy isn't very good.'"

Once revived, Y&R New York started gaining new clients and new business from existing clients. "In one year we won something like a billion three in new business," recalls Bell. "If we just counted the new business from that year it would've made us something like the 11th largest agency in the world. It was huge."

Until He Finishes His First Novel

Throughout his career in advertising, Bell continued working on his creative writing, producing four screenplays and selling one. The movie was two days away from getting produced when the investors pulled out.

Recalls Bell, "It was one of the worst days of my life. I'm still not sure if it was a good thing or a bad thing. I've had a lot of fun making ads."

Then when he moved to London to take the job with Y&R, he started writing another novel, perhaps as a flashback to his post-college days trying to be a novelist in Europe. He finished writing it after he moved back to New York.

"I was living in Connecticut and I wrote on the train coming in every morning and going out every night," says Bell. "I wrote at lunch hour, whenever I could." Titled *Nick of Time*, he self-published the book as a POD (or publish on demand). His goal: "Just to get it out there," he says. "Just to have something." This time he had some success because it enabled him to sell its screen rights to Paramount and they asked him to write the screenplay. "I wrote the first draft," says Bell "and that's where it stands right now."

...And Has a Hit with His Second

When Y&R was sold to WBP, Bell decided to leave to work on his second book full-time. Called *Hawke*, it was Simon & Schuster's lead fiction title for the summer of 2003. The book reached the best seller list and he's since released three additional books in the *Hawke* franchise, giving him a second career in the field where he had originally set his sights. "I now work 9:00 to 1:00 most days," says Bell. "But it's not work for me. It's fun."

SELECTIONS FROM BELL'S BOOK

—— BANK AMERICARD ——

When Bell was working on a portfolio to show agencies in New York, he ran across an article suggesting that America would soon be a cashless society. The headline came to him and he sketched out this ad for a credit card and included it in his early portfolio.

Yukon Jack.
The Black Sheep of Canadian Liquors.

YUKON JACK

Bell created Yukon Jack in the early '70s. "The creative director told me that the client was always looking for a product that could beat Southern Comfort," recalls Bell.

"All I knew was that the product was going to be Canadian whiskey with honey in it.

"I liked the idea of a guy who was all by himself. I wanted him to be real macho, a tough guy, a loner.

"Those ideas lead to the concept and once I had 'The Black Sheep of Canadian Liquor,' I felt I could write these things forever.

"I'm proud of Yukon Jack because I came up with the concept and it turned out to be a huge success." It is still a product today.

VOLKSWAGEN

Here's an example of using current events to create memorable, timely advertising, a technique that was popularized by DDB.

Former peanut farmer Jimmy Carter was now president. He was well known for his simple lifestyle. Because of gasoline shortages in the late '70s, Carter decided to discourage the use of limousines by his White House staff.

Taking advantage of VW's economical gas mileage, Bell cranked out this ad over a weekend, and it ran in the *New York Times* and *Washington Post* on the Monday that Carter announced the new policy.

Rabbits eat peanuts.

A little friendly advice from Volkswagen for those of you who have to get to work on your own.

It won a gold One Show Award, Bell's first.

"I always assume that people are smart and will appreciate someone who takes the time to give them a little humor and intelligence," says Bell. "And I always try to give people something back for taking the time to read my ad."

The VW Thing was one of the first assignments that Bell worked on at DDB.

"The headline's fun, " says Bell. "But it also tells you something about the Thing—that they're tough cars. They're built to stand up.

"The headline is not a joke. It's cute, but it says something. It has a point. It sells."

—— MEMOREX ——

Do demo commercials need to have boring, straightforward presentations?

Of course not.

Here's an example of an engaging way to demonstrate a product, one that tells a story.

In this commercial, a girl cries as her hero hops into his Porsche and speeds away, whereupon she hits rewind and watches it yet again. "Is it love? Or, is it Memorex?"

Bell shot this with director Joe Pytka over a Thanksgiving holiday with a very limited budget. But, with a strong, simple concept the story itself delivers.

"I think that writing commercials—not so much print—really teaches you to make characters come to life very quickly," says Bell. "You don't have a lot of time in a 30-second commercial to say, okay this is the harried mom, this is the dad, who are these people and what are they all about. So you learn how to rough in characters very quickly. You also learn how to tell short stories, in 30 seconds with a beginning, middle, and end."

By the way, Bell used this knowledge when writing his novels. "Basically a book is just a bunch of scenes strung together," says Bell. "And they all have to have a point."

—— PIRELLI ——

Thinking back on his years in advertising, he says, "You couldn't ask for better training than Bernbach for ten years and then Leo Burnett for ten years." It's what enabled him to be successful at Y&R. And while DDB and Burnett shaped his

thinking, Y&R didn't change his thinking about advertising. Of his years at Y&R, he says, "I tried to change their thinking."

Here's a print ad that resulted from his efforts at creating a creative culture, one that was created while he was living in London. While he didn't serve directly as the writer or creative director on this ad, he helped foster the environment that enabled its development and it is now considered one of the best ads from its era.

——— *Hawke* ———

Not only did Ted Bell write these novels, he had a hand in creating the advertising for his second novel, *Hawke*, helping it land on the *New York Times* best seller list. This shows that once you understand how to create effective advertising, you don't lose it—even if you leave the industry and styles change.

THE PURPOSE OF ADVERTISING,
AS WELL AS IMPORTANT ADVICE

As mentioned, Ted Bell believes that "you either have it or you don't."

He claims that after having looked at hundreds of beginning portfolios, he could tell you within four ads whether a person is going to get a job or be successful.

Says Bell, "You get the trick of doing good ads. You just get it. You just know how to do it. Or you don't."

So what's the trick of doing good advertising? To figure this out, we must first gain a basic idea of what an ad should do. Bell believes that its purpose is not to show how cute or clever you can be. Rather, its purpose is to communicate the advantages of your particular product or service in a way that makes the audience notice, makes sense, and gives the audience a reason to act.

And what type of work gets his attention? Bell recalled one ad from a creative's portfolio that particularly impressed him. The ad showed two windows. One looked out on clouds in the sky—from above the clouds. Underneath the clouds was the line, "The $599 View."

The other window looked out at rolling hills and the sun setting over a little town. Under that window was the line "The $79 View." At the bottom, it just said "Amtrak" and had some body copy.

"The ad showed an understanding of advertising," says Bell. "Clearly the train ride offered a more scenic and less expensive way to travel than air. That ad showed consumers the benefits of riding the train with a simple, intelligent, and witty message." Bell hired this individual, who went on to run Burnett's Tokyo office.

This person presented a fresh idea. A new way of looking at an old problem. "The quality of surprise, the freshness, is the trick," says Bell. "You have to hook people emotionally. You've got to give them information and make them see things in a new way."

But once you have an understanding of advertising and these basics down— basics that many experienced creative people even forget—how do you proceed?

Here are some of Ted Bell's thoughts on developing a sample portfolio as well as building your career.

Forget the format: Some schools and many advertising books recommend that your portfolio contain three campaigns—one for package-goods, one for a durable, and one for a service. Bell doesn't buy that. "I believe if you understand advertising, you can work on anything," says Bell. "There's no package-goods guy, no car guy. Really good people can work on anything. And *want* to work on anything. A truly brilliant art director treats a matchbook cover like a two-page spread in *Time*."

Remember, slick don't stick: "Twenty years ago beginning books were very rough. Today, even fresh grads can create tight comps. But if people hiring these kids are smart, they'll look past the glitz," says Bell. High-priced leather portfolios and weird gimmicks turn Bell off. He's seen a lot of slick portfolios that have no fresh ideas. And he suspects a glitzy portfolio may be an attempt to compensate for a lack of creative ideas. Says Bell, "Sometimes a guy knows in his heart that he doesn't have very many good ideas, so he's got to make them look good."

Learn the fundamentals: Your book has to show that you can think in terms of advertising—that you understand what the job is all about. The right advertising school can help you do this. "It's a real shortcut way to learn the fundamentals," says Bell. "If I had known about these schools when I was trying to get a job, I probably would have gone to one."

Read the annuals: It's another way to learn the fundamentals. "Beginners who don't go to a school to create a portfolio still have a chance," says Bell. "A great idea is a great idea even if it's a pencil-drawn stick figure on 8 x 10 notebook paper." Bell suggests that you find the ads in the annuals that you think are great and discover what they have in common. Says Bell, "Try to figure out what makes the ads fresh." (Look for more about the importance of annuals in later chapters.)

Record interesting images and ideas: "If I'm watching a movie and I see something funny or I see something on the street, I sort of file it away. It's like a novelist who overhears a conversation and jots it down," says Bell. "He doesn't know what he's going to use it for, but somewhere down the line you'll see that conversation in a book. You'd be surprised at how many famous advertising ideas first saw the light of day on a cocktail napkin. In fact, I'd say the cocktail napkin is one of the essential tools of the advertising business."

Emphasize the idea: "If a copywriter writes great body copy, that's terrific. But I have to see a great headline concept first. If he's a writer and his art direction is a little weak, I don't get bothered by that. A copywriter can even come to me with an ad scribbled on tissues. As long as I can understand it and it has a great headline, I'll consider him. That's how much I care about fancy presentation," says Bell. As for an art director, Bell says, "If his art direction is weak, obviously I'll get bothered by it. Really good creative people are ambidextrous. Good writers are strong visually and good art directors are strong conceptually."

Improve existing ads: Bell learned how to create advertising by redoing the advertising in the newspaper and magazines. "Look for ads, tear them out, stick them on a wall, and see if you can do them better," says Bell. "That process made me start to think about how to do great work. That was the basis for building my portfolio."

Let it hit you immediately: Bell believes the first ideas are often the most valuable. He observes, "Most people will tell you that their first idea is what they usually end up doing. When it takes weeks and weeks to come up with a concept, you just ain't doing it. If I keep asking, 'How's it going' and I keep hearing, 'We're working on it,' I don't hold my breath. We had a game at DDB, 'Blitzkrieg Advertising.' One person says a product name, the other blurts out the first headline that comes to mind. We played it all the time. It helped."

Start with print: In agencies like Burnett, DDB and Y&R, beginners used to work on print, then, after a long time, television. But that's not true today. Bell believes this is a mistake. "Print is how you learn concepts. Print forces you to have an idea on a page," says Bell. "So you learn the discipline. In television, you have more going on, so you can hide a weak idea."

Stay away from radio scripts in your portfolio: "Nobody has time to read over radio scripts," says Bell. "At least not me. Creative directors want to see your ideas, how you see the world. A strong headline, a visual, a little copy—six to nine truly new, great concepts—that will get you hired."

Use research appropriately…: When it comes to post-production research, Bell still doubts its value. Bell believes that up-front research should enlighten the creatives about the realities of the marketplace. Creatives should be provided with as much information as possible before they begin working on a project. "I don't need people in the shopping mall telling me they do or don't like my ads. If they're so creative they should be here and I'll go out in the shopping center and offer my opinions," says Bell. "But as far as getting information up front, the more you know, the better off you are. Partnership between disciplines is so important."

…Forget research altogether: When putting a book together, it's difficult to factor in relevant research. Beginners should just figure out a product and come up with a great ad. "What research would have led to the Amtrak ad?" asks Bell. "Everybody knows it costs a lot more to fly than to take the train. Everybody knows when you look out of a plane you see clouds and when you look out of a train you see landscape. The writer didn't need research. He needed common sense and an original point of view."

Team up: For copywriters, Bell looked at the ideas, the headlines. And for art directors, he looked for tasteful art direction and ideas. To cover both sides, Bell suggests teaming up. "If you're a writer, find a partner who wants to be an art director and work together," he says. "Look for an art director who is as great a writer as you are. The best art directors are very conceptual. They know how to write their own headlines and come up with their own ideas. And the best copywriters always have a very good visual sense. These disciplines, at their best, are never mutually exclusive."

Make it tasteful: "I think a lot of this business is taste and intelligence," says Bell. "It's a sense of fitness. Style. Of how things should look. There are beautiful ads and there are ugly ads. When in doubt, go with the beautiful."

Go against the grain: Bell learned many lessons while working with art directors such as Helmut Krone, Bert Steinhauser, and Charlie Piccirillo. One of those things was "When everybody yells, whisper. When everybody is running, walk. Go against everybody's sense of what's currently the right thing to do. People are always talking about trends in advertising. I don't want to know about trends, except to know what to avoid. Trends are what already have been done. I want to start a new trend. And as soon as it becomes a trend, I want to start something else."

Keep it simple: "Just about every ad I've ever been involved with has been very simple," says Bell, "in terms of the idea, the layout, the copy—everything. That was a very good lesson to learn early on. Don't let the art direction get between the consumer and your idea. Don't make the work too hard. We didn't go running around the halls saying, 'Look at this ad. It's really great. It's really complicated.'"

Show your enthusiasm: "If you really have a passion for the business, that comes across and helps you," says Bell. "It comes across as you talk. People sense that you're going to have energy. Or you're not. And who would you rather having working for you? The guy who loves the work."

Protect your ideas…: Bell believes that those who succeed in advertising have very strong opinions about what is good. "Great advertising is a very fragile thing," says Bell. "The minute something is created, there are a million people who want to kill it for a variety of reasons." The challenge, according to Bell, is that once you have an idea that you know in your gut is great, you should see it through and get it done. Says Bell, "That's tough to do."

…And fight like hell: Bell believes that the best way to fight for your ideas is to show your unwavering commitment to them. "It's a matter of saying loud enough and long enough that 'This is great!' and sooner or later, people will say, 'All Right. Do it. Maybe you're right.' That's the secret," says Bell. "Fight like hell for your ideas. Because that's all you have to sell."

Move with resolve: Bell recalls a scene from the novel *The Last Tycoon* as an example of the type of focused determination needed to achieve a goal. In it, the Irving Thalberg character is flying from Atlanta to Los Angeles. He's interested in airplanes, so he visits the cockpit. He looks at the mountain ranges and asks the pilots, "If you were to put a road through that mountain range, where would you put it?" The first pilot answers, "I guess I'd put it over there, where the valley is, that ravine, and go all the way through." The copilot then answers, "I'd go through the valley." "No," the character says, "If you're going through these mountains, go right through the middle." Says Bell, "This is a guy who understands how to get things done. You just go. This is what we're going to do. Do it."

Don't make excuses for weak work…: Bell dislikes hearing a copywriter or art director with a portfolio say, "I have to apologize for some of these ads. They're not what I really wanted to do. The client killed my best stuff." There are millions of stories about what you wanted to do that didn't happen. Bell has heard them all and isn't interested. "What it comes down to is how you write is how you think. This is you," says Bell. "If your portfolio isn't a representation of your thinking, change it."

…Especially with clients: What is true in presenting a portfolio is also true when presenting work to a client. "Don't give them any bull, because they know," says Bell. "If it's not good work, admit it. Say, 'You know what, we can do a lot better than this, and we will.'" In addition to helping you sell better work, Bell believes this will help you bond with your clients.

Don't ever take a bad ad to a client: Bell has a foolproof way of ensuring that you can fill your portfolio with great work that has been produced: don't give the client a chance to buy a bad ad. "If you never take them a bad one, they can't ever make a bad one," says Bell. "That's what I used to say to my creative group all the time. You know the reason we've got a lot of bad ads is that we're taking bad storyboards out there. If you never take them a bad one, then they can't make a bad one, can they?"

Maintain your vision during the creative execution phase: While a client can't buy a bad ad if they don't see one, the execution of the idea is also an important factor in creating *effective* advertising. This may require you to serve as a buffer between the clients and the director when clients want to change things on a shoot and to use your sales and people skills to the fullest. "Once again, I'd just tell them the truth," suggests Bell. 'I'd say something like, 'Yeah, we can shoot it that way, but it wouldn't be very good.'" Bell warns, however, that some clients would get angry when they heard this, because they believe that since it was their money, they want it done their way. Bell always resisted that response by reminding clients that they were paying him a lot of money to help them figure it out. In addition, he would say, "Don't buy a dog and bark yourself. You hired me and I'm going to tell you what I think." Bell also always worked with such top-end talent as Joe Pitka. "Joe terrified everybody," says Bell. "We didn't get a lot of backtalk from people when Joe was the director."

Recognize that everything that sells is advertising: "People talking about 'new' advertising are full of it," says Bell. "I once heard a speaker say, 'We're not even going to call it an ad agency anymore. We're going to call it a sales creation unit.' And I thought, 'What is this guy talking about?' All we do is advertising. Whether we do a 60-second TV commercial with a big budget or a 2-inch ad in the back of the newspaper, or a beer coaster, it's an ad and should be made great. A great direct response ad is a great ad with an 800 number on it. Even a sign in a store showing you where the beer is should be a great sign."

Become a legend: While Bell preferred hiring young punks for his creative teams, he believes that once you get how to craft an ad, you never lose it. His reason for hiring beginners was because they weren't conditioned by agency cultures that tolerated the development and sale of less-than-stellar creative product. Bell also believes that clients prefer meeting with younger creative people. So how do you, when you're an old punk, get over these tendencies? Unless you own the agency, become a "legend." Bell points to a friend of his, Peter Murphy. "He was a writer at DDB when I arrived there and he was already a legend," says Bell. After DDB, Murphy went to Riney in San Francisco and worked on the Saturn campaign that helped that agency win the business. He then went to Y&R in New York, where he worked for the rest of his life. "Peter was probably 60 when he died," says Bell. "He was brilliant. He was one of the best writers in the building. He had it. He just was a great writer. If you've got talent you don't lose it mid-career." But in addition to his skills, he had a reputation that made clients want to work with him.

A SPECIAL POSTSCRIPT:

A LOOK AT TWO ADVERTISING GIANTS

Throughout this book, you'll be hearing about the contributions of Leo Burnett and Bill Bernbach to the field of advertising. Ted Bell was one of the few who worked under the "shadows" of both. (Leo had already passed away when Bell joined the Leo Burnett agency, but his influence was still greatly felt.)

In 1987, while serving as president of Burnett, Ted Bell presented a speech to the Adcrafter Club in Detroit. In it, he described the opposing personal styles, yet parallel advertising philosophies, of Bernbach and Burnett.

They both revolutionized the advertising industry. Bell's insights into their ideas can help us understand how they created a world of advertising that was big enough for both of them.

Let's take a look at excerpts from that speech.

"Leo Burnett and William Bernbach. Any list of advertising giants must include them. Why is that? What did they do? What made them tick?

"Since I've been fortunate enough to work in both of their shadows, I thought it might be interesting to offer a few comparisons in an effort to discover whether these giants left any tracks of lasting value.

"As I've said, people who met them for the first time were always surprised to discover that each was so short.

"But then, they never saw either man standing on his wallet!

"Leo grew up a small-town boy, and graduated from the University of Michigan. Bill, born August 13, 1911, under the sign of Leo, oddly enough, graduated from the streets of Brooklyn and then New York University. Bernbach was an English major with a smattering of philosophy.

"Leo left his post in Detroit as ad manager of the old Marmon Company to found his agency in Chicago at the height of the Depression, 1935. I'm sure many of you have heard the story of Mr. Burnett's apples. He was told that anyone crazy enough to open an advertising agency in those times would soon be selling apples on the street.

"'Maybe so,' Leo said, 'but first I'll give 'em away.' I'm glad to say we're still giving them away by the bowlful, all around the world.

"Bill Bernbach wrote his first ad while in the mailroom at Schenley, and went on to become creative head of Grey Advertising, New York. In 1949, Bill left Grey to start a new agency with Ned Doyle and Maxwell Dane.

"He opened his doors with this engaging manifesto: 'It will be known as Doyle Dane Bernbach and nothing shall come between them, not even punctuation.'

"I always liked that a lot. As it turned out, nothing ever did come between them...except time.

"In the beginning, and always for that matter, Bill and Leo were copywriters. Both founded their agencies before the flickering dawn of television and both shared a profound and powerful love of the printed word.

"And both men, I would argue, built their agencies and their reputations by simply revolutionizing the way we, as writers and art directors and marketers, talked to people. They felt that to talk to people, or better yet, with them, was far better than talking at them. Both believed fervently in the essential humanity and dignity of their audience. Both were intelligent enough to realize the simple fact that people simply aren't stupid. Give people credit for a little intelligence and they'll pay you back a thousandfold. With trust, and better yet, belief. As Bernbach once said, 'Yes, there is a 12-year-old mentality in this country...every six-year-old has one.'

"Until Bill and Leo, a lot of advertising consisted of jabbering away about this or that product claim, a laundry list of attributes, singing product strategies. Advertising didn't seem to spring from the real world where people lived.

"I think one of the things that made them great was that they were the first to recognize that logic as the basis for advertising is illogical. That the human brain is an organ of survival, and as such it searches not for reason, but for advantage. Everyone yearns for a better life, everyone is in the never-ending pursuit of happiness, everyone longs for freedom from the menial.

"Bernbach and Burnett realized that people make decisions based not on fact, but emotion. It's not how people think about you, but how they feel about you. As in 'What do you think of your new car?' Answer: 'I like it.'

"It all sounds simple, now, but Leo and Bill were first. And they were right. As a result, they changed the course of advertising forever, and both men, as you may not know, entered the Copywriters Hall of Fame on the same day!

"Very few people know this, but Leo and Bill were actually friends. They met frequently for lunch in New York during the sixties at Bill's favorite restaurant, the Four Seasons. At a corner table in the Grill Room, where George Lois once went down on his knees to kiss Bernbach's ring, some real power lunches took place. Oh, to be a fly on that wall! Here was a study in contrasts:

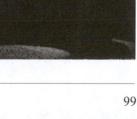

"Leo, with the ever-present Marlboro dangling from the lower lip, dusting his lapels with ashes, presenting the rumpled appearance of one who sleeps in his suit to save time...

"Bill, who never smoked or drank, ever dapper in his pale blue English shirts, clearly a man who abhorred any imperfection in dress or manner. A kid from the streets, who'd done all right for himself.

"Leo, shy but gruff in his opinions about the advertising business. On this subject, he threw his body into the discussion.

"Bill, ever attentive, his ice-blue eyes leaping to life as ideas boomed in his mind...smooth, quiet, persuasive.

"On Leo's side of the table, surely a dry martini. Leo was even known to carry his own tumbler of gin and vermouth whenever he traveled by air. 'I just don't trust airplane gin,' he used to say.

"Bernbach, minus a drink or cigarette, but always the teacher using his hands to try to carve his ideas out of thin air, for Leo to see.

"Two giants, locked in mortal combat, not with each other, but in a mutual rebellion against all that was shoddy or banal or second-rate in a profession they both loved.

"What thoughts filled the air at those now distant luncheons? What signposts were being hung out to point the way as our business was being moved in new directions, as these two tiny titans pulled the levers?

"I'd like to share a few of their thoughts with you. Here are the thoughts of the man on one side of that long ago table in the Grill Room, Bernbach:

- We must ally ourselves with the great ideas and carry them to the public.
- We must practice our skills on behalf of society.
- We must not just believe in what we sell, we must sell what we believe in.
- For creative people, rules are a prison.
- Dullness won't sell your product; but, neither will irrelevant brilliance.
- I warn you against believing advertising is a science. Advertising is an art; nothing memorable ever emerged from a formula.
- The product, the product, the product. Stay with the product. Simple.
- The truth isn't the truth until people believe you.
- I don't want scientists, I want people who do the right things. I want people who do inspiring things.
- Let us blaze new trails. Let us prove to the world that good taste, good art, and good writing can be good selling.
- The real giants of advertising have always been poets—men who jumped from facts into the realm of imagination and ideas.

"And the thoughts of the gentleman on the other side of the table, Burnett:

- An ad must make no pretense of being anything but an ad. It must not attempt to snare the reader by pretending to be something else. It must say, 'I'm an ad and proud of it. I have something important to tell you and here it is.'
- The problem is how to be believable, sincere, and warm but colorful and provocative at the same time, with a good honest ring to our words.
- I have learned that any fool can write a bad ad, but it takes a real genius to keep his hands off a good one.
- I can't give you a formula for success. But I can give you a foolproof formula for failure—just try to please everybody.
- I have learned that the greatest single thing to be achieved in advertising is believability.
- As I have observed it, great advertising is deceptively and disarmingly simple. It has a common touch without being patronizing.
- I don't think you have to be 'off-beat' to be interesting. A truly interesting piece of advertising is 'off-beat' by its very rarity.
- Most writers, when they become sincere, are merely dull.
- A small thought on a slick paper in full color won't live. But a big thought on a scrap of cardboard will live forever.

"If there were arguments long ago in the Grill Room where the giants sat, they may have been about the check, but they certainly weren't about advertising. On that, they seem to have agreed. I wondered earlier about the legacy of Leo and Bill.

"In fact, Leo himself wondered out loud one morning about the same thing. He knew very well what he had built, and, as he was nearing the end of his career, he knew what he would be leaving behind. So, as was Leo's way, he also left very wise instructions on how to keep his spirit and dedication alive. And a warning of what would happen if we don't: To take his name off the door.

"It would be fair of you to ask me what these old codgers have to do with now. Not nearly enough, would be my answer. Certainly, the current business of business and the business of advertising bear little resemblance to Leo's world, or Bill's. In the end they left us with this:

- You make a good product.
- You don't take shortcuts.
- You take pride in what you make and you tell the truth.
- You don't allow success to breed arrogance, because you'll never outsmart the American consumer. They'll always find you out, and they are very slow to forgive.
- You recognize the dignity and humanity in people and they'll recognize it in you and believe you."

(MUSIC UP)
COLLINS (SINGS): I CAN FEEL IT

COMING IN THE AIR

TONIGHT...

OH LORD.

(MUSIC UP)

WELL, I'VE BEEN WAIT-ING FOR THIS MOMENT FOR

ALL MY

LIFE...

OH LORD...

OH LORD.

ANNCR (VO): So exception-ally smooth...

(MUSIC UP)...

...

...

...

...

...

...

...

ANNCR (VO): The night belongs to Michelob.
SINGER: I CAN FEEL IT COMING IN THE AIR.

Susan Gillette

"If you're good, you have a lot more control over your destiny than you think you have."

Susan Gillette moved from being a copywriter to a creative director by the age of 27, and, by 40, became president of DDB Needham's Chicago office. After retiring from her presidency several years later, she continued to work as a strategic consultant for the DDB agency network, showing that creative people can go beyond the traditional agency positions of copywriter, art director, and creative director.

She currently consults for and serves as a member of the board of directors of DDB Worldwide. In addition, she acts as Dean of their corporate university.

Gillette feels that a lot of creative people waste their talent because they are dreamy types who don't take charge of their careers.

In this chapter, we'll look at the career of someone who has taken control of her career, has taken it in unusual directions, including "retiring" at 40, at the top of her game. And we'll examine more basic ideas for putting together a portfolio and finding a job in advertising.

Gillette was born in Philadelphia. Her family moved to Villa Park, Illinois, a Chicago suburb, when she was 13. She attended Northern Illinois University (NIU) and graduated in 1972 with a major in English literature and a minor in psychology.

STARTING POINTS: TALENT AND INTUITION

Gillette believes all creative people start out with good intuition and a conscious understanding of human nature. "The rest," she says, "is trial and error." In other words, creative people can get more polished over time, but the underlying talent is innate. Says Gillette, "You can nurture talent. You can mature talent. You can improve talent. But you can't ordain it. People either have it or they don't."

Gillette had the typical creative personality: dreamy, preoccupied, forgetful, self-critical. As a child, she was a worrier, always feeling guilty about something.

In the fourth grade, for instance, she went through a "save-the-world" period and wanted to give all her birthday money to the church. Says Gillette, "I wanted to be a nun and I wasn't even Catholic. I was a pretty weird kid."

This worrying and guilt gave her a chance to learn how things affect people and, in turn, how to cause that effect. "That's what great advertising creative is really about," she says. "It's like, I can make you laugh; I can make you cry. Creative people take great pleasure in being able to elicit emotions from others."

Like many creative people, Gillette credits her somewhat turbulant childhood for helping to cultivate her talents. "I lived in three different states for 6th, 7th, and 8th grades. I went from being comfortable and popular in 6th grade to being the 'new kid' two years in a row at a vulnerable age. Peer groups in middle school are notoriously brutal. It was a real sink or swim situation for my self-esteem. Fortunately I learned to swim—and write."

Gillette says she "wasn't very goal oriented in college." She took her first full-time job because her parents wouldn't let her lie around the house for more than a week after graduation. She tried teaching and decided it wasn't for her. She considered graduate school.

Since she'd always enjoyed writing, she looked under "writer" in the Chicago Tribune classifieds. There were two jobs listed. She interviewed for both, lied about being able to type, and was offered a position as a writer/secretary in a small suburban telecommunications firm.

The job was more fun than Gillette had expected it would be. She worked with two young designers from IIT. Her boss was a 30-year-old who drove to work in an orange Corvette. She was soon promoted to assistant ad director and began writing trade articles and speeches for the vice president, as well as technical materials.

But she saw herself getting complacent in her job, and she didn't like that. Also, she didn't have an engineering background to truly understand what she was writing about and had no desire to learn the technical side of the telecomm industry.

Luckily, not long after the restlessness set in, she was asked to write some ads for a trade campaign. She enjoyed writing the ads, which she mentioned to her brother. He, in turn, directed her to a friend of his, Mike Cafferetta, who was, at the time, a creative director at Leo Burnett.

When she showed Cafferetta the ads she had written, he suggested she put a spec portfolio together. He advised her to begin by studying the *Communications*

Arts advertising annuals. She got her hands on the annuals from 1968 to 1973—which she thinks were classic years for advertising. She "decoded" the ads in the annuals to figure out what made them great. She took away the headline to see if the visual still worked, she removed the visual to see if the headline still worked.

What she learned was the Doyle Dane Bernbach format: A picture communicates one message, words offer another meaning, and combined they send a third message. For instance, the headline, "You don't have to be Jewish to love Levy's" has one meaning, but accompanied by a visual of an Asian child eating rye bread, the ad has another and makes you smile. For Gillette, great ads are this juxtaposition of verbal and visual messages. Unless you have an extremely powerful message, she believes words alone rarely make a great ad. (For another take on the DDB format, see Roy Grace's chapter.)

With her book near completion, Gillette quit her job with the telecommunications firm. Her boss reacted by telling her he thought she was making a mistake—that she wouldn't make it in advertising.

"But failure wasn't something I was concerned about," says Gillette. "I was a kid and didn't care. I hadn't achieved anything I defined as success, so I wasn't giving up anything. Except a paycheck."

Once her portfolio was complete, Cafferetta provided Gillette with a list of contacts. She called each of them and found that they were very receptive to seeing her. But none had an available position. Some, however, referred her to other people. This generated a second list.

Discovering a New World

Even with help, she found her job search frustrating. On the positive side, however, it gave her an opportunity to see what kind of agency she wanted to work in and what kind of people she wanted to work for.

Says Gillette, "Some people I interviewed with were so rude, I said to myself, 'Good, I'm glad you don't like my book. I don't like you either, and I wouldn't want to work here even if you paid me.'"

At one agency, she was ushered into an office where the interviewer stood with his back to her while he hung awards on the wall. She sat there for over twenty minutes before he turned around and acknowledged her.

This agency had a campaign running for Smile Gum, and they had created a slogan that said "Say Cheese and Smile." Gillette's book contained a campaign for Carefree Sugarless Gum. One ad showed a dentist sitting in his own chair playing solitaire and had the line, "Your dentist will hate you for this." In other words, the gum is so good dentists will hate you because you'll never need them again. Gillette's interviewer told her the ad was terrible. "There's no appetite appeal," he explained.

"This guy obviously had no sense of humor," Gillette observed. He directed her to look at his chewing gum campaign.

Gillette critiqued the creative director's campaign by saying, "Say Cheese? Cheese and gum are the most unappetizing combination. It makes me think the gum tastes like cheese. That's terrible."

She says she feared the guy was going to throw her out of the room because of her response, but she was not apologetic. "Gall is something I've always had," says Gillette. "I had it in the beginning of my career, and I'll always have it. I've developed a bit more diplomacy than I had at 23, but not much." She laughs.

On the other hand, Gillette offered to work for Jan Zechman for free, because he was a great copywriter. Zechman turned her down because he said it wouldn't be fair. But he promised that he would hire her in two years. She didn't expect to hear from him again, but two years later he called and offered her a job.

Taking the Bus to Success

After 30 or 40 interviews over the next three months, she was hired as a copywriter at a small agency named Stern Walters for the same salary she had been making at the telecommunications company. At this agency, she worked for Larry Postaer, who would become one of her mentors. Gillette honed her print writing skills and won some awards for the work she did for the Chicago Transit Authority, the public transportation company. One of Gillette's favorites was a 15-second commercial with the headline: "Introducing a new economy model." As the headlights go on, the viewer sees that the vehicle is a bus, not a car. This was the most expensive commercial she worked on at Stern Walters. It cost $7,000, but it had a strong selling idea. She was soon promoted from copywriter to a copy supervisor.

But after two years, she decided it was time to move.

When Gillette arrived at the agency then named Needham, Harper & Steers (which merged with Doyle Dane Bernbach in 1985), she had to start over as a copywriter. But she understood that working on national accounts would have a different set of demands. Says Gillette, "I was savvy enough to know that if I was good, it wouldn't take long to be promoted again." As luck would have it, Keith Reinhard had just been promoted to Chief Creative Officer of Needham, Harper & Steers. "I've always been blessed with good timing and good luck. Keith, a true genius in our business, has had an incredible influence on my career."

From the Fast Track to the Mommy Track

At that time, creative groups were loosely divided according to media. And with a strong print book, she was assigned to the print and collateral group. It didn't take her long to decide she wanted to do McDonald's commercials. But she was in the wrong group.

She took control when she was asked to write some print materials to introduce a new McDonald's sandwich called the McFeast. When Gillette and her art director did the print and collateral, they also did a television commercial: "I never waited to be asked to do anything. Since no one else was working on the TV spot yet, we sold the entire package. The next time we did it again." After the second time, management promoted her to the television group.

At 31 she turned down the opportunity to become deputy creative director. She was pregnant and was unsure about the demands of motherhood. She didn't know how she would feel after having the baby. But she knew she was going to need more time with her child to be the kind of mother she wanted to be.

"I was a psychology minor," says Gillette, "I really understood that there were these couple of years for me to make an impression on my kids." She went from the fast track to the mommy track.

She calls this her proudest moment. "I'd have to say that was the gutsiest thing I've ever done," says Gillette. "But it was also easy. And it was the only thing I could do emotionally."

It was risky. Even today, many corporations still penalize talented employees for taking time off to raise a family. They hold back promotions. They question the person's loyalty. But the fact that her career had come relatively easily to her helped her decide to take the risk. She figured she could always get work in advertising. "Talent gives you a sense of security," she observes.

The 60 Percent Solution

Her boss was skeptical of her working part time, but she made a deal with him to work six hours a day, skip lunch, and work at home—for 60 percent of her salary. She retained her title as group creative director. But she lost her group.

During her first year as a part-timer, she did everything nobody else wanted to do. "All the garbage." she says. She wrote an in-house Crusade of Mercy campaign, speeches for the then-president, posters, and matchbook covers. "For one year my biggest media buy was the back of the bathroom door," says Gillette. "But it was okay with me."

Gillette then got involved in pitching new accounts. She helped pitch Sears, which Needham won. She pitched Michelob Lite and won that account. Then she won more work from Sears and some from Kraft. People began asking to be in her group—even though she didn't have one. What's more, after she had helped win the business, the agency knew that she had to be involved with producing the work and servicing the accounts, so they gradually began letting her build another creative group. Over the five years that she worked part time, she estimates she helped win approximately $150 million worth of new business.

"At that point, I think I was the most underpaid person in advertising," she says. "But I didn't care. I still worked part time. I had a real group again." Gillette would get home at 2:00, put her kids to bed at 10:00, and spend a couple more hours working. Sometimes, she'd go back to an editing suite after her children had gone to bed. Other times, she'd work two weeks straight because they were pitching a new piece of business and then she'd take some time off.

When she traveled she took the children with her. "It was flexible," says Gillette. "And that was what I wanted."

Michelob and Michigan Avenue

During her tenure as a part-timer, she developed her most famous campaign, "The Night Belongs to Michelob."

At the time, she was working on Michelob Lite, a brand that lacked a big budget, and she wanted a chance to work on the big-budget Michelob campaign. But because clients are possessive about their creative talent, she was asked not to work on that account. If she did, they were afraid the client would feel his brand was not getting the attention it deserved.

Gillette again took control of her career. She did a little research and discovered that there was a product called Michelob Dark. This brand didn't have an ad budget. And it wasn't taboo for her to work on it.

She started thinking about the meaning of darkness and night imagery. While walking across Chicago's Michigan Avenue bridge, she came up with the line, "Nothing's the same after dark." She knew she had it.

Recalls Gillette, "I started laughing because I knew it would sell the moment I thought of it."

The next morning, she talked with her art director, Bruce Ritter, about the imagery she had envisioned. They put together a commercial knowing that they were actually trying to sell a Michelob campaign and sent a cassette of it to the client saying, "We know you don't have a budget for Michelob Dark, but isn't this kind of provocative?"

Ten minutes after the clients saw the commercial, Gillette received a phone call from them telling her they loved it, but that they had no budget for the product.

Gillette suggested that maybe, with a little rewriting, they could use it for Michelob. With the client's interest in her campaign, Gillette obtained permission to work on its creative development. Says Gillette, "It ticked off a few people who were working on it 'officially.' But we proceeded to do ten commercials."

It took nine months for Gillette to sell the campaign, which was developed around a very simple idea. At the time, consumer sales were sluggish because Michelob was perceived as a "special occasion beer." Part of this was the result of a campaign that said "Weekends are made for Michelob." Gillette's ad expanded that perception and said that night was a special time of day. So, says Gillette, "It was for a special occasion that came every night of the week." Though Gillette was responsible for the creative rationale behind the campaign, she credits Joel Hochberg, her boss at the time, for the tagline "The Night Belongs to Michelob."

Promotions, Pressure, and Perspective

After five years of part-time work, Hochberg, who was becoming president of the agency, asked her to return to a full-time schedule and become creative director. "Joel was incredibly generous and supportive," notes Gillette. It was difficult for her to turn down the offer. She doubted that another agency would offer her a similar position after five years of working part time. Says Gillette, "You are most valuable in a place where the clients trust you." Since this might have been a once-in-a-lifetime opportunity, she decided to try it.

"It was like going from 0 to 60," she says. "As involved in my group as I was, it was different running the agency's entire creative department." She believes that once you rise to the position of creative director, your biggest challenge is to control the creative process by making people feel good about their work while keeping them out of trouble.

Creative people, she claims, love to hear themselves talk; they always think they have the right solution. Gillette's role was to make sure the work was not only artful, but strategically sound and could be sold to the client. "Sometimes," she says, "you get work that is none of the above."

Gillette feels that getting promoted early helped her career; she quickly learned that she'd be responsible for everything. She was going to get credit for work that was successful and suffer humiliation when it was not.

"I'm still not sure I was ever a great creative director, because I would always come up with my own solutions to problems," she says. She believes this is human nature. "You see a problem and your mind looks for a solution. I'd ask myself, 'Do I suggest the solution, or do I let them get there themselves? Do I tell them what I would do, or let them figure out what they would do?'"

Gillette's answer depended on the deadline. "If we had to go to the client the next day with inferior work, you have to push for a solution. Hopefully, I can say, 'Boy, this seems off to me. Here's why. Here's what I think you need to do. You guys go back and figure out how to do it.'"

In 1991, Gillette was promoted again—to president of the Chicago office. "I loved being a writer—and I still do. I could be very happy as a copywriter," she says. "But as a creative person, your ultimate fantasy is to be in control of everything."

She believes that being president of an agency is just a different kind of pressure, a different level of problem solving. She compares her promotion to going from composer to conductor. "You step up and you're just as concerned about the solo that night and the excellence of the performance," she says. "But you tend to have a different perspective. You worry about more things. You know if you can't keep the house full, you can't pay these people—and if you can't pay these people, you lose your best soloists."

Gillette's philosophy as president was much the same as it had been throughout her career: Every piece of work should be as good as it can be. That includes the idea, the words, the pictures, the music, the film, the nuances—everything.

When a copywriter writes a couple of headlines and thinks she has written an ad, she is disappointed. "I probably went through a pad a day," says Gillette. "I'd write a hundred headlines before I'd be happy, and I'd rewrite the body copy 15 times."

All of a sudden, Gillette had to deal with new perspectives. She was no longer just a manager of creative people; now she also had to manage account people, strategic planners, and media people.

"I realized that even though I didn't have their skill sets, they're people and they're motivated by a lot of the same things that motivate creative people," she says. "Indeed they're idea people, and some of them are very creative in how they do their jobs. It was a bit of an eye-opener."

"It's a team sport."

One thing that Gillette did as President was to reassign offices so that creative people were not sitting in a separate enclave. Rather, they were put into teams with strategic planners, account, and media people, all sitting together. Plus, she disbanded the dress code. While DDB/Chicago wasn't necessarily the first to make these changes, they were among the first. "You couldn't tell who was who," says Gillette. This, Gillette believed, leveled the playing field. People from the various disciplines began listening to each other. "Creative people can learn things from marketing, strategic, and smart media people," says Gillette.

Gillette's restructuring of the office was inspired by an insight she got when she moved out of the creative department. "While creativity is important, advertising is not a solo sport," she says. "It's a team sport. Strong ideas will survive a lot of different people commenting on them."

From President to Dean

In 1994, just after DDB/Chicago landed the Helene Curtis account, Gillette took early retirement to spend more time with her children. "I'd been instrumental in bringing in that business, and I knew that they'd be very upset to come to the agency and have me disappear," says Gillette, "so I offered to stay involved in the transition as long as they needed me."

Gillette worked part-time on Helene Curtis for a year and then made the transition to corporate consultant, overseeing special projects for the agency network.

For example, she did research on women's advancement in the company. "I'd say that at this point in my life, I shifted a lot of my goals into the people area, instead of staying focused on a piece of creative or on a particular business objective," says Gillette. "I love DDB, and I'm glad I've been able to stay involved and have an impact on the organization. I'm also very okay with the fact that it's in this whole different arena. I think it's an arena that's really important."

In 2002, Gillette also took over a newly formed role of Dean of DDB U, an agency-wide corporate training program. "The thought behind DDB U is that we've got some really great tools at this point—strategic, research, and media planning tools—but they're ineffective unless we teach people how to use them. The same is true of management skills. People are generally promoted to management because they're good at their craft, not necessarily because they show strong people skills or managerial ability. Most of us learned through trial and error, just kind of practicing on people until we got better at it.

"You can do it that way, but if we can mentor them and help them learn management skills, then the whole thing is just going to work better."

Having a corporate training program goes against the trend for ad agencies. The few that existed have been eliminated over the years in an effort to cut expenses. But Gillette sees the importance of such a program. "Advertising agencies have not put as much emphasis on HR, training, and people programs as GE or big consumer goods companies," Gillette says. "It's a shame because our industry is a service industry and our product is people, to an even greater extent than someone who manufactures an actual product. Agencies deal in intellectual capital, and the people who produce that intellectual capital have got to be happy, well-tended, well-nurtured, well-trained, and well-versed in the company culture and philosophy."

Gillette describes DDB U as a virtual operation. In addition to Gillette, there's a day-to-day manager of the program—Raquel Suarez, who has experience in corporate training and adult education—and a DDB U leader in every office in the world.

"It is pretty much a volunteer army," says Gillette. "We use some consultants, but mostly we use the best and brightest of our own people to train other people in the company in the tools, tactics, and skills that they need."

Gillette's outside interests have evolved over the years as well, first focusing her energy on her daughters and the things that interested them and then on helping some social causes that interested her.

"I don't think that's so unusual," she observes. "There are years in your life where you're really focused on your career, and when you step back from that then you focus on life in general and the broader perspective."

Gillette was on the National Advisory Board of the Salvation Army for five years. In addition, she serves on the advisory board of her alma mater, Northern Illinois University. And, as you'll see in her portfolio section, Gillette writes ads for her church. "I use the abilities I've acquired over the years to make a positive impact in the things that I think are important."

She says that even today each problem sets her mind off in many different directions. She believes this is not a result of talent, but how one's mind is wired.

Gillette uses herself as an example. "I always hated to lose. They could keep rejecting my work, but I would keep coming back with another great idea."

She feels this kind of competitiveness was ultimately good for her clients as well as her career. "I want my clients to win in the marketplace. I want them to beat the heck out of their competition. I'm very goal directed. Win the business. Build the sales. Win the awards. Focus on the work. My success has been a result of that relentless focus."

A FEW SAMPLES FROM THE DREAM PORTFOLIO

— PUBLIC SERVICE SPEC WORK —

Students of advertising are often told to avoid public service ads in their portfolios. There's a perception that they're easy to do. But Gillette believes that to write a great public service ad is to write a great ad. "Besides," she says, "it gets to people, and it's more fun to do than toothpaste."

Her early portfolio included this public service spec ad, which presented a different kind of "feminine protection." The body copy told women that they had a right to carry condoms to prevent venereal diseases.

Ironically, her public service work for preventing sexually transmitted diseases didn't end with her spec book. Years later,

she's still creating ads to inspire people to protect themselves against AIDS. "They do not have the same kind of headlines or executions," says Gillette. "They're not as flip. VD is curable; AIDS is not."

SEVEN YEARS IS A LONG TIME TO WORRY ABOUT A ONE-NIGHT STAND.

Gillette chose the American Cancer Society for public service work because her grandmother died of breast cancer.

One public service campaign in her early portfolio was this ad to encourage women to examine their breasts. The copy included simple instructions on how to conduct the exam. Gillette wrote this in 1973, before mammograms were easily available.

In 1985, she pitched and won the American Cancer Society of Illinois, which is still a DDB/Chicago client.

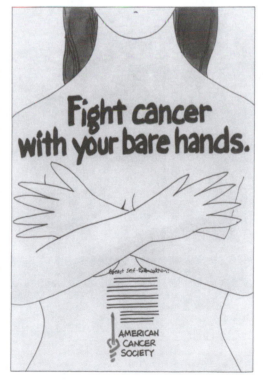

Fight cancer with your bare hands.

AMERICAN CANCER SOCIETY

FRY NOW PAY LATER

Prolonged exposure to the sun will give you more than a deep, dark tan. It will give you deep, ugly wrinkles before your time — and make you ten times more likely to develop skin cancer.

American Cancer Society®

So slather on the water-proof sunscreen SPF 15 or higher and take it easy on the sun bathing. Your beautiful, healthy skin will thank you for it.

Then, in 1984, she wrote this ad.

It is a good example of juxtaposition in advertising—the DDB format that greatly influenced Gillette early in her career (see page 105). The headline, "Fry Now, Pay Later," means one thing by itself—an ad for buying cookware on credit. And the visual, without the headline, sends a pro-sun message.

But together, the words and visual clearly communicate a different message. "I look for a strong understanding that words alone—or pictures alone—do one thing, but when pictures and words come together, they do a third thing" she says.

"When I see someone who understands that, then I know that person understands the power of print advertising."

—— Polaroid ——

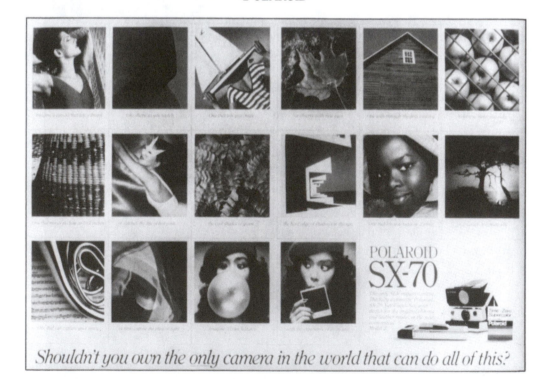

Shouldn't you own the only camera in the world that can do all of this?

Although the agency had the Polaroid account for only two years, Gillette is proud of the work she and her group produced. The account was out of New York and split between the pre-merged Needham, Harper & Steers and Doyle Dane Bernbach, which made it difficult to service.

This award-winning work didn't have headlines—only poetry under the photos. But the pictures told the entire story and were best complemented by an unconventional format.

"There is no formula for good advertising," says Gillette. "An innate consciousness of the power of words and pictures and an ability to put the two together in a magical way is what makes somebody a good print writer."

—— McDonald's ——

"I'm proud to have made commercials I like without big production budgets," says Gillette. "Except for the talent, this McDonald's commercial was produced on a very low budget. We used Michael J. Fox before he was Michael J. Fox. Copy credit goes to Jim Glover, who I coached through his first dialogue spot. It was shot by my former art director, Jon Yarbrough."

McDonald's did so many commercials in a year that Gillette was able to experiment with writing dialogue, humor, or anything else she wanted to do. It gave her a great training ground with instant gratification and national exposure.

Gillette worked on McDonald's for seven years. "I went from being a copywriter to a group creative director on McDonald's. I worked on everything that McDonald's sold, and I was heartbroken when we lost the account. I was so upset," she recalls.

"The client called and assured me it wasn't the creative. That call only made me feel worse, because that was all I had control over. The week I was made president we got back part of the national McDonald's ad account. That was a great promotion gift. It wasn't cause and effect, of course. Keith Reinhard worked relentlessly to win back McDonald's. He was obsessed and successful."

——— WINNETKA CONGREGATIONAL CHURCH ———

Here's proof that you don't need a big production or media budget, a global client, or a trendy, hip brand to create smart, provocative advertising; all you need is a strong idea and great execution. "They're 'get your butt in here' kind of ads," says Gillette. "They're very retail oriented."

The ads were designed because people assumed that this was more a conservative church—from the outside, the building looks like a bank—but it's actually a more liberal, more inclusive type of place.

Created with Jim Retzer, a long-time art director at DDB/Chicago, these *pro bono* ads appear in a local weekly newspaper.

The content of the ads change according to the season and in response to current events.

"It was an attempt to have a voice in the community," says Gillette.

"It's been very interesting listening to older members of the church—people who I thought might have felt we went a little over the edge," says Gillette. "They say things like, 'This is really interesting,' 'We really like these ads,' and 'We like the fact that we're saying things in the community that are getting attention.'"

SOME BASIC ADVICE
FOR CREATING SOPHISTICATED ADVERTISING

"A lot of advertising is like Chinese food," says Gillette, "it's okay, it tastes good, but it just goes away." She believes good advertising should make people say, "'Oh, I never thought of it that way.' It should have impact and stick with you."

But what makes substantial advertising?

"Going for the kill is an instinct that good creative people have," says Gillette. "They have a laser-like ability to pull everything together, to harness all the elements and give them power."

Gillette looks for ads that look different, sound different, or take something from a slightly different perspective and then "nail you" with their relevance.

She says great ads stop you when you first look at them, then you stop and enjoy them for a while. A young copywriter once told her that the best ad research would be to put a bunch of ads in a room and let people walk around and see which ones they stopped at. "First it's stopping power," says Gillette. "Then it's staying power. It's that little insight that makes the ad speak to you and helps the product fill a void the reader may never even have known he or she had."

Here are some ideas to help you create ads that speak to your audience:

Embrace the joy of discovery: "I think somebody could have tried to teach me how to make ads, but I'm not sure it can be 'taught' to everyone," says Gillette.

"There are a lot of kids taking communications courses. Few of them will be great copywriters or art directors." Gillette suggests you decode award-winning ads to see why they work. Question the visuals, headlines, words, and layouts.

"See what excites you about them, and then see if you can apply the theories to your own advertising."

Find a trusted counselor in the business: Gillette suggests that you ask a professional advertising creative—a creative director, writer, or art director—to look at your work "with a clear eye" for honest feedback and advice.

"I had someone do that for me," says Gillette. "He looked at my stuff and said, 'Get rid of this. Get rid of that. This spec stuff is really good. Get rid of this other stuff, it's distracting me.'

"When we're young, we don't always know what's good and what's not good, what's going to impress people and not impress somebody, so it can't hurt to have somebody look at your stuff before you unleash yourself on the world."

Edit—then edit some more: Your portfolio should continually evolve.

Don't be shy about trying stuff, changing stuff, and, if necessary, doing more. According to Gillette, that's what it takes to get a job.

"I'd go to one person who said he or she liked one thing and hated another thing, so I'd reconsider or rewrite the hated one," recalls Gillette. "People had differing opinions. It made me think about the strengths and weaknesses of each piece. It was a process of elimination.

"Over time, I kept in the things that everybody liked and eliminated things that nobody liked, and then I'd try to write more stuff that everybody would like. The odds that you're going to get a job on your first interview are very unlikely."

Think like a strategic planner: "Before there are ads, there is a strategy. You have to decide who you're talking to, who your audience is, and what the intended message is.

"Then you try to find an insight about the product that makes a connection between the potential consumer and the product. And that's the role of strategic planning," says Gillette.

"I don't expect creative people to be market researchers. I don't expect them to have marketing degrees. Fortunately, at agencies, we have an entire department to do the strategizing. But I do expect creative people to have a working strategy in their heads for the products in their portfolios. You really can't develop an ad without one."

Set deadlines: "There are two great creative stimuli," says Gillette. "One is the noose, which means we either have to come up with the solution by tomorrow or we all die. And the other one is problem solving by thinking around the problem.

"You think about other things, sometimes related things, and always have the problem in the back of your mind." Gillette believes both methods are effective. "If you're having trouble finishing your portfolio because you have all the time in the world, try the 'noose' method. You just might surprise yourself. Sometimes sorting through too many options just gives you a headache."

Think beyond print, TV, and radio: Print, television, and radio speculative work is still the way most beginning creatives are judged within the industry. However, Gillette suggests that you bring along other types of samples for interviews.

"It's certainly critical for you to have strong print and TV creative abilities," she says. "But when I see a creative direct mail piece, I become grateful that there actually is such a thing. There are also a lot of possibilities in some of the newer mediums or in having ideas that cross mediums. I think talent is talent."

Identify the agencies where you want to work: Gillette recommends that you try to get a working knowledge of what agencies are producing which ads. "There might be an agency with a famous name, but its Chicago or Detroit office is not in the same league," says Gillette. And target agencies that produce work that is compatible with your sensibility. There are different styles of good creative approaches. You'll go farther in an agency whose philosophy and approach resemble your own. If you can't assess your style yet, just choose an agency whose work you like."

Find a great boss: "When you take your first job, you can't be picky. After that, try to get to a place where you can work for somebody you respect and who cares about you personally. It makes a big difference who you work for—how smart they are, how nice they are, whether or not they're going to nurture your talent—or try to squelch it," says Gillette. "Postaer, Hochberg, and Reinhard helped me grow my talent and advance my career.

"Some advertising people are jealous of the talent and intelligence of the young people under them. When that happens, a brilliant young creative can begin to think he or she is untalented. You have so much to learn, especially in those early years. You can't do it completely by yourself. Especially at the beginning."

So what should you look for? In addition to the willingness to mentor, Gillette thinks you should find "someone who fits your style and produces work you admire. You're probably more likely to succeed this way than if you get a job by randomly picking an agency out of the phonebook."

Show you want to work for the person: "Let's face it, bald flattery still works," says Gillette. "If I were a young kid, I'd find the two or three people who are doing the best work and I'd annoy the hell out of them. I'd say, 'You're the person I want to work for, not your company. I saw the new spots you did, and I think they're incredible, and here's what I like about them, and I think I could learn a lot from you.' We're all human, and if I really thought somebody wanted to work for me, that would hold a lot more water than someone who I thought was just desperate for a job and willing to take any port in the storm."

Look at your own life: "Write ads for products with which you have a lot of familiarity," says Gillette. "Don't try to do Porsche advertising if you don't know cars or have one. Do something that hits close to home. Breast cancer was something I wanted to work on because my grandmother died from it. If you pick a product you use, then you've already fallen in love with it—you already have a great sense of it—so work backwards and figure out why you fell in love with it.

"What is it about that product that you really like? Then you have to figure out how to stop someone who'd never seen the product and is experiencing it for the first time with something witty and incredibly insightful. It's almost like the chicken going back into the egg."

Have a notion of sales: "A lot of kids coming out of school think that they're getting jobs at the Art Institute. But they're not. You really have to sell products.

"You can't just be a clever writer or be able to compose a stunning layout or visual," says Gillette. "You have to communicate a sales message.

"A talented advertising person creates a selling idea people can't dismiss. The reader has to engage with it, relate to it, and be moved by it."

Develop a new product: Gillette finds new product ideas intriguing. "It shows me the art director or writer is someone who not only knows how to draw or write, but also thinks about consumer activity."

In Gillette's beginning book, she included an ad for a cordless hairsetter—which became a real product ten years later. "When I was in college, it was a pain to have all these small electrical appliances, blow dryers and hot rollers, plugged into the same outlet. The idea for the product came from my own experience," says Gillette.

The ad's headline read, "Isn't it time you cut the cord?" Says Gillette, "The ad wasn't that great, but the idea for the product was smart. It solved a problem that existed in real life."

Turn up the "provoca meter": "I was really trying to get people to pay attention to me," says Gillette of her portfolio, which she describes as being very sassy, sexy, and irreverent, but very well written. She believes that the world is not waiting for a new ad. She says, "Advertising should continuously strive to surprise, delight, and move people."

Look at an idea inside out: At DDB, extensive research is used to guide creative direction and determine strategy. But, for beginners, this is difficult to find and incorporate into a campaign. To compensate, Gillette suggests you simply look at your own reactions to advertising.

"I did this when I wrote my Carefree Gum campaign for my spec portfolio," recalls Gillette. "I hated the original campaign. I didn't believe dentists recommended sugarless gum because I figured everybody's basically a mercenary. So I tried to look at the ad and take the flip side of it. Look at a campaign that's running and turn it inside out. See if you can argue the other side of the case.

"I don't expect young creatives to understand marketing. I do expect them to understand ideas and logic and the power of the unexpected."

Put the in-house work in the "outhouse": When Gillette began her job search she included some poetry she wrote in college as well as product letters and a company newspaper from the telecommunications firm in her portfolio.

One interviewer handed Gillette the poetry and said, "Save these for your boyfriend." He then handed her the product letters and said, "These prove you can spell. Don't show them to anybody." It was the kind of blunt assessment that is worth a lot to a beginner.

Make sure everything in your book is your best: While Gillette recommends that you eliminate your in-house work from your portfolio, she will make an exception for great in-house advertising. "If you can honestly say that your in-house advertising is provocative and high quality, then of course show it," says Gillette. "If it's in-house piece for some obscure product or service, that's fine. People win awards with that kind of stuff. But, if it's trade advertising that's sort of mediocre, which is kind of what I got to work on before I got to an agency, then it won't convince anybody that you're brilliant. All it's going to do is make them nervous that that's the best you can do.

"You have to ask yourself, is this going to be evidence that you're willing to compromise or is it going to be evidence that you're great? We all know that we're willing to compromise to eat. Just don't put the evidence in your portfolio."

Show your work to everybody: "Give your ads to normal consumers—your mother, your dad, your peers—and see if they get it. See if they understand the ad and if it makes them respond," says Gillette.

"Showing it around also keeps you from humiliating yourself by presenting a concept that's already been done. You might have written something that was actually written by somebody else—which happens a lot," she says.

"If people feel your ad is vaguely reminiscent, leave it out of your book. At the end of the day, telling a successful creative director who's critiquing your book that your Mom 'just loved that one' probably won't turn the tide."

Make them feel it: "At some point, a copywriter and art director cross over from wanting to tell you or show you everything to wanting to make you feel something," says Gillette. "When you cross over, you're no longer an art director or a writer. You're an advertising person. Every great person I've worked with is a hybrid."

And make it slick: Agencies today are less inclined to take the chance on someone with a rough book, warns Gillette. The samples in a beginning spec portfolio should look as good as any finished ad.

"Back in my day, you could get hired with a very humble portfolio. I did my own art direction. I had strong ideas, but it looked like doo-doo. It was just typewriter type and my own little chicken-scratch drawings," says Gillette. "But the ante has been raised by portfolio schools. At this point people expect a certain level of polish."

Start small: Gillette advises beginners to start at a small shop. At Needham in her first round of interviews, Gillette was told that she didn't want to start there because the agency wasn't good for beginners—they'd probably ignore her and leave her thinking she was not good. This was advice Gillette did not want to hear. (She admits she would have taken a job from Jack-the-Ripper.) "Kids out of school can be extremely talented and not very useful at a big agency like DDB," Gillette says. "We expect a lot of self-sufficiency. We would fully admit that you either sink or swim if you come in the door here as a beginner. I'm not sure I would have ended up president of DDB/Chicago if I'd started there."

Learn to convey an idea in a headline: Gillette believes this is a good a way of focusing and galvanizing your idea in a short amount of words, even for a TV spot. "For a while I was asking junior creatives to bring in idea cards," says Gillette. "Before you show me a storyboard, write the idea of the commercial in one sentence. It wouldn't have to be a clever phrase, but it would have to be succinct and it would have to make me think that it was an interesting idea. If you can get impact with that one phrase, it could be the punch line for the commercial. It doesn't necessarily have to turn into a print ad." For an example, Gillette pointed to the Michelin campaign. "It's a print ad. It's a baby in a tire, and a set of words. So, baby in a tire is the idea, and that's a surprising visual. The idea could have been a print ad.

"On the other hand, Budweiser's classic 'Whasssup' campaign doesn't work in print. It's not a print idea; it's more of an audio idea. It's a linguistic thing. It's a whole different kind of an idea."

Include print ads in your book: While print advertising is becoming a less dominate medium, having it in your portfolio could help you land the job. "Print tends to pop out more when flipping through portfolios," says Gillette. "People don't have much patience when they're looking at portfolios, and headlines tend to grab you. Emotional subjects—like HIV, condoms, child abuse, life-and-death kinds of things—are things that will move people to react. If you can do something that's emotional, sensitive, and tactful, then people will respect you. People also respect a new take on an old subject."

Keep interviewing: "Persistence is something a lot of young kids don't have," says Gillette. "It's like they think they're going to go on two or three interviews and get a job." Gillette claims to have gone on more than 30 interviews before she found her first job in advertising. "If you believe in yourself and you're good, you will get a job eventually. Don't be too proud to take a job in a promotional or direct-marketing agency. Just don't stay too long or you'll be pigeonholed as a specialist—unless you want to stay in that area."

Find where you fit: "One doesn't have to produce TV commercials to be a card-carrying creative," says Gillette. "There's all kinds of creativity out there today. The Internet is full of outlets for creativity. People can bypass TV and print media so easily, yet the web allows them to become really engaged with a brand on a whole new level.

"The whole dot-com thing was a wakeup call for our industry. All of the sudden agency art directors were looking a little old fashioned, and the dot-com people were looking like the new wave. It's shifted back a little.

"But the truth is, thanks to integrated marketing, there are all kinds of creative jobs out there, and I don't know that one is inherently better than another. If you want to be creative, take the job that somebody's handing you, be creative, and then figure out where you go from there. If you're using it as a stop over, that's great, but you might fall in love with it and decide to stay. That's great too."

Move on: Staying in unrewarding positions for a long time strikes Gillette as odd. "I've had people come in at age 30 and say, 'I've been at this terrible in-house agency for eight years.' Why? Unless you have an amazing tale, like you've been supporting two blind maiden aunts. If you had gumption you'd have quit," says Gillette.

"I know of no one who has created garbage for nine years and gone on to be an award-winning copywriter. How can you survive nine years of garbage and have the soul of a great copywriter or art director?

"This doesn't apply to someone doing *good* small-market advertising and then going to a big national shop. All these people usually lack is media exposure. A small regional agency is a great place to start."

Cheat: "Anything you can do to get attention is okay as far as I'm concerned—as long as it's not stupid or illegal," says Gillette. "I confess I did not have a package goods ad in my fortfolio. A CD at Burnett told me my work was too funny. Which didn't disconcert me at all, but left me believing I'd probably not fit in at Leo Burnett circa 1975."

Gillette broke many "rules" in her quest to find a job in advertising. "Use all of your creativity and your sense of humor. You're not just selling your book, you're selling yourself."

Look beyond advertising: "I believe that creativity is a commodity that is very sellable. The ability to write, think, and problem solve in a creative way is not something that all people have, and whenever you have an ability that other people don't have, it's a sellable commodity," says Gillette.

"Go work for a congressman writing speeches. Design a website. Start a blog. Go work for the local newspaper. If you can't write, take pictures or design things—packages, products. People sometimes think that big advertising agency jobs are it. Maybe that's your ultimate objective, but there are certainly lots of other paths to being creative."

POSTSCRIPT:

YOU AND THE FUTURE OF ADVERTISING

The field of advertising is continually changing. Here is what Susan Gillette has to say about the future of advertising. It may help you decide where you fit in.

"People who think that advertising is about writing good ads will be disappointed. Advertising is about solving problems for clients. It requires thinking beyond the page. Some copywriters and art directors can do that. And some cannot.

"Those who can't really don't want to solve a client's problem; they don't want to sell product; they don't want to be involved in the "dirty" part. They just want to create art. But it's not about selling art. It's about the art of selling. (And never forget that the first person you have to 'sell' is the client.)

"Advertising and communications is an exciting field for people who love change. It's depressing for people who just want to go back to the '60s and write a great headline or TV commercial.

"The notion of what advertising is has changed and is going to change many times within the next ten years. What isn't going to change is the need for creativity and a powerful selling idea.

"Artfulness, entertainment value, and simplicity have never been more important. If the media keeps changing as exponentially as it has in the last couple of years, and I believe it will, how will we reach people? How will we talk to them? We have to find even more remarkable ways to stop people. They can already hide from us like never before. They can zap us and click us into oblivion.

"The people who will really make a name for themselves in the future will be people who go beyond the page. Not just great copywriters. Not just great art directors. But the people who see beyond the barriers, the visionaries. The people with the next generation of big ideas.

"You'll still have to be an expert in the traditional forms—the world's best headlines, the world's most stunning layouts—but you'll also have to go beyond what is traditionally known as advertising. There may be a new form of advertising.

"Integrated marketing is here to stay, and if you learn to use all the weapons in your arsenal, it's incredibly powerful.

"TV isn't always first anymore. Sometimes a direct marketing campaign is first, or as in the case of Altoids, outdoor.

"It's looking at the problem and seeing opportunity in places where, in the past, we probably wouldn't have looked.

"In the past, you probably would have automatically played the TV card. We do a disservice not to think about packaging, displays, and all the other creative elements that touch people. Creativity is limitless and valuable. You are not an advertising person—you are a creative person. The future for creative people is full of new promise.

"Through it all, the most elusive element of the marketing mix is magic.

"Clients don't always know how to create it, but they know when it's there.

"The elusive thing that makes Nike cooler than the other sports brands is because it's been injected with magic. Both from inside the company and from their marketing communications partners. It's true of all the brands that have had wonderful brand building, marketing, and advertising. It has actually made those brands more successful than the brands that don't have it.

"The best CEOs and the best marketing guys out there would absolutely rather have it than not have it. If you are a person who can create magic, then you can do something that not everyone else can do.

"It's that intangible 'plus' that brilliant creativity brings to a product. It's transformational. Having been exposed to X, you come away with a changed perception of the brand.

"If you are a person who can create that magic, then you can do something that not everyone can do. It's a valuable commodity, and that's not going to change."

No. 2 says he tries harder.

Than who?

We wouldn't, for a minute, argue with No. 2. If he says he tries harder, we'll take him at his word.

The only thing is, a lot of people assume it's us he's trying harder than.

That's hardly the case. And we're sure that No. 2 would be the first to agree.

Especially in light of the following.

A car where you need it.

The first step in renting a car is getting to the car. Hertz makes that easier for you to do than anybody else.

We're at every major airport in the United States. And at some airports that are not so major. Ever fly to Whitefish, Montana? Some people do. And have a Hertz car waiting.

No matter how small the airport you fly to, if it's served by a commercial airline, 97 chances out of 100 it's also served by Hertz or by a Hertz office within 20 minutes of it.

In all, Hertz has over 2,900 places throughout the world where you can pick up or leave a car. Nearly twice as many as No. 2.

Can't come to us? We'll come to you.

We have a direct-line telephone in most major hotels and motels in the U.S. It's marked HERTZ and it's in the lobby. Pick it up, ask for a car, and we'll deliver one to the door. You often can't get a cab as easily.

What kind of car would you like?

When you rent from Hertz, you're less likely to get stuck with a beige sedan when you want a red convertible. We have over twice as many cars as No. 2.

Not only is our fleet big, it's varied. We do our best to give you what you want. From Fords, to Mustangs, to Thunderbirds, to Lincolns and everything in between. Including the rather fantastic Shelby GT 350-H.

Who's perfect?

When you rent a new car from us or anybody else, you expect it to be sitting there waiting, ready to go, looking like new.

On that score we claim no superiority over our competition. They goof once in awhile. We goof once in awhile.

Except when we goof it bothers us more because people don't expect the big one to goof. And to make up for it, if our service is not up to Hertz standards we give you $50 in free rentals.* Plus an apology.

No. 2 gives a quarter plus an apology. And advertises that he "can't afford" to do more.

We feel the other way about it. We can't afford to do less.

Besides, the $50 comes out of the station manager's local operating funds. This tends to keep him very alert...and our service very good.

Hot line.

When you're in one city and you're flying to another city and you want to have a car waiting when you arrive and you want it confirmed before you leave, we can do it for you. Instantly. In any one of 1,038 U.S. cities. No other rent a car company can make that statement.

The major reason we can do it is because we recently installed one of the world's most advanced reservations systems.

After all, with the supersonic jets in sight and one hour coast to coast flights in prospect, you'll need some quick answers. We can give them to you today.

About credit.

If you've got a national credit card with most any major company, you've got credit with us.

About rates.

You can rent a car from Hertz by the day and the mile, by the weekend, by the week, by the month, by gift certificate, by revolving credit, by sundry other ways in between.

We offer all these rates for two reasons. To stay ahead of competition. To get more people to rent cars.

When you go to rent a Hertz car just tell the Hertz girl how long you want the car and roughly how much driving you'll be doing. She'll figure out the rate that's cheapest for you.

Speak up No. 3.

Is it you that No. 2 tries harder than?

Hertz

Amil Gargano

"If you don't believe in what you're doing, how can you expect anyone else to believe it?"

So says Amil Gargano, creative leader and co-founder of Ally & Gargano, one of the hottest and most influential shops of the '60s, '70s, and early '80s. He explains, "The last thing to do is to make ads. The first thing to do is become informed. Knowledge is a weapon. The more you know about a product, the more you can convey its merits to consumers. With knowledge comes conviction. And that conviction is transferred to the work you create. When you believe in what you're doing, you get others to believe it, too."

Gargano's reputation is based on much of that belief. He was the creator of many breakthrough campaigns for such clients as Volvo, Hertz, Pan Am, Fiat, Saab, Polaroid, MCI, and Calvin Klein. He has won hundreds of industry awards, holding the record for the most gold medals won in one year from the One Show.

He has been elected to the Art Director's Club Hall of Fame and to the One Club's Creative Hall of Fame.

In 1991, he left Ally & Gargano and founded a new agency, Amil Gargano and Partners, with one client—Showtime. This agency grew to also include such clients as Alabama Power, the Blackstone Company, Astra Merck, and Audiovox, as well as projects for American Express and NYNEX.

During his agency years, Gargano served on the board of Helen Keller Worldwide. He also served for many years on a creative advisory board for the Partnership for a Drug-Free America. And, for more than 25 years, he taught a post-graduate level communications course as a visiting professor at Syracuse University.

He closed his agency in 2001 to concentrate on writing an autobiography of his years at Ally & Gargano.

Today, while working on this book, he splits his time between New York and Florida (he recently sold his boat to Ed McCabe).

He has been married for 40 years and has a grown son and three grandchildren. His son works in the advertising industry.

COMPARE THIS CAREER

What attracts many people into advertising? Gargano has his own simple answer: nothing. They just drifted in from other careers. "A lot of people have wandered in with ambitions of becoming serious artists and writers," he says.

Gargano, in fact, was one of those people. As a child, he wanted to be a fine artist and, later, a commercial illustrator. He started working toward those goals in the fourth grade after a teacher identified his artistic abilities. She suggested that his parents send him to art classes after school. So two days a week, after his regular classes, he attended the William's School in downtown Detroit. And his father picked him up on his way home from work. "That's where I developed a real interest in art," says Gargano.

From Korea to Cranbrook

He then attended Cass Tech in Detroit, a high school that emphasized art, music, and science. Later, he entered Wayne State University. But his education was interrupted by the Korean War.

He spent 21 months in the service. Fifteen months were spent on the front lines. "I was discharged early because I had combat experience," he says. "I started thinking about what I wanted to do and I found that I didn't have enough money to go away to school."

Back home, he registered at Cranbrook Academy of Art. He financed his education with the help of the GI Bill and by working as a part-time salesman in a men's clothing store. "I was one of two veterans," Gargano says. "The school was in the suburbs of Detroit, an enclave of automobile executives. Everyone was affluent, and the surroundings were palatial."

Finding himself uncomfortable in these surroundings, Gargano stayed for only one year, and left to find a job. Friends suggested he apply at Chrysler. But his portfolio wasn't really cut out for a position in America's automobile capital. "I wasn't interested in drawing automobile parts," he says.

Nevertheless, he was offered a job designing the lettering for car interiors. "I didn't want to spend my life with a group of men in shirt sleeves trying to decide whether to use script, serif, or san-serif type," he says, "so I rejected it. And the guy doing the hiring was outraged because the job paid $100 bucks a week—a lot of money at that time."

From Detroit to New York

Then, he learned of a job at a place called Campbell-Ewald—the Chevrolet advertising agency. "I thought, advertising? What a terrible business!" he recalls. "Advertising in the mid-'50s was so bad, you couldn't even parody it because everyone would assume you were serious."

But since agencies commissioned artists for illustrations, he took the job, expecting it to bring him closer to achieving that goal. In his first job, he cut mats, and completed mechanicals and patch work for the art directors. "I became their hands," he says. "And on weekends and evenings, I'd work to develop a portfolio that would land me a job in a Detroit art studio."

Then on Christmas, six months later, he tried to resign in order to look for a job as an illustrator. "I was so naive," he says. "My parents were direct, honest people who taught me to be up-front with everyone. I couldn't imagine looking for a new job on someone else's time. You didn't take advantage of anybody who had hired you. That would be immoral. Today, that seems ridiculous, doesn't it?"

But the aspiring illustrator's attempt to quit was met with protest. To his surprise, his boss, Al Scott, told him that he had been planning to promote him to assistant art director after the holidays. "He told me," says Gargano, "and this is what got me: 'In advertising you create the ideas and give them to an illustrator. As an illustrator, you wind up rendering art directors' thinking.' This intrigued me."

In January of 1956, Gargano took on his first assignment as assistant art director—doing industrial ads. "In those days," says Gargano, "a copywriter would give the art director a yellow piece of paper with a headline that had already been approved by the account executive. So I took the information, looked at it, and designed the hell out of it. The result didn't make much advertising sense, because the design had no relationship to a selling concept, but it looked interesting and different from the other ads being done. The agency loved it. I look back now and cringe."

After eight months, he was promoted to art director; then to group art director. At 27, he became vice president. "I was just beginning to understand what advertising was about," he says, "because I became immersed in it."

He studied the New York Art Directors annuals and began to notice the work of Doyle Dane Bernbach (DDB) and other up-and-coming agencies. He was impressed—more by the design elements than the concepts, but he began to understand how to really communicate with people—that what you say and how you say it is what gets people to read and believe your ad.

"I began to examine why I stopped to read certain things," he recalls, "and what interested me. I knew other people would be attracted the same way."

He did not study television commercials because art directors back then weren't part of the process. "Most of them were abominable, anyway," Gargano says. "They were predominately singing commercials. It's not that things have changed much. They've just gotten a lot more slick."

He had always wanted to work in New York. The work coming out of agencies like DDB motivated him further. He spoke to his group supervisor about wanting to move, saying he would prefer to stay with Campbell-Ewald and work in their small office there. "I told him if you ever need anyone in New York, you can count on me," says Gargano. "I'd volunteer."

In less than a year, the opportunity arose. It happened because Carl Ally, then an assistant to the president of Campbell-Ewald, had his eye out for new opportunities and noticed how fast New York agencies were growing. He asked to be sent there to try to cultivate new business. With some reluctance, management agreed.

In New York, Ally heard that the Swissair account was looking for an agency. He called them, made a pitch and won the business.

To service the account, Ally needed fresh talent. Says Gargano, "The New York office was a sleepy place where people were hiding comfortably." That was Gargano's cue. "Carl Ally was someone I had worked with sporadically back in Detroit," Gargano says, "and we hit it off extremely well." He moved to New York, along with Jim Durfee (also from Campbell-Ewald).

A few months later, the agency also won United Technologies. But the work they were doing wasn't what Campbell-Ewald management had in mind. Complying with clients was more important than vigorously defending ideas. Consequently, the trio left for other jobs agreeing that, should the opportunity arise, they'd start their own agency.

Getting Acquainted with Greatness

During his first few years in New York, Gargano spent much of his time becoming acquainted with the city. He became even more familiar with DDB's work and watched for it.

"Most of the advertising at that time was not very compelling," says Gargano. "But DDB had tremendous appeal. They told things the way they were, did it in a way that was startlingly original—in a language that everyone spoke."

Because DDB's work was so remarkably different from previous advertising, Gargano studied it to learn the elements that made it work. He'd walk to the subway station in New York and see the ads for Levy's Rye Bread. Or open the *New York Times* and see an ad for Orbach's. In the process, Gargano's attitude toward advertising changed from contempt to inspiration.

"There was a famous ad that Bob Gage of DDB did for El Al," he remembers. "It simply said that El Al has shrunk the Atlantic by 20%. And they had this dramatic photograph of the Atlantic Ocean with the corner cut and rolled back 20%. At other agencies, this ad would have never been conceived or approved. Instead, they would feature a big, stupid airplane—like that was the thing people were buying. But people don't buy an airplane; they buy an experience. An airplane's just the vehicle to get you someplace. Knowing that, DDB took advantage of a simple, powerful idea that people would find unusual and engaging."

He spent many hours talking with Ally and Durfee about advertising. "We were all from Detroit and trying hard to find our own advertising philosophy to help change the industry. We used to talk about why certain ads were effective. And what individuals were creating real innovation. We became students."

Much of what Gargano saw bothered him. Historically, there was a definitive agency hierarchy. The account person had absolute control. Copywriters were number two; followed by research and media. "The art director was last on the food chain—a renderer, a pair of hands," he says. "I was outraged by this caste system—mainly because there wasn't any overwhelming thinking taking place by any of these people to begin with." Bernbach, however, liberated art directors. He gave them equality to copywriters. That appealed to him.

Developing a Vision

In addition, the three of them had their own opinions.

Their philosophy departed from DDB's humanistic, emotionally engaging approach. They went after a harsher, more combative style. They wanted to challenge the audience with reasons to buy one particular product over another, but in ways that hadn't been done before. They wanted to differentiate themselves—with a style that would be their own.

"We said to ourselves that information is the crucial element to creating persuasive advertising. It's a weapon. You can bludgeon your competition with the right information," says Gargano.

"We believed in taking a consumer advocacy position. What's in it for them? We had tremendous contempt for advertising that was of an insidious nature. It was often tasteless, patronizing, and mindless in its presentation to people."

In 1962, with those thoughts in mind, they pitched an unknown account, Volvo, and won the business. Carl Ally, Inc., was formed. "Because Carl was ten years older and had a strong personal sense of entitlement, he insisted that his name be on the door exclusively," says Gargano. "Our first advertising for Volvo pioneered comparative advertising. What we did for Volvo was define the character of the automobile to the public. Gave them a new set of criteria for buying a car: durability, longevity, and safety. A strategy that endures 40 years later." The agency then went on to create some of the decade's most significant work.

And Putting Your Name on the Door

By 1977, Gargano wanted recognition in the agency he had helped found. "Look," he told Ally, "my contributions have equaled yours. In fact, in some respects, I think they've exceeded yours, so I think my name should be on the door too."

Ally agreed and the agency's name was changed to Ally & Gargano.

But then, in 1978, the agency lost three major pieces of business and billings dropped from $54 million to $26 million.

Carl Ally had been chairman and CEO for 16 years. He suggested that Gargano take over the agency to revitalize it.

Gargano agreed on the condition that he be made the controlling shareholder, something Carl had insisted upon for himself in 1962. "We believed that we could function as equals within the agency, but someone had to ultimately make the hard decisions," says Gargano.

"To his credit, I can't think of many people who could step aside the way he did. So I took over the company in April of 1978. And we got lucky and had five remarkable years of growth and recognition for our work."

By 1983, Ally & Gargano reached nearly $160 million in billings. "Then someone had the bright idea to take us public," says Gargano.

"It sounded good at the time. But it was the biggest mistake of my business career. It was a disastrous period in my life. The whole company changed. We had always believed in a broad distribution of equity in the agency. We wanted people to feel that it was their agency, too. Employees had a tremendous sense of loyalty to the agency. When we went public, that sense of camaraderie and family was lost."

Soon shareholders and analysts were coming at Gargano from every direction. His board of directors knew nothing about the advertising business. He was approached by a lot of agencies interested in acquiring them. By 1986, Gargano could see that the agency was vulnerable because of its size.

Marketing Corporation of America (MCA) provided a solution. They proposed an acquisition that would keep the integrity of the organization intact. After eight months of negotiations, MCA acquired Ally & Gargano. The two cultures were incredibly disparate, but MCA wanted an agency with a creative reputation and philosophy and was willing to defer. So, Ally & Gargano was to be dominant in the relationship. And MCA's name was to be dropped. "It's been fully integrated," Gargano says. "And the inevitable outcome was a completely different agency."

By 1991, Gargano wanted to run his own agency again, and so Amil Gargano and Partners was born. "I have strong feelings about entrepreneurship," he says. "What interests me is being in control of my own fate. If you don't own it, you don't control it. I just want to work guided by what's important to me—unencumbered by extraneous people. It sounds a bit selfish, but that's what makes me go. I need that. I'm pathologically incapable of working for someone else."

Forming a new agency also gave him an opportunity to get back to what he enjoyed about advertising. "Years ago someone said that advertising is no business for a grown man. I'm bored out of my mind sitting in a meeting with 14 brand managers talking about inconsequentials for six hours. They start to dissect stuff that is absolutely absurd. I think, 'What am I doing here? Why am I sitting here wasting my time? My life is going by!' That's the part of the business I've tried to divorce myself from."

Gargano ran that agency for ten years and then closed it to write the story of his career going up to the sale of Ally & Gargano to MCA.

Once he completes his book, he plans on writing, directing, and producing a full-length documentary, a career option he's been considering for more than ten years—ever since he produced his first award-winning documentary.

With his new career choice, he remains dedicated to controlling his own fate—this time going so far as being unencumbered by having to meet the needs of a client.

COMPARE THIS PORTFOLIO

—— VOLVO ——

When Ally, Gargano, and Durfee pitched the account, Volvo was trying to enter the American market and did not have an identity. What's more, they were up against Detroit, which was just beginning to downsize their products by coming out with compact cars like the Valiant, the Corvair, and the Falcon.

Their first ad showed a Volvo, Valiant, Corvair, and Falcon competing in a race. The Volvo was out in front, and in the back were a Renault and a Volkswagen. The copy simply said, "Volvo will outperform Valiant, Falcon and Corvair and get almost the same gas mileage as the Renault and Volkswagen."

Later ads, like this one, talked about other ways this car was better than Detroit cars, taking Volvo out of the import arena. "Rather than compete with dozens of import cars that sold less than 50,000 units combined in the United States, we said, 'Why not compete with cars that sell 2 million units in the United States. And we'd be the only ones competing with them.' That's the basis on which we

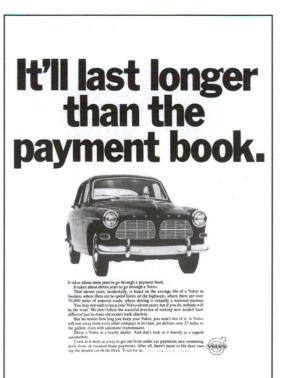

It'll last longer than the payment book.

tried to compete and redefine Volvo," says Gargano. "Instead of just concentrating on the craft of making ads, the real strength of Ally & Gargano was its ability to find new ways of thinking about a product or service."

—— SHEARSON LEHMAN BROTHERS ——

When Shearson awarded this account to Ally & Gargano, the investment community was under siege. It had lost credibility among investors. The problem: how do you restore confidence?

Gargano thought that having Shearson profile the way investments can support companies who are working to improve things would cause investors to have a higher opinion of the company.

"Our cities need rebuilding. Bridges are falling down, buildings are collapsing, and roads are horrible," says Gargano. "And Shearson has identified a company addressing this problem. So here's an opportunity for investors to make some money—because first of all, you have to appeal to their sense of greed—and also do something fundamentally worthwhile for society."

Ecology and health care are two other issues Gargano addressed for Shearson. "People usually make money at someone else's expense, but these ads give people a chance to make money while helping other people."

Gargano contrasts these ads to Shearson's major competitor. "Merrill Lynch says we're a 'tradition of trust' and they show bears getting transformed into

bulls. And they spend millions of dollars to produce that transformation technique. Does that do anything other than engage in the technique of advertising?"

On the other hand, this campaign enabled Shearson to demonstrate virtue and trust. "We were being responsive to a problem," he says, "not just making ads."

—— Hertz ——

Avis, a DDB client, had been publicly ridiculing Hertz for four years, in one of the greatest ad campaigns ever.

Even without using the name, everybody knew whom Avis was talking about. And Hertz's market share was declining rapidly. Gargano believes the reason they got this business was they were the only ones to tell Hertz management that it was time to tell Avis to shut up.

"We were the ones who said you have to assault them because there's no virtue in being second."

In addition to attracting customers, the campaign provided impetus, philosophy, and stature for Hertz that management couldn't do with talks and sales-meeting rallies. "We ran it for 90 days," says Gargano, "and it killed Avis' campaign. It was aggressive. Confrontational. No nonsense."

Gargano argues that this campaign was not risky (see advice section). "There's a lot of talk about taking risks. The argument is it gets people's attention. I believe that work like the Infiniti introduction took the wrong direction. I don't know how it was sold, but it took a big risk. I would never create or try to sell that to a client because I have no conviction about it.

For years, Avis has been telling you Hertz is No.1.
Now we're going to tell you why.

We're No. 1 because we're better at helping you get to where you're going.

A car where you need it.

The first step in renting a car is getting to the car. Hertz makes that easier for you to do than anybody else.

We're at every major airport in the United States. And at some airports that are not so major. Ever fly to Whitefish, Montana? Some people do. And have a Hertz car waiting.

No matter how small the airport you fly to, if it's served by a commercial airline, 97 chances out of 100 it's also served by Hertz or by a Hertz office within 20 minutes of it.

We also have locations throughout the downtown and suburban areas of every major city.

And because you don't restrict your travel to city areas, we don't restrict our locations to city areas. We're also out in the country. And out of the country, too. Windy Hill Beach, South Carolina has a population of 100. It has a Hertz office. Chichiri, Malawi in Africa has a population of 2,059. It has a Hertz office.

In all, Hertz has over 2,900 places throughout the world where you can pick up or leave a car. Nearly twice as many as No. 2.

Can't come to us? We'll come to you.

We have a direct-line telephone in most major hotels and motels in the U.S. It's marked HERTZ and it's in the lobby. Pick it up, ask for a car, and we'll deliver one to the door. You often can't get a cab as easily.

What kind of car would you like?

When you rent from Hertz, you're less likely to get stuck with a beige sedan when you want a red convertible. We have over twice as many cars as No. 2.

Not only is our fleet big, it's varied. We do our best to give you what you want. From Fords, to Mustangs,

*There's one thing you have to do for us though: fill out our Certified Deposit form and mail it to our main office in its self-addressed envelope. Upon notification we'll send you $50 in rental certificates.

to Thunderbirds, to Lincolns and everything in between.

And because we know that travel can be a bore if you travel a lot, we've even got something to ease your foot. The Shelby G.T. 350-H. If you know what cars are all about, you'll know what this car is all about.

What kind of service will you get?

When you rent a new car from us or anybody else, you expect it to be sitting there waiting, ready to go, looking like new.

On that score we claim no superiority over our competition. They goof once in awhile. We goof once in a while. Except when we goof it bothers us more because people don't expect the big one to goof. And to make up for it, if our service is not up to Hertz standards, we give you $50 in free rentals.* Plus an apology.

No. 2 gives a quarter plus an apology. And advertises that he "can't afford" to do more.

We feel the other way about it. We can't afford to do less. Besides, the $50 comes out of the station manager's local operating funds. This tends to keep him very alert. ...and our service very good.

Hot line.

When you're in one city and you're flying to another city and you want to have a car waiting when you arrive.

and you want it confirmed before you leave, we can do it for you. Instantly. In any one of 1,038 U.S. cities. No other rent a car company can make that statement.

The major reason we can do it is because we recently installed one of the world's largest private electronic reservations systems.

After all, with the supersonic jets in sight and one hour coast to coast flights in prospect, you'll need some quick answers.

We can give them to you today.

About rates.

We probably offer more kinds of rates than you care to know about.

You can rent a car from Hertz by the day and the mile, by the weekend, by the week, by the month, by gift certificate, by revolving credit, by sundry other ways in between.

We offer all these rates for two reasons. To stay ahead of competition. To get more people to rent cars.

When you go to rent a Hertz car just tell the Hertz girl how long you want the car and roughly how much driving you'll be doing.

She'll figure out the rate that's cheapest for you. She'll get it out of our rate book that states loud and clear, that people must use the lowest applicable rate on all reservations.

About credit.

If you've got a national credit card with most any major company, you've got credit with us.

A businesslike way of doing business.

If you own your own firm or are instrumental in running one, you know what a nightmare billing can be.

Have your company rent from us and we'll help ease the nightmare. We can even tailor our billing cycle to fit your billing cycle.

We'll bill by the rental, by the month, by division, by

department, by individual, and by blood type if it'll help you.

And now about trying hard.

No. 2 says he tries harder. Than who?

Hertz

"Instead," he says, "this hard-hitting response was a logical next step in light of Avis' actions. That is not risk taking. It's determining a strategy based on events and choosing the message that will provide the best results.

"To their credit," says Gargano, "Avis' campaign established a standard of how to conduct business in the rent-a-car industry. They promised a different, caring attitude by their people, clean ashtrays, windshield wipers that worked, and a full tank of gas."

—— PAN AM ——

Gargano's goal for advertising is to make consumers say, "I never thought of that company in that way." Here's an example of how he did that for Pan Am.

Since all of Pan Am's destinations were offshore—and America is inhabited by immigrants—he created a campaign introducing the idea that foreign travel is an opportunity to discover one's heritage. It showed Japanese Americans visiting Japan. Western European Americans visiting Europe. And African-Americans visiting Africa. "Air France was talking about serving French meals, TWA was offering three kinds of entrees and two different feature films, and Braniff was having their stewardesses wear different fashions," says Gargano. "But an airplane is supposed to take you someplace. Nobody gets on it for the ride."

All of us come from someplace else.

Picture this if you will.
A man who's spent all his life in the United States gets on a plane, crosses a great ocean, lands.
He walks the same streets his family walked centuries ago.
He sees his name, which is rare in America, filling three pages in a phone book.
He speaks haltingly the language he wishes he had learned better as a child.
As America's airline to the world, Pan Am does a lot of things.
We help business travelers make meetings on the other side of the world. Our planes take goods to and from six continents. We take vacationers just about anywhere they want to go.
But nothing we do seems to have as much meaning as when we help somebody discover the second heritage that every American has.

America's airline to the world.

See your travel agent.

Just once, you should walk down the same street your great-grandfather walked.

For another example of finding substantive points of difference, Gargano looked at Pan Am's tag line. Since they pioneered commercial aviation—they were the first airline to develop international capabilities and they worked with Boeing to develop new airplanes—they had a line that said, "The world's most experienced airline." But when their account was with J. Walter Thompson, they dropped that in favor of "Pan Am makes the going great." Says Gargano, "That's not an advantage. That's just a slogan. It's a line. Given the choice, which airline would you rather fly on? The world's most experienced airline or an airline—any airline—that makes the going great?"

—— MCI ——

According to Gargano, the first rule of comparative advertising is the company must have a superior product. "Otherwise, why make comparisons?" he asks. "You can only do that if you have a better product."

Back when these commercials came out, MCI, for instance, offered people an alternative to AT&T at a 50 to 60 percent savings on their long distance phone bills. "That's a superior product benefit—a significant point of comparison," says Gargano. "It has enormous appeal. Most of the world is struggling to get by on their salaries. Telling them that they can save 50 percent on their long distance bills will get their attention."

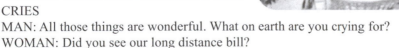

MAN: Have you been talking to our son on long distance again?
WOMAN: NODS AND WHIMPERS
MAN: Did he tell you how much he loves you?
WOMAN: NODS AND WHIMPERS
MAN: Did he tell you how he's doing in school?
WOMAN: NODS AND WHIMPERS AND CRIES
MAN: All those things are wonderful. What on earth are you crying for?
WOMAN: Did you see our long distance bill?

ANNCR VO: If your long distance bills are too much, call MCI
Sure, reach out and touch someone.
Just do it for a whole lot less.

137

ADVICE TO HELP YOU
SEE ADVERTISING IN A NEW WAY

What makes a great advertising professional? According to Gargano, the real route to greatness is to get people to think of the brand in a new way—use your creative skills to find strategic, innovative ways to (re)position brands. "Ad making is a craft," he says. "You can develop it over time by observing good work and developing your own writing and art direction skills."

To help ad professionals and beginners alike focus on this issue, Gargano has been sharing his ideas with MFA students at Syracuse since 1973. He has also spent many hours lecturing at other schools around the country—always emphasizing that strategic development is the foundation for all advertising.

"You have to build the strategic definition of the product or service within tangible parameters," he says. "It cannot be some big, innocuous strategy like 'quality and value.' You can go into any boardroom and hear the chairmen and the minions say the same, boring thing, 'We're quality and value.' Those are the watchwords and they've been for the '90s—and the '60s, '70s, and '80s.

"But that's not a strategy. That's an objective."

In his MFA seminars, his first assignment is to have students pick a product they know and like, and then define an objective. "They have to decide what they want their ad to do," he says "Who do you want to reach? What do you want for them to learn from the ad?

"Then, in just a couple of sentences, define a strategy of how they intend to accomplish their objective.

"Most of the time it's clearly articulated, but when someone shows the resulting ad, it bears no resemblance to what that person wanted to achieve."

Gargano believes this happens because advertising people have been narrowly trained in the business of just making ads. "They get caught up in puns, visual techniques; everything is tortured and manipulated beyond belief. It's frantic with the technique of advertising. That is not very different from what takes place in this industry day by day from New York to L.A."

To help you get beyond the technique of creating advertising to the substance of actually solving problems for client brands, here is some of Gargano's advice:

Know your product: "Get immersed in your subject. Any good writer is going to do that," says Gargano, "and become extremely knowledgeable. Become so well armed with the facts, you can defend any position you take for a product.

"Simple, straight-line thinking. Simple, declarative language. That's the way it happens—not torturing a headline, or manipulating the graphics.

"There is no substitute for knowing what you're talking about and being informed. And there are no short cuts. Get smart."

Analyze the features: "In forming a strategy, begin by analyzing the characteristics," suggests Gargano. "For example, if a boat or a lawn mower is manufactured in a special way, pay attention to the details.

"Take the collective pieces of information and try to find some overview.

"Then state in simple language—so you don't get derailed by your own cleverness—a summary of ideas that make the product important.

"Stick to simple language and, instead, put life into the concept. You can dress it up once you know where you're going.

"Then you can play with the language and the visuals, but not until you know you've got a vigorous idea."

Remember to make it compelling: "Nobody buys a magazine for the advertising. It's a chance encounter," Gargano reminds us.

"You come across it purely by happenstance. If it's interesting, you read it. If not, you don't."

Gargano makes his ads compelling by insisting that all his work provide some information. So consumers gain some value by reading the print ad or paying attention to the commercial on television.

"If it has tremendous relevance and strikes some essential truth in people, an ad can produce astounding results," he says.

Pursue clients who want to shake things up: Gargano recommends working for upstart clients—like Federal Express—because they're innovators. They're companies whose leaders have the courage, brains, and conviction to want to change things.

"Look for the kind of clients who want to change things, who want to do something, who want to be responsive, who do not want to settle for the status quo and business as usual."

Work without fanfare: "I admire guys like Bob Gage," says Gargano. "He said, 'I don't want to run anything. I simply want to do the work.'

"That has great appeal to me. The people who do the work and let it speak for itself are the ones I respect the most."

Get a good liberal arts education: "In college, I became as captivated by my liberal arts classes as by my art classes. I became as interested in English, history, and anthropology as in art," says Gargano.

"A liberal arts education is an excellent foundation for any advertising person, because in the course of an advertising career, you encounter diverse subjects. You need a broad knowledge base from which to draw in order to respond effectively. And liberal arts tends to amplify and broaden your awareness."

Be as informed as possible: "I'm into information," says Gargano.

"I surely want to know what I'm doing. I want to be able to have a strong point of view and conviction about something, because that's what makes the difference," says Gargano.

"I rely on market research during the learning period. What do people think? There are some people who tend to dismiss research or use it very sparingly. But I don't think you should resist information."

Use market research as a point of departure to something larger: "A lot of agencies and clients make the mistake of thinking that focus groups are going to provide new insights. At most, they're going to tell you what most everybody already knows," says Gargano.

"If you ask somebody in a shopping mall for their opinion, they'll give you an answer; but it won't be the answer—it's only part of the answer. Research is a stepping-stone to someplace else.

"There are certain things that people say that will strike familiar chords.

"But you'll never get a focus group that's so bursting with brilliant new ideas that you can say, 'That's it!' It doesn't work that way."

Tie the concept to the product: "Your product shouldn't be shoehorned into your commercial. It should not be something that, for example, makes people laugh and then says, 'Oh, here, by the way, is the advertiser's name.'

"That's not advertising. That's filmmaking." Says Gargano, "A good ad is something that brings out some fundamental piece of truth. When people look at it and unconsciously say, 'Yeah, that's true, that's worth considering.' That's the sign of a good ad."

Rework existing ads: In putting together a portfolio, Gargano suggests taking existing ads and improving them. "Many years ago a young journalist, who aspired to be in advertising, brought in his portfolio. He was a very quiet, introspective man, but I was absolutely dazzled by his ability to dig salient facts out of body copy and use them as the lead," Gargano recalls.

"He took a series of ads and reworked them using what he found to be more pertinent information in the body copy. And he improved the ads.

"His art direction was terribly crude, but it didn't matter. He found new ways of positioning the products. It was the best beginner's portfolio I'd ever seen."

Avoid risks…: "When I'm on a panel at a seminar, what I hear repeatedly is 'We have to get clients to take risks.' But the worst thing you can do is tell a client to take a risk," observes Gargano. "Clients don't want to hear about risks. They may be well established in their careers. They may have families, a mortgage, and car payments, the whole catastrophe.

"In comes a young art director and a copywriter who want them to take a risk. In effect, risking the client's job. That's not what they want to hear.

"Even some senior people with big reputations talk about taking risks.

"It's madness. Dumb. It's the wrong language to use with clients."

...Focus on the strategy instead: "Minimize the risks and go for a line of thinking that's progressive," says Gargano.

"So you can tell your client 'We've thought about your product very carefully and feel we have an opportunity to make tremendous inroads in our competition's market by taking this approach.'

"Get them to the point where they can comfortably say, 'Yeah, that's right. That will help my career. That will help pay for my kids' college years.'

"This doesn't mean your work can't be breakthrough. I've done a lot of breakthrough work, but it was never positioned as being risky."

Encourage accountability: "Accountability is essential. There is a definite correlation between running advertising in the marketplace and counting the results," says Gargano.

"Before a client spends $5 or $50 million on an ad campaign, find out what people think. Then afterward, find out how their perceptions have changed. Or put an 800-number on the commercial. The results will validate the strategy—and justify spending money on advertising."

Find inspiration everywhere: "I'm stimulated by being alive and just observing life," says Gargano. "I once saw a 66-year-old tenor saxophonist who was filled with as much life and talent and zeal as any young jazz musician. He was funny. He was brilliantly talented. And I was inspired by the man. So where do you get the source for inspiration? All over the place."

"Comfort the afflicted and afflict the comfortable"—sign in Carl Ally's office: "Carl Ally liked the little guy," says Gargano. "That was one of the many things we had in common. We both grew up poor, not that we were wanting for clothing on our backs or food on the table.

"That may be a part of our iconoclastic, irreverent, but honest approach to the business. We didn't want to do traditional advertising—what was expected. We wanted to deal with the truth. The way things are. Warts and all."

Be the kind of person others want to be around: "I think that personality is as important as the work being presented," says Gargano.

"I've made the mistake of hiring some people who had great portfolios, but were arrogant.

"Prima donnas without team spirit.

"Now I ask myself if I'd look forward to walking into their office and chatting with them for a few minutes. I want to be around people who enjoy producing everything from a commercial to a matchbook cover. These people love what they do. They're inspired. Alive. They have energy. And they make everything they touch important. So everything they do has a wonderful consistency."

Keep your values in check: "There aren't too many people I admire in this business," says Gargano. "But outside of this business, I have many.

"One of them is a successful ophthalmologist, who started an organization called Sight Savers International. He's dedicated his life to curing blindness among impoverished people and regularly travels to Mexico and performs eye surgery.

"They come to him barefoot and wait for hours in a sweltering heat for their operations. A day or so later, these people, who've been blind for much of their lives, take off the bandages and can see. Talk about the heroes in this world—and nobody even knows him!

"And then I sit in meetings talking about shampoo and dandruff for hours."

Prepare yourself for instability: As a beginner, you may not earn much and some agencies may keep you around because you're relatively inexpensive.

But as you move up, know that you have very little job security. "If you're lucky enough to earn six figures and have a good job, but haven't achieved superstar status, you're vulnerable," warns Gargano.

He notes that, when there are cutbacks, those people are often the targets. They're the ones cut out of the business and replaced by younger people who may not perform at as high a level, but will work for a third of the salary.

"The pool of unemployed people who may never get re-employed in this business is big. It's a tragedy."

Explore different alternatives: "Advertising provides people with a background and the technical skills that can transfer to other related careers. That makes it valuable as well as interesting," says Gargano.

For an example, look at Gargano's career change (as well as Ted Bell's career change; see Chapter 4).

"As you progress in this business, you learn new skills and are provided with different job alternatives. So advertising is one of the more compelling careers for young people. Unfortunately, the ad industry hasn't provided enough openings for beginners. We steal young people from other agencies and spend the other time firing the people who've been around for a long time."

POSTSCRIPT 1:

IN DEFENSE OF COMPARATIVE ADVERTISING

Comparative advertising has been attacked through the years.

According to some critics, it lowers the esteem of both products. According to others, people don't remember which product was the better of the two being compared.

But we have shown in this chapter that comparative advertising can be a very powerful technique. Here are some more of Gargano's comments on this topic:

"Comparative advertising usually gets a bad rap because, many times, the comparisons don't make any sense—like products with a huge pricing difference such as a Volkswagen and a Mercedes Benz—or it lacks strong distinctions in product comparison, so the consumer doesn't remember which product is really better.

"It's just like other forms of advertising that have been criticized because the people creating ads did not know what they were doing.

"Humor has been wrongly criticized because most of the ads aren't funny and don't try to sell anyone on the product.

"Everybody thinks they're a gag writer. And radio is the most abused medium of all. Because, many times, the junior people get the radio assignments and think it's their chance to become the next Mel Brooks.

"But when it's done right, it works. Look at Federal Express.

"You can do a bad testimonial. You can do a bad demonstration.

"You can do a bad slice-of-life (which is usually redundant).

"And, you can do a bad comparative ad.

"Our criteria are simple. You have to compare reasonably like products.

"Let's say, you're in the market for a car at between $12,000 and $15,000. What are your choices? What would you look for? Which cars are selling in that price category and are they of comparable performance characteristics?

"Of course, you must also have the superior product. Otherwise, why make the comparison?

"If the comparisons are weak or irrelevant, it only lowers the esteem of the products you're advertising. Look at Pepsi Cola, a BBDO client. Do you think that some of Pepsi's gain in market share was achieved only because they said they were the 'Pepsi generation?'

"That's part of it, but that message came in the context of aggressive taste comparisons. I bet you could see Coca-Cola's market share diminish as Pepsi's rose because people preferred Pepsi over Coca-Cola.

"The American Association of Advertising Agencies has published standards that explain the do's and don'ts of comparative advertising. There are some guidelines that make a lot of sense. You compare similar products of equal value. And you don't compare irrelevant features.

"I once gave a speech to the American Marketing Association and took the two ad techniques that were most commonly denounced: comparative advertising and humor.

"I did a reel of comparative advertising and I showed the results.

"Then I did a reel of humorous advertising and showed those results.

"There was no point of contention. There are numerous case studies to prove that if comparative advertising is done correctly, it can be enormously effective."

POSTSCRIPT 2:

THOUGHTS ON SOCIALLY RESPONSIBLE ADVERTISING

Professionals in every industry sometimes face ethical issues. Advertising professionals are no different. But advertising is seen by millions of people and decisions concerning ethical issues can often have a greater impact.

Although most of the people profiled in this book made a point of sharing their concern for sound ethics and social responsibility, back in 1991 for the first edition of this book, Gargano spoke at great length on the direction advertising is taking and its impact on society.

While his comments are more than a decade old, they are just as relevant today. Here are some of his remarks:

"I've often said that the kind of person you are is revealed in the most inconsequential acts you perform throughout the day. So people do reveal who they are through their work. And certainly when people create advertising, they reveal a tremendous amount of information about their character.

"When I look at the work that is highly regarded by young people today, it tells me something about them. And, I find the bulk of today's work very disturbing.

"So much of it is created for shock value. All under the guise of being cool and hip and street-smart. I'm angered when an ad attacks my Italian heritage—or, trivializes human suffering, minorities, the handicapped, and even death.

"People think 'Hey, we're cool. Don't take it all that seriously.' But it's wrong. It's socially irresponsible because it trivializes. It's petty and degrading and encourages young people to embrace the same viewpoints.

"Death and violence have become something we casually accept because it's abundant on our television screens. A former president of Columbia Pictures noted that in a typical American film, 164 people get killed. And those deaths are never reconciled in the plot. No one ever thinks about the consequences of an individual's death—whether the individual was a villain, hero, pedestrian, bystander or whatever. Did he have a family? Did she have a husband? Were there children? What were the consequences of that death?

"It's never even brought up. The director simply cuts to the next scene.

"I can't believe those messages don't seep into our psyches. If children continue to get heavy doses of casual death on television, I've got to believe that over time it contributes to increasing crime and violence.

"Sometimes people lose sight of the power of mass media when they assume 'You can do anything you want to. You can be outlandish and immoral if it's tongue-in-cheek.' I find that irresponsible and offensive. There has to be a sense of responsibility on the part of the people who create the ads and the clients who approve them."

If this resembles your agency's organizational chart, give us a call.

Fallon McElligott Rice, 701 Fourth Avenue South, Minneapolis, Minnesota 55415, Telephone 612-332-2445

Tom McElligott

"I hate advertising."

"I hate watching bad commercials. I despise most of them. I really do. Ninety-five percent of the advertising out there is either just wallpaper or is aggressively bad," says Tom McElligott, co-founder of Fallon and its former creative director (see Chapter 12 for more information on the founding of Fallon).

"But then, there is about 5 percent that is mildly pleasing—or sometimes is absolutely wonderful. At that point, it's art. Yes, it's selling, but it's selling artfully."

When it's great, he loves it. And while he was working in the industry, he loved creating it. McElligott injected humanity and originality into his writing.

He wanted his work to touch people. And it certainly touched the advertising community. Clios, One Show pencils, and New York Art Directors awards are just a few of the prizes his creative genius brought him throughout his career—more than enough to earn him a place in the One Club's Advertising Hall of Fame in 1991.

McElligott's high standards, idealism, and integrity also led the American Association of Advertising Agencies (4A's) to choose him to develop an ad campaign aimed at improving the industry's image.

But, despite his enthusiasm for the craft of advertising, he kept a realistic outlook. "Frankly," he said back in 1991 while still running an agency, "I'm not prepared to die for this business. I love it—and I love to work hard—but some sanity has to enter the picture."

For sanity's sake, he enjoys reading, camping, canoeing, and sailing.

In 1989, McElligott started another agency—McElligott Wright Morrison White.

While founded with great industry fanfare, this promising agency disintegrated in 1992 due to an internal power struggle. Since then, McElligott has kept a low profile.

He worked for a short time as a copywriter with the Martin Agency (see Mike Hughes, Chapter 8), but was drawn into agency responsibilities that he didn't want and left the industry again.

Called the "J.D. Salinger of the advertising industry" by one of his associates, he checks in on friends from time to time but most claim that they don't know his current activities or how to reach him.

DRIVEN BY THE NEED TO SUCCEED

Low scholastic performance? An unsupportive dysfunctional family? No connections in the business? Those are typical reasons people use to explain a lack of success. But they shouldn't really hold anyone back.

Just look at McElligott's career. He experienced all of those conditions, and instead of looking at them as a reason for failure, he used them as motivation for success.

As a high school student, McElligott was a classic underachiever. He graduated at the bottom of his class—a very large class at Fargo Central High School in North Dakota. "I surely didn't study," he says, guessing that his lack of academic achievement was a result of his home life.

"I came out of an incredibly screwy family; I think quite a few creative people do," he says. "That led to low self-esteem and a lack of confidence."

But his high school years were not totally unproductive.

In fact, when he was 14, he restored an old car. "This was a very creative project," he says, "because I made something happen. I would call up companies in Detroit and ask for car parts. I've thought about it in recent years and realized that that project was a lot like working in an ad agency."

After high school, McElligott spent three years in the Marines where he turned his low self-esteem into confidence.

He left with a determination to put his intelligence to use.

"I learned that I didn't want to carry a rifle the rest of my life," he says.

He entered the University of Minnesota and, to his surprise, enjoyed a successful academic career as an English major. He discovered 18th century literature and made plans to go to graduate school so that he could teach it. But those plans were expensive, because the GI Bill, which had financed his pursuit of an undergraduate education, would not apply to his graduate degree.

McElligott had other financial pressures.

It was the late 1960s, and he and his wife were expecting their first child. The role of husband and father weighed on him and he felt a rising need to make money, but he had little idea of how to apply his education.

Meanwhile, he worked evenings at a local brewery as a tour guide. It was at one of the brewery's parties that he discovered a classified ad for copywriters in a copy of *Advertising Age*. The job paid $12,000 a year—double the salary he expected to earn as a teacher. (Back then, you could buy a new car for $2,000!)

Consequently, he decided to take a detour from graduate school until his wife could resume her career as a nurse. He planned to write ads while working out a financial plan that would let him return to grad school.

"I'd never studied advertising. I thought copywriting was something you'd do in a law firm," he recalls. "That's how little I knew about the business."

Later, McElligott looked in the classifieds of the local newspaper and found an ad for a position at Dayton Hudson's, a department store in Minneapolis.

The position had been open for a long time because the copy chief, a perfectionist, had sent each candidate home with several ads and asked that they be rewritten. If the copywriter improved the ads to the copy chief's satisfaction, he would be hired.

Apparently the copy chief wasn't impressed by anyone he'd seen. McElligott took him up on the challenge.

"That evening I sat at the dining room table rewriting the ads and discovered what I had been missing in the first 25 years of my life. I absolutely loved it. I had a wonderful time writing them." McElligott returned with his ads and got the job.

In retrospect, McElligott feels his ads weren't really very good. "I'm sure I'd look at that work today and wonder how I ever got hired," he says. "But they were probably a little better because I was so passionate about writing them. So they showed enough promise to get me hired."

McElligott loved writing for Dayton Hudson's, even though he wasn't very clear on how to do it. He was a good writer, and he had good ideas, but most of his ads were derivative. "What I managed to get on paper was taken from this room in my head that was full of slogans, headlines, and graphics that I had accumulated over the course of my 25 years," he says.

"They weren't fresh and they weren't like the work I'd later do. But they were good enough. And I was one driven, passionate young guy who desperately wanted to do great work."

At Dayton Hudson's, he was asked to produce everything from two-page newspaper ads to small quarter-page ads. He found this to be great experience. "The wonderful thing about starting in retail is that you're forced to write quickly and produce a lot," says McElligott. "Many copywriters don't know what it's like to have a tremendous work load.

"In an agency, an ad or a campaign can consume weeks of their time. There's nothing like coming into your office on Monday morning and knowing you're responsible for producing 18 different pieces of work by Friday."

Within two months, he was promoted, and he began supervising people with much more seniority. Eventually, he also wound up writing all the broadcast for the store. He loved it.

The next stage of his career happened by accident. At a local garage sale, he met a copywriter who suggested that he consider working in an agency; the copywriter said that an in-house retail agency was no place to spend an entire career.

But McElligott was still very naive. He was happy writing and too busy working to investigate alternatives. Yet he realized that the retail industry was small.

If he wanted to work for a quality organization, his choices were limited. Apart from his employer, there was just Neiman Marcus, Bloomingdale's, and a few others.

Consequently, he took the copywriter's advice and researched and found several ad agencies in the Minneapolis/St. Paul area that interested him.

He applied to Campbell-Mithun and Knox Reeves, plus Leo Burnett and Needham, Harper & Steers in Chicago. "I sent copies of my ads, which were not good at all, but they were good enough to get responses."

At Campbell-Mithun, he was offered a job with a very good salary. Later the same day, he was offered a position at Knox Reeves for $1,000 a year less. "I took the job at Knox Reeves because it looked like it offered more opportunity."

"It was a more creatively driven agency in those years, but it was not great. Ron Anderson, who became my friend, was creative director, and he clearly had a passion for creating advertising," says McElligott about his long-time friend. "When you find someone to share that with, that's something."

Ron Anderson inspired McElligott as a mentor and provided him with insight, stability, and editing over the next eight years. More important, he helped McElligott develop the ability to critique advertising, to distinguish his better efforts.

"Some work tickled me more than other work, but I couldn't tell which ads were good or just dumb. Ron could." One night McElligott left Anderson about 50 rough ads for the Minneapolis Police Department. "When Ron returned from a meeting, he was so excited. He called me and said, 'There are a couple of ideas here.' And I responded by saying, 'Oh really? Which ones?' I really didn't know.

"I'd had a pretty good afternoon at work and was generally pleased, but Ron knew which ads were stronger."

Over the years, McElligott became much better at judging his work. But even today, he has others take a look.

"You never stop needing an editor," he says. "I firmly believe, even if you're pretty sure, you owe it to yourself and your client to let other people look at it and to listen what they have to say about it."

Around this time, the creative director of BBDO noticed McElligott's work, called him up, and invited him to talk. "He complimented my work, but said that it looked like Minneapolis work. He then said that as long I compared my work with the best work being done in Minneapolis, I'd never be better than Minneapolis.

"That was key. It was like an epiphany.

"He suggested that I buy all the awards annuals I could find, and study them."

The eager young writer followed this advice and spent evenings poring over the outstanding work of the time. "I was absolutely knocked out by the work of Ed McCabe, Neil Drossman, David Altschiller, and Martin Puris—all the wonderful New York writers. And Bill Bernbach—the greatest ad man of our time," says McElligott. It was a different league of work. He found it to be powerful and honest and wanted to emulate it.

Meanwhile, his career kept progressing. With help from Anderson, he was made copy chief at Knox Reeves in 1974. This forced him to manage projects that he felt were over his head, but he was ambitious. He accepted the position after Anderson agreed to be his partner. After years of working together, McElligott continued to find Anderson's presence reassuring.

"Being promoted at Dayton Hudson's and Knox Reeves was very helpful in both cases. It pushed me," he says. "And it did some good for my self-esteem."

McElligott's talent was honed enough to earn him a creative director position after Knox Reeves merged with Bozell and Jacobs. The larger merged agency had offices in Chicago, Dallas, Los Angeles, and Montreal. McElligott's role was to act as a troubleshooter, which required him to travel with Anderson to those offices—either to save accounts or to acquire new ones.

"I was living quietly in Minneapolis with my family. Everything Midwestern and intact. Yet every other week I was getting on airplanes to work on major national accounts—British Airways, Max Factor—no easy trick in this market," he says. "It was an opportunity to be exposed to account responsibilities I would have had to go to New York to find."

As a result, McElligott was learning that creating a good campaign wasn't enough, that he'd have to embrace the side of the business he most wanted to avoid—the marketing side. He had to become more sophisticated about marketing strategies in order to defend his work. That realization came after presenting campaigns he felt were terrific, original, and powerful, but were rejected.

"Ron (Anderson) and I would fly off to Dallas with a satchel of wonderful work, present the work to the client and have it dismissed.

"I didn't like that. I had worked hard. I wanted to see the fruits of my labor mean something.

"That's when I began a real transition. I began to really think about the client's product in the competitive environment and to approach selling powerful, original work in a completely different way.

"It quickly became obvious to me that good writing was good salesmanship. I would track its success. I'd provide the client all the comfort I could. So they could understand that I was a disciplined, responsible steward of their dollar."

By 1979, McElligott began asking his staff to present their work in the context of the marketing strategy. "I'd have my staff bring me the strategy, put it on the wall and put their work next to it, and I had them tell me how their work tracked from the strategy. And then whether they had created something original."

With this change in outlook, McElligott was ready to move on.

He considered moving to New York or Los Angeles. But, instead, he chose to put the needs of his family first and stay in Minneapolis. He had established solid working relationships with Nancy Rice and Pat Fallon—freelancing with them in the evenings.

So the three of them decided to start their own agency.

"I had grown out of room," he says. "I wanted a real agency with real accounts. I also wanted to create an environment where things could happen and direct a creative staff that would make things happen."

The goal of Fallon McElligott Rice was simply to create fresh, original, powerful advertising that was strategically sound. "My contract with people coming into the agency went like this: 'I want you to do the very best work of your life—or don't come. If you put in the time and are committed, I guarantee I will sell your work, maybe not all the time, but most of the time. If we have an account that consistently will not buy great work, I'll not let you suffer. I will not have you go off and turn out wonderful work that I've asked you to do and then have it shot down again and again. We'll resign the business.'

"Virtually every creative person I hired heard me say that," says McElligott. "I did not want good people continually bummed out after turning out brilliant, disciplined work."

That was a major commitment, but Fallon McElligott Rice lived up to it.

"We resigned a fair amount of business," he notes. "So I got people to produce wonderful work."

McElligott operated very simply. When something didn't meet his standards, he had the creatives go back and do it again. If they still defended their work, he would take a group of six to eight people, go into the agency's conference room, and have them select the best three or four pieces. He then usually selected the final ad from that group.

"I'd discuss my picks with the team and if they disagreed with me, I'd change," he says. "I make mistakes. And I didn't want to stand in the way of good work or stop interesting things from happening. Quite the contrary."

Partly because of this process and a shared feeling of fairness, there was little turnover at the agency. "We believed that if an ad was terrific, it should get produced. In fact, if it was terrific and it didn't get done, everybody in the agency knew about it and was sympathetic. No one went off to his or her office alone feeling terrible."

Eventually, Fallon McElligott Rice's innovative, effective, and creative work helped the agency grow to 140 employees—and put Minneapolis on the advertising map. Their success also attracted many companies interested in acquiring them, and the partners finally sold to Scali, McCabe, Sloves (SMS) in 1985.

Within a year, McElligott could see the agency changing. It was still a good agency with good people doing good work, but it wasn't the same to him.

SMS had paid a substantial amount of money for the agency, forcing them to shift their focus from developing the best creative to improving the bottom line.

"We weren't in a position to resign Federal Express when they became the world's most obnoxious client. I saw reams of work go off to their office in Memphis. I promised the staff that wonderful work would be sold, but our sell rate plummeted from 80 percent to 20 percent. For some agencies that isn't bad, but we weren't used to working that way."

This upset McElligott. Unlike Lee Clow, who is not opposed to presenting more work until the client is satisfied (Chapter 18), McElligott believes that if a great ad is created—one that is strategically sound—then it should sell, unless, of course, the client has a good reason for not buying it. "I may redo an ad a few times because this is a service business," he says, "but I despise it."

Unhappy with the direction the agency was taking, McElligott broke his contract in 1988, which forced him to take a year away from the industry.

McElligott returned to the industry in 1989, joining Chiat/Day, where he spent nine months. He had arranged to spend a week in Minneapolis, then a week in New York, London, Toronto, or Los Angeles. But within a few days, he could see that he'd be perpetually on the road. "Chiat/Day is a very interesting agency," he says. "And I continue to admire their work, but it is basically 'loony time' there."

So after being away from his son for more than five months and earning 163,000 miles on Northwest Airlines in nine months, he knew he couldn't continue.

"I decided I'd better return to Minneapolis," he says. "In fairness to Chiat/Day, they bought me a wonderful place in Greenwich Village. But my wife and I made a commitment to put our kids through school in Minneapolis.

"My family has remained intact throughout the ups and downs of my career. It's a huge part of my life."

So, in 1989, McElligott found himself again starting an agency with several other partners: McElligott Wright Morrison White (MWMW) in Minneapolis. But he wanted to create a difference between his new agency and Fallon.

"At Fallon, especially in our early years, we were happy just to create a good ad," he says. "The difference at MWMW was that we were looking to make those ads fit within a brand personality, which sometimes meant giving up brilliant moments. It also meant forgoing the pleasure of knocking off one wonderful 30-second spot that didn't fit the brand personality or tone of voice."

For an example of an agency producing work that built long-term brand personalities, McElligott looked to Leo Burnett. "What they've done is commit to not only a strategy, but to a brand personality that is pretty consistent—and recognizable by the consumer— over many years," says McElligott. "Given the great amount of advertising that consumers see, the only way to build equity with them is to have a reasonably consistent brand image."

But those mutual goals at MWMW eventually faded, and within a few years after the group had opened its doors, McElligott's agency partners instigated a "palace coup."

While he was away judging the 1992 Cannes Film Festival in France, they tried to remove him from his creative director position and fire his copywriter. Their actions led to the quick demise of the agency.

For several years, McElligott kept a low profile and took a sabbatical from advertising. He resurfaced again, however, in 1996 as a copywriter for the Martin Agency. "He's an old friend, and he called me one day out of the blue," recalls Mike Hughes (Chapter 8), adding that McElligott hadn't stayed in touch during his break from the industry. McElligott said he wanted to be a copywriter again and thought that the Martin Agency was the best place for him to work.

"It was so cool. Incredibly flattering. I gave him a little office with no windows. All the writers and art directors were kind of in awe," says Hughes. "He did a terrific campaign for us (Wrangler Jeans)." This campaign included a commercial where a herd of cattle ran down Wall Street, requiring them to close down this street for a day.

Hughes calls McElligott a natural leader. "It was impossible for him not to take a leadership position," says Hughes. "His intelligence about the business is just remarkable. He talks in that quiet voice, but he's so forceful in his thinking. Everybody listens when Tom speaks. It's not just because he was the legendary Tom McElligott. It was the force of his thinking."

What Mike Hughes couldn't figure out was a way to keep McElligott isolated from the outside world. From the moment he landed at the Martin Agency, reporters wanted to talk to him and he didn't want to do any of that. "It became the advertising business again," says Hughes. "He wasn't just the advertising copywriter that he wanted to be."

McElligott stayed at the Martin Agency for about a year before taking another sabbatical from the business. Today, he keeps a low profile and checks in with industry friends only about once a year.

Said to be in great shape, rumor has it that he is bicycling through Europe. "If Tom called me tomorrow, I'd have him back," says Hughes. "He's such a constructive force."

A PORTFOLIO FILLED WITH POLISH AND PASSION

——— State of Minnesota ———

Early in his career, McElligott learned that a great ad needs a dominant element that communicates very quickly. "Whether it's a headline, a startling photo, or something else, it has to be sufficiently original and arresting to stop you and get your attention," he says. "Then it has to be honest enough and intriguing enough to keep your attention while moving the ball forward in the selling process."

He believes that good creative people have an understanding of how the page works. They understand that adding elements to a page reduces the importance of every other element, while removing an element raises the importance of the remaining elements. "It's a simple rule," he says.

McElligott learned this from Tom Donovan, the executive art director he worked with at Knox Reeves. "He was a great teacher," says McElligott. "If you pushed

him, he would say things like, 'I don't want to use that visual because it will rob the headline of its importance' and 'If you make the headline bigger, you're going to ruin the photo.' So he knew what had to happen."

This ad, created in 1978, is a result of that schooling. There are many elements to this ad, but each is proportioned in a way to easily guide the reader through it. "If nothing in the ad is very important," says McElligott, "then it's not a very important ad."

— The *Wall Street Journal* —

"There's nothing like watching television and having an absolutely terrific commercial come on," says McElligott. "It's a wonderful thing and it's well worth pursuing." An example: this commercial for the *Wall Street Journal*. Notice the fair amount of humanity in his writing. "A good ad or commercial restates a problem that dozens of other people have tackled, but finds a different way of saying what others have said," says McElligott. "It's far easier said than done."

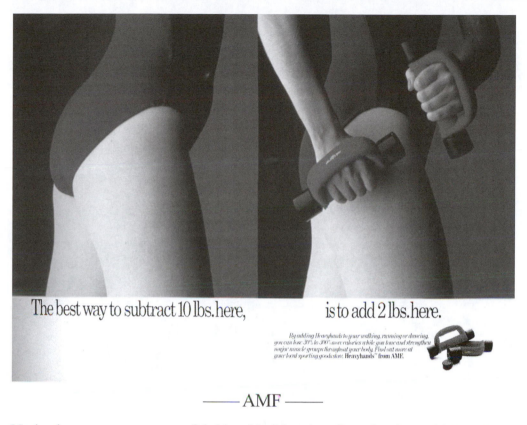

The best way to subtract 10 lbs. here,   is to add 2 lbs. here.

By adding Heavyhands to your walking, running or dancing, you can lose 30% to 300% more calories while you tone and strengthen major muscle groups throughout your body. Find out more at your local sporting goods store. Heavyhands™ from AMF.

—— AMF ——

Notice how sparse yet powerful this ad is. Now imagine what it would have been like if information about weight loss, as well as information about the company, were added to it. When creating an ad, McElligott likes to limit the amount of information that he includes in it. "For many years—and to some degree today—clients had a tendency to want to cram more into an ad. They're paying for it. So they want to give every possible piece of information that can help them make a sale," he says. "But if you pile on six different type faces, four different visuals, a logo, three pieces of copy, and God knows what else, the ad won't have any real power."

Get rid of these handles,   with these handles.

By adding Heavyhands to your walking, running or dancing, you can lose from 30% to 300% more calories while you tone and strengthen major muscle groups throughout your body. Find out more at your sporting goods store. Heavyhands™ from AMF.

ITT LIFE

Here was a product innovation that needed announcing to potential customers—reduced insurance premiums to nonsmokers who were fit and trim.

In typical style, McElligott wrote hundreds of headlines before choosing which ones he'd use in the campaign. In addition, like most of the ads he wrote, this one shows his tendency to use dry wit and irony when communicating.

By the way, according to an article in *Print Cases Book 6: The Best in Advertising*, the photographs for this ad—all of the same man—originally appeared ten years earlier in a magazine article that McElligott and Nancy Rice had remembered seeing. They tracked down the photographer and bought the rights.

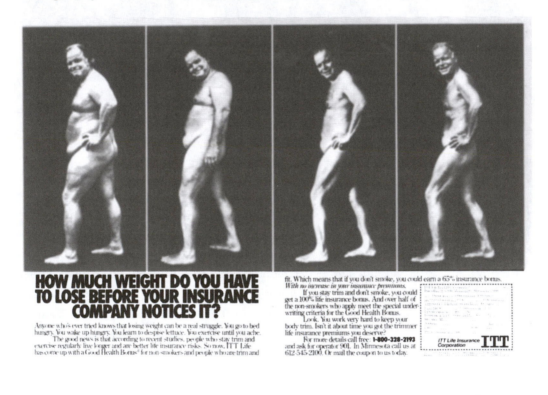

PORSCHE

According to McElligott, advertising is pleasing when it makes its point in an original way. "Originality is wonderful," he says. "When I see originality in a book, movie, architecture, or painting, I'm delighted. There's too little of it in this world."

Advertising isn't much different. "It has to sell, but if it sells with wit and originality, it's delightful," he says. "In the mundane daily life we all live, when you're in your car and look over at the side of a bus and see a truly wonderful piece of advertising, it's a moment of pleasure.

"You don't have to know anything about advertising to be delighted by it. And the pleasure of that moment reflects on the product. That's the greatest thing that can happen to the product because it gets the credit for delighting people."

In addition to showing how originality can sell, this newspaper ad is an example of communications developed within a long-term brand personality. All of the Porsche ads created at Fallon McElligott communicated with this attitude.

ADVICE FOR CREATING A SUCCESSFUL CAREER

What makes a great advertising persion? McElligott speculates that it's passion, intensity and a strong drive to succeed, more than education or even talent. "There are a lot of talented people around," he says. "But without the fire in their guts, a good talent can go to waste."

So when hiring, McElligott looks for an aura of intensity. "I am not talking about good salesmanship," he says. "Quite the contrary. I'm talking about somebody who is so intense I'm not sure I want to be in the same room with him or her. I was a driven, intense guy with an enormous, dysfunctional need to succeed. It's not unlike the great American entrepreneurs outside of advertising. Success is a way of overcoming other things in their lives."

He looks for people with intensity, combined with drive, a sense of originality, and an ability to see things differently than other people. He feels that everything else can be taught—the strategizing, and the ability to write good sentences and paragraphs. He notes that "Over three or four years of copy chiefing, you can make a kid literate."

So if you're extremely driven—and want to be guided by one of advertising's greatest practitioners—here are some ideas and suggestions that may help you along. Please note that while the following advice—as well as the other comments from McElligott in this book—comes from interviews for the first edition of this book, it is as powerful and pertinent today as it was back in 1994.

Don't be afraid to take an unconventional path: *"*People who create effective advertising have the ability to come at problems from a fresh perspective," says McElligott. "They have a slightly askew point of view. And often travel unconventional paths, which force them to stand at the sidelines and see something from a slightly different perspective. I can't make this a blanket rule, but it's a pretty good one."

Take a course in art direction: *"*Art direction is more methodical than copywriting," says McElligott. "It's a little closer to a profession. It's still a craft, but art directors have to have the basic mechanical tools. They have to know typography, composition, and all kinds of things that begin to resemble a body of professional knowledge."

Know the rules—and break them: McElligott believes that good advertising is about breaking rules. If you create within the rules, you can't be fresh. And freshness is what disarms consumers. That means, according to McElligott, "Great advertising should make your client's palms sweat a little."

But when you break the rules, McElligott warns, "Know the consequences. Certain things simply have to happen in a print ad or commercial," he says, "so breaking rules is great, but first understand the tradeoffs."

Study the annuals—again: Like so many of the other creative geniuses found in the pages of this book, McElligott believes the best way to start a spec book is to get the One Show annuals, New York Art Director annuals and *Communication Arts* advertising annuals—and study them. "Start to understand why some of these ads are really special," he says. "If you bring the annuals into your life, in effect, you're bringing in the graduate school of advertising. You're getting a glimpse into the minds of some very good creative advertising people. You have to start somewhere. Even Picasso was influenced by other painters. His early work was derivative."

Identify products you want to advertise: "Get into the Zen of thinking about concepts," McElligott suggests. "Pick five or ten products you might like to advertise—pens, cars, batteries—anything. Start a file for each one. Put all your roughs in there. Start thinking about each product. Relax. Page through the annuals and consider whether an interesting approach to one problem would make sense for your product. For example, would an approach for BMW make sense for Shaeffer pens?"

Collaborate: "A beginning art director should enlist the help of a beginning copywriter, so the copy will be as crisp and effective as possible. Beginning copywriters need the help of a beginning art director who, in turn, will help the visual be as powerful as possible," says McElligott. "Even when putting a beginning book together, it's important for the art director and copywriter to share a firm grasp of the concept and how it applies to the goal of the campaign."

Be resourceful: "There's a lot to be said for using scrap art. Use existing photos. And get type set," says McElligott. "You can put together a pretty convincing ad with very little money and it'll look close to a real one. We do that for presentations. I know that we have more resources, of course, but good spec ads don't have to be expensive."

Polish your portfolio: "Beginners should strive to create ads that are as original and polished as the ads I see in the One Show or the *D&AD*. That's the fastest way to get a job. If you show a book that has six or eight ads close to that caliber, you'll almost certainly get a job. In a way, creating a good portfolio is a huge accomplishment, but it's not that complicated," McElligott says. He also thinks that polishing the ads is important for another reason. "I like to think I can see an idea. But, sometimes, I'm amazed at how terrific some ads become when they're executed," he says. "And I suspect I'm not the only creative director who sometimes does not fully appreciate where an idea can go when it's in its roughest form."

Share with your partner in a way that works for both of you: "I've never been the sort of writer who wants to sit in a room staring at an art director for five days.

When working with Nancy Rice, for example, she'd go away. I'd go away. Then we'd meet, share ideas and tweak the ads until they did what we wanted them to do," he says. "It was a strong collaboration. It often works that way for creative teams."

Go for volume first: When McElligott writes, he churns out a huge pile of ads, sometimes 30 different variations on the same concept. This helps him move past the easy solutions and loosen up. "You have to get past the stuff everybody else does," he says, "and that requires a lot of hard work." Sometimes he creates five or six hundred roughs before he finds four or five ads he loves. "I'll look the next day," he says, "and usually one of them is far, far better."

Talk to the consumer one-on-one: Advertising is most effective when it speaks to one consumer rather than to an enormous audience. "The problem with so much advertising," he says, "is that it speaks from a podium. I think—with rare exceptions—advertising copywriters tend not to understand that it's an extremely personal thing to sell something to somebody. Of course, the best writers find that out fairly quickly. But if you look at the whole body of American advertising, you will find very little that actually touches people."

Use simple and casual language: McElligott believes writing should reflect the kind of dialogue you hear between individuals. When it does, it has a truthful, special quality that lends the advertising credibility. "It quickly became obvious to me that good writing was good salesmanship," he says, "so the less formal the language is, the better it is. And if you're writing in the vernacular, sentence fragments are appropriate."

Fulfill the strategy: "I don't know that young people have to be fully familiar with the entire process of strategizing, but I think they at least need to have respect for it. They must have a general awareness that they are responsible for fulfilling a strategy. So the work should never be so obviously wacko that it would never stand a chance of being produced," says McElligott. "Then, once in an agency, it must track. It's a very, very shallow victory for some kid to go off to an awards show and pick up a gold medal for something that didn't work. That can't last a lifetime. And that's not good for a career."

Make your work defendable: McElligott believes in pre-testing and post-testing. "So I'm at the point now where I will absolutely not take a piece of work to a client when I can't strategically track it. I want to be able to take clients through the strategic process. Ultimately, something has to happen in the marketplace. Because what we're doing is selling. And if we're not selling, then we're doing something wrong and we can't be proud of it."

Seek advice: "At some point, you'll have so many roughs that you'll need to have some objective input to help evaluate which ideas have the most potential," says McElligott. "Without feedback from others it will be difficult to create a spec book. So this is where you need to be pretty resourceful because editing or mentorship is not easy to come by, especially from really good people." McElligott says he has helped several beginners through this process, reviewing their work and helping them decide on which rough concepts to pursue, as well as which changes to make.

Persevere: "Getting into the advertising business requires resilience and tenacity," says McElligott. "You can't be crushed when people don't return your phone calls or letters. Simply hang in there. And then do some brilliant ads for your spec portfolio. And you'll surely get a job."

Keep up: The speed at which the advertising industry changes hinders effective advertising education and also complicates the advertising professionals' need to keep up. "When I returned to advertising after a year away," says McElligott, "I was astonished at how fast things had changed. It took me six months just to catch up."

Don't hide your intensity and originality: Many good creative directors can sense the kind of intensity and originality that fuels a beginner's career. McElligott has relied on his ability to sense these qualities in people he has hired. And his instincts have paid off. Many of the writers he has hired who exhibited drive have become extremely successful. While they had varied levels of education, they all shared an intense need to succeed.

Postscript:

PREPARE FOR THE STRUGGLE

Throughout this book, we've heard that advertising is a shrinking field, that many experienced people are looking for work, and that it's getting harder to break into the field.

Let's hear about that from someone who has experienced those ups and downs.

"A lot of people are drawn to advertising today. There are hundreds of wonderful applicants coming and going whom I can't hire and I feel very badly for them.

"There is virtually no place for them because the business has become considerably smaller. Far smaller.

"When I started out, it seemed tough. But it wasn't as tough as it is now.

"Whatever I did in 1970 was good enough to get me into the city's premier department store. But not today. Not with what I had to show them.

"In fact, with what's happened in this business, I doubt I would get in. I had a lot more enthusiasm than I had ability. Today, I see young people with fairly polished starting books who are relentless in their pursuit of success.

"It's that combination—really—that does it.

"The most important thing about the whole ad game is to be damn sure you're really passionate about it. It's no place for people who aren't sure they want to be there. There are a lot of midcareer advertising people on the streets of New York, Chicago, and Minneapolis who are having a very tough time—and it's especially bad to have a tough time when you're in your late thirties or in your forties.

"In the last five years, the advertising industry has taken a hell of a beating. Yet, it still attracts people for all the right reasons. I was attracted to it because it can be great fun. It's creative, it's challenging, and it changes every day.

"So I don't want to discourage anybody, but people have to be prepared for real ups and downs. To get into the business without that knowledge would be a big mistake. It's pretty commonplace for people to lose their jobs a few times during their advertising careers. And, unless you understand that—really understand it—advertising can be brutal."

CREATING BETTER WORK –
SOME INITIAL STRATEGIES

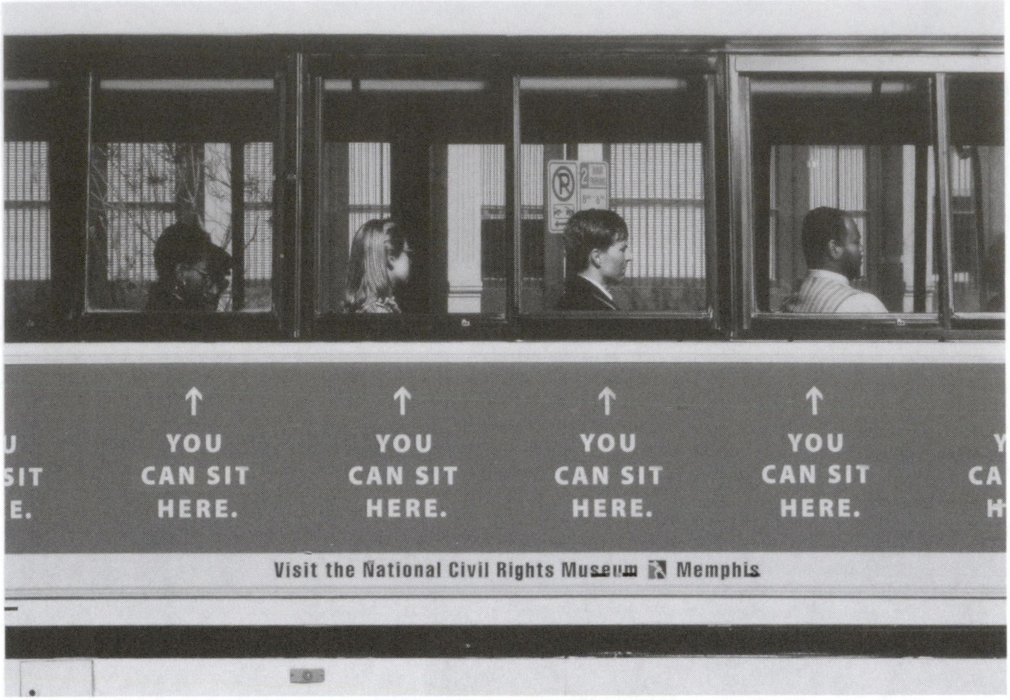
YOU CAN SIT HERE.
YOU CAN SIT HERE.
YOU CAN SIT HERE.
YOU CAN SIT HERE.
Visit the National Civil Rights Museum Memphis

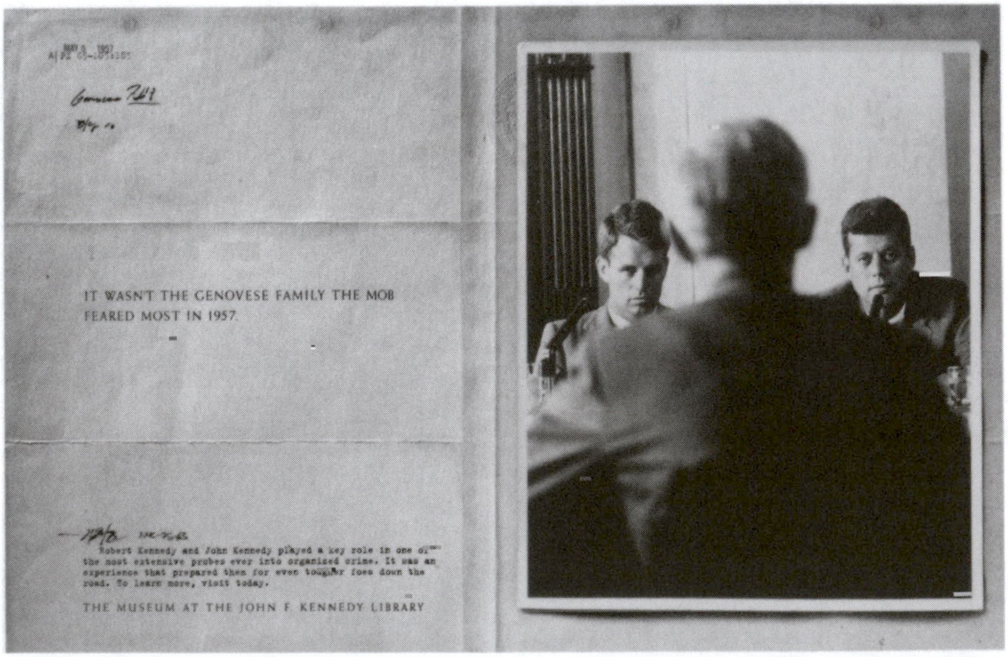
IT WASN'T THE GENOVESE FAMILY THE MOB FEARED MOST IN 1957.
Robert Kennedy and John Kennedy played a key role in one of the most extensive probes ever into organized crime. It was an experience that prepared them for even tougher foes down the road. To learn more, visit today.
THE MUSEUM AT THE JOHN F. KENNEDY LIBRARY

Mike Hughes

"I never felt entitled to any of my jobs."

"Ad agency creative departments are such chronically unhappy places," observes Mike Hughes, President and Creative Director of the Martin Agency in Richmond, Virginia. He believes that most ad agency creatives are cynical, especially when it comes to how they approach management. "If a creative can keep a freshness of attitude, that person will find that the more senior people in the agency—the people who tend to do the hiring—will gravitate toward him or her."

Mike Hughes is a creative who has the ability to keep a fresh attitude. And, because of that, he has been able to help build an agency that boasts that spirit as well.

The result: *Ad Age* says The Martin Agency is one of three best creative agencies in the world. *Adweek* considers Hughes as one of the nine best creative directors working in America today, citing his integrity as one of the reasons for including him. His creative department has won trophies from virtually every major advertising award show.

A former director of the American Association of Advertising Agencies and chairman of its creative committee, Mike also has served as a director for the One Club for Art and Copy in New York. He's served as the American judge for the Cannes Advertising Festival and has been a leader in the Advertising Council's post-9/11 Freedom and Homeland Security campaigns. In 2006 alone, he's been tapped to judge the ANDY Awards, the Kelly Awards, and the Shark Advertising Awards in Ireland.

He is a graduate of Washington and Lee University, married, and the father of two sons. His youngest son, a graduate of Yale, is a technical director for a theater at a college in New Jersey. "He calls himself a carpenter," says Hughes. "He also teaches there. I can't believe he's my kid, because I can't do anything with a hammer or a screwdriver."

A WELL-CRAFTED SUCCESS STORY

While many creatives say that their drive for success was born out of an unhappy childhood, Hughes claims the opposite, describing his childhood as being "blessed." Says Hughes, "I come from a wonderful family—a loving mother and father, hard working, pretty solid middle class." Born in Washington, he has lived in Richmond, Virginia, since the age of five. "My mother's family is from here," he says. "I have cousins all over town."

To earn a living, his father first worked as a print production manager for a couple of ad agencies in the '40s and '50s. "In those days, once the layout and copy were approved, the project would be turned over to a production manager who'd supervise the setting of type, the photography, and the keylines—all of the things to put it together," he says.

Then in the early '60s, his father left print production to sell typography to ad agencies. "He represented the Philadelphia Typography Company," says Hughes, "back when there were typography companies."

But the business was changing at that time, and his father started dealing with art directors who would order their own type. His father didn't like what he was seeing. "Partly, he defined himself as a salesman of typography services," says Hughes. "But it was also the craftsmanship of being a production manager. He was appalled that some people who didn't understand the craftsmanship of the business were getting ahead; he was appalled by art directors who didn't really understand what could be done with typography."

His father and mother, however, had huge respect for the creative people in the business and thought that they were "inspiring" and "cool."

While Hughes was exposed to production early in his life— he grew up with typography books on the bookshelves of his childhood home—he claims to know little about it. "I am remarkably naïve about the technical side of our business," he says. "I swear there's not a single typeface I can look at and tell you that I know its name. And, while his best subject was math, he always thought it would be better to be an English major in college. "Those people just seemed smarter and wiser," he says. "I think that it probably came in part from my parents' admiration for the creative people."

But he didn't want to become a copywriter; rather he wanted to be a journalist, an interest that began while attending a Catholic military high school. "The local newspaper had a youth page," recalls Hughes. "And each school had a representative. I got that position and started writing a lot of stuff for them—because they paid by the column inch."

By accepting a lot of assignments, Hughes learned how to tell a story and how to get to the point quickly. "We were getting more publicity than the other schools around town because I was writing so much and the newspaper was publishing all of it."

This led to a summer job at the newspaper that lasted throughout high school and college. "One summer in college, I lost my driver's license for too many speeding tickets," he recalls. "A reporter in Richmond without a driver's license isn't much use. The editors kindly put me on the copy desk for the afternoon paper. I wrote 25 headlines in the morning to go in that day's paper. They brought in the stories and told me the number of lines, columns, and letters per line they needed. It was like doing little crossword puzzles. The headlines needed to be clear. Looking back, many of them weren't, but I turned out a lot of stuff."

As an aspiring journalist, Hughes worshipped the *New York Times* and the *Washington Post*. "But my editor encouraged me to read the *New York Daily News*, because of its more populist, guy-on-the-subway kind of writing," he says. "That taught me to make sure my writing was clear and straightforward, something hugely helpful in advertising. The discipline of figuring out my thinking, what's important and what isn't important, and what a reader would be interested in was also great experience for advertising, where one often doesn't have as interesting subject matter as newspapers."

When Hughes graduated from college, he was moving toward a magazine editing position. "It felt right," he says. "I thought I had to move to New York to do that. I didn't know how to go about it. So I thought, 'Maybe I'll try advertising for a while.' My dad, of course, knew all of the agency people here and got me an interview with Dave Martin who was just starting what was then this agency, which was called Martin and Woltz."

But Martin didn't hire him. Rather, Martin arranged for Hughes to meet with Harry Jacobs, who was then president of Cargill, Wilson, and Acree, which was among the leading ad agencies in the South at that time. Recalls Hughes, "Harry later became president of The Martin Agency and my mentor, but at that time, he didn't give me a job. Harry just didn't have an opening. I think he would have given me a job if he'd had an opening."

Jacobs sent Hughes to the Richmond office of Clinton E. Frank Advertising. They had Reynolds Metals account and offered Hughes a job to work on it—his first job in advertising. And his first assignment was to write a full-color brochure to promote Reynolds Do-It-Yourself Aluminum: sheets of aluminum for use in making things around the house.

"As a reporter for an afternoon newspaper, I went in early in the morning and wrote my stories quickly so they could be in the paper that afternoon," says Hughes. "After getting my first assignment on the first day, I was in my boss's office 20 minutes later with the brochure all figured out and written. He said, 'What's this?'

I said, 'The assignment you gave me.' He said, 'But we take days to do it.' I said, 'What do you mean you take days?' I had a whole lot to learn."

While Clinton E. Frank was not considered a creative powerhouse, Hughes learned the importance of figuring out a selling strategy, approaching the client with integrity, and being responsible for meeting the goals of the client. "It's not just about creating clever ads," says Hughes. "It's about giving people information that changes their behavior in ways that are good for them. If I have a concern about portfolio schools today, it's that kids sometimes graduate thinking that it's all about doing award-winning advertising when it is really about doing the craft as well as you can do it and doing it in a way that benefits your sponsor, your client."

After a few months on the job, his supervisor told him that he had real promise for the ad business—and if he were still working at Clinton E. Frank in 18 months, he would be fired. "I was told I ought to go to a better agency," recalls Hughes. He stayed at the agency for exactly 18 months, resigned, and got a job as a copywriter for Martin and Woltz. Then an agency from Norfolk, Virginia, Lawler Ballard, opened an office in Richmond, and he went there as co-creative director for the next 18 months.

Lawler was striving to be known on the national level, and when he became a co-creative director of the Richmond office, the agency gave Hughes a small amount of stock and asked him to sign to a contract that required 90 days notice to terminate. But Hughes was going through a lot of life change—he'd married an account executive from Lawler—and he was talking to other people about opportunities and possibilities. "I was interested, but I had this 90-day clause," he says. "So I turned in my 90-days notice not quite sure what I was going to do."

At first, agency management tried to talk Hughes into staying, but they soon found another writer in Richmond who was able to start right away—Nina DiSesa, who is now Chairman of McCann Erikson in New York—and paid Hughes for the 90 days of his contract. "Since it was a small office, they didn't need both of us," he says. "All of a sudden I was free and had 90 days pay. It was great. I had quit but got the equivalent of severance, and that set me up in my own freelance business."

He found that he loved it. "I've never worked harder in my career than when I was doing my freelance business. And, I never had a slow day. Right now the freelance market is crowded, but it was far less crowded back then."

After freelancing on his own for about a year, Bill Wynn, who had been a creative director at an agency in Richmond, joined Hughes. "We had five or six employees," says Hughes. He found that many of the smaller agencies in Richmond didn't have full-time creatives, and he worked regularly for them. He also landed business from outside of the area. "I don't remember how we found them, but there were a couple of agencies across the country," he recalls. "We had a big agency client in Fort Wayne, Indiana. They became one of our biggest clients, maybe even our biggest client."

Hughes Wynn charged by the hour. "I did every job from the ground up," he says. "I did not go back through files and try to find old things. I found that I could be incredibly fast, and I was willing to work. I worked a lot of 20-hour days."

Hughes also brought his new wife into the business. "I married a woman who had a son, and we quickly had a second son," he says. "While she didn't work full-time, she helped out as a combination of office manager, account executive, and writer. We were young, in love, and working together all of the time. We enjoyed it."

Meanwhile, the partnership between George Woltz and Dave Martin dissolved, and Woltz left to start another agency. "Dave kept The Martin Agency," says Hughes. "He asked me to become its creative director, and I decided not to do that. The agency probably only had 30 people at the time, but I was just intimidated by it. I thought, 'That's too big.' I was afraid I wouldn't know what to do. I was only 28."

When Hughes turned down the position, Martin got Harry Jacobs to join as president and creative director. "Harry hired us as freelancers," says Hughes. "He was such a legend in advertising in this part of the world that when he called and asked to see my portfolio, I couldn't do it. I was scared to death. I couldn't show him my crummy work."

But while he'd never entered awards shows, some of the agencies where he'd freelanced entered his work. "It did pretty well," he says, "so Harry saw it and hired me to work on some projects. He introduced me to a new level of advertising. I decided I could learn a lot about the creative process and advertising from Harry. So although I was intimidated, working with Harry was also a joy. We hit it off from day one. And the first things we did ended up in all of the national award books."

After they'd done a few projects together, Jacobs started talking to Hughes about joining The Martin Agency. "I felt funny about it because Bill Wynn and I had a good thing going," he says. "And I was making twice as much money freelancing than I could make at The Martin Agency. But it was a chance to work with Harry Jacobs and to learn. Bill understood and was great about it. We remained terrific friends."

From $4 Million to over $360 Million

When Hughes joined The Martin Agency, he thought he was going to be a copywriter. "My first day, Harry comes in with a little sheet about me," he says, "and I'm down as associate creative director, which had never been mentioned to me." Clients included some local industrial accounts, a local theme park, and an agricultural account. "Our TV commercials were for the ag account. We'd do four or five TV commercials a year, and they often ran on Nebraska farm shows at 4:00

in the morning. But we started getting into the national award books, and our peers started talking about us. Advertisers would come and tell us, 'I have friends who work in agencies in Los Angeles, and they say that you guys are pretty good.' That was how we got new business, and it grew from there." They went from $4 million to over $360 million in billings.

"My job hasn't changed... but my title grew."

Jacobs focused on maintaining the agency's creative vision and turned the day-to-day responsibilities of running the creative department over to Hughes. "I sometimes feel that my job hasn't changed since I started," says Hughes. "But my title grew. Harry became Vice-Chairman and Chief Creative Officer, and he made me Creative Director." Jacobs retired in 2000.

As for client services, John Adams is the account-side counterpart to Hughes. "He started on the PR side the year after I left the first time. We have a fabulous, very collaborative relationship," says Hughes. "I make the company's creative decisions, but he knows that I don't hesitate to ask his advice and encourage him to give advice on his own. We don't report to each other. I bet nobody at the agency knows to whom we report. I'm not sure we even know." Hughes laughs, adding that they're now part of the Interpublic Group. "But we're remarkably independent. The same people who ran the company before IPG run it now. Our financial guy stays in touch with IPG. And we're good corporate citizens. When they have something we think we can learn, we go and learn it."

And while The Martin Agency currently maintains service offices all over the country, the creative, except for interactive projects, is developed in Richmond. Says Hughes, "As a creative, you can hide in other agencies, but not here."

Outside of work, Hughes has had to face health challenges in recent years. His stepson was diagnosed with HIV-AIDs in 1998 and died in 2002. The same year his son was diagnosed, his wife, Ginny, discovered that she had cancer. And he learned that he had lung cancer. "I am a lifelong non-smoker, but I still came down with lung cancer," he says. "The morning after I first got the diagnosis—it was during a regular check up—*USA Today* had a little chart that said only 85 percent survive five years, and it's been over five years now, so I consider myself incredibly lucky."

"...To another level."

All of these health problems inspired Hughes to rededicate himself to advertising. "It surprised me," he says. "It's not that we were wealthy, but I could have retired. I decided what would be fun is to see if we could take our agency to another level. It's been a little frustrating because, like ad agencies everywhere, we've had to spend a lot of time playing defense and just keeping even the last couple of years.

While we're doing better than 90 percent of the agencies out there, I came back with the intent of being pretty aggressive about trying new and bigger things."

What were his goals? Hughes explains: "Every once in a while a company can be a good presence in the community. Corporations had always talked to customers from across the table. They were in a coat and tie, a little intimidating, and off to the side. But Doyle Dane Bernbach got people to think differently about corporations through its Volkswagen advertising. Wieden+Kennedy's work for Nike over the years has helped us realize that there is an athletic, competitive spirit inside all of us. I want us to work at that level. It's hard to build a plan for that—DDB and Wieden+Kennedy didn't know when they were starting to do those things—but that's the kind of impact that I want us to make."

Hughes, however, is still proud of the agency. "Our agency seems to be a company with a lot of heart," he says. "It demonstrates itself in the way we treat each other, respect our clients and suppliers, and act in the community. I hope it also shows up in the work we do and our style. If we do our job right, the advertising will reflect the client, but it will also reflect the people who make it. If the environment in which it's created is arrogant or cynical, it's going to be reflected in the final advertising."

Hughes is also proud of the former employees who've gained industry fame. "I think it's great," he says. "Bill Westbrook (Creative Director and President of Fallon) worked with us twice, and Jelly Helm (of Wieden+Kennedy fame) worked with us twice, and Luke Sullivan worked here. Who knows? Maybe Luke will end up with us again." But he is more proud of the people who have stayed at The Martin Agency. "I'm so lucky that I get to go to work every day with a group of people that I love," he says, "especially when I'm doing something that could be important."

A PORTFOLIO WITH HEART

Brainstorming roughs from Jacobs and Hughes exploring various strategic and creative directions.

—— BANK OF VIRGINIA ——

Here's an ad Hughes created with Jacobs. "The first time I sat down with Harry to make ads, we never talked about ads," says Hughes. "All of a sudden I started learning the strategic side of the business. Harry put outlines together of possible directions we could go. He said, 'We could have the client speak for himself like Frank Perdue, or we could take an approach that is based on consumer needs, on the product innovation, or on the product difference.' If we did an ad from customer needs, what would that mean? If we did it from the client's point of view, what would that mean?' It was all about thinking. So that when we finally developed the ads, they were strategically sound."

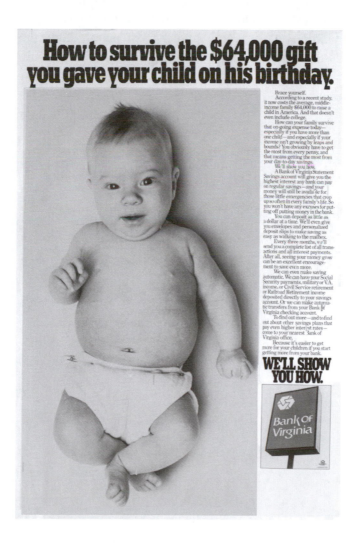

KING'S DOMINION

When Hughes first started working on King's Dominion at Lawler Ballard, he hated it. "On Monday mornings, I'd get the numbers for how many people went to the park that weekend," he says. "Nobody cared about the cleverness of my radio spot or the filmic value of my television commercial. It was just the numbers. And they could be brutal. But then I embraced it. I said, 'Okay, if that's how they're going to measure it, that's what I'm going after.' I became extremely results-focused."

But he still didn't give up his dedication to craftsmanship. "I wasn't going to give up my determination to create work that was charming and compelling," he says. "I was going to do that, but also take on the challenge of getting results. I got more competitive. At that time there were two theme parks in Virginia, King's Dominion and Busch Gardens. That brought out the competitive sense in me. I wanted to beat Busch Gardens every week and get more people through the turnstiles. I found that made the business more fun. I was still concerned with what my peers thought of the work in terms of its creative values, but I also was just as concerned about getting results."

—— Newspaper Association of America ——

Inspired by his father, Hughes looks for care in the craftsmanship of the ad. "It's harder to find today because we've gone through some rather free-ranging design fashions in the last ten years," he says. "And it's harder to tell who has a true sense of design. But if you look at artwork, Picassos are so exquisitely designed. There's a lot of imitation work that might still be Picasso-like, but they don't have the same craftsmanship and sense of design. Just painting a woman who has three noses on the side of her head doesn't make it art. A big part of what makes the difference is sense of design and craftsmanship." This example, from a campaign created by The Martin Agency for the Newspaper Association of America features various leading ad creatives demonstrating Mike Hughes' sense of design and craftsmanship.

HOW TO CREATE A NEWSPAPER AD BY LEE CLOW

I'm an ART DIRECTOR. And I've always felt that the opportunity to design an ad for newspaper was a special creative opportunity. But newspaper is a special medium. It's URGENT, not yesterday or tomorrow but TODAY so the message has to demand ATTENTION.

Therefore, I believe there are TWO KINDS of newspaper ads.

1. The "A picture is worth a 1,000 words" approach. You start with a great big beautiful page, you put an incredible-looking new computer or car or perfume bottle on it and write a headline that says "TA-DA!" Maybe a little copy that explains the importance of this new design, this new concept, this new fragrance. And "VOILA!" It's virtually a POSTER.

2. The "8 or 900 words can be worth a 1,000 words" concept. This is the "we have A STORY TO TELL YOU" approach. This approach must respect the audience, their intelligence, their sense of HUMOR and their CURIOSITY. But a well-written interesting ad can SEDUCE a reader into spending 4 or 5 minutes with you (a lot more than a 30-second TV commercial). CAUTION, if you don't make it SMART AND INTERESTING people can just turn the page.

I BELIEVE that an ad that lands in-between "the poster" AND the "we have a story to TELL YOU" approach WILL FAIL to stop the time READER who is spending time WITH the newspaper for news.

Sitting with a newspaper in the morning and a cup of coffee will always be one of the MOST INTIMATE media experiences there is. And the opportunity to connect with someone using a page you've created will continue to be one of the MOST REWARDING challenges for someone who loves to make ads.

LEE CLOW is Chairman/Creative Director of TBWA WORLDWIDE. He is a member of the One Club Hall of Fame, the Art Director's Hall of Fame and the Museum of Modern Arts Hall of Fame. His work has also been honored by the Newspaper Association of America's Athena Awards and can be viewed at www.naa.org.

The New York Times

How does he tell if a person has a true sense of design and the craftsmanship? "It comes through the consistency of the portfolio and the conversation," he says. "It's a realization that design isn't just about the graphic placement of things. It's about the thinking behind the placement and how the thinking is ordered. I think that's also true of the writers. It's the flow of the words and the flow of the logic throughout the case that is being made. When you find somebody where it consistently comes through in places where you know it's not just chance or luck, but rather through some sense of purpose, then that person is worth his or her weight in gold to me."

—— CAREER BUILDER ——

What is an ad "concept?" Hughes once thought about getting an agency dog and naming him Concept. Says Hughes: "I figured that if he ever ran out in traffic and got killed, we'd all come in and say, 'Our Concept got killed.' Seriously, I once asked some of my partners, 'How do we articulate the idea behind a campaign when we talk about it?' The easy answer is that it's the idea that informs and shapes the communications, but I think that answer often gives people an easy out because they come up with a gimmick, device, or tactic and say that it's the concept. What I'm really looking for is something that is so fundamentally true on a very human level and then is exquisitely expressed. Some things we see strike us as true, but the

expression of it is not very involving. Some things get us very involved, and then when we explore, it just doesn't feel right, because it's not true for the brand or for the audience. I want both brought together."

—— The John F. Kennedy Library Foundation ——

"One of the harder things for me is to appreciate the success we've had and the fact that our work has often been acclaimed," says Hughes. "The Volkswagen and Avis ads I saw when I was a kid were such magnificent pieces to me. They got me

WHEN YOU'RE CARRYING THE WEIGHT OF THE WORLD
ON YOUR SHOULDERS, WHAT'S 34 MORE POUNDS?

THE MUSEUM AT THE JOHN F. KENNEDY LIBRARY | Columbia Point, Boston thinking about business in a whole new way: that business could be accountable as human beings, interesting, and have wit and charm. I always feel that we're coming short of those incredibly high standards. When a client compliments our work, I have been known to say, 'Well, it could be so much better.' I want to change every spot when I show our agency reel to new business prospects or to the board of directors of clients. I want to rewrite and redesign every print ad. People say, 'Let it go.' My partner did a cartoon once of me at the top of a mountain, and the thought bubble from my head said, 'Boy, we still have a long way to go.' But I don't think I've ever been at that top."

—— UPS ——

Even though business-to-business advertising gets a bad rap, Hughes still loves it. "I think it's such a huge opportunity, and it can actually be pretty good for your ego, because it's not quite as hard to stand out with your craftsmanship and ideas," he says. "Our work is mostly consumer today, but one of the campaigns that put us in the map back in the '80s was for the electromotive division of General Motors, which built locomotives."

In some ways, UPS, the biggest client for The Martin Agency, is a business-to-business client. "I told the UPS chairman that I want us to take a very aggressive

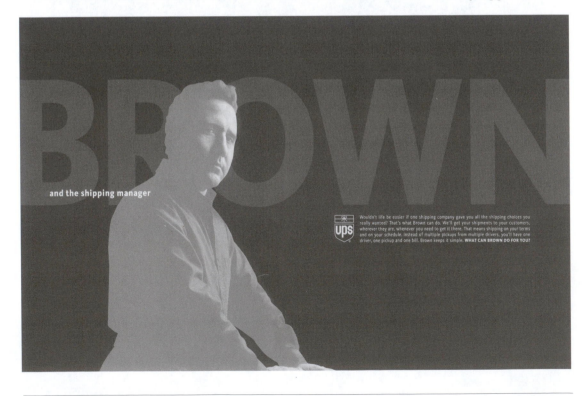

stance in telling their story because every time people go to FedEx, DHL, or else-where, I've failed as a copywriter. I haven't made it clear to them why they should be sending every package via UPS, no matter if it's ground, overnight, or interna-tional. I want to get their numbers better than their competitors' numbers."

The agency's campaign, featuring the tagline "What Can Brown Do for You?", has created the highest awareness numbers of any campaign ever tracked by UPS. Additionally, it has helped strengthen their position as a leader in the shipping business while adding awareness of their world-class services in the fast-growing logistics/supply chain management category.

—— BERNIE'S TATTOOING ——

Hughes also looks for entertain-ment value in books. "I think that the importance of keeping your audience interested and involved is sometimes undervalued in ad-vertising today," he says. "But what is universally valued is the ability to make a strong selling ar-gument about why someone should consider your product, point of view, or service."

Why does this happen? Hughes believes it's because many company leaders tend to work out of the logical, mathematical part of their brain. "That part helped them succeed," he says. "So when they look at the case that they want to make, they think of their audi-ence as being like them, which is very ordered and logical in their thinking. But it's much mushier than that."

Hughes explains the benefits of creating emotional interest and involvement: "With no camera

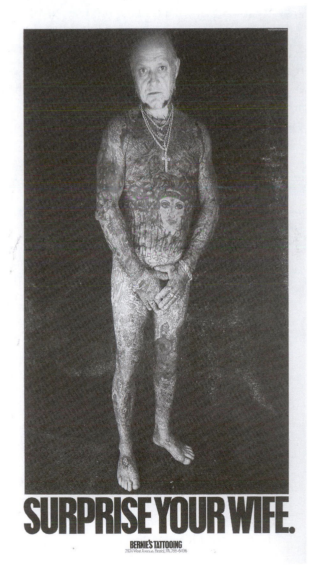

SURPRISE YOUR WIFE.

BERNIE'S TATTOOING
2824 West Avenue, Bristol, PA, 215-45496

heritage at all, Sony had no business becoming a leader in digital cameras. It drives the camera folks—Olympus, Nikon, and Cannon—nuts. Sony came in because of this mushier feeling that consumers had that Sony could somehow make technology easier, friendlier, and more reliable. What did Sony know about making good pictures or lenses or anything like that? What Sony did know is how people respond to their brand and the products that come out under it in those mushier ways."

HOW TO CRAFT YOUR CAREER

Looking back over his legendary career, Hughes says, "I never felt entitled to any of my jobs. I never felt that there was any reason that I should be hired. I was a guy off the street. And, I felt extremely lucky when they did hire me." Hughes didn't have a spec portfolio when he started. "I had a couple of freelance brochures, but I mainly had newspaper articles that I wrote in college and high school. I could never get away with this today," he says. "But in those days, ad schools didn't exist."

Hughes believes that it's harder—if not impossible—for people to break into advertising today if they don't go to a portfolio school. "It's awfully hard to stand out in the crowd and compete, especially when there are people coming out of these graduate schools of advertising who often have very strong portfolios. Plus, people from ad schools have demonstrated the interest and know the language."

But he points out that it's not impossible to break into the creative side without attending a portfolio school. "We had a young writer in our department who first got a job in the operations department," he says. "Some of the creative people probably can't even find the operations department. But they occasionally sent out e-mails to the staff, she volunteered to write them, and they were funny. They were really a stitch and demonstrated a fun way of thinking. All of a sudden I got e-mails from people saying that I ought to give her a chance. So we gave her little opportunities. Then she came up here and became a full-time writer with us."

Whether you decide to attend portfolio school or not, here is some advice from Mike Hughes to help you succeed:

Write headlines by the thousands for one ad: "We need people who come in willing to work hard, listen, go back, and do it again and again and again," he says. "When I had an assignment, I'd literally just keep working at it. And when I met Harry Jacobs, he became such a great editor for me because I would narrow down my thousand headlines to maybe a hundred and take them to him. He'd then mark the ones that he thought were cool and sometimes he'd say, 'None of them.' I'd go back and write a thousand more. I'd be up all night writing headlines. You need to keep that attitude strong."

Show your craftsmanship: In advertising awards shows, Hughes believes that many judges are looking for originality. But he first looks for the fundamentals. "An old technique, a gag, a touching moment that brings a tear to your eye can be impressive if it's done well," he says. "I look for extraordinary craftsmanship, human understanding, and some sense of 'smart.' It's harder to see right now, because the current fashion of advertising allows all kinds of very un-design-y kinds of things. But the best of those have a lot of craftsmanship."

Keep trying: As you may recall, Hughes wasn't hired the first time he applied to The Martin Agency, and others have the same story. "We have a bunch of people that we didn't hire the first time," he says. "Sometimes it cost us a lot more money to hire them later. Getting the right job is such a combination of luck and timing. Martin and Woltz actually came after me because they were getting a food-related account and they thought my experience on Reynolds Food Service could be helpful."

Start working: "There's a lot to be said for just getting the first job and just doing some work," says Hughes. "If it is not a great place, don't stay forever or even that long, but just start doing it—make some ads and brochures—which was basically what I did. Too many of the kids right out of portfolio schools only want to work for Fallon, Wieden, or Goodby. But a career is a marathon; it's going to be going for a long time. You don't have to be a creative director at 28. Just start learning your way around the business: what works and doesn't work, how to sell things, and when to shut up and listen. Jeff Goodby didn't start at Goodby Silverstein, and Dan Wieden didn't start at Wieden+Kennedy. They started at places that were nowhere near as good as those agencies."

Then start building your career: Hughes suggests that once you start working, find better places to go. "Earn those places in the other shops," he says. "You'll probably appreciate them more when you do go to them. People who start in Goodby and leave are forever disappointed in their other agencies, and when they were at Goodby, they didn't think it was that good."

Work on anything: "Some people say, 'I'm a TV person' or 'I don't do small space trade campaigns.' But those people aren't going to get jobs here," says Hughes, "because one of the things you have to demonstrate is a real enthusiasm for the craft no matter how it's applied, whether it's a brochure, matchbook cover, small space ad, or huge TV campaign." Hughes also believes you should be willing to accept less-than-glamorous client assignments. "Typically, first jobs involve doing rate ads for a bank and schedule ads for an airline," he reminds us. "Very few people get a spread for Nike as their first assignment."

Accept the creative challenge: Hughes believes that successful creatives should possess the unusual combination of insecurity and confidence. "It's having the total insecurity that even a matchbook cover or brochure will be hard to do—a challenge to figure out—and the total confidence of being able to say, 'I'm a professional and I will figure it out," he says.

Don't be afraid to show b-2-b: Hughes says that having b-2-b in your portfolio can actually help. "Showing that you can figure out how to do a business-to-business ad will probably demonstrate your depth a lot faster than a simple visual with a snappy headline," he says. "With a b-2-b ad, both sides of the brain have to be engaged, not just one or the other."

Learn to write long copy: Hughes thinks it's a shame that young writers don't put more emphasis on learning to write a good long copy ad. "It's not that one should often write long copy," he says, "but it develops thinking and your craftsmanship skills. And it teaches you how to tell stories. The column inch didn't mean writing long stories, it meant writing a lot of them."

Spend time figuring out the solution: "I don't care about the number of concepts a team brings me as long as they're good," says Hughes. "When I suspect that somebody hasn't gone through the work of figuring it out, I'll send them back. What feels contemporary in the conceptual process today is a strong emphasis on a clearly stated concept. They certainly don't need to be as headline-based as they were 30 years ago, but I do find myself very suspicious of people who don't work like crazy to figure out the best way to say something."

Get someone to make you his or her project: "As far as putting that first portfolio together, I suggest finding a mentor at an agency," suggests Hughes. "Don't try to get the top person. He or she is going to be too busy. Try to find a young writer or art director to be your mentor to take you under his or her wing, work with you, and then help you get a job someplace. Writers and art directors tend to know a lot of other writers and art directors, and they'll help you if they take you under their wing and they feel that you are their project. Those mentors are invaluable. Most of the people we hire come because someone in the creative department is really behind them and advocating for them."

Sell the logical part: Hughes suggests that you don't try to sell the entertainment value. "Sell the logical part of what you're doing," he suggests. "The entertainment part is just the bed that it rests on. And the logic doesn't have to be visible. In the old Levi's 501 Blues campaign, it was hard to exactly articulate the selling argument that wearing Levi's was cool, but it was unmistakable in its connection with its audience. Something inside your head made the logical connection. It didn't have to be in your face. But I suspect that it would be a harder campaign to sell today than it was in 1988. I think it would still work extremely well right now; however, businesses think that the way to get the best ROI is to make their selling argument very straightforward and clear."

Sell internally: "Be sure to present your work to your boss, the creative director, or even your friends down the hall. Don't just hold it up and say, 'Isn't this a cool ad.' Think about your presentation: how you define the job to be done by the ad and the target audience. We might be hiring you initially because we think you have some kind of talent that we can use for our clients' benefit. But what you want to demonstrate is that you're a thinking person beyond the clever writing or flashy art direction."

Read magazines: Hughes considers himself to be a magazine fanatic and reports that this helps him stay current. "It's a combination of relying on a few magazines and randomly picking others. I think *The New Yorker* is, in a sense, a weekly miracle, for its in-depth journalism. I also think that the *New York Times*, the *Wall Street Journal*, and *USA Today* are all daily miracles. It is an honor for my advertising to appear in them. I don't pretend that I read all of the deepest magazines. I will occasionally go through a *Harper's* or an *Atlantic Monthly*. I see the *Economist* pretty regularly, but I also love *Vanity Fair*, *Esquire*, and *Gentleman's Quarterly*. My wife and I are also big movie fanatics and go to the Sundance festival most years. Staying up with that kind of pop culture is important."

Develop your sense of 'taste': "Your own particular take on things is important, but to have some sense of taste that is developed, and not just what comes to you intuitively, will be helpful," Hughes suggests. "Go to museums. Study the paintings. Go to all kinds of movies from big blockbusters to little independent films with awfully small production budgets. Develop a sense of what sounds right and what doesn't sound right, an eye for what looks right and what doesn't look right, and what is appropriately disruptful and dramatic—which is how you get people to look at your advertising—and not just chaotic."

Think non-traditional: "A young person getting in this business today who considers only traditional media is going to have a very limited career," says Hughes. "Traditional advertising is not going to go away. But we need innovators right now. We need to find new ways to get through to consumers. More people will go into a Wal-Mart store in a given week than will watch any single TV commercial or TV show. Only the Super Bowl will beat a Wal-Mart store. You have to think about point of sale: What can I do there? How can I reach people in ways that don't clutter the environment, aren't offensive, are constructive, are welcome additions to the landscape and still let me convey my message?"

Don't set long-range goals: You may want to set five-year goals, but Hughes warns against setting 20-year goals. "Don't say, 'I want to be creative director of a top-ten agency' because you don't know enough about yourself yet," says Hughes. "As you move along, some of it will happen naturally. No matter what, Tom McElligot was going to become a creative director. He might be the best copywriter on the planet, but he also had creative director skills. Other people, even if you give them the title, don't really become creative directors. They just become writers or art directors with new titles. It's a different set of skills."

Decide if you really want to become creative director: "Some people should become creative directors, some shouldn't," says Hughes. "It's the difference between the coach and the player. Most writers can stay at writing something for hours and hours. Being a creative director requires patience with things like client meetings and working out knotty personnel problems. And, a fabulous writer is probably more valuable on any given day than a fabulous creative director. There's a reason the players get paid more."

If you ever get laid off, use it as a chance to create your vision: "While I've never been laid off, I know from so many friends how it can play games with your ego and confidence," says Hughes. "It can give you an unwarranted sense of insecurity. But you will bounce back. For a lot of people I know, the layoff made them more determined to seek their own vision, figure out what they want to do, and find the place that is best suited for them. I also think going through something jarring in your career, like a layoff, can help settle you down and become more sensitive to the hopes, fears, and personal idiosyncrasies of the client. Some of the best people we've ever had here were people who had been laid off at other companies. It's not an experience you'd wish on anybody, but it can be a great learning experience."

Look at your career as a race with hurdles: "Sometimes you want to make your career into a race, but, if so, it's a race with hurdles," says Hughes. "You see all of those hurdles and you think, 'I could go so much faster if those hurdles weren't there.' But this is a hurdle race; it's not a flat track race. People who take a more realistic view, but still set their standards and sights as high as they can, are the ones who become more valuable."

Postscript 1:

PLANNING AT THE MARTIN AGENCY

Throughout this book, we've heard about the importance of planning. It's a key skill to have, even if you're not a professional planner. But every agency has a different approach to this discipline. Here's Mike Hughes' description of The Martin Agency's version of planning and how he uses planning to help his staff develop better, more creative advertising:

"Planning at our company has evolved from the two strains that we've heard about: one of them from the last 50 years of marketing and the other from the last 15 years of marketing. It's a combination of the account planner, whose responsibility is to think from the consumer's point of view and find the connection with your product or service. The account planning discipline has historically grown from that.

"The other part of it is strategic development. That comes from the company's point of view. What are we trying to do? What is true about our company and our product or service and our sales approach? What is true that we can take out into the marketplace? You have to think about the company's goals and how we're going to get there. We take this corporate strategic approach and marry it to the consumer account planning strategic approach. That's basically what most of us have today: some hybrid of those two things.

"The planner's responsibility is to make sure that our work will accomplish our goals. Some terrific people need outside help doing that. They might be terrific at their craft of finding ways to articulate what needs to be articulated and making ads and commercials that are lively and interesting. But they may not be the best strategic thinkers, in which case an outside person can help. I am probably better at the strategic side than I am at the creative side. I don't know if I'm naturally the best big-idea person, but I am a person who's pretty good at figuring out what needs to be done.

"It's hard to figure out from a portfolio if a person has planning skills. You can only get clues about it from the conversation. There are parts of it that you can teach. And, some creative people don't need planners because they think that way and do it themselves.

"The nice thing about an agency is you can bring together a bunch of people with different skills. Sometimes when I look at an art director, I see someone who is just fabulous at design and execution, but may not be the best strategic thinker. I think, 'How can I take advantage of what this person does and let this person do the best work of their career while teaming them with somebody that will make sure that it's all purposeful.' As a creative director, I try to bring those different kinds of skills together."

POSTSCRIPT 2:

LESSONS FROM HARRY JACOBS ON
HOW TO CREATE A GREAT AGENCY

As you may recall, Mike Hughes dissolved his freelance agency in order to work with Harry Jacobs, and he credits him with being the visionary behind the success of The Martin Agency. "Harry got people to think at a more professional level," says Hughes. "I've had the fortune of working with some wonderful, wonderfully talented people, but Harry remains the best art director with whom I've ever worked."

But how did he turn around The Martin Agency? And, what did he teach Hughes about creating an environment for great work? Let's hear the answer right from Hughes:

"It's rare to find someone who can create a creative environment by the force of his or her will and talent. In most of the cities that have had creative breakthroughs, there were one or two people who created that new kind of environment in that market, whether it was Ron Anderson in Minneapolis or Harry Jacobs in Richmond, McKinney in Raleigh, Gossage and maybe also Riney in San Francisco, and Wieden in Portland, and even Bill Bernbach in New York. For most of us, we need to have had the ground cleared at least a little bit for us. Maybe we can clear more ground, but getting started is hard.

"Creating that kind of environment is an act of confidence, and most creative people can't muster that on their own and pull it off without arrogance.

"When Harry Jacobs would go into a room and a client was used to running tiny little ads with a different message on each one, he'd say, 'No, this is what we're going to do: We're going to do a spread ad to announce the new program, and then we're going to follow it up with these large-spaced, dramatic, very pointed ads. You're going to get more than your money's worth. It's going to pay off much better than those little cockamamie one-at-a-time things.' Other people would say, 'We have the media numbers that say we need this many insertions.' He'd say, 'No, no, no, this is what's going to work.' And he'd have the confidence in himself and what he was doing to sell that to an audience that, like most audiences, is pretty timid about taking those bold steps.

"He started doing that at a pretty young age. I certainly couldn't have done it. I have more confidence today, but today I'm not put in those situations. Typically, advertisers don't come to our agency unless they have some of those beliefs. We built a staff that has those beliefs. I hope to build on those beliefs, but the first effort has been done.

"Harry said that he'd made a mistake early in his career by trying to change everything overnight by clearing out a creative department. That kind of agony wasn't productive. What Harry did was expect the best of the people around him. He expected work that was clear and dramatic, but still focused. He knew how to lead people to create award-winning campaigns, but he never talked about award-winning campaigns. He talked about doing work 'that'll just blow your socks off' or 'blow the doors off.'

"He didn't come in and immediately change all the staff. Rather, he made people more responsible by taking care of the nuts and bolts and gave them a sense of possibility. When I started full-time at the agency, he and I went aside and put together what we called then our 18-month plan. I guess we're now in about month six. He said, 'We have to convince the people in the agency that we can do great things. We have a bank in town that does a lot of advertising in the local papers. That's what our people see.' So we concentrated on making those local newspaper ads for that bank just world class. When people see that it's a possibility, they rise to higher levels.

"Harry showed us one ad at a time and one campaign at a time that we could do things that were a little more dramatic, a little smarter, a little more human and real and touching. He showed us by doing some of it himself, but also by demanding it and expecting us to keep going back and doing it over and over until we got it right.

"Some people who work at agencies that aren't doing very good work try to build a little quality shop within the bigger organization. That's incredibly hard to do. Consistently doing great creative work is a conspiracy between the top management of the agency and the creative department. Once people demand it, expect it, and demonstrate that it can be done, everybody else gets fired up because if one guy can do it, they can do it too and beat him or her. You want that healthy competition."

After we paint the car we paint the paint.

You should see what we do to a Volkswagen even before we paint it.

We bathe it in steam, we bathe it in alkali, we bathe it in phosphate. Then we bathe it in a neutralizing solution.

If it got any cleaner, there wouldn't be much left to paint.

Then we dunk the whole thing into a vat of slate gray primer until every square inch of metal is covered. Inside and out.

Only one domestic car maker does this. And his cars sell for 3 or 4 times as much as a Volkswagen.

(We think that the best way to make an economy car is expensively.)

After the dunking, we bake it and sand it by hand.

Then we paint it.

Then we bake it again, and sand it again by hand.

Then we paint it again.

And bake it again.

And sand it again by hand.

So after 3 times, you'd think we wouldn't bother to paint it again and bake it again. Right? Wrong.

Roy Grace

"A lot of kids come out of school today and all they've learned to do is think. They can't execute their ideas."

"They can't even communicate them visually on a piece of paper," said Roy Grace, an advertising legend who passed away in February of 2003.

"It's moved away from the craft. It's like a surgeon who knows all the techniques, but is unable to use all the instruments."

Like a Surgeon

Roy Grace was surely a "surgeon" who knew how to use all the tools. He art directed some of the most groundbreaking work ever to come out of DDB. He won numerous Clios, One Show awards, and Cannes Lions, as well as many others. The Museum of Modern Art in New York has four of his commercials in their collection. According to Barbara Lippert in a March 10, 2003, article in *Adweek*, "His monumentally award-winning body of work moved advertising from the flat and formulaic, the impossibly perfect and shiny, to the conceptual, more succinctly observational and enduringly funny."

In this chapter, we'll investigate one aspect of creating a groundbreaking ad—graphic invention—as well as other "tools" you may need.

In addition, we'll meet a very original and important player in the history of advertising.

Before he started his own shop with former DDB copywriter Diane Rothschild, Grace worked his way up to the positions of chairman of Doyle Dane Bernbach/U.S. and vice chairman of the board of The Doyle Dane Bernbach Group. Said Grace, "I doubt if these were titles you could really put on a business card."

THE GREATEST 14TH CENTURY TALENT
IN THE 20TH CENTURY

If you have the talent, you can succeed. It may take many interviews. It may even take many jobs. But once you find your home, you'll know it. You'll thrive. And you'll create the type of advertising you've always wanted to create.

That's one major lesson we can learn by looking at Roy Grace's career. But that's not all. You'll also learn some of the creative problem solving methods of a truly original personality.

Roy was always interested in doing creative things. His passion was ignited for what he calls a very shallow reason: It stole attention away from his bright older sister. "When I was very young—about five—I drew Donald Duck and my mother and father oohed and ahhed," he recalls. "From that moment on, I knew art was for me."

His schooling reinforced this interest in art. In grammar school, the academic subjects bored him. And like any bored but bright child, he got into trouble. School officials constantly sent for his parents. The only subject he excelled in was art, which prompted his teachers to recommend he apply to the High School of Art and Design (then known as the School of Industrial Art).

It was not something he'd considered, but it seemed interesting, so he applied. To his astonishment—he felt that others taking the entrance exam were more talented—he was accepted by the school.

Bored by the academics and teachers, he became the class clown. He constantly made wisecracks and acted inappropriately. Once, for instance, he covered his entire face with loose-leaf paper reinforcements. "Let's put it this way," he said, "I certainly wasn't voted the most likely to succeed."

What Grace did learn from a very young age was "craft." Throughout his education, he constantly worked with his hands, learning many different techniques and, more important, learning how to visualize. He studied printing, photography, three-dimensional design, and paper sculpturing. He learned chiseling, lettering, retouching, drafting, cartooning—every subject aligned with the commercial arts.

"It gave me a sampling of what was in the real world," said Grace. In addition, by gaining knowledge of these things and practicing them, he learned other forms of visual communication.

"I really prepared for the 14th century," said Grace, something he sees as a plus. He explains: "Kids aren't prepared for the 20th century or the 21st century. There are certain things to know, and I'm not talking about the concrete production of an ad. I'm talking about knowing how to approach problems on an intellectual level. They don't seem able to do this."

At 17, when he graduated from high school, he was ready to work and interested in making money. He didn't know what he wanted to do, outside of the fact that it should be something to do with art or illustration.

His job search strategy consisted of looking at building directories to find the advertising agencies and studios and then going up to the receptionists and announcing he wanted a job. "It was awful," said Grace. "That entire summer of 1954, I remember literally walking the streets, getting depressed, and being discouraged by employment agencies because they said I needed this and that."

A Perfectionist Learns His Craft

Finally, through a friend of his father, he learned about Famous Studios, the East Coast division of Paramount Studios. They produced all the animation for the Paramount cartoons—Popeye, Tubby, Baby Huey, Tom and Jerry, Little Lulu, Casper the Friendly Ghost—and ran it like an assembly line. First, an animator made the initial drawings. Then an "in-betweener" drew the rest. Next, an inker took these drawings and, after following a series of preparatory steps, traced them with a fine quill pen. Finally, an opaquer painted the figures. The studio gave Grace a job as an apprentice inker.

At first, he thought he could never do the job, but he turned out to be a natural. An inker had to produce 60 to 80 frames a day. Grace would produce nearly 120.

More importantly, he learned that often a task that looks impossible, with enough practice and determination, becomes a piece of cake. "It taught me that there's no challenge too great," he said. "You just have to make up your mind you're going to do it. And not run, but attack."

But it wasn't long before he grew bored and restless, so he quit. "I was never good at finding another job before leaving one," he says. "I was very impulsive."

At that point, Grace wanted to become an illustrator. To do this he needed more education, so he began taking night classes at the School of Visual Arts. But these courses did not put him any closer to developing a career goal. Instead, Grace learned that illustration might not be the best thing for him.

At the same time, he had begun working at studios as a messenger. He thought this was a great way to learn key lining and paste-up. He planned to work his way into a bullpen. "Sometimes they gave me a break and let me clean the rubber cement off the mechanicals," he said. "But nobody would ever teach me."

With his career stalled and people being drafted, Grace and a group of his friends decided to enlist. Ironically, he became an illustrator in the army, drawing tactical equipment in a little Washington, D.C., spy unit. He'd get blurred photographs taken from a moving car along with sketches of machines and weapons. He was supposed to interpret them, but he didn't. Without an engineering or military background to understand the photos and sketches, he'd make things up. "I'd put a bolt on it if it looked good," said Grace. "I wish I had those drawings. They were really nice. Again, I kind of taught myself and had 18 months of practice. So I got pretty good at it."

When Grace was discharged from the army, he landed his first big job. The studio made packaging mechanicals, the most precise and, thus, most difficult kind of mechanicals because dies were cast from them. Since he had never done them before, he lied to get the job. "I was heading into deep, deep trouble," he said.

Within a few months, Grace was fired. "I felt awful," he said. "I was devastated. Nobody likes to be told they're inadequate. But I couldn't do it. It was really more than I could manage at that point." (Note: This happened in 1958, and the studio was still in existence when Grace was voted into the Art Director's Hall of Fame in 1986. At the induction ceremony a man came up to Grace and said, "You're not the same Roy Grace that..." and Grace said, "You fired over 20 years ago." The man responded, "We should have kept you.")

Not to be discouraged, Grace went to another studio, one where the work wasn't as precise. The new skills he'd learned in his previous job made him a star. He liked that. But after two months, he asked for a raise because of his rise in status. When they said no, he quit. From there followed jobs at studio after studio, as well as at a printer—they offered a layout, mechanical, and printing for the price of printing alone anywhere else—and at a now-defunct trade publisher.

At the same time, he went back to school—Cooper Union—studying at night. "This really opened up the world for me," said Grace. "It all came together. Everything just kind of lit up for me. I began to understand thinking and concepts."

Entering the World of Advertising

One teacher, an art director/supervisor at Benton & Bowles, offered Grace a job as an apprentice. This was approximately his 25th job. "I knew nothing about advertising at all," said Grace. "It wasn't my goal. In fact, I fought it for years. It felt kind of crass to me."

He continues, "I really wanted to become a graphic designer. I wanted to design posters, book jackets, record albums. I liked the feeling of graphic design. The two dimensionality of it. The elegance and aloofness of it."

Grace admired the work of Paul Rand, particularly his book jackets, and Rand's innovative logos such as IBM's. He didn't realize that this great designer was also working in advertising with Bill Bernbach.

Back then, the creative revolution was just beginning. People were doing things that felt exciting and interesting to Grace, and he wanted to be part of it. A creative director at Benton & Bowles was trying to get the agency to join the creative revolution and had hired such future creative leaders as Amil Gargano and Ed McCabe. "This guy tried," said Grace, "but management wasn't ready for it."

At this point, Grace's portfolio contained more ideas than completed ads. "What I wanted to do was demonstrate my thinking and my ability to be graphically inventive, which, by the way, is what's missing from art directors' books today."

Grace defined graphic invention as "finding a new page." It's laying out the ad a little differently, doing something that's never been done before, finding a way to graphically communicate the idea rather than expressing it verbally.

Grace took to advertising very quickly. Within six months, he went from an apprentice to working on national campaigns. He was a "star" again. Then a photo rep suggested he send his portfolio to Grey Advertising. He doubled his salary.

Grey was frustrating. Immediately, they had him working on television commercials. He'd never art directed television before, and he was in over his head. But he hung in there. He learned, for example, that with print, you work in space, and with television, you work in time.

"You learn by doing," he recalled. "That's the best teacher in the world. Also, you learn by failing. Nobody does anything that's an immediate success."

His first commercials were for Pampers. "Thank God, I blotted them from my mind. From P&G's point of view, they were a resounding success," he said. "From my point of view, they were a resounding failure. These were the old style of commercial—babies in diapers and side-by-side faucets. You know, one diaper absorbs. And the other doesn't."

To the Promised Land...

After more than 27 jobs—quite a lot for a 26-year-old—Grace went to Doyle Dane Bernbach. He stayed for 23 years. His portfolio was filled with roughs for ads he wanted to do that had been killed at either Grey or Benton & Bowles.

"I had produced some ads," said Grace. "But in my book, I basically had spec. They [DDB] wanted to see how I thought."

Grace had wanted to work at DDB "for a long time." But he was afraid to apply because he thought they wouldn't hire him. He didn't want his fears confirmed.

As he explains it, "I didn't know what I would do if I couldn't work there because I felt there was no place else for me to work."

To avoid rejection, he kept stalling. He'd promise himself to do one more ad to make his portfolio better. "I probably stalled for six months, which is an eternity for me," he said. "I usually do things pretty quickly.

"Finally, I took a deep breath and sent the book. I didn't present it. They wouldn't see people. Books were lined up by the thousands. Everybody wanted to work there. And, amazingly, they called me."

DDB offered him a job for less than he was earning. "Everybody who went to work there at that time had to take a cut," he recalls. "That was part of it. But I refused. And they hired me anyway. I couldn't have been happier. It was as if I had died and gone to heaven. To be working at Doyle Dane Bernbach was like being on the 1927 Yankees. They were hot. There was no other place at that point."

Grace was nervous about refusing to take the pay cut, but he had already begun to understand a hiring pattern at the agencies. "When I went to Benton & Bowles, they asked me to step into a room, figure out my expenses, and tell them the least amount I could possibly live on," he said. "I did a very honest evaluation, and they offered me less. Then when I went to Grey, they offered me a certain amount, but the day I started, they tried to give me a pay cut because they just lost an account. I decided to be obstinate. And it worked."

After bouncing through so many jobs, what kept Grace at DDB?

Simple. His ideas were produced.

"All the stuff I had been trying to do at the other agencies found a life there," he said. "I was allowed an enormous amount of freedom from virtually the first day I walked in. They let me be on my own. It was very loose, and I liked that."

Bumps in the Road

Grace's 23 years at DDB were not always smooth sailing. And he strayed twice from the fold. The first and most instructive time was shortly after DDB opened their first office in Germany. They asked Grace to create some Volkswagen ads for the German market. He did, and they were so well received by Bernbach, DDB decided to run some of them in the States and offered him the job of Co-creative Director of the German office.

To Grace, it seemed like a great opportunity—here was a chance to be a creative director just two-and-a-half years after beginning as an apprentice. So he jumped at the chance and went to Germany. He agreed to go for three years, but after less than six months, he knew he had to return. "I just felt I was out of the business," he said. "The creative revolution was happening in the States, and I was in a backwater. And with DDB growing, I was afraid they wouldn't take me back."

Around that time, Wells, Rich, Greene was becoming a hot agency, and he'd received an offer from them. So he figured he'd work there and went back to New York without telling anyone. "I was still a little crazy," said Grace. "I had a girlfriend (now my wife), and I holed up in her apartment.

"Bill Bernbach called me there and said he wanted to talk. I was shocked he would call. He said, 'Look, we want you. If you don't like it there, we understand, just go back and stay there a little longer until we can find a replacement.' I was so floored by the generosity, in view of the fact that I did not fulfill my agreement, that I felt incredibly obligated to him."

Even though the job at WRG was for considerably more money, Grace returned to Germany for a few more months. Then when he came back to the States, he went back to being Art Director/Group Supervisor at DDB/New York.

Lessons Learned

What did Bernbach do to instill this loyalty? Grace said it was because he loved doing great advertising. "With most agencies back then, management was crusty, cynical, and narrow-minded. You'd have to bludgeon, sneak, and manipulate an ad into existence. Bernbach was open, exuberant, and encouraging. And he loved what you loved. The work coming out of the agency showed that."

Of his working relationship with Bernbach, Grace said, "I always wanted to please him. There was no doubt about that. When you brought an ad or commercial to him and he liked it, his level of enthusiasm was intoxicating. I was five years old again, drawing Donald Duck, and my mother and father were 'oohing' and 'ahhing.' There was that same elixir. I was getting respect and admiration from the best. What could be better than that? That seductive brew."

He also enjoyed learning about new businesses. "You can find yourself in the middle of the desert in the Southwest, in a factory in Yugoslavia, in a balloon in Morocco," he said. "And you're studying some esoteric part of something you didn't even know existed six months before."

Ultimately, Grace worked his way up to Chairman of DDB. But this didn't mean much to him. "You know what it meant?" he asked. "It meant the same thing it meant when you were a kid: that somebody else didn't get it. It pulled me away from what I really liked to do, which was the advertising. It got me more and more involved in the management, and that's one of the reasons I quit. I just wanted to get back to advertising."

Grace also quit because he felt the agency had changed when it went public. "Instead of wanting to be the best," said Grace, "DDB wanted to be the biggest." He says this change in emphasis took place slowly.

A final reason—and the driving force behind his leaving all his previous jobs— he felt he no longer could do his best work. "I just felt very frustrated," he said. "And that same feeling led me to quit every single job I've ever had."

A Clean Slate—and His Name on the Door

Grace founded his new agency in 1986 with writer Diane Rothschild, who was a creative director at DDB. One day, after a particularly frustrating meeting, he asked her if she'd like to go into business with him. She said, "Sure."

They opened their doors without a client. Grace felt he shouldn't solicit any of DDB's clients. "Because of my position as chairman," he said, "I didn't think it was ethical."

In addition, he wanted a clean slate. His last year at DDB had been a difficult one. He didn't want to carry any of that baggage with him. "I really wanted to let the scar tissue heal as much as possible," he said. "And take a fresh new look at things."

Grace and Rothschild began with five people and a willingness to "wait and see what happened." He and his partner built the company up to 100 employees and $160 million billings by developing groundbreaking work.

And into the Sunset...

Then in May of 2000, he retired. "I just walked away, because that's what I wanted to do," he said. He didn't want to sell or merge his agency, because if he did, he'd have had to make a commitment to stay with the newly formed entity for a minimum of three years. "I just got sick of sitting in meetings and nothing ever happening, just talking and very little doing," he said. "I got sick of the business aspect of the agency, constantly chasing clients that, ultimately, I really didn't even want. I just found that the whole nature of the business had changed dramatically from when I really enjoyed it." He also felt that after being in the business for more than 40 years, the fire went out. "It got to be awfully repetitive," he said.

Diane Rothschild merged the agency with Jerry Della Femina, and she retired late in 2002.

After leaving Grace & Rothschild, Roy did some consulting as well as a small amount of lecturing at such East-coast schools as Syracuse University and at a few ad agencies, including Young & Rubicam. "I enjoyed it to some degree," he said, "but not enough to really pursue it."

He also spent his time sculpting, carving, painting, playing tennis, and reading. "I'm into doing a lot of stuff with my hands," he said—still a craftsman. "I had a show, and much to my surprise I sold some of my work," he said. "But then I got too intense about it and started thinking of turning it into a business, and I found I wasn't enjoying it so I passed, and I'm just really doing it for myself now."

He found that he enjoyed retirement. "There's a whole other world outside of advertising," he said. "Advertising was something I was intensely involved in and something I truly loved. And I've found that I was able to move that interest and energy into other areas."

Unfortunately, he developed prostrate cancer, something he reportedly kept from his friends in the industry, and just three years into his retirement, Roy Grace left us—with great sadness and many words in his behalf from an industry that appreciated his talent and dedication.

He is survived by a wife of 37 years as well as a son and daughter. Both of his children work in the visual arts, one designing computer graphics and the other designing window displays.

A PORTFOLIO FILLED WITH GRACE

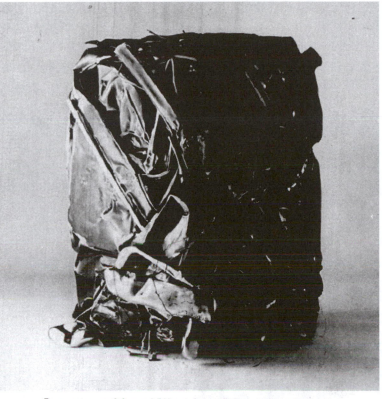

Every now and then a VW runs into a little trouble at the factory.

That hunk of junk was well on its way to becoming a Volkswagen, when it ran into a stone wall; a bunch of hard-nosed inspectors who pull enough parts off the line every day to make the equivlent of 20 cars.

Or 2 freight cars full of scrap.

There are thousands of inspectors who literally pick every Volkswagen to pieces every step of the way.

If there's a little scratch in a fender, it gets scratched. If there's a little nick in a bumper, it gets bumped.

Wherever ten people are doing something, there's an inspector to undo it. For the paint job alone, no less than 8 inspectors check every VW.

All that inspection doesn't mean the work isn't done carefully. The men who make the VW make it very well. The inspectors just make it perfect.

—— VOLKSWAGEN ——

Roy Grace worked on Volkswagen advertising for 20 years. The overriding strategy was that Volkswagen was a smart buy—aren't you smart to buy one?

Grace's paraphrase of the strategy was "Look at those dummies. They have to put a lot more money in the gas tank, and they get stuck in the snow. It was really a smart buy." He didn't know if anyone ever wrote out that strategy. "But that's what it turned out to be," he says. "We just did it unconsciously."

The first ads in the campaign were done by legendary art director Helmut Krone. Two of Grace's ads, the one that began this chapter and the one shown above, were among those that caught Bernbach's attention, prompting Grace's promotion and transfer to Germany.

For a later example of Volkswagen advertising, take a look at Ted Bell's portfolio.

IBM

AND

AMERICAN TOURISTER

In these ads, the visuals expressed the idea and the headlines simply commented on it.

For example, with American Tourister, the visual communicates the suitcase's strength much more than any headline can. Back when he created the ads, that style was new and inventive.

Grace saw the need for graphic invention in a beginner's portfolio. "You can see it in virtually any good ad," he said. "But I can't show something new to explain it because, by definition, it hasn't been done yet."

—— Volkswagen ——

Here's another commercial art-directed by Roy Grace that used unexpected humor—and a taboo for car advertising. Much like today, the other carmakers of the time were focusing on performance and prestige, but Grace took a different tack. Notice how this innovative, slice-of-life spot reinforced Volkswagen's message that it was a smart buy. To see the entire spot, go to www.adbuzz.com.

Male Voice Over: *I, Maxwell E. Snavely, being of sound mind and body, do bequeath the following:*

To my wife, Rose, who spent money like there was no tomorrow, I leave $100 and a calendar.

To my son, Rodney, who spent every dime I ever gave him on fancy cars and fast women, I leave $50... in dimes.

To my business partner, Jules, whose motto was "spend, spend, spend," I leave nothing, nothing, nothing.

Finally, to my nephew, Harold, who oft time said, "A penny saved is a penny earned."

And who also oft time said, "Gee, Uncle Max, it sure pays to own a Volkswagen..."
I leave my entire fortune of $100 billion.

—— J & B ——

"We were looking for something young and contemporary so we could shed J & B's old fuddy-duddy image."

Grace recalls, "We were to replace a campaign that featured a bottle of J & B, a sword, a dragoon helmet, and some lead soldiers. We knew we wanted it to be fresh, a little bit disarming, and a little bit wacky.

"We were looking for something that had a lot of 'legs' so we could do a lot of ads from it (this is critical to Grace in his approval of a campaign). So we put it through all those filters, and we thought along very precise lines."

Grace said he tried to stay away from puns in headlines. "I do visual puns," he said. "I hate puns, and I've always stayed away from them. For me, they're a cheap shot. But J & B seemed so wacky, so overdone, and so excessive that it seemed appropriate for the audience we were trying to reach.

"The frightening thing is, visual puns seemed to have caught on, and I see more and more campaigns based on them."

—— ALKA-SELTZER ——

"It's amazing, wherever I go, this one comes up, and it begins to become something I want to escape from," said Grace.

It was the first to have a commercial within a commercial. While many argued that this ad didn't help sell the product, it is now in the Museum of Modern Art and the Clio Hall of Fame. In fact, it was voted the best commercial of the last 25 years.

Of its creation, Grace said, "We were looking for situations where you're forced to overeat. We were working under the rule that you could not show a glutton in a commercial. Our own experience in food shoots—where you're forced to eat stuff for hours—was a funny, interesting idea."

—— RANGE ROVER ——

You typically buy a jeep for about $16,000 or $18,000. How do you justify buying what is essentially a $40,000 jeep? And how do you communicate that on a very small budget?

"We had to create an aura of something really special," he says. "There was a slow hammering out of the strategy with the client."

The first ad consisted of a big, white Range Rover covered in mud on a white page. The headline was simple counterpoint—"Introducing the most beautiful vehicle in the world."

Precisely how sturdy is a Range Rover?

No this sturdy.
Ten tons of careening boulder would undoubtedly turn even a Range Rover into a convertible.

Short of such an inconvenience, however, you can reasonably expect a Range Rover to bear up under some considerably unreasonable conditions.

In fact, with features like a 14-gauge steel chassis and welded frame, Range Rovers routinely survive not merely for

decades, but for decades in jungles, deserts and the cold tundra.

So it's hardly surprising that Range Rovers here hold up so well they retain

their value better than a host of comparable cars. Including some with names like BMW and Mercedes.

And even at a starting price just under $39,000, that makes Range Rover one of the smartest investments on the road. Or off it.

Why not call 1-800-FINE-4WD for a dealer near you?

After all, when it comes to building an uncommonly strong vehicle, we leave no stone unturned.

RANGE ROVER

"Nobody had ever introduced a new car with a speck of dust on it, let alone dripping with dirt," says Grace. "I thought it was really revolutionary for the client to accept it and encourage it." That's partially what Grace was talking about when he mentioned the need to be graphically inventive. Today, however, it's common to see SUVs covered in mud. So to show mud on a vehicle would no longer be graphically inventive. The goal would now be to find something else that was never shown—or to express the message in a new way.

As for this ad, it shows what Grace called the "one plus one equals what" process. "The picture is one, the headline is one, and the reader is forced to come up with two," he said. "The information is communicated to you in a more profound way, because you're the one who comes up with the solution. Nobody told you that it was the strongest one on the road."

To sum up the overall campaign, Grace said, "We just looked for dramatic ways to express the strategy to show that Range Rover was the best off-road vehicle in the world and was also a luxury car."

Who says that a product demonstration has to be boring?

Grace and his writing partner found a new, irreverent way to demonstrate the strength of this product.

"I look for fresh solutions," said Grace. He would rather have hired people who are in danger of being absolutely wrong than being timidly right. "There are so many ads that are okay and nice and it's hard to find something wrong to say about them," he said, "but the ads that are exceptional are usually a little irreverent, foolish, or dangerous. Some even cross the line and get the creative in trouble with a client. Exceptional advertising is like walking a very delicate tightrope, but if you don't have the courage to take a chance, you'll be doing mundane work forever."

At the same time, Grace recognized that a new idea now would be an old one by tomorrow. "When anybody has a new idea, it's co-opted and becomes common," he said.

THREE PAGES OF ADVICE BASED ON
THIRTY YEARS OF ADVERTISING EXPERIENCE

When Grace left the ad industry, he didn't like the direction it was going. "You'd often find yourself in a room with somebody who just took a course in marketing and they had no idea what they were talking about.

"I found that there were a lot of clients who had little or no respect for the power of advertising. They basically didn't have an understanding of how useful a tool it could be to change people's minds, to move them, to motivate, persuade, and, ultimately, to have them try your product."

Unlike Hayden (see Chapter 3) and others, Grace also believed that the growth of promotions and integrated brand marketing took the focus off the more powerful aspects of advertising.

"When you think of consumer advertising, you think primarily of television," said Grace. "And television is theater. It's entertainment. Because of that, I think that it just carries more weight, more excitement, and more sex appeal."

He also recognized that the economy during the George W. Bush administration was clouding his views. "Whenever you have an economy like we have now, which is obviously not a good one, not a rich and vibrant and positive atmosphere, you have a pull that affects advertising.

"It happens in many different ways, but on a basic, human level, you have clients whose business is not good. Therefore they're less adventurous and more conservative, and I think that has an enormous effect on the level of creativity that you see."

Grace believed the result was more people in the industry who were less visionary. "A climate like this favors people who, by definition, are more conservative. Agencies get scared and become more concerned with holding onto their business. This calls for people who are less willing to take risks, more eager to build secure relationships with clients than to create bold new frontiers."

This, however, should not affect the level of creativity you show in your portfolio. "I think I would still try and be as creative and bold as possible," he said. "I'd like to think that whoever you have to see, be accepted by, and, ultimately, be hired by would have the imagination and good sense to look for what is the best, rather than what is the safest."

Grace also saw the industry returning to more creative standards—but just not yet. "I don't think it's a closed door. I have to assume that human nature, invention, and imagination are still as valid today as they were yesterday," he said. "It's just maybe a period right now where we're not going to see anything as rich and imagined as we did maybe 35, 40, 25 years ago."

His overall advice then: "I think that you definitely have to come in as if creativity is still absolutely king." So how do you create a bold, new frontier? While Grace couldn't tell you exactly how (if he could, it wouldn't be fresh—or new), he gave you some ideas to start your thinking:

Forget advertising schools: Some schools are just factories, Grace believes. "You see the same ads from book to book, and you don't know who did what," he said. "It's a very hard job [teaching] not to fall into a rut, and I think some people have." And don't think that your portfolio will be lost in the shuffle because of your lack of school credentials. Grace said he would look at anybody's book.

Don't suffer for your craft: Grace doesn't believe in enduring miserable working conditions or long hours. "I believe in working hard," he said, "but doing it in a normal lifestyle. I like being home with my kids. I think I can count every weekend I've worked on one hand. Keep everything in perspective and have fun while working. And if it stops being fun, get out."

Run with your first idea: Grace believed that the first idea is usually the best. "I've never been one to dwell on a problem," he said. "If it takes three seconds to have an idea, it's too long. If it takes 30 seconds, I panic. I go, 'Oh my God; I'll never solve this.' I'm a student of the school that the solution should become apparent in one big explosion within the first few seconds. Once you understand the problem, the answer should be there."

Redefine the problem: "Sometimes this is the hardest, but the most important thing to do," said Grace. "Often, if you have difficulty solving a problem," he said, "it's the way that problem is defined that is creating the difficulty. By redefining it, you can understand it."

Research before you create: Grace encouraged research before production. "Research helps you paint a perfect target or, at least, a near perfect one," he said. But after production, Grace avoided it. "You're measuring, in essence, the immeasurable," he said. "There are just too many variables, too many unknowns. It's a waste of money and a waste of time. If it worked, I'd be the first to subscribe to it. There would be no failures in the marketplace."

Work in a fantasy world: "No person in his right mind is going to look at a beginner's solution and expect him or her to know the absolute, exact temperature of the marketplace," said Grace. "I saw many, many books where solutions didn't make sense because beginners didn't know the marketplace. But I didn't hold that against them. There was no way for them to really know. Within their defined world, their view made sense, and I accepted it."

Show it with attitude: Nowadays you'll hear a lot about attitude. Grace thought attitude was probably the latest version of image, or even position. And he defined it as the tonality you want to convey in an ad, the point of view.

"Attitude is maybe a little snottier than tonality, but essentially it comes down to the same thing," he said. "You have to have one voice—one tone—in a campaign. That voice has to be appropriate to the product. What's right for a J & B is certainly wrong for a Mount Sinai Hospital."

Learn to "dance": "Very few ads that come out and make a direct statement are good," said Grace. He believed direct headlines are good when you have something concrete to say, like announcing a cure for cancer. "You wouldn't want to play around with that," he said. "Because you really have something to say."

The rest of the time, Grace believed, you have to entertain. "With the vast majority of advertising, you don't have product superiority or real news," he said. "What you have to do is dance a little bit. Part of what you're selling is a good feeling about the product and a positive image of it."

Take calligraphy: Grace took years of calligraphy and found it forced him to think visually. "It teaches you about negative and positive shapes in a way that nothing else can," he said. "That's critical in designing a page. It helps you know how big a headline should be and how small the body copy could be."

Try humor: Grace felt that a commercial should be entertaining while conveying its message, which is why he used humor. "I think it really helps," he said.

"When I first started in the business, humor was a negative. People said funny advertising didn't work. Now, everybody tries to do it. But it's hard to do."

Believe in yourself: "I was fired three or four times in the beginning—once for turning over a pot of ink on my boss," said Grace. "If there's any message here, it's that if there's something you really want to do, and you really believe in it, persevere and it will happen. It really will. You've just got to keep hanging in there."

Use your skills elsewhere: An advertising background could help you in other occupations, such as sales promotions and other selling areas. "The skills may not manifest themselves immediately," said Grace. "You may not be creating advertising, but you are creating that same bond between a seller and a consumer. This may sound ludicrous, but one person I know went from being an art director in a large agency to running a birdseed store. Ultimately, what he does is sell. That's just where he wound up. I think a lot of people are winding up in positions like that, some form of marketing, which is not the sophisticated, electronic marketing they've known in the past, but still allows them to use a lot of their fundamental skills."

POSTSCRIPT 1:

HOW TO TELL A GOOD IDEA FROM A BAD ONE

There's no easy way to tell a good idea from a bad one. However, Grace developed a checklist that may help. He went through this list automatically and unconsciously. You may wish to eventually develop your own criteria; his list provides a great start. Here is his list and what he has to say about each point:

1. "Is it relevant to the product? Does it bear some relationship to the product?

2. "Is it the kind of idea that's never, ever been done before by anybody else for this category?

3. "Is it an idea you can do many variations of? Could it last for many years?

4. "Is it not only informative, but entertaining? People don't come home at night to watch commercials. And they don't open a magazine to read the ads. Does the message move you? Is it dramatic? Is it impactful? Will it attract somebody's attention?

5. "Does it make people think? That's critical. Do people participate in the ad? Do the little motors in their brain start running, so they're actually involved in the premise? And is it motivating and persuasive?

6. "Do I like it? If you like the advertising, there's a good chance the audience will like the product.

"*Finally*, when I first see it, do I get a tiny tingling in my stomach? Does it make me nervous? I like ads that make me nervous because they're a little dangerous and new. You don't get nervous when you're seeing something you've seen before.

"No doubt there's something you get from experience. When I was far less experienced, how did I know? It felt right. I could not articulate it, but it felt right. And I was prepared to logically defend every part of the ad. I asked myself: Why am I doing this? Why is the type so big? Why am I choosing this type? Why am I choosing this picture? Why is the headline expressed this way? Why is the copy like this?

"Feeling great is only the beginning. It's important that you're also able to logically justify your feelings. You know, it would feel great—probably—to walk out of the window of my office right now and fly down 20 stories. But when you hit bottom, it's not going to feel so good. That same process is in place when you create something.

"What I do is create the ad and then try to analyze why it works. You come up with something that just feels good to you, and then you investigate your premise. You check to see if it's right. Sometimes you go back and say this won't work. It doesn't make sense. Then you find a way to make it make sense."

Postscript 2:

MORE THOUGHTS ON GRAPHIC INVENTION

Throughout this chapter, we've talked about the need for graphic invention and that it is missing from most beginners' books. To help you understand what that means more fully, here are more thoughts from Roy Grace:

"The solution to most advertising problems is verbal. While I think that it is beginning to change with the advent of computer-based work, it's still true in that advertising is mostly a verbally dominated field. Most art directors come out of schools more as writers than art directors. That's because, in school, they're forced to think conceptually, which is fine. But they're also forced to think verbally rather than visually, which I think is horrible.

"In addition, art directors have to think executionally.

"Art direction is like running a little factory. You work with the writer to come up with the headline, you may come up with the idea, or you may even come up with all of it. But then you have to manufacture the product. To produce the ad. And that requires a lot of knowledge.

"Now, I've hired scores of young art directors out of school, and, believe me, it's astonishing to see how ill prepared they are to be art directors. They're good at thinking, but they're not able to put something down on a piece of paper that helps sell an idea. That's because they don't think visually any more. They think verbally. The whole revolution of the '60s was a revolution in thought. Art directors and writers sitting together and thinking has dominated so much that it's swept everything else aside.

"The other way of approaching it is to come up with the visual idea first. If you can come up with an arresting visual idea, you've got a leg up on the competition. And with the right visual idea, the headline writes itself. Take a look at the Range Rover ads.

"Or take a look at the J & B ads. They're not exactly the same as what I'm talking about. But they're close. Virtually every ad has a visual invention in it. They're pictorial creations, little visual puzzles. Not blatant black-and-white concrete, absolute statements. You're forced to participate in them, to come up with your own conclusions."

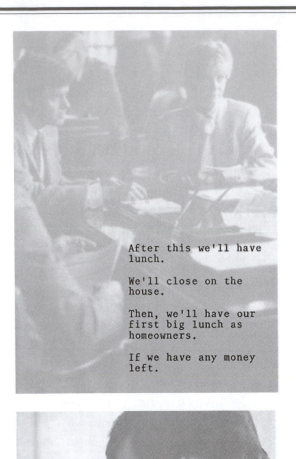

After this we'll have lunch.

We'll close on the house.

Then, we'll have our first big lunch as homeowners.

If we have any money left.

Margaret and Tom Fitzgerald
Age: 30, 31
Married; no children yet

Income
Combined Salaries ... $42,000
Bonus ... 2,000
... $44,000

Assets
Home Equity ... $20,000
Furniture, Misc. ... 10,000
Cash, Savings ... 8,400

Estimated Expenses
House Closing Costs ... $4,000
Mortgage, Property Tax, Insurance ... 10,000
Income Tax ... 9,200
Auto Loan and Insurance ... 2,400
Food, Clothing, Misc. ... 14,000
... $39,600

Needs
To protect housing investment
To develop a long-term investment strategy

Answers
John Hancock Homeowner's Insurance
John Hancock Universal Life
John Hancock IRAs
John Hancock Growth Trust

Tom and Margaret Fitzgerald closed on their house this morning. Their first house.

A short while later they talked to us to find out ways they might protect this investment and discover other investment options.

A John Hancock representative furnished them with the recommendations you see above. Maybe you'll see in the plan we described for them an opportunity for yourself.

Contact your nearest John Hancock representative for more information or a current prospectus.

Real life, real answers.

John Hancock
Financial Services

John Hancock Mutual Life Insurance Co., Boston, MA 02117, John Hancock Variable Life Insurance Co., John Hancock Property and Casualty Insurance Cos., John Hancock Advisers, Inc. /Stockbrokers, Inc.

I love you
little Jenny Katherine...

I want to tell you something
very, very important.
Daddy got a raise.

Bill Heater
Age 30
Married, two children

Income
Single income ... $35,000

Assets
Car, Furnishings, Etc. ... $9,000

Expenses
Income tax ... $8,500
Rent ... 8,500
Food, Clothing, Insurance ... 13,000
... $30,000

Needs
Long-term security for his family
To build investments

Answer
John Hancock Variable Life:
Life insurance with a range of investment options:

Stock Account   Total Return Account*
Bond Account   Aggressive Stock Account*
Money Market Account

Two things happened in Bill Heater's life which caused him to think about long-term security for his family and his opportunities for investment: the birth of his daughter and a raise in pay.

To satisfy both needs, he decided to buy an insurance policy. He wanted a plan, though, that would work hard for him. One that would provide both the security of life insurance and investment options.

A John Hancock representative recommended our Variable Life product. Not only does it guarantee a death benefit, it offers him the opportunity to make money on his policy through a variety of investment options. Furthermore, he can periodically change investments as his needs or market conditions change.

Perhaps you can identify with this situation or one similar to it. If you'd like more information about John Hancock Variable Life, including charges and expenses, please contact your John Hancock representative for a prospectus. Read it carefully before you invest or send money.

Real life, real answers.

John Hancock
Financial Services

John Hancock Variable Life Insurance Co., Boston, MA 02117 *Available April 1986.

Don Easdon

"A lot of creative people normally think a little off-center.

That's an asset."

"Good artists and writers have a unique point of view," says Don Easdon, President/Owner of Red Advertising in Boston and who, earlier in his career, reinvented the design language of advertising, particularly in the automotive and financial categories. He is always looking for fresh images and messages and has an ability to convey life in a way that is subtle, yet attention-getting. In this chapter, we will look at how you too can create unique work by drawing on a truly unique source—yourself.

In his more than 35 years in the industry, Easdon has created hundreds of commercials for such clients as John Hancock Financial Services, Charles Schwab, Anheuser Busch, Gillette, Dr. Pepper, Toshiba, and AT&T. His efforts have won him much industry recognition: ten awards at Cannes including four Gold Lions and a Grand Prix, eleven Clios, four One Show awards, and twelve Andys—to name a few.

But Easdon's career has had low points as well. Only dogged determination seems to propel him. "You get to the point where you'd die for your work. Nothing is more important," says Easdon calmly. "I'll be trying to make a certain thing happen. And, I will make it happen even though others don't think I will. You have to be naïve enough to keep positive; but if you lose that, you're dead."

CREATING A BIG BANG WITH A WHISPER

Easdon believes that there's a feeling of "sameness" to most advertising, a result of creative people following the industry's accepted "methodology." "There's a certain way to write headlines," he says, "and a certain way to compose layouts."

But how do you learn to break away from this and create truly unique advertising? He suggests you look inward. "It really does come out of your personality," he says. "As soon as you put away the award books, you usually do great work. And you really stand out."

To fully understand this view, let's look at Easdon's career. His big bang began with a chirp—his fourth grade teacher asked the class to draw spring birds and her reaction to his bird was so positive he was inspired to become an artist.

Fearing that he wouldn't make money as an artist, he decided to study architecture. But while attending the University of Connecticut, he got a job in the school's promotion department. He enjoyed this and changed his career plans again, this time deciding to become a designer. He put together a portfolio of mostly design work, though it included a campaign for Webster's Dictionary. He designed the ads with plenty of white space, a small picture of a dictionary in the corner, and an enlarged definition from the book. Since the editors had taken a progressive approach and included the word "ain't" in the dictionary, Easdon showed an enlarged definition of this word, with the headline, "Dictionaries ain't what they used to be." Says Easdon, "My first book was really naïve."

But he never had to use his book because in his senior year, one of the promotion pieces he created for the university caught the eye of someone in New England's largest agency, Wilson, Haight & Welch in Hartford.

"All those horrible projects no one else wanted."

He was hired as an assistant art director and was teamed with the then-assistant copywriter Ted Bell (Chapter 4), also in his first job. "I worked on all those horrible projects no one else wanted," recalls Easdon. "I did ads for crutch tips—those little rubber tips on the bottom of crutches—and ostomy bags." Those ads gave him a chance to learn production and type. "You don't get the glamorous assignments when you start."

Easdon's career developed quickly. After a year at this agency, he was hired away by an agency in Providence, Rhode Island, because—like his first job offer—someone there had seen his work. "Like so many agencies," muses Easdon, "you had to work at this place to be able to remember its name."

But he yearned to be in New York. And, from the shop in Providence, he got his chance. He moved to what he calls the "Korean War of advertising"—a small New York agency. He should have suspected the job wouldn't be easy when the man who hired him quit on his first day. Easdon felt as if he'd been left to the wolves. Working on GAF film, Maidenform, Jean Nate, and a host of Bristol-Meyer antiperspirants, Easdon functioned as an "idea factory" in a "workaholic" environment. "It was creative direction through intimidation," he recalls. "Management tore boards up in front of you."

"The only thing that keeps you sane."

With tight deadlines and the bulk of his work being for television, Easdon was forced to learn how to draw storyboards quickly. Since one art director there was able to produce them with very little effort, Easdon studied his technique. "He'd draw cartoon figures and put a couple of dots down for eyes," says Easdon. "Then he'd draw a nose, go on to the tie, and sketch in the hands." This disconnected way of drawing worked for Easdon. "I started drawing this way, and now I can crank out a storyboard in a few minutes—and draw it pretty well—where it would have originally taken me half a day to draw it."

To maintain his sanity, Easdon did a tremendous amount of freelancing. "It's the only thing that keeps you sane while you're doing junk," he says. "It gives you the control that creative people want out of life." One of his accounts was a store in Connecticut called the Common Market. A pre-famous Martha Stewart worked there in the food department. For one project, he pitched Ralph Lauren and did some work with him. Easdon still recalls these early freelance campaigns with fondness. Meanwhile, he learned like crazy, perfecting his graphic design and production skills. Says Easdon, "People today don't put in their time to learn the basic skills."

Winner—"Ad of the Month"

Easdon left this shop to take on a short-term job at another agency, and after three months, he sent his book to Young & Rubicam/New York, where he was hired as a junior art director. Eager to do great work, he went to his creative director three times a day and said he'd be happy to work on anything. The creative director respected his initiative and rewarded him with a choice assignment—a double-page print ad promoting Puerto Rican tourism. Almost immediately, he and a photographer headed for Puerto Rico.

But Easdon was apprehensive. The shoot was very expensive, and, like Koelker with the 501 campaign, he was unclear about what he'd need. He planned to crop the shots into narrow vertical strips of images no deeper than an inch. Easdon had the photographer shoot and crossed his fingers. Then he planned to take the pictures, blow them up, and arrange them into the vertical scheme. He could only go by instinct to know if it was working or not. If it didn't work, he felt he'd be looking for a new job. But he found wonderful slices, put them together, and created an innovative, provocative ad. It won "Ad of the Month" at Y&R. Ironically, the prize was a trip to Puerto Rico—where he'd been every week since he started his job.

But while he gained recognition at Y&R, he lacked an understanding of the importance of concept and strategy. "I came into the business as a designer," Easdon says. "I was more interested in how it looked." This insight came to him in London during a long shoot for a Dr. Pepper campaign. "At the time, it was the largest production in Europe outside of a movie—like $3 million for eight spots," he recalls. "It was a big deal."

The $100,000 Fake Cherry Tree

One of the commercials he was shooting was supposed to look like an old Japanese Kung Fu movie, and dialog was in Japanese. He brought in workmen from Japan to create an ancient Japanese-style house and had them burn the floor and then wax and buff it—just "the way it had been done in Japan." He even spent nearly $100,000 on a fake cherry tree for the set. "It was an unbelievably beautiful set," he recalls. "I was so detailed—so anal—about making it real."

Easdon was checking the set for accuracy when his boss and a senior creative director at Y&R, Lou DeJoseph, told him to calm down and focus on the idea. Recalls Easdon: "He said, 'Don't look at the details. What we're doing is a very unusual commercial. It's very different, very individual. We're not doing a Coke commercial. Dr. Pepper people tend to be very different drinkers, and that's the idea of the spot.'"

"So it's not really about the Japanese?" Easdon asked. When his boss answered, "No," he realized that much of his energy was being spent in the wrong place. After that, he started to focus more time on the idea. "I had done all of the commercials," he says. "I had come up with them, but I never quite understood the simplicity of the idea. I was so much into the execution that I just glossed over it."

"Once I put myself in the position of the customer, I did better work."

Easdon's new center of attention was reinforced when the senior account team on Gillette encouraged him to work with research people. "These really brilliant people would come at it from a totally different side," he says. "It was all about how people felt. I think that formed me more than anything else. Once I put myself in the position of the customer, I did better work." That process also helped him see that his own feelings weren't entirely unique. "I realized that if I followed my feelings, I could anticipate trends," he says.

As a result of his work on Puerto Rican tourism, Right Guard and other Gillette products, Dr. Pepper (for which he won his first Clio), and other accounts, Easdon was promoted to associate creative director.

A Big Fish in a Small Pond

But then after 12 years at Y&R, the lack of greater advancement opportunity dictated that he move on. The highest position he felt he could achieve at Y&R was group creative director. "I'd decided to be a big fish in a small pond. I'd gotten divorced and wanted a different kind of lifestyle away from New York." Hill, Holliday, Connors, Cosmopulos (HHCC), a small but significant agency in Boston, offered a position as an Executive Vice President, Creative Director, which he understood to imply hands-off, high-level decision making. But the long title didn't accurately portray the position. HHCC gave everybody big creative director titles and put emphasis on creating ideas, not managing others. And the creatives lived and died by their work.

Easdon's first assignment was to pitch John Hancock. "I killed for that category because my father had been assistant chairman of the board, executive vice president at Equitable Life Insurance. He died young as a white-collar grunt. In my mind, I was doing the campaign for him," he says.

"Why can't we do that?"

"I remember when the idea for Hancock clicked," recalls Easdon. "I was watching a TV documentary about a women's band. But I was thinking about Hancock and realized I was stimulated by the style of the documentary. I thought, 'Why can't we do that?' At that point, 'slice-of-life' advertising had bad connotations. But I thought the commercials could be done in a documentary style."

Easdon's creative partner, however, presented a stumbling block. "He was an ex-DDB guy, and when I presented the ideas, he'd play back something from the awards books. Everything was within the confines of that box. It had to be from the awards books. So I couldn't do anything fresh with the guy." Frustrated, he started working by himself. But he needed the help of a copywriter.

"A good partnership is 80 percent chemistry and 120 percent respect."

One day, Easdon wandered into Bill Heater's office. Heater was working as a technical writer. "He stood about 6'5", wore a big lumberjack shirt and a full scraggly beard, and never said a word," says Easdon. "Secretaries would walk into the elevator and take one look at Heater and walk out, but he wouldn't hurt a flea." Heater listened to Easdon's complaints and then asked about his idea. Easdon started talking but then walked away after Heater's phone rang.

Four hours later, Heater came into Easdon's office and threw down a piece of green paper. "Green was his trademark," says Easdon. "Everyone has their little affectations." On the paper was a rough of how the copy might work.

It was the beginning of the campaign. Easdon realized he could do the kind of work he wanted if he could work with Heater. So, he went to management to ask to change partners. They listened and things started clicking. "That's the difference between having a bad partner and a good partner," he says. "You really need someone who listens and you in turn can listen to. A good partnership is 80 percent chemistry and 120 percent respect."

When the Hancock campaign came out, it signaled a new approach. "It was the beginning of my creating a more respectful brand of advertising. It was quiet, a bit intense, and, hopefully, intelligent," he says. "And, I tried to make everything seem fresh—every element." He isn't sure how this "quiet" approach originated. "I just like very subtle, unobtrusive things—something that is a little more human, approachable and respectful of viewers' intellect. I don't like advertising that is in my face and tries to 'sell' me. I grew up with repetitive advertising and annoying jingles [of the '50s]. It put a bad face on advertising."

The Hancock account gave Easdon the credibility he wanted. He won the Cannes Film Festival, Grand Prix, as well as many other awards. The agency built off that success and doubled their billings. It was his first big success.

With Easdon's newfound status—he followed up the Hancock campaign with a groundbreaking campaign for Wang—and his agency's committed strategic team, he was asked to help Nissan introduce a new luxury car brand to America—Infiniti. Instead of introducing the car with an attitude of arrogance typical of the category, Easdon wanted to create a sense of "specialness" for the new brand. The team looked at every element of traditional car advertising. "It was zero-based advertising," he says of this controversial campaign. "Instead of sitting down to design ads and write headlines—the methodology of the business—we asked ourselves: 'What is a car beyond styling?' and 'What is a luxury car experience?' We started at the beginning and even questioned the concept of luxury. What is luxury?"

Easdon wasn't allowed to look at the car before he created the campaign. Yet everything he had heard about the experience of the new car sold him. He decided to use the same approach. To do that, he compared the Infiniti's experience to nature. "I never looked at it as a teaser campaign like the rest of the world did," he says. "I'm very happy with the result. It created a car brand with a personality that was true to the Japanese spirit—yet relevant to Americans."

In addition, while many people in the ad industry disliked, and even mocked, the campaign, several polls reported it to be among the most well-known campaign of the '80s. Still talked about today in the ad industry, it continues to influence the langauge and style of luxury car advertising.

"The toughest job I ever had."

In his four-and-a-half years at HHCC, Easdon did exactly 156 commercials. He then freelanced and thought about starting his own agency. But in 1991, he was asked to join Backer Spielvogel Bates (BSB) in New York, whose forerunner (the old Ted Bates agency), ironically, created much of the repetitive advertising of the '50s. The offer: To become the agency's Executive Vice-President, Executive Creative Director and help turn around their fortunes. The agency had already lost several accounts and many more were on their way out. After his arrival, the client exodus stopped—even keeping one that was about to walk out the door—and the agency won a few new accounts.

However, he was unhappy at BSB and only stayed for two years. "It was probably the toughest job I ever had," he says. " I didn't feel creatively fulfilled. I'm not like a lot of creative directors who are good with the story and can take over a conversation in a big room. I tend to be a little bit more introspective."

He claims he's much better one on one. "But if I know everybody in the room I'm pretty comfortable. When I was working at HHCC, I would sit in the room with 20 people and it felt like I was having a one-on-one conversation because I knew everybody." He relates this back to being insecure. "A lot of creative people are," he says. "I am more comfortable if my work precedes me. Then I feel like I've made my statement through my art, my work, and that becomes my strength."

Red

When he left BSB, he landed a freelance project from Y&R for AT&T.

He then formed an agency in Boston with his old writing partner and landed Anheuser Busch and several other well-known accounts. The agency, Heater Easdon, was off to a promising start. But after a falling out with Heater and a divorce from his second wife, he resigned, moved to the West Coast, and started over. He named the new agency "Red" after his father's nickname and got Charles Schwab as an account. "I was at the bottom, owing money," he says. "And I end up getting one of the biggest and most lucrative accounts of the time."

But he found himself commuting to Boston to see a girlfriend. "It was very difficult. I was either flying to see her or she was flying to see me," he says. "And it was very expensive." As luck would have it, the chance to move back to that area soon presented itself. His former account partner, Steven Gugio, called and asked if Easdon would be interested in returning to his old agency.

Easdon was not comfortable with returning to his old place, but if they opened a Red Advertising office in Boston—"So we'd be on both coasts"—he'd move. Gugio agreed and under the Red banner, they took over existing accounts and picked up additional work. Easdon eventually severed ties with Red's West Coast office. "My partner out there and I split everything."

While he's been able to land new business on this side, Easdon recognizes that the ad industry is going through a tough time right now. "It's the worst I've ever seen it," he says. "Creatively, it's just boring. I don't even watch TV anymore. There isn't a lot that's fresh. And that's really too bad."

"You get it visually. Then you read it."

To keep his work fresh, Easdon applies personal impressions and experiences. "I used to talk about the design being more of a frame for the message," he says. "But now, it's less. Now I tend to go right to the emotion. You get it visually. Then you read it. I think this way is much more involving. And I'm doing a lot more print advertising than before. It's been fun, but it's also been necessary."

He also continues to draw on his training from Y&R and put himself in the position of the customer. "I tell clients that our job is to be the champion of the consumer, because you're too close to your product or service for you to step outside and look at it from their point of view. They'll always be your customers, but they don't look at themselves as customers. They look at themselves as the owners of the product," he says. "Clients don't own the product, customers do. It's an extension of them and not an extension of client. I think that's a hard concept for some clients to understand."

Clients Are Smarter

But while he sees creativity and originality lacking in most agencies, he believes it's more important than ever. "Ad agencies are now more like production companies. They are less about media and servicing the account and more about creative production," he says. Likewise, he believes the balance of power has shifted. "[Strategically,] clients are smarter than most agencies right now. The really smart account people have matriculated over to the client side because they have more control."

Red Advertising continues to thrive—even during the down economy—both as an agency serving its own clients and as a creative resource for bigger agencies. Easdon has survived the low points of his career and has come full circle in another part of his career: he has started working again with Bill Heater. Where this will take him should be interesting.

A QUIET PORTFOLIO THAT GETS ATTENTION

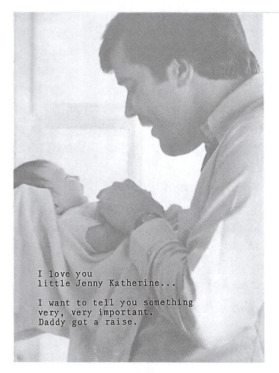

——— John Hancock Financial Services ———

John Hancock Financial Services wanted a product-oriented campaign. Most creatives would have been turned off by this request, but Easdon took it as a challenge. He felt he could market the products if he presented them in a very low-key manner and thought that "slice-of-life" could be a successful technique—if it were presented through a fresh approach. Until that point, slice-of-life advertising was rarely interesting.

But Easdon knew it could be wonderful if he controlled the feel, making it more like a movie or a documentary. Decisions concerning the type, film texture, pacing, pauses, and lights were all filtered through the concept.

The ads were intentionally quiet, so people wouldn't feel they were being sold. The first viewing would stop you because of its then-fresh structure. The next time you saw it, you'd pay a lot more attention. "Oddly enough, by then, people paid so much attention," recalls Easdon, "that tests showed they could repeat the copy verbatim."

——— Wang ———

By the time Easdon began working on Wang at Hill Holiday, he had learned to trust his instincts. This was at a time when MIS (management information systems) professionals were fond of talking in jargon. "I had no idea what the hell they were saying. It was like being in the army and hearing conversation that was all acronyms. And it was pretty consistent. I recognized I could use this 'techno-jargon' to do a campaign."

The campaign targeted the MIS people in companies who were already inundated with computer industry magazines and direct mail pieces. Easdon felt that although television would reach a much broader audience than necessary, it would have a greater impact.

As predicted, the techno-jargon in these unorthodox television commercials turned off some people but it created in-

GIVE US A DAY
TO MAKE IT WORK FOR YOU.

WANG MAKES IT WORK.

stant empathy with MIS directors and was very successful at evolving Wang's image. "That was good for Wang," says Easdon, "because they were not seen as being as high-tech as other companies. The aim was to show how high-tech they actually were."

—— AMERICAN ORIGINALS ——

Easdon has done a lot of new product work for Anheuser Busch. "We came up with new beers to go up against the micros," he says. For instance, he created a line of beers called American Originals. "They were basically the beers that were around a hundred years ago," he says. "Anheuser Busch had a black and tan, and they had something called Faust. They had wonderful labels. They were very authentic. And they still had the recipes. So I brought them back. We worked on everything from how the products looked to how they tasted, because Anheuser Busch had to adjust them for modern tastes. It was a pretty successful launch."

——— Red Label ———

Ironically, another beer Easdon worked on was called Red Label. "It was never meant to be much more than what I call 'the other side of Budweiser,' the big mass market of beers," he says of this print campaign. "This one was very fashion directed and oriented toward media like *Vanity Fair*. That was really fun. Anheuser Busch is more for *Maxim* and places like that."

Easdon ended up using a young fashion photographer from New York. "He took what I would call 'story pictures.' You look at them, and you wonder what the heck is going on. You have to figure [them] out. They're a little strange."

In one ad, for instance, there's a woman taking a bath in a backyard, and there's a party with people drinking beer in the foreground. "It came out of my own experience. When I was in Mill Valley, I had a bathtub in the backyard. But it makes you stop and think—'What's *that* all about'—and that's all I really wanted to do. I just wanted to involve the viewer with a bizarre little story."

—— Bingham McCutchen ——

Easdon believes that creative people have a duty to bring new ideas to clients and help reinvent categories—it doesn't matter if it's a car, financial services, or even a law firm. He points to his client Bingham McCutchen, an international law firm, as an example. "We've taken a very boring category and reinvented it," he says. It sounds really boring—a law firm—but we do really nice ads for them."

He believes the reason is twofold. First, they dig deep to understand the audience and, as Easdon says, "Mirror something that is shared." Secondly, the client wanted to stand out. "The senior partner who runs it is an entrepreneur. He relates. He knows that to stand out, you've got to take some chances." This does not mean that Easdon takes undue risks. "We test every ad with about ten of their partners, one on one. We hire a guy to do that, and we get a good sense if it's going to be a home run or a disaster. We only go with home runs, which I like. They won't run anything unless people really love it."

The result: "This client has literally tripled in size since we've gotten it and is now one of the biggest law firms in the United States," says Easdon "The advertising is an extension of their personality and it draws in all kinds of new clients, and more importantly, makes them *the* place to work."

—— LL Bean ——

Easdon feels that using media in unexpected ways can be as provocative as unexpected messages, and this retail campaign is an example. A contrast campaign—bad holiday experiences versus good holiday experiences—he took another look at the use of vignettes and the typical structure of a 30-second spot. "Instead of a 30 or even the conventional two 15s," he says, "why not break it anytime I want?"

"You could use a spot of 23 seconds and one 7-second spot, or a 9-second spot and an 11-second and a 10-second spot—as long as you end up with a 29.5-second spot with a half second fade. Next, switch out the pods and use new ones, and you have a 30-second spot that is constantly being refreshed with new information."

Easdon believes that it's the traditional ending and fade as well as the continual refreshment of the content that makes it effective. "People never get to the stage where they think they've seen it before and shut off. This is especially important in the retail category," he says. "You need to view the constraints of the medium as advantages, not as limitations. Think of it like judo—use the weight of the constraints against it. Instead of fighting them, go in that direction, only more so."

—— SABIAN CYMBALS ——

What makes an effective ad? Easdson believes it's when the piece is provocative yet inviting, is able to communicate a new consumer insight, and creates a bond between advertising and viewer. Another key is that it conveys the experience, such as these ads. They were "written" by Sabian drummers in the language of drummers. Visually they capture the spirit and unique sounds of each drummer. Each one works as an ad, a signature piece, a poster, and perhaps even a drumming lesson.

—— BUDWEISER ——

Here's an example of Easdon's "more respectful form of advertising." Together with Heater and director Joe Pytka, he created a Budweiser commercial that showed two policemen, soon to go off duty, in conversation. One tells the other of his brother-in-law's lucrative position selling municipal bonds and his own frustration at not making a lot of money.

The other officer responds, "You wouldn't want a yuppie job like that; it's not going to make you happy. Why would you want to do that? What it comes down to is, you wouldn't want to have a Bud with a guy like that, would you?" Then the other officer looks down at his shoes and says, "Nah." And they go off.

The only mention of Budweiser is the reference to "have a Bud...." "What I like to do is give people a free sample of the experience," says Easdon. "Whether it's a print ad or a website or a promotion—any kind of communication—it should offer some sort of free sample of the experience."

—— Infiniti ——

Easdon and Heater began working on the launch of Infiniti in a Japanese garden in Kyoto. "We were trying to figure out why this garden was so intriguing," he recalls. "It was beautiful. Simple. But after a few minutes, I realized I wasn't looking at the garden. It's just a place that makes you feel very comfortable. The garden lacked visual information. After a while, my thoughts wandered. The simplicity and familiarity of it made me very comfortable. Try staring out the window for 30 seconds. Be aware of what goes through your mind. You see a building—the building doesn't change—and your thoughts start to wander."

By using a nature scene, Easdon found that it brought greater focus to the announcer. "The scene became a frame, if you will, for the message," he says. That's

CAN THE AVERAGE DRIVER
TELL THE DIFFERENCE BETWEEN AN INFINITI
AND A TRADITIONAL LUXURY CAR?

There are differences of philosophy between a car designer raised in Bavaria and one raised in Kyoto. Not so much on what is fundamentally good engineering, but on what luxury is.

Here's the view from Kyoto:

Infiniti cars are designed for the driver. Its luxury personality is fully experienced at highway speeds as a touring sedan. Even an inexperienced judge of automotive performance will appreciate the ability of an Infiniti to respond accurately to the will of the driver.

The key idea is 'the will of the driver.' For it says that a car is designed to make the driver's experience more enjoyable. That an Infiniti, while it has an impressive road presence, is not a car that you own to impress, but a car that you own to drive.

In line with this are the car's simple, natural curves—the lack of gadgets and ornamentation. The use of natural materials for the car's interiors.

These things we believe, show a difference in approach to luxury. Differences which are easy to discern and which depart from traditional standards.

The point is not to make a case for which brand of luxury is better. Only to say that you can judge Infiniti cars on their unique character as luxury-class automobiles.

Call for more information to make your own evaluation or for the name of the dealer nearest you. 1-800-826-6500.

Thank you.

created by Nissan

INFINITI.

225

where the "executional" element of nature came from. Creating an analogy between the Japanese experience and nature was designed to make consumers feel very comfortable with an alien concept.

"People knock subtle advertising," says Easdon. "They say it doesn't sell hard enough. Give me a break. If there is something in the concept that articulates a feeling that the consumer has felt, but has not been able to articulate yet, then the ad has done a service. Empathy has been created. A bridge between the service and the consumer has been created. And that is an accomplishment."

—— CHARLES SCHWAB ——

Meet these Schwab customers going public with their investment experiences.

Howard
Marian & Rich
Forbes
Holly and daughter Alexandra

These Schwab customers have generously chosen to share their investment experiences to demonstrate how they use the tools and services now available through Schwab. They are real people like you and their decisions are their own. We invite you to follow along and learn the process of investing, as they create their financial futures.

www.schwab.com — CharlesSchwab

Easdon created this campaign in the beginning of the '90s dot-com boom. "It was aimed at making people feel more comfortable with investing online because there was a lot of fear about that," he says. "So I created a campaign where I allowed people to basically sit behind investors ranging from a complete novice to a very sophisticated retired millionaire and watch how they invested and used the tools that Schwab offered. [It] was interesting because it was topical: If something happened in the marketplace, I ran quarter page ads in the *New York Times* that showed how these four sets of investors responded."

The campaign succeeded in part because, typically, viewers could relate to one or two of the investors. "I especially [related] to one couple, Ray and Marian, and I did some really nice spots with them," says Easdon. "They were really charming people." Early on, this account was the mainstay of Red's West Coast office, but when the client contact left Schwab, the relationship ended.

ADVICE FOR CREATING UNIQUE ADVERTISING

Easdon looks for "idea people," new hires who don't necessarily have the most polished portfolios—or all of the skills. "I think that people in general are ten times better than they were, but there's a sameness among a lot of creative people. They come in for interviews with incredibly similar executions. But I rarely see new ideas or innovative executions, someone who excites me with their ideas and problem solving. They're hard to find. They're rare.

"Those rare people follow their instincts, which is what enables them to be confident—and their personalities are so strong that they can't help but put themselves into their work," says Easdon. "And they're immediately successful. They just scream ahead."

Easdon suggests that you use your instincts to figure out the feelings that people can't articulate and translate it into campaigns that form bonds with consumers. "The real trick is to be able to integrate the message in a non-selling way so people can feel comfortable with it," he suggests.

For copywriters and art directors, Easdon has seemingly contradictory advice. On the copy side, he finds short stories in portfolios to be intriguing. "A lot of the work is so polished that you judge it against work that's already out there," he says. "You have to because it looks like it's been printed. I think it makes it harder for them." As for art directors, he's tougher. "I'm really much tougher on art directors because it's my forte," he says. "If I were starting all over right now, I'd make my portfolio look as real as I possibly could. Either way, I wouldn't want to have anything get in the way of demonstrating my skills."

Here's some additional advice from someone who looks at things differently.

Don't get into the business: "The advertising industry is probably worse now that it ever has been," warns Easdon. "It's hard. It's rewarding as hell, but it's competitive. It's like being a baseball player. You'll either be a real star or you'll end up with an antique store in New England. Emotionally, that's very difficult. Every campaign I've ever worked on has taken a couple of years off my life. I will say that the old advertising structure is dying. If you follow the tried and true ways, you will not fit in this new creative environment."

Ignore awards books: Unlike so many other creatives, Easdon says that to do your best work, you should ignore the awards books. "People who look to awards books and are directly influenced by them are doing work that is probably not as good as the originator had done," he says. Easdon explains that some creatives have built their careers on a certain type of advertising style, and they vote for the work that represents that style, even though it may not be right for the particular client. He sees the awards books, however, as a valuable tool for learning the basics of advertising and for keeping current. "You have to stay current," he says, "but award books are not any more important than picking up a magazine or watching the newest hot movie."

Use yourself as a resource: Rather than looking to awards books as an idea resource, Easdon encourages creatives to look into themselves. "As people put their personalities into their work, their work becomes more unique. If you're brash, you'll do brash work. If you're sophisticated, you'll do sophisticated work," says Easdon. "So, you should have the confidence to let your work reflect yourself. During the last executions of the John Hancock campaign, which I didn't work on, they showed a woman who suffered from stuttering. She worked on a computer, which helped her feel very eloquent and articulate. It was a wonderful commercial. The reason I believe it was so good is because the person who wrote it also stutters. He put himself into his work."

Trust your instincts: "I trust my instincts. People will come with work for me to review and I always have a visceral reaction," says Easdon. "You have to listen to your instincts, and even though you feel inarticulate, just start talking about it and try to find the words for what you feel. After a while, you get used to articulating what your gut is telling you. I know that sounds basic, but that's it."

Explore new approaches: Easdon finds American awards books dull. "But I pore over Japanese magazines and films. They approach things differently," he says. "A trend in advertising was to put down their own products. They'll trash their own product! I found that intriguing. So, I'm drawn in."

Recognize you need others: "Nobody does great work by themselves," says Easdon. "If you succeed and think you've done it yourself, you're either egotistical or you don't recognize reality. It's impossible to do it yourself." Easdon credits much of the success of his work to having great partners. For many years, it was Bill Heater. "You need somebody who listens and someone whose ideas are worth listening to. Bill and I had our differences. But we'd talk them through. Where copy was concerned, he had the final say. But where art direction was concerned, I had the final say. It was just a wonderful relationship, and it helped create a lot of good work."

Make fear your friend: For Easdon, fear is a big motivator. Fear of not being successful drove him to create his best work. And when he finally won recognition with his Hancock work, fear of having had his career peak motivated him to work harder for his next major success.

...But be confident: Easdon is very sensitive to the insecurities every creative feels. "Everyone is intimidated by the blank page. The blank page makes you feel like every day is your first day. That feeling never goes away. You don't know how it's going to happen, where the ideas will come from, but they come."

Preserve fresh ideas: "Nobody's idea is great at first. Learn to build on it. It's like playing with a little tinker toy, a puzzle, or Lincoln Logs; fiddle with it until it works. Even bad ideas can foster brilliant campaigns. One day, I was reviewing an atrocious campaign. It was so bad. I smiled and tried to find something nice to say about it. But in trying to find something nice to say, a great idea came up."

Respect the client: Unlike many advertising people who believe clients are naïve and uncreative about advertising, Easdon sees them as a valuable resource. "Clients know the brand and have the responsibility of policing the brand." And many agency people have moved to the client side, so today clients are more sophisticated about both sides of advertising.

Be positive: "Good advertising people have to be confident and brash enough to come out with something different," says Easdon. "You're naked when you come up with something totally brand new—that can make you nervous. A fresh thought is easily killed. Anything new doesn't thrive in an environment of negative thinking. Think positive and surround yourself with positive people."

Make terrible assignments terrific: "Most people think that the only way to create great work is by working on flashy products like jeans or perfume. The Hancock campaign, before I worked on the account, showed a scale of justice with a miniature family on one side and on the other side a hand putting weights on the scale. It suggested term insurance to balance out the family's needs. It was awful—the challenge was to create something fresh. Any product or service has the potential for fresh ideas!"

Understand the product's most basic value: "A car, for instance, is basically just transportation," says Easdon. "If you're writing an ad for a car, also understand why it's styled the way it is and the other emotional factors that motivate the consumer. So it's best to start at zero and question everything before you start to develop approaches."

Don't impose your personal style on your client's products: "Use only the parts of your personality that match your client's personality," advises Easdon. "You certainly communicate through your personality, which is the only way to work instinctively anyway. And sometimes there's just a good match-up."

Reach for the audience with visuals: Like the target audience, Easdon feels that an ad must stop him to gain his interest. "I want to be startled. I look for things I haven't seen before. At award shows, I'll only put my glasses on to read the copy if the ad works on a visual level. If it's not interestingly designed, I won't even look at it. If it is, then I read it."

Reflect society: "Advertising doesn't drive society. Society drives advertising," says Easdon. "And good advertising people are a barometer of what's happening. The better ones can articulate what's happening in society before society articulates it. If you don't do it, someone else will. If I didn't do the Hancock campaign, it would have been done six months later by Prudential. I just had the right opportunity and the luck to be able to execute it first."

Keep it consistent: Easdon usually looks for a unique yet consistent approach in a beginning portfolio. "I can learn something from that," he says. "The more people put their personalities into their work, the more uniqueness you can see. And if his or her personality is fairly consistent, that uniqueness should be seen throughout the portfolio."

Stay involved with the culture around you: While the advertising industry is filled with young people, Easdon doesn't think age is a factor. However, the experiences and knowledge that creatives take in are big factors. "You can only output what you input from your experiences," says Easdon. "People dry up fast when they don't get involved in the culture around them and just work instead. You have to constantly get excited about things. One of my creative directors when I was at BSB worked there for years and created the classic Anacin spot with the hammers-in-the-head graphic. I was absolutely fascinated by this guy. I always learned something from him. He was a vault of information."

Look at limitations as assets: Easdon has learned to look at the advertising specifications that clients make as assets instead of as limitations. For example, Avis requires that 20 percent of Avis print ad space and 20 percent of commercial airtime be devoted to the car. That's because General Motors supplies the cars and finances their advertising. An employee at Avis is even paid to figure out the exact percentage of space and time on each ad or commercial. Rather than look at that as a limitation, look at it as an asset and work to discover ways of using the car much more creatively, making it a much more integral part of the communications, rather than just being an add-on. Similarly, Hancock wanted to mention numerous products in each communication. Rather than just tack a list of products on at the end of each piece, Easdon found a way to employ the product orientation in his creation of a breakthrough campaign. (See portfolio section.)

Keep it classic: For new business, Easdon recently put together a reel of his work, which he had not done in more than ten years. "I'm always afraid to do that because some of it's dated," he says. "But I looked at it afterwards, and every single thing would hold up today. You could run every single one. You wouldn't even know it from the execution, because I'm always conscious of keeping fashions to a fairly classic level."

Consider the ad's context: People look at an ad in relation to the other ads on the air or on a page. Keep that in mind when you're coming up with ideas and deciding on an execution. The context may affect how the commercial will be received.

Work in all media: "Most creatives think the only way to make it is by doing fashionable, hip TV campaigns. I thought so. The truth of the matter is, it's the other media that give you an opportunity to be really creative," says Easdon. "And doing a billboard is as important as doing an entire campaign."

Filter the execution through the idea: Easdon suggests you think of an idea as a pair of glasses. "Put on the glasses and look through them at the type, the visuals, the sound, every element," he says. "Make sure everything is filtered through the idea."

Make your boss look good: "If you make your boss look good, you go farther. No one is going to hire anybody who's not going to make them look good," Easdon reminds us.

Freelance: At some agencies, employees caught doing freelance were fired on the spot. But Easdon realizes that most beginners need freelance work to survive. "I tell people that they can freelance, if it's not for a conflicting account. It makes you better," he says. "It's also very fulfilling because you don't have all the management layers."

Avoid tantrums: "I've quit a number of jobs," says Easdon. "I quit on Wang. I quit on Infiniti. That works against you in the long run because people think you're some kind of prima donna. At this point, I should be mature enough to convince people of my point of view without a tantrum."

Keep your hands on: Easdon believes creative directors get out of touch when they're promoted up and no longer do the work. "I'm a working creative director," he says. "I've found that I lose my edge and confidence when I'm not involved. And I found I lost interest in the business when I stopped working myself. That's not good for a career. I know I have a pretty decent portfolio, but that doesn't matter. It's what you did last week that counts."

Show clients that you care: "A client wants to see that you're enthusiastic, interested, and fully committed to their product or service," he says. "They don't want to know about your other clients. They want to feel like you're a dedicated soldier and that you don't have an ego getting in the way. That's a prerequisite."

POSTSCRIPT 1:

ART DIRECTING ON THE COMPUTER

Many creative leaders believe that computers limit creativity and feel that art directors should think through the idea before touching a computer to execute it. Don Easdon takes a different approach and feels that computers can enhance creative ideation. Here's his take on creating with a computer.

"A lot of people feel that the computer is an enemy: but I feel that it's helped evolve art direction in a very positive way.

"I did a print campaign for Lotus Notes that was never produced. I wanted to do it from five or six different directions—from a cartoon strip for the novice to a highly, highly technical article. So I did this very editorial look. I changed the typeface for each one. Each message had its own editorial look and feel. Then I managed to put them all on a double-page spread so that it just looked really eclectic. I thought it was great. But I could have produced it so much easier on a computer.

"This was way before everybody else was doing editorial-looking advertising. I showed it to the head of Lotus before they were taken over by IBM. He looked at me like I was out of my mind, but I still think it was one of those things that would have just stopped people. They would have spent time looking at it.

"That was pre-computer, and it was hard for me to do because it was just so much work to put things together. I was pulling things from magazines to get a sense of what I wanted to do. It could have been much easier if I had the right tools.

"Software like Quark or Adobe Illustrator is amazing. I used to spend thousands of dollars to see what different typefaces would look like because I literally had to set them. Now it's just a matter of seconds. I can really see what the color is going to look like.

"Even when I had the right tools, Bill would get crazy because I'd be on the computer trying to learn it. Now I know it. I don't even think. I just do stuff.

"I think that creative directors and copywriters get fed up with art directors who use a computer—and feel that it's limiting—because they see them working with their hands and don't think they're working with their brain. They don't realize that the computer has become an extension of the art director.

"Even with a computer, you still have to have a perspective and an idea before you start. There are a million images on Getty. What are you going to do? Just look at images and hope something sparks you? You still have to start somewhere. The computer just tends to give people a bigger range and a lot more choices than they ever had before, and that's important."

POSTSCRIPT 2:

CREATIVE DYSLEXIA

Throughout this chapter, the importance of drawing from yourself and relying on all of your attributes has been explored. That using yourself as a resource and putting yourself into your work is a key to success. Another important lesson of this chapter was to look at limitations as assets. All of these points are rooted in something that could have been used as an excuse not to succeed, but in fact helped propel Easdon forward in his career. He's dyslexic. Let's take a look at what Easdon had to say about dyslexia. (Hopefully it inspires you to look at all of your attributes as assets.)

"I recently read in a psychiatric journal that a lot of graphic people are compensating for something. I'm dyslexic. If you think black, I think white. And I'm always surprised that you are thinking black. I'm not a very organized, methodical person like a lot of copywriters or account executives who run agency businesses. I find that I cannot concentrate on the organization. I go right to the feeling of what I want and work backwards from there."

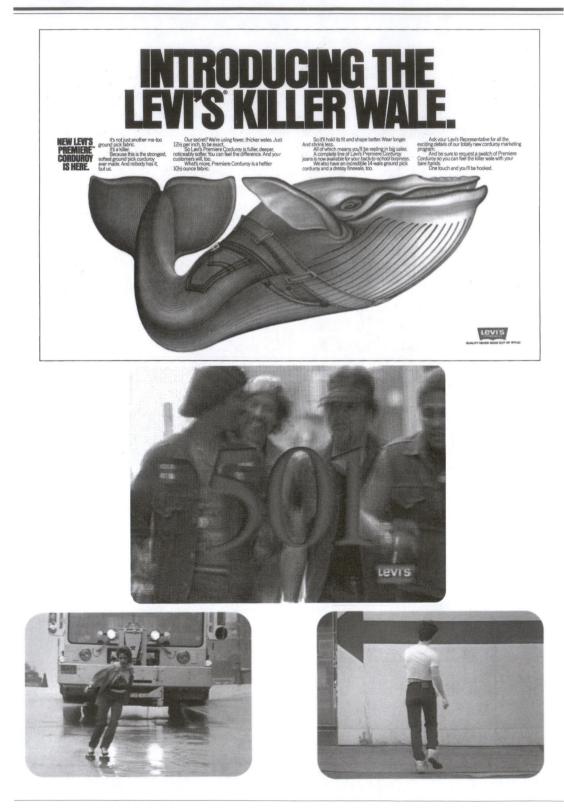

Mike Koelker

"Too many people try to back into an ad."

"They try to apologize for it being an ad. I don't mean that you can't be clever. But I do mean you have to get at it," said Mike Koelker, a long-time creative leader of Foote, Cone & Belding.

Koelker's success came in part from his willingness to approach advertising—as well as his career—head on. Always with directness, honesty, and humility. He created one of the greatest "lifestyle" campaigns ever for Levi's 501 jeans, winning numerous awards in the process. It was even selected by the Smithsonian Institute for their permanent collection of landmark American advertising.

His work building the Levi's brand, according to *Ad Age*, helped usher in "San Francisco's creative renaissance."

While best known for his work with Levi's, he also created campaigns for the California Raisin Advisory Board (the dancing raisins), Agree Shampoo, Clorox, Supercuts, Tone Soap, Epson Computers, Pacific Bell, and Italian Swiss Colony wines. "I didn't like doing wine advertising very much," he said, "because I don't like vineyards. They're boring, and they're hot." He also served for many years as Corporate Director of Creative Development for Foote, Cone & Belding/USA.

Prior to joining FCB/San Francisco, Koelker spent ten years in a variety of copywriting positions—he wrote for a department store, a daily newspaper, and several small agencies. He broke into copywriting while working toward a bachelor's degree in social work from Augustana College in Rock Island, Illinois.

A native Midwesterner, Koelker moved to San Francisco in the mid-'60s—even though he claimed not to enjoy the relaxed California lifestyle—and lived there the rest of his life. A heavy smoker, he succumbed to complications from lung cancer and passed away in 1995.

A SMALL STORY WITH BIG RESULTS

While most beginning writers and art directors dream of starting at a big agency, working on glamorous accounts, and creating big-budget television commercials and glossy print ads, that might not always be the best strategy for success.

In this chapter, we're going to look at another approach: the "humble, but confident" approach, which extends from job search techniques and strategies to the actual creation of advertising.

From the beginning of his career, Mike Koelker was in a position to know that this approach can work. Born in Omaha and raised in Chicago and Shenandoah, Iowa, he's one of only two people featured in this book who became familiar with advertising as a child (the other is Mike Hughes). His mother was a copywriter and art director for Bozell & Jacobs in the 1940s.

An average student, he dropped out of college for a year and worked in a number of jobs. He drove an ambulance, worked on road construction, and even embalmed people in a mortuary. When he returned to college, he became interested in sociology. "I got fascinated with the way society plays on a person's mind," he recalled. "So much of what we, as a society, value and believe is actually learned."

In addition, he took a basic advertising class and was fascinated by it.

Because of these two interests, he decided to transfer to Augustana College in Rock Island, Illinois, only to discover that while the school offered sociology courses, they did not, at the time, have any advertising courses.

Since he was interested in advertising, he decided to apply for a job in the ad department of the daily newspaper in nearby Davenport, Iowa.

At first, they wouldn't interview him. But, every day for two weeks, wearing the same inexpensive suit, he went to their office.

Finally, his perseverance paid off, and he was given an interview.

He told them he wanted to write advertising, pulling the goal out of the air because he couldn't draw and was too shy to be a salesperson. They hired him.

The pay was low, but he didn't care. He was proud to have been offered the opportunity. And he loved it. To manage, Koelker worked part time and attended school part time.

Upon receiving his bachelor's degree in social casework, he decided to become a clinical psychologist and applied to the University of Omaha, in his hometown. At the same time, he sent a letter to Brandies, an Omaha department store, to apply for a job as a copywriter. The retailer liked the young writer's letter and his samples from the newspaper and hired him immediately.

Koelker credited the letter for getting him the offer. "I didn't want to appear to be a smart ass," he said, "because I was young and there was a lot I didn't know.

But I wanted to appear very confident in my ability to meet challenges. That sounds like a lot of MBA hogwash, but it's really true. It comes across if you write the letter correctly. You just have to find the right tone of voice."

Koelker planned to work part time and go to school part time, using income from advertising to support himself while attending graduate school.

But after one semester, he realized that his interest in clinical psychology, social casework, and everything else related to sociology had faded. The fact was, he loved writing ads. "I don't know any way to say it other than I just loved sitting down at a typewriter with a blank sheet of paper and making something happen," he recalled. "I got to the point where I took internal pride at being able to start a sentence with any word, finish the sentence, and make it work. The volume of work I did was just tremendous. Some days, I'd literally write all day long just as fast as I could."

The variety was tremendous as well. He wrote ads for hardware, baby clothes, women's clothes, lingerie, men's suits, sportswear—every department. Plus, he wrote image ads and seasonal ads.

After two years, Koelker wanted to experiment. He'd only done print ads, and he thought that by moving to an agency he would have the opportunity to write for radio. Writing for television was inconceivable to him.

Again he sent his samples and a letter saying something like, "I have never worked for an advertising agency. I know it's different. I know it has to be infinitely more difficult. But I think I can do it." This "humble, but confident" approach worked again. He was hired by a small agency in Omaha.

From there, he moved to a larger agency in Omaha and, under the direction of a co-worker, refined his talents. "Throughout my life I have been able to identify people I could learn from," said Koelker. "I'd attach myself uncompromisingly to those people. They'd help me write better copy. They'd look at my headlines and say, 'This is stupid, this is crap, why are you doing it,' and then coach me into creating something better."

One day, the agency lost a big piece of business and had to trim staff. "They cut the guy who had always helped me, but kept me because I got a lot of work done and was cheap," he recalled. "When they let him go, I was crushed. I worked there another three months and realized I hadn't grown so much as a quarter of an inch since the day he left."

Not long after, Koelker's mentor phoned from Kalamazoo, Michigan.

He'd landed a job as creative director and wanted Koelker to come work for him. Without hesitation, Koelker accepted and headed for Michigan. Once there, he discovered the power of art direction.

"In my excruciatingly painful manner, I did my copywriter's rough and went to the art director with it," said Koelker. "He was out of Chicago, which was big time, and he looked at it and replied, 'What's this? I don't want to see these roughs. If you have an idea for an ad, let's sit down. We'll talk about it. You'll talk about what you think. I'll talk about what I think. And we'll see where we go from there.'"

It was an enriching experience. He learned the value of leaning on the talents of someone else 50 percent of the time. He felt that learning to work as a team to find solutions was the most wonderful thing that had happened to him in his business career to that point.

For the first time, he was working in a partnership. He learned that two people could work as one and be very productive. "I learned that, sometimes, you may have to give in, even if you think you're right, for the sake of the partnership. No ad is worth destroying a partnership," he said. "I also learned to contribute in unforceful ways."

After two years, Koelker felt he'd learned all he could and was ready to move on. "By then, I was conscious of the need to grow and learn," he said. "You have to work for people who are far more talented than you are, so they can teach you how to do things."

He applied for copywriting jobs at three agencies: Tracy Locke in Dallas; McCann Erickson in Portland; and an agency called Meltzer, Aaron & Lemen in San Francisco. "I thought, what's to lose?" said Koelker. "I didn't know anything about San Francisco. California was like a rumor to me. I had always lived in the Midwest and had never gone anywhere. I'd never even seen an ocean."

Koelker's inquiries were met with interest. Tracy Locke flew him to Dallas and offered him a job. He recalled that they seemed nice and the atmosphere seemed fun. McCann Erickson flew him to Portland and came close to offering him a job, too. Meltzer, Aaron & Lemen (MAL) met him in the Detroit airport to talk. He liked the opportunity, but decided against them.

He wrote MAL a letter saying that he had decided on Tracy Locke instead.

A letter came back from MAL's creative director. "It was the cleverest, best-written letter I'd ever read," recalled Koelker. "I phoned him the next morning and said, 'I have to work for anybody who can write that well.' It was probably the best decision I have ever made, because, of all the people I had worked for, this guy was the best. He was brilliant and insightful. He was able to look down a long piece of copy and find the headline. And he was right every time. It was a killer."

The creative director also helped him perfect his ad writing style. "I learned to look at a piece of copy as a visual element, not just words," said Koelker. "I started looking for balance in my copy—short sentences, long sentences, short paragraphs, long paragraphs."

From there, Koelker went to Honig-Cooper & Harrington (HCH), where he got an opportunity to create for television. It was a Levi's commercial, and he was terrified. "I thought I had to speak some special language to do TV ads," he recalled. "I thought I had to know about zooms, cuts, dissolves, and reveals and how to write the visual directions." But then his art director told him to let the film director take care of all that, and he became comfortable with the medium.

Five years later the agency merged with FCB—a merger that Koelker compared to Jonah merging with the whale. But it suited both parties well.

While FCB was huge, their San Francisco office was small. Likewise, while HCH was the largest independent agency on the West Coast, they were small on a national scale. The merger strengthened FCB's position and gave the San Francisco office the global capabilities that major clients had come to expect.

After the merger, Koelker was promoted to Associate Creative Director, then, in the mid-'80s, to Executive Creative Director. During this period, he created his most famous campaign—the 501 "Blues" for Levi's (see portfolio section).

Koelker remained involved with the Levi's account for the rest of his career, but as FCB's North American Director of Creative Development, his days were also spent helping the creative people in all of the agency's offices.

To do so, he wrote long memos addressed to a person named "Al," exploring his feelings about strategic development and about how creative people and account people can best work together.

"Account people don't normally work in partnership," he said. "But once they start working on a creative project, they become vital to the partnership. This takes sensitivity on everybody's part. It also means that there can't be rulers. A person can't pull out all the stops and win by position or title."

Within the San Francisco office, he used a laissez-faire style of management to supervise his staff. "I manage by hiring," he said. "If you hire good people, not necessarily award winners, provide them with an open climate—it brings out the best in them—be available to help at any time and with anything, you don't have to spend much time managing anyone."

Why did Koelker manage this way? His answer was simple: "Every now and then, I have to feel like I'm doing something useful. I can't let that change. Whether I work on 501s or Dockers, my work is important to me. To do that work takes time. I have to be able to trust people to carry on without me."

He took a medical leave of absence in March of 1995 and passed away in June of that year.

A VERY REAL PORTFOLIO

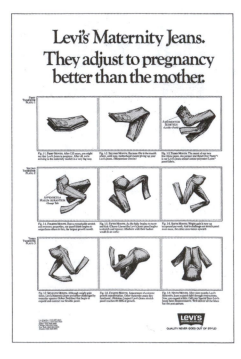

—— LEVI'S ——

Here are two examples of early Koelker print advertising for Levi's. They are also examples of how to charm people without apologizing for asking them to read feature-oriented product advertising.

"Consumers do not want to sit around and fumble their way through word games to get to the point," he said.

"You can be clever, seductive, charming, romantic. You can do all that. But you have to give people some idea of what you want from them—what they're supposed to be thinking.

"Give them some clues as to where you're going. Don't just dance around or play word games. Don't apologize."

Chances are, they're not talking about our jeans.

Nor is it likely they're discussing how Levi's 501 jeans are made of a special denim that shrinks in the wash to fit only you. Your waist, your thighs, you.

Indeed, they probably don't even care that it's like having your jeans custom tailored. For a personal fit ordinary jeans can't match.

But they *are* wearing Levi's 501 jeans. And they do appear to be enjoying themselves.

And that's good enough for us.

—— Levi's 501 ——

Prior to 1984, Levi's didn't have wide enough distribution to justify national advertising. Consequently, their advertising focused on the variety of products they made—cords, denims, skirts, and the variety of colors. But they were willing to gamble with focused brand image advertising.

Since 501s (button-fly jeans) had the widest distribution, Levi's decided to experiment with them. But people didn't know about 501s. Button-fly jeans were barely available on the East Coast. And the public had difficulty accepting buttons in place of zippers.

To address these problems and build awareness, Levi's management favored the upbeat lifestyle approach Coke and Pepsi were using in their advertising.

But Koelker felt that most lifestyle advertising rarely reflected the average lifestyle. "I would walk down the street, and none of the people were that blond, that happy, that handsome or beautiful as lifestyle ads suggested. And young people didn't spend their lives playing volleyball on the sands of Malibu. They'd just hang out."

What Koelker created was a campaign capturing real people doing real things. "After we ran the campaign for three years, we went around the country asking kids to imagine a door to the Levi's world," he said. "What's behind that door?

"They didn't say that it's a world where everybody wears Levi's. Instead, they said it is a world where I'd be welcome no matter if I were short, thin, fat, tall, a different color, or in a wheelchair. It didn't matter. I would be welcomed in that world. That's the world we wanted to build. Kids got it, even though we never explicitly said it."

And the results of his work can be seen in one simple statistic: Within 36 months, Levi's sales jumped from 9 million to more than 30 million pairs of jeans a year.

—— 501 BLUES ——

Here is an example from the television component of the 501 Blues campaign.

In most commercials, according to Koelker, agencies take a jingle and work it into many different musical styles. Instead, he wanted every commercial to have a completely different piece of blues music from different musicians, yet all with the same upbeat feel and attitude.

He also wanted to find a director who could capture real life, a task he found frustrating. He and his partner went through close to a hundred reels. They all looked alike. "After four weeks, I suggested we just pick a reel out of that stack," he recalled. But then, a producer told him to look at a documentary on black street musicians that a director had done in South Africa. It was soulful and honest—exactly what he wanted.

With the right director signed, the next step was to decide what to shoot.

At this stage, most agencies do storyboards. Koelker, however, didn't want that. "If we did storyboards, it wouldn't have reflected life. It would have been a Marin County copywriter and art director imitating life," he said.

They also decided to shoot in New York. "We wanted to shoot strong people," he said. "California kids were not particularly strong.

They are handsome, nice, and into tofu, but it isn't hard to grow up in California. It's hard growing up in New York. You've got to be tough to survive."

Once in New York, their plan was to avoid using commercial actors. While they did use a few struggling stage actors, most were real people the casting director found around town. And during the casting sessions, instead of asking them to do something particular, they were told to do whatever they wanted to do. One young woman said, "Okay, I'm going to serve you coffee." She went out, got coffee, brought it in, and served it to the group. She was hired.

The team gathered the events they thought charming from the casting session and structured them. Then they decided on locations and a general scenario that would best reflect them. And the 501 campaign was born.

—— WOMEN'S 501S ——

Initially women were buying men's 501s, so the company saw an opportunity and decided to gamble on the female market.

They brought out a 501 cut for women. Their goal was to achieve the same kind of cult status that the men's jeans had achieved.

The result was a commercial that opened with a woman sitting in the back of an open car. And then, in the distance, she sees a guy walk out of a house.

She stands up, turns her back to the camera, and yells, "Travis, you're a year too late."

That was it. Research found that women absolutely despised it. It made them angry. Everyone wanted to know who he was and why he was a year too late.

People even discussed it on radio talk shows.

But here's the surprise. "It sold more jeans than any other single Levi's commercial," said Koelker. "It worked because everybody thought about it, talked about it, and wondered who Travis was. So it added a sense of mystery to the jeans. And the whole idea behind a cult item is that there's a sense of mystery."

Once the jeans were introduced, Koelker created the print ad on the preceding page. In addition to showing how he captured the attitude of the 501 Blues campaign in print, it shows how words and sentences create a visual element.

"The eye needs relief from long sentences," he said. "But every once in a while the mind hungers for a long sentence filled with information. It can't be: fact, fact, fact. But it can be: fact, charm, charm, fact, charm, charm."

—— DOCKERS ——

Here is another example of how Koelker used reality as a creative resource.

"I'm fascinated by reality," he said, "because I think it can be filmed in really interesting ways and can be very persuasive. We take it for granted. We never look at it. It's fun once in a while to let the camera look at life, and we go, 'Yeah, that's the way it is. Ain't it happy. Ain't it sad. Ain't it something!'"

And this is also an example of how Levi's various brands continued moving away from copy-heavy, feature-oriented advertising after the success of their 501 Blues campaign. With the growing importance of "branding," it's a trend that continues today.

A REALISTIC APPROACH
FOR PUTTING TOGETHER A CAREER

Koelker recognized that beginning copywriters and art directors are in a bind.

They need samples to get experience. But they don't get samples until they have experience. To make a beginning spec book, he suggested you start with print. "That's something tangible," he said. "Television is a committee job."

He suggested taking a magazine, tearing out 12 ads you find interesting, studying them, and finding the basic point they're trying to communicate.

"Every ad starts with a problem," he said. "Around here we say the word 'strategy,' but it's really a problem. Maybe people don't know about the product. Maybe there are misconceptions about the product. Maybe people think it costs too much. Maybe the world just needs to be told that the client is a good, friendly, big-hearted company."

Then he suggested that you try to figure out the problem from the ad. "What are they trying to communicate? That it lasts longer? That it's beautifully designed?"

Once you have the ads figured out, find a new way of communicating the message without violating the tenor—or attitude—of the campaign.

"Do that 12 times and you've got the foundation for a portfolio," said Koelker. "And you've got enough to talk to somebody. And say, 'I don't have an inflated value of what I'm going to be doing when I walk through the door with absolutely no experience. You're going to ask me to do the grunt work. The backups. So I have a portfolio of backups.' That would be so refreshing in this business.

"Realistically, a beginner is going to be asked to continue a campaign someone else started. No one is going to ask you to come up with the next great campaign for Chevrolet. They're going to ask you to continue some advertising campaign that's been proven."

If you want to take a humble but confident approach to breaking in and succeeding in the industry, here is some more advice from Mike Koelker.

Be sure to pay attention, because while these thoughts date back close to a decade, they could still help you succeed today:

Dump the non-advertising school samples: "I will not look at people who come in with portfolios of newspaper articles they wrote in college, short stories, poems, any of that stuff," said Koelker. "It's all well and good, but what's the point? That's not this business. This business is a lot crueler than that."

Learn how agencies operate: Koelker suggested that beginners study advertising for at least one semester just to learn how agencies work and are organized.

"I talk to kids in colleges every once in a while and they don't even know how a commercial happens. They think the client says what to do. They should know that the assignment goes to an agency, to writers, and art directors. They present it to the client. It gets changed. And, finally, a director gets it. Beginners should know how agencies make money."

Work hard before trying to break in: Sometimes beginners take Koelker's advice and put together a book based on existing ads. And sometimes they don't. "A lot of them don't come back because it's work to sit down and do that. So they give up. But, hell, writing one ad is work. It's work once you get here, so it doesn't hurt to do a week's worth of work before you come here."

Find the strategy in existing campaigns: "Anyone can look at an ad and figure out the strategy," said Koelker. "Write that down as a presumed strategy statement. That's your analysis of what they're trying to do and shows you can work within a strategy. Then show how you'd extend the campaign. Show how you'd do it differently. Enhance it and make it live longer in the marketplace. That's not to discredit the previous execution; it's to demonstrate you'll be able to understand your first assignments."

Team up: "As early as you can, team up and start building a portfolio. You're both going to need it," he said. "Ideally, a would-be copywriter should team up with the would-be art director to put together a sample portfolio. Even if you are not interviewing as a team, you can talk about the working relationship."

"The creative director will realize you have an idea of what the business is all about." Without an art director, he believed that writers shouldn't try to draw. Rather, they should just draw a rectangle on the page and describe the visual. If that feels uncomfortable, he suggested cutting pictures out of a magazine to use for the visual. Likewise, he believes art directors shouldn't try to write.

Cultivate varied styles: Beginners should be able to create ads using varied styles—aloof, factual, warm, but always with an attitude that says, "This is really important and now listen carefully."

Art directors should also have varied styles—rich, whimsical, or dynamic, yet always engaging.

Koelker looked for that ability to be different depending on the situation. "I like to see variety in a portfolio. I like to see work that's straight and buttoned down and work that's loose. I don't like to see headlines that are all puns. I also want to see headlines that are brutally direct and give an unexpected view of the product."

Avoid humor: Despite the fact that humor is so prevalent at awards shows, Koelker thought that beginners should avoid it.

"You might want to try a little bit of it to show that you have an amusing streak, but don't dwell on it, he said. "Humor tends to fall flat in print. Very few print ads are really hysterically funny. And without the benefit of somebody professional reading a radio script, very few radio scripts are funny. Most creative directors look for the 'solid stuff' in a portfolio."

Do the unexpected…: "I like to see people try the unexpected. That's the biggest thing I look for. And clarity. People in advertising are usually more experimental than clients, and clients are usually a little more experimental than consumers, who tend to be very comfortable with Madge, Marge, and Harry out in the kitchen.

"People say they hate it—and they probably do—but it's far more comfortable."

…And be rationally outrageous: "Don't worry about being rejected because your work is unusual, but have good reasons for having done what you did.

"If you sense your work is perceived as a little too off the wall, have a good rationale and defend it. You can say something like, 'Maybe I'm reaching a little far, but it seemed like a legitimate shot at it.' It's easier to pull back than it is to stretch."

Be likeable: "I don't know if I've ever looked at a portfolio and said, 'We have to hire that person.' I really base the hiring decision on what kind of person he or she is," said Koelker. "Do I like this person? Is he or she nice? Would this person be pleasant to be around? Can I talk to him or her? Do I feel comfortable?

"It's very subjective, and it's very narrow. When I'm interviewing, all I have are my own opinions. If I like the person, and I think the person's work is good enough, I'd really try and hire him or her."

Start small: Unless the agency has a formal training program (which is very rare these days), Koelker suggested that copywriters and art directors start at a small agency where they need help with non-critical assignments and have enough time to help beginners learn the business.

Although FCB has hired graduates from The Art Center who have worked out well, the agency prefers hiring people with experience. "We tried hiring beginners, but without a full-time manager, they don't get the coaching they need. They end up sitting here and rotting. It's not fair to them. It's horrible.

"Unfortunately, we're an agency full of people who want to do the work, not manage the staff," said Koelker. "I came up from smaller agencies. I was lucky. I had good people every step of the way to help."

Don't whine: Koelker noticed that many beginners often want their work to be considered "hip and cool" and were discouraged when clients suggested changes that detracted from this "coolness." "But clients don't want to hear that their own comments aren't hip and cool," he said. So he suggested that beginners pause and say something like, "That's an interesting point. Let me give it some thought."

Then look at what the ad is trying to accomplish. Maybe your approach isn't consistent with what you were trying to do or what you agreed to try to do. But after looking at your work, if you still believe in your approach, be able to support it with a logical rationale that supports the agreed-upon strategy.

Respectfully submit your ideas to your partner: "I've learned you can hurt someone's feelings when you step on their ideas. You have to be careful. You have to be sensitive, or you won't have a long-term partnership. No ad is worth jeopardizing the partnership. When somebody tosses out an idea, don't trample all over it," suggested Koelker. "You nod, even if your first reaction is horror at the stupidity of it. You try to build on it. You go, 'Gee, that makes me think we could do this, too.' Maybe it will go nowhere. Because as you extend it, it gets even worse, and then it becomes apparent to both of you."

Give in to your partner once in a while: "Even if you're absolutely convinced you're right, it's important to occasionally let your partner win," said Koelker. "Maybe you've won three in a row. Winning four in a row could destroy the partnership. Your partner won't contribute like he or she used to."

Rise and fall with your partner: "In an ideal partnership, both partners think, 'Gee, I hardly did anything, the other one did it all.' Even if you get talked into doing something that you don't think is entirely right, you go along with it.

"At the next level, if it's rejected you bail out your partner. You came up with it together by whatever route got you there.

"That's where you are, and that's what you show and defend."

Brainstorm without paper: "To come up with an idea, I keep thinking about the problem," said Koelker. "My partner and I work differently than most creative people.

"We never kick around ideas. We always kick around the problem. We talk about it. We ask ourselves why we think the client said what he did. Why they want what they want.

"We never have a scrap of paper in front of us. We just keep talking until we have eliminated a thousand possibilities, and then we start to work. And the ideas just come out of what sounds almost like business school talk."

Draw the client into the partnership: This was one of the keys to Koelker's success with Levi's, so it's a point we should really think about. He suggested that you don't look at the client as an adversary. "They are giving us a tremendous amount of money and entrusting us with the fate of their company," he said. "They have their company to run. We have advertising to do. We need each other. And I want to work in partnership with my client. I do my thing and he does his, but that doesn't mean we don't meet on our little lifecycles. There are lots of little meetings, and suddenly you find the job has been approved and you can't even remember when. So everything you can do to draw the client into the creative mix is great."

Don't get stuck, get information: You have to know everything about the product in order to say something significant about it. Someone Koelker once worked for told him that if he couldn't come up with an idea, he probably didn't have enough information. "It's really true," Koelker agreed.

"Or you may have a pile of information, but there's nothing in it that leads anywhere but to the conventional and the ordinary. If you are trying for something new, you need some sparkling pieces of information that hasn't occurred to the competition."

Ignore post-production research: Like many of the people featured in this book, Koelker put little value on post-production research. "At its best, this is a pedestrian and pretty mediocre gauge of an ad's potential. If you have a lot of money in your advertising budget, then I suppose it helps. But it's probably better suited to packaged goods than to anything that really wants to break through the clutter of television. If you need to make a small budget work like a big one, then you need creativity. You need the unexpected, and the unexpected never tests very well in the beginning." And remember all the research that said women despised the Levi's "Travis" commercial—the one that "sold more jeans than any other Levi's commercial." Go figure.

Recognize the absurdity of awards: "I don't care much for awards," said Koelker. "Or entering contests. They're silly. If you have ever judged an advertising show, you'd understand why the humor spots always win. By the 18th spot, you're a zombie and so bored that anything that elicits a response from your brain makes you say to yourself, 'I'll vote for that.' It isn't necessarily good because it sells the most product or is even the most creative. It's just that you're so bored looking at a reel of 100 commercials. So if you laugh, you give it a check mark, and with enough check marks, it wins."

Prepare yourself for the tension between business and art: "When you run a business, you attempt to make everything 'win/win.' But creative work is unfortunately not 'win/win,' but 'win/lose.' Either your idea gets sold or it doesn't," he said. "There's really no in between, except appalling mutations, which sometimes happen. That's when a piece of work evolves to a point where it has no integrity any more; it has no soul. It's just more advertising on television. And, God knows, that's the last thing we need in this world."

POSTSCRIPT:

INTEGRATED MARKETING COMMUNICATIONS

When the first edition of *How to Succeed in Advertising When All You Have Is Talent* was in development, the field of integrated marketing communications was just emerging. But what is IMC? And why is it important?

As an early practitioner of it, what Koelker had to say about this area during its emergence may give you a clue.

"Doing nationally renowned television commercials is still a great way to advance. But there isn't really all that much room for advancement in this business. This industry isn't that large. So beginners had better get out of their minds that only broadcast advertising is important.

"And I can tell you that integrated marketing communications is the way it's going. The wave of the future. The key is to do it with topflight creative people so it doesn't look like typical promotional advertising.

"With integrated marketing communications, everything a client does speaks with the same level of creativity—and with a single voice.

"We're doing that with Levi's right now. We're setting up a design group within our creative department. It's not a separate department like at most agencies. We're bringing in the best designers we can find to do outrageous point-of-sale. We're even helping our clients do hang tags.

"We're putting the same creative horsepower against that as we're putting against network TV. I know that because I'm working on it myself. I'm doing network TV, and I'm doing hangtags. And I'm having a ball! It's fun to do.

"The client loves it because it's all important. In the case of Levi's, they want all of their communications to retailers to have the same voice, the same look and feel as their network advertising. Then everything pulls together.

"Clients are saying that they intend to spend less and less in broadcast. They're not going to cut it out completely because it's still a great way to reach people fast and with high impact. But they're saying that they're going to spend more on integrated marketing communications—if we can make it work for them. And they want it to work for them because their dollar goes further.

"So beginners should think more along those lines.

"The times really are changing."

8

BUILDING YOUR CAREER

Nancy Rice

"Make sure that you merchandise yourself in your early years."

"Making people aware of your unique qualities and strengths is really important," says Nancy Rice, an ad industry icon and co-founder of two highly regarded agencies, including Fallon McElligott Rice. "If you don't do this for yourself as well as you do it for your clients, then your career isn't going to go as far."

Rice is someone who knows how to merchandise creativity through national and international advertising awards shows. She's won numerous gold and silver medals in the Clios, the One Show, the Andy's, the New York Art Directors Club, the Athenas, *Graphis*, *Print* Case Books, and *CA*. She was also featured as one of Esquire register's "Men and Wormen under 40 Who are Changing the Nation" as well as one of only two women worldwide featured in D&AD's *The Art Direction Book*. In 2006, at age 58, Rice was inducted into the New York Art Director's Club Hall of Fame.

A 1970 graduate of the Minneapolis College of Art and Design, Rice began her career three days out of art school as a storyboard artist at Knox Reeves Advertising (which later merged with Bozell and Jacobs). After her first year, she was named an Assistant Art Director and worked her way up to Vice President, Senior Art Director.

In 1981, after meeting her future partner, Tom McElligott, she became one of the five founding partners of a major creative force, Fallon McElligott Rice. Five years later, she left to found Rice & Rice Advertising, Inc. Her trek then led her to DDB Needham/Chicago for eight years, to Ogilvy/Chicago for a little less than a year, and then back to Minneapolis to BBDO. Now Nancy Rice has come full-circle and followed her heart to higher education—first as Worldwide Creative Director of Miami Ad School and now as full-time faculty and co-ordinator of the Advertising Program at the Minneapolis College of Art and Design. Rice says she is "committed to challenging and inspiring the future talent of the ad industry."

A CAREER WITH ATTITUDE

We've already learned about putting a portfolio together and creating great ads—as well as other pieces of communication. We've even addressed what to expect in your first job.

Now we need to explore ways to make your career blossom. We've touched slightly on this subject when we looked at Susan Gillette's career in Chapter 5. But in this and the following two chapters, we'll focus on ways to turn that initial talent into a successful career. We'll also continue to look at great ads and collect more good advice that will help you create them.

Nancy didn't start out as someone determined to become highly visible in the industry. In high school she was the class artist, drawing the event posters and doing the school bulletin boards. She figured there must be a way to make a living at it. So, she applied to the Minneapolis School of Art. Back then, says Rice, the college had a reputation as a fine arts school. It wasn't known as a terrific school for graphic design, much less advertising. But her older sister went there, and it did offer a degree in graphic design. So she became a graphic design major with a printmaking minor.

"In my second year, another student let me know about a job opening at a local art studio." The studio did finished illustrations, conventional key lining, and comp layouts for local ad agencies. She landed a job there cleaning shelves, cutting mats for the illustrators, and running errands. How did she get the job? "I cut great mats," says Rice, "and I was willing to work for practically nothing."

The job gave Rice more than money, it gave her an opportunity to get a feeling for what ads are like while being developed. "We'd get work from local agencies to comp up so they could present their ideas to their clients. I'd be mounting the work to make it look nice and would be saying, 'Can you believe this?' and 'What if they did this?' I rethought the projects the entire time I was there."

Nearing graduation, Rice planned to become a full-time employee at the studio. Instead, she was fired—by someone who liked her. Rice's supervisor (and one of the studio's owners) said, "It's not that we can't use you. It's that we don't think this is what you should be doing. You really ought to be at an ad agency." To urge her in that direction, he offered a list of people she could go see to get herself started.

Feeling hurt, she took his list, then went to the phone book to make her own list—of competing studios. She planned to go to work for one of them. "I'll show these guys," she thought to herself.

But, with many recent grads on the street looking for their first position at illustration, layout, and design studios, competition was stiff. So she decided to include some of suggestions on her ex-bosses' list just in case.

The last interview was in an office building she couldn't find. "The address just didn't make any sense to me," says Rice, "and, I didn't have a car. I took the bus and was on foot." She arrived an hour-and-a-half late—at Knox Reeves Advertising—and met with Tom Donovan, the Executive Art Director. "He seemed like a nice guy, and asked me to wait to see the Creative Director."

When the Creative Director, Ron Anderson, looked at her portfolio of student work, he hired her on the spot. Still determined to work at an illustration or design studio, she figured she'd stay until she found something better. Nancy stayed for 11-and-a-half years, eventually becoming VP, Senior Art Director. "I started in May of 1970 (three days out of art school) and stayed there until I left to form Fallon McElligott Rice. It was a great job, and I loved it!"

But Rice says her book back then would not compare to student books today. It wouldn't get her a job anywhere. She believes she got the job because she could draw and the agency's storyboard artist was quitting. "Lucky for me, a lot of people coming out of art schools majoring in graphic design couldn't draw. Still can't. That skill got me in the door. Which was all I needed."

Rice also notes that she was aggressive about making it known that she needed a job, wanted the position, and could start immediately. She thinks this helped. "It certainly was not my portfolio," says Rice. "I had some clunky package designs, some hand type renderings, some life drawings that were not particularly wonderful, and a few conventional keyline skills that weren't at all marketable."

Her first year, she mostly assisted more senior art directors—helping them comp their ideas and render storyboards. "A number of us there (about six or seven) were just out of school. We weren't assigned to any particular piece of business. We were like buzzards looking for anything that fell off the tables of more senior people," she recalls. "We took projects they didn't want and tried to make something out of them."

First Lessons

Rice learned something back then—the more she did, the more work her boss gave her. "It was like being thrown in a pond and getting bricks tossed to you. If you didn't sink, you'd get another one thrown to you," recalls Rice. "So the better work you did, the more you got."

Rice admits, though, it wasn't a very nurturing environment. She didn't have anyone assigned to train her. "You had to find it," says Rice. "This is someone else's quote, but it basically describes my creative director's management style— 'The Mushroom Theory'—which was keep 'em in the dark, feed 'em shit, and watch 'em grow. Somehow it worked for a lot of us there. Our CD was definitely not a micro-manager. He did give you feedback if you sought it out. I had to ask for my first raise after about a year-and-a-half," said Rice. "I was almost in tears. I asked, 'Am I doing okay or what?' 'Yeah, kid,' he said, 'you're doing great.'"

In addition to her creative director (Ron Anderson, later chairman of Bozell), the executive art director, who had first interviewed her, became her mentor. "He was very patient, and he'd calm me down," Rice says.

For instance, the first time she was assigned to cover a photo shoot, she didn't know what to do. She wondered how to get from the layout to the final photo—and was afraid she'd get fired for not knowing. "I'd been working there a year and nobody told me how to art direct a photo shoot. Pretty basic stuff."

She came in shaking. She wondered how to tell her boss that she didn't know what to do, and the executive art director took her through the process. "A lot of things in my early years were learned that way," says Rice. "I learned very early not to be afraid to ask questions, no matter who it annoyed. And I'm still learning. I don't think you ever stop."

Since she didn't get much feedback from her superiors, she just did things that made sense to her and her writing partners. "We figured out what turned us on, what turned us off. We also talked about how we wanted to be spoken to as consumers," says Rice, "and we used those insights as a guide."

For example, one of Rice's first campaigns was for West Publishing, one of the largest publishers of law books. West wanted to market their legal books to high school libraries. Since Rice and her copywriter partner were closer in age to high school students than anybody else at the agency, they got the assignment. "We had to do ads that would pique the interest of high school library purchasing agents and key decision makers," says Rice. "We just did it from our own young perspective— why we'd be interested in reading an excerpt from a law book while in high school. The client also wanted to incorporate a direct response coupon. We didn't know anything about the science of coupons, so didn't come in with any pre-conceived notions. Most creative teams ran screaming from 'coupon ads' in those days. We thought they were cool."

Their solution: a print campaign explaining that students need—and want—to know their rights. In one ad, a row of people waited for a job interview with a Native American student in the foreground. The ad said that students should know their rights, and the laws against discrimination, when applying for a job. These and other issues affecting their lives are contained in these books.

Another ad showed students protesting. A third one created controversy for the publisher, because it contained a visual of a pregnant teenager (Rice, though a bit older than a teenager, was even the model for the comp layout). "We thought there was a growing need for kids to be aware of their rights," says Rice. "And the campaign was very successful for them."

Like that campaign, most of the early campaigns Rice created were for clients of Knox Reeves' industrial division. "They didn't call it trade or 'business-to-business' advertising back then," recalls Rice. "This division was in the basement—three damp floors below the rest of the agency. The young teams were put on business that came out of that group. There were just a couple of people who worked down there. They were much older than the rest of the agency. And they were given all these down-and-dirty industrial accounts that no one wanted to work on except us. We saw these assignments as opportunities."

Rice and her peers were fascinated by the problem of trying to sell law books to libraries or refrigeration units to movie theaters. They'd ask themselves, "How could we make this interesting?" "I guess unattractive and dull products that were invisible to the consumer created a challenge we found exciting," says Rice. "It gave us the opportunity to do something wonderful and unexpected for the category and stand out in the publication. No one explained how a trade audience differed from a consumer audience, or what a sales force, a dealer, or a distributor was. They just sent us a job ticket, the size of the ad, and a stat of the logo. We had to figure it out for ourselves. Perhaps it was our naïveté that helped us do terrific stuff."

Rice realized that the people who bought business-to-business products were consumers, too. "Obviously if the product was good and performed a service, we would find its strength, where it could compete and win," says Rice, "and we did unusual, but relevant work."

The main thing Rice learned early in her career was that anything has the potential to be the subject of a powerful piece of communication, even on a small budget. "I've found that the bigger the budget, the glitzier the product or service, the more restrictions there are on the creativity," says Rice. "It's also harder to get through the layers of management on bigger pieces of business, both on the client and agency sides."

Anything Can Be Great

An event that cemented Rice's attitude that an ad for anything can be great—and resulted in her first award—was an ad she created for a local liquor store. Her first challenge was to create a message that would be approved by the city liquor commissioner. This store had a huge selection with the lowest prices. However, state law prohibited them from directly stating that they were the cheapest. They had to find a way of communicating this message without actually saying it. Their solution: a visual of a wine bottle with only the price sticker. The headline read, "Of the 2,500 labels we sell, the most impressive is the one we stick on in the store."

All the ads for the store were created on a very tight budget. Rice had to hand press the headline herself. She and a photographer went over to the liquor store, pinned up seamless paper right in the aisles, and shot the photograph themselves. Even the newspaper created the half-tones. "This ad and others won all sorts of awards." In one competition, this ad won in a category in which the US Army had entered. "That's when it genuinely occurred to me that it's the strongest idea that counts. It didn't matter that we produced our ad for around $100. And the Army had God knows how much," says Rice. "It told me I was on the right track. Don't be uptight if you don't have a flashy client or budget. What's important is the idea, how you say it, and that it's graphically refreshing."

During her 11-and-a-half years at Knox Reeves (later Bozell & Jacobs), Rice took on more and more responsibility. She worked with many different writers and became Executive Art Director and one of the first female Vice Presidents within that organization. "That was where I met Tom McElligott," she says. "He was just another staff writer I worked with from time to time."

The Next Stage—FMR

Her partnership with Tom McElligott led to the next stage of her career. Fallon McElligott Rice (FMR) came about because three people got together and decided to start an agency. Rice was not the first pick for Tom's partner. "Tom and Pat (Fallon) had worked together as freelancers," says Rice. "Their creative partner was my creative director, Ron Anderson. Somehow, the timing wasn't right for Ron. When I was approached, they had already decided to start an agency."

Rice took about a month to consider the move before she signed on. Once she decided to join them, the team chose two more partners and planned for a year before they resigned from their respective agencies and formed FMR.

During that year, they developed a business plan while McElligott and Rice did more freelance projects together, establishing themselves as a creative force prior to opening. Their goal was to have highly visible and award-winning projects ready to go as accounts. They wanted to use these projects to set the tone for the agency and help recruit employees. "A lot of agencies are built on a strong creative philosophy, but the philosophy isn't universally held by everyone in those organizations," said Rice. "We wanted to set up what we thought was the ideal situation—where everyone involved in the agency truly believed that our only edge was creativity."

"We wanted to be the best creative agency in the nation," said Rice. And they wanted to do it in Minneapolis. "We all had families and great lives here," she adds. "We didn't want to leave."

National Recognition

FMR was successful from the beginning. Some of their early ads won awards that brought them national headlines. They wanted the recognition for two reasons. First, they knew this would make potential clients notice the work they were doing. And they knew this would help them recruit top talent. "We merchandised the new agency through the national headlines we got by winning the awards," Rice says. "We liked that kind of visibility. So did our clients."

Rice's philosophy of advertising was manifested—as well as universally embraced—at FMR. "There wasn't an army of people who had different views of how an agency should work," she says. "Everyone was working together." Because of this, FMR was only small for a short time. "I guess the small and tight part was really only in the first year or two," says Rice. "Then we grew."

With FMR, Rice achieved everything she wanted—being part of an agency totally committed to creative advertising. "It was a great experience," says Rice. "I loved the clients. I loved the staff. I started doing some of the best work of my career. We were able to attract a lot of national clients that we first thought would never come to the Midwest."

All of FMR's clients—from a local church and a camping gear manufacturer to the *Wall Street Journal* and *Rolling Stone* magazine—genuinely believed that smart, well-targeted, thoughtful advertising with a creative edge could influence their bottom line. "I did my best work for clients who truly believed that," says Rice.

To this day, Rice doesn't discuss why she left FMR. She notes that there were growing ethical differences between her and some of her partners. However, she says that it had nothing to do with the staff, the clients, or the kind of work they were doing, and she remains very positive about the whole experience. So, after five years as a founding partner, Rice left to form yet another agency.

A Small Agency, Then a Big One

Her new agency, Rice & Rice Advertising, Inc., made a conscious effort to seek out clients that had a commitment to social responsibility and taking care of the planet. Many of them were also Fortune 500 companies. "This was long before it was trendy," says Rice. "I've always felt strongly about environmental issues and parts of society that don't seem to get a fair shake." Nancy and ex-husband, Nick, ran the award-winning agency for five years.

Rice was then sought out by a much larger agency, DDB Needham/Chicago. "I never considered leaving Minneapolis, but it was the right offer at the time. It was a wonderful experience as it was a very energetic office. Susan Gillette, who hired me, was President and absolutely marvelous. She was a true inspiration." And, Rice loved living in Chicago.

This was her first real experience with a worldwide agency network. "I had worked with Bozell & Jacobs for a few years after Knox Reeves was bought out by them, but that didn't really give me a sense of a close alliance of offices and certainly not a worldwide network," she recalls. "For me, that was the inspirational part of going to DDB. I realized that our ideas had the opportunity to be used on a global scale. That was very exciting. It was great sitting in meetings, listening to the genius of Keith Reinhard who eventually ran the global network. I loved being a part of it. Of course, I was also exposed to much larger clients than before."

After eight-and-a-half years, she joined Ogily/Chicago as a Managing Partner for a brief time, working on Sears. "I learned a lot about retail, largely from my partner, Marlena Peleo-Lazar, now head of creative for McDonald's Corp." When Rice's client from Sears left to take the leadership of the BBDO/Minneapolis office, Rice knew it was time to leave, too, accepting his offer to join the same agency back home in Minneapolis. "Big time homing instincts kicked in. I loved Chicago, but Minneapolis has been my career home and my physical home for most of my life. I really had an urge to return."

Following her position at BBDO, Nancy again listened to her instincts. She made a major career move and spent two-and-a-half years as Worldwide Creative Director for Miami Ad School. "After 32 years in the business, I took a step back and tried to figure out what I enjoyed about my day." Rice discovered that she liked helping the younger people working in the agency become better creatives. In addition, she knew that she enjoyed education, having led seminars at the Cooper Union and Syracuse University as well as speaking with students at other schools.

Rice chose the Miami Ad School, because she felt she'd do better with older students, people who had a little more life experience under their belts. She also felt that undergrads lacked focus due to too many other academic commitments.

She had another reason. Ron Seichrist, the head of the Miami Ad School, the person credited with inventing portfolio schools, had been one of her early teachers. "I was in the first graphic design class he ever taught, and he talked about a vision like this, but I was too young to know what the hell he meant," recalls Rice. "I guess I wanted to go back to my first teacher and learn some more."

Today, Rice continues her commitment to training the future of the industry. She's moved on from the portfolio schools and is leading the Advertising Program she's written for her alma mater, the Minneapolis College of Art and Design. While she's complimentary of the post-grad portfolio schools in general, Rice says, "Something's wrong when these talented students have to go to school for six years to be ready for the industry. That's why I'm now focusing on the undergrads at MCAD. These students are truly fantastic. Glad I'm not competing with them!"

Outside work, Nancy's always been family-oriented, spending as much time as possible with her daughters and new grandson. "Tables have definitely turned, though," says Rice. "They now have busy schedules I have to work around!" Both daughters are fine artists living and working in the Chicago suburbs. "After living in Chicago for eight-plus years, it's my second hometown and I still love it. Hope one of the girls always stays there so I have a place to crash when I'm in town."

Most of Nancy's friends also work in the industry as art directors, writers, designers, photographers, and illustrators. "It's a fun industry," says Rice. "So many talented people to help make your work wonderful. I still believe, as someone once said, that creativity is the last remaining legal means of gaining an unfair advantage over your competition."

ADS CREATED WITH AN ATTITUDE FOR GREATNESS

Rice begins her creative process by drawing little boxes with visuals and headlines. She and her writer partner go through the thumbnails and pick out the best ideas. They decide which might work best as magazine or newspaper ads or as posters or direct mail, or as something completely different. "Some are better for photography, some illustration, some as all type. Type is a great visual."

Typically, this is as tight as Rice gets before deciding which ideas to present. "Then everything stays up on the wall so the entire team can tweak things and stay in the loop with what's happening," says Rice. Her next stage is doing a bigger rendering, blowing up the thumbnails in the copier to keep the graphic balance.

Rice recognizes that everybody works differently, but even with tight computer comps, it's the idea that's king. "You shouldn't have to get tighter in your portfolio to show a great idea. Sometimes it's important to make them tighter, especially if you're a kick-ass art director/designer. It depends on who you're trying to impress. There are no rules."

—— THE EPISCOPAL CHURCH ——

This campaign was started by McElligott and Rice a year before founding FMR. When they started the agency, it became one of their first accounts. The client, Rev. George Martin, followed Rice when she went on to form Rice & Rice (and years later, performed the wedding ceremony for one of her daughters).

The concept for the original campaign began with the client, who wondered, "Why can't we run intelligent, witty ads that invite people to join us in worship?"

Each execution explores a different position taken by the Episcopal church: that people are part of the "family" and will find a home there; that it shouldn't be just parents who attend but also children; that church explores all aspects of life: world hunger, nuclear power, materialism, etc. "There were also some strong ads against TV Christianity and the moral majority," says Rice. "Those were the only alternative forms of worship the campaign attacked."

Rice believes this campaign is another form of evangelism. "It's getting the word out in a way that's closer to selling a car, so people will be more interested in hearing what we have to say." She adds, "All we're trying to say is here's a community that feels a certain way. If you feel the same, come join us."

Rice worked on the campaign for over five years. The work also led to projects from the National Episcopal Church as well as their Native American Field Office in Oklahoma.

—— ROLLING STONE ——

The One Club called this campaign one of the ten best of the 1980s. It was the only print campaign to make their list. It very simply repositioned the magazine in the minds of potential advertisers. This was one of the last campaigns she created at FMR.

Rice thinks that each piece of communication should have one idea and not try to say everything. "Have one strong message that can be communicated and acted upon or thought about," she advises.

—— RICE & RICE ——

Here's proof that any piece of communication—regardless of format, budget, deadline, size—can be a gem.

Many creatives look at little announcements as something to get out of the way quickly.

On the contrary, Rice looks at them as chances to do something wonderful. This one was featured in *Adweek* and also won in the One Show. Her daughters' birth announcement won an Andy (she listed her daughters as the clients).

"From the get-go I volunteered to do anything, birth announcements for colleagues, invitations to the local ad club, anything." Says Rice, "What's worked for me over the years is the belief that I can make something out of anything."

—— GOLD'N PLUMP CHICKENS ——

"It's exciting to take a fresh viewpoint to solve a problem," says Rice.

"Coming in without a lot of preconceived notions is an advantage." In this case, it was especially true.

Rice believes every piece of communication should be thought of as a clear roadmap to information. "The fewer detours and barriers you set up, the better chance you have to communicate quickly to customers. They have short attention spans and much better things to do than read ads. You want them to know you appreciate they've taken the time to stop, look, and listen. You want to reward them by giving something of value to take away." She adds, "That's the approach I take with everything—have I made this easy and compelling?"

— SUCCESSFUL FARMING —

Rice estimates that 80 percent of her career has focused on selling business-to-business related products and services, while 20 percent has been selling to the general public. She says she likes working with consumer-related clients because of the high visibility of the communications. But she loves the challenge of working with the complexities of a business target. Among her b-2-b clients were high-end office products, agriculture, publishing, salon products, and financial advisors. "You learn a lot working with a diverse mix of clients," she says, which is one reason she has yet to consider going to the client side. "It seemed limiting, just focusing on one client, every day. I like a lot of varitey."

Clearly, whatever the challenge, Rice tries to look at each from a different point of view. What seems like a dull product to some isn't dull to the people who want it.

Finally, most advertising challenges within certain categories have some similarities. "You can apply a number of the same principles no matter what the assignment is," she says. This was a trade ad for a publication most of us will never see. Rice created something that not only won awards, but gained the magazine lots of recognition.

SOME KERNELS OF TRUTH FROM NANCY RICE

You've already heard Rice's most important advice—that since any piece of communication can be great, you should try to make it great. "This attitude helped me when I started and still does," says Rice.

She thinks it's beneficial to create invitations for seminars, agency parties, small-space ads, sales kits, materials for agency pitches, mail aheads, leave-behinds, Christmas cards, and even birth announcements. "I'd even give away my time to do projects like these," says Rice. "It's amazing what you can make out of them. And the pieces can start getting you some visibility."

Rice says she often hears excuses like "I never get to meet the client," or "I never get to sell the work." Her response: "Who cares? If you decide that the account is a dog or feel it's an insignificant piece, your attitude is never going to work for you." She thinks that you have to sniff around and make it great. Once you have something, then you have a right to complain. "There are so many students that are browbeat into producing a good book with someone standing over them saying move this here and that there," she says. "And that's really not the way it works, because if they can't do their book a second time, they're out of there. Talent is a price of entry. You need to become a profit center."

But talent and attitude is not enough. There are other things you must consider. So to help you along, here are some more ideas and suggestions from Nancy Rice.

Go for variety: "You can't have a book full of double-page spreads and expect to get a job with that," warns Rice. "You need to show how many notes are on your scale—that you have a variety of approaches to problem solving, whether you're a copywriter or an art director." She also wants you to recognize the convergence of media and that traditional methods are out the window because people can choose when they're being contacted. And she expects you to embrace all media and not be frightened that an idea has to reach another culture in another part of the planet. And she expects to see a variety of clients in a portfolio—not just a selection of small retailers or just big brand ads. Rice thinks it's also important to have a variety of partners. "You need to have a book that reflects what you can do on anything, with anyone."

Show you can write: "There are lots of books that have gone very, very visual, and copywriters aren't showing that they can write," observes Rice. "They need to show that they can write. They need to show that they're versatile."

Team up: Like Ted Bell (Chapter 4), Rice thinks that aspiring art directors and copywriters should work together. "The majority of good schools really push that team spirit and let you know you are not all by yourself. It's your group that influences the ideas that go into an ad."

She adds, "It's smart to work with a teammate while putting portfolios together. Back when I was at an agency, I even said, 'Well, look up this person we just interviewed the other day. Here's her address. She has some good ideas; you have some good ideas. Why don't you get together and work on your books?'"

Learn to be a quick study: In advertising, you have to be able to get up to speed quickly. "I heard this put best by a copywriter during a new business pitch. We were pitching a technical medical product, and the prospective client was concerned we didn't have medical experience. The copywriter said, 'When changing agencies, I started my last week at Agency X finishing some spots for Crispy Wheats and Raisins. I ended that same week at Agency Y writing trade ads for Honeywell Mach 4 Torpedoes.' Inside an agency you'll have to change gears quickly, often in the same day," says Rice.

Find good-quality products and services to work on: "It's hard for me to manufacture the 'up,' the passion and energy, that I think is necessary to sell products and services," says Rice. "If I thought a product was a dog or the people on the client side were dogs to work with, I had trouble providing a good service." Even early on, Rice turned down working on a product she didn't believe in. "If I thought it was genuinely bad," she says, "they'd find something else for me to work on."

Picture someone very specific: Rice believes you should be able to say, "This is the person I want to convince that this is a relevant piece of information about a service or product at this certain point," because this helps you focus your message. To find out what would be the most compelling piece of information as well as the key benefit to someone, Rice believes in research. "Find out what the customer wants and if the product or service can deliver it. Learn all you can about both. That's where the 'aha' comes from," she says.

Say only what matters: "I think it's important to find the strongest attribute of a product or service," says Rice, "to find an arena where you have a chance of winning." How? By knowing the product, the people who will buy or use it, and the competition. "There may be 15 important things to say, but you must separate out those things and only communicate what will be perceived as a benefit."

Execute your ideas: "One thing that attracts me to a book is the ability to put great ideas down in fresh and exciting ways. Hey, I'm an art director. Show me what you've got under the hood! I want to know that you don't need three assistants to render your ideas," says Rice. "I'm not talking about layout skills, but how you create a balance between emotion, execution, and directness. It's hard to teach that. It's less important to have things highly comped and rendered. It's more important to have a great idea in a rough form than a bad idea perfectly rendered—unless you're going for a layout position, which is what I did in the beginning. I didn't know at that point that my ideas were any good. At the time, I competed where I could win."

Learn to sell: Rice reminds us that you should always have a reason why you did something. "It's cool," doesn't cut it. "Develop the ability to speak persuasively with different types of people, especially linear thinkers. Young artists are not necessarily used to that. Learn to reason with them and to have good negotiating skills.

"Be prepared to answer questions about your work and defend it. Your work is a constant audition. You have to have the ability to sell it all along the way."

Make sure the team supports the idea: "Many times a team member will not have the same vision you have and will end up sabotaging the effort," she warns. "That's the most frustrating. When you sell an idea to a client, it's important that everybody supports it. No matter what, you really have to present a unified front. Even with a client who doesn't like to be sold. Especially if you're asking your client to stick their neck out and do something different—a.k.a. 'risky'—that's all they'll need, a hole. If the client is not sure that you're sure, they'll look for an opening to think, 'Hey, wait a minute, they're not really convinced of this.' It can take just a little to put the skids on a great idea. So, if someone's going to sabotage the effort, find out quickly, and don't bring them to the table."

Don't take it personally: "One of the most important things for a young person to learn is that you have to have a fairly thick skin. If you get criticism, whether or not it's productive, you have to realize that it is about the work and not you," says Rice. "It's not because they don't like you, it's because something isn't working. Some very fine work will not go through. That is just the way it is. It doesn't make you any less of a creative person. It's just, for one reason or another, it didn't fly."

Develop the ability to keep rethinking work: "Work will get rejected," says Rice. "Your idea might not fly with your partner. Your creative director may reject it. Your supervisor, creative director, and everybody else could be loving it, and then you get to the top and someone doesn't like it. Develop the ability early on to take your losses quickly and move on. Keep alive the ability to go back to the well and develop new stuff. More often than not, it'll be better stuff, smarter stuff."

Promote (merchandise) yourself: "Hey, that's your profession, selling. So why not take some quality time to promote the most important brand you'll ever represent—yourself. There's a lot of good work out there that's great, but the creative teams that came up with the stuff are anonymous. Their bad," says Rice. "Creative people should make sure they're visible with their work—whether it's through award shows or simply through joining advertising clubs and meeting people."

Know where you're interviewing: Rice recognizes that not everybody can or wants to work in New York, Los Angeles, Chicago, or some other major advertising center of the universe. "When you're actively interviewing, it's more important to know about the agency, the creative director, and their clients than the true market situation of the ads in your portfolio," reminds Rice. "If you have a target city, get to know the agencies there and who's doing the good work. If you've set your sites on a particular agency no matter where, get to know what's going on with them and get smart about what they're doing well."

Get a job: "A lot of times, your first job won't be the best," says Rice. "But it gives you access to other talented people and a lot of great resources. You can start building or re-building your portfolio. You might be in a group that might not be doing the best stuff, but you're getting a paycheck and experience, not to mention paying back those student loans. In addition, if you think, 'I can't believe what they're doing, this could be wonderful,' then do your own approach and put it in your book. In addition, if there's another young person at the agency who has the same fire in their belly or even at the agency next door—hook up, talk about each other's accounts, and make two books happen. Some legendary teams have started just that way."

Freelance: "There are a lot of decent little businesses that can't afford huge agencies. It's too bad a number of these places aren't a little smarter and advertise that they'd produce a good campaign if a young creative team wants to come in and do it," says Rice. "Find a client who won't burn you; make sure the client can at least pay your out-of-pocket expenses. Then use it as a way to get some good work produced and to merchandise yourself."

Volunteer for pro bono work: "Good ideas are good ideas no matter who they're for," says Rice. "Actually, pro bono work is not that easy. You can run into a lot of 'well-meaning' committee members who don't know much about advertising but have a lot to say about it and your ideas nonetheless. But, on the other hand, it can be fantastic. It benefits a good cause, and it gets you working with clients. Who cares whether you had to sit in a meeting and go through eight months of work to produce some advertising for someone. Is it good work? Did it do something for somebody?"

Enter awards shows: "There's been a lot of industry whining about whether creative people are doing real work for awards shows," says Rice. "They'll go and create some ads and give them to the local dry cleaner who runs them in the local newspaper. Then they enter them in shows and get a lot of publicity and awards.

"I think people who create terrific work for little clients should be rewarded, not punished. You tend to find more of that being done in agencies where people aren't being given the opportunity to do good work; they'll go out and seek things like that." Awards shows can get you some peachy job offers. The One Show is considered one of the top job-networking shows in the country. Make it a goal to be there as a winner, student or otherwise, as soon as you can."

Treat vendors with respect: "Most people in this business have quite a few jobs along the way," says Rice. "The people who will stick with you and work with you (and help you) wherever you go are the suppliers—the printers, photographers, typographers, illustrators, etc. So make sure they're treated as team members."

Rice warns that you should always remember you're building a career that will span many places and not one position at one agency. "I don't say that to be disruptive to the agency team spirit," she says, "it's just that, although I've only had five advertising jobs, most people at my level have had seven to twelve."

Be prepared for coincidences: "I've had my ideas show up in someone else's book. Once it was an ad that a client had rejected. There was no way the person could have seen it. So I hired him because I knew he was thinking along the same lines as me," says Rice. "But replicating an idea—either on purpose or by mistake—happens quite a bit.

"I've done it. I've gone all the way to production with an idea, then found it in a 20-year-old awards book. There's just no way you can know everything that's been done. Just hope your client feels the same way."

Show you're hungry: Rice believes that your presentation is important. "If there were five people interviewing for a position and they all had great art direction and great ideas, the one that would get it is the one who showed the desire, the drive.

"That person must really want the job," says Rice. "Show that you're willing to take any type of assignment and that you're aspiring to do great work. Most people come in wanting to work on the agency's prime accounts. The reality is, you're not going to get a shot at those."

Get a life: "It's important to have time away from your agency, time to travel, read, go to films, listen to music, play with the kids," muses Rice. "If you want to think of it from a materialistic point of view, all those experiences will make you a better ad person. It gives you material to draw on. Dull people make dull ads. If you want to touch people, you have to be in touch with real life." When she's not working, Rice enjoys cooking, remodeling, gardening, canoeing, music, and travelling, as well as visiting her two daughters and their families in Chicago. "I always spent a lot of time with my daughters outside of work, even when it wasn't very popular with my business partners. That can be, and still is, perceived as a negative in the industry—especially for females—but I never cared. Family's forever. So many collapse when their career changes because they've also sacrificed their family and friends along the way."

Have outside interests: "I think it's important, not just for a creative person's life-long education, but also for their emotional survival to have a life beyond their job," counsels Rice. "You want to be an interesting person for your partner to sit across the table from."

"With an industry in constant flux, this is especially important. When clients cut their budgets, advertising is often the first item to be slashed. So, if your agency is the one affected, guess what?! It's so important to know that your life doesn't begin and end with your job (no matter how much you love it). People can get very hopeless when shit hits the fan. Your talent doesn't vanish just because your position does. Have faith in your talent, and have a positive real life and support system of family and friends to be part of while you decide what's next."

Be open-minded to people who are less experienced than you: "They bring fresh ways of looking at things. Sometimes a student will get hung up if their partner is a semester or two behind them. Just be open to ideas coming from everywhere. When someone doesn't know all the 'rules,' they're not afraid to break them."

Keep your eyes and ears open: "Ideas come from everywhere," says Rice. "Sometimes the best ideas happen on a boat or in a shower. It's your life outside the agency that gives you your ideas." Rice believes it's important to talk and listen to everyone. "Bounce ideas off other people," she says. "Not necessarily your creative teammate, but others in the agency—the receptionist or the accountant.

"Clients have wonderful ideas, your kids have ideas, even your next-door neighbors have ideas."

Be an information junkie: "You have to just hunger to find out everything you possibly can. Find out what's missing from the brief," says Rice. "Nowadays agencies have armies of intelligent people looking for information. But never forget that just because you're a creative person, that's still part of your job.

"Often the creative person can find a business idea just as much as an entire research department can, as good as they are. Don't forget that you're a businessperson, too, and you can come up with these insights also."

Look for idea people and problem solvers: "Each department within an agency is basically another creative department," says Rice. "I've found some of the most talented people in the media department. Just idea people.

"They're everywhere in an agency. They're in design firms. They're trend specialists. Each client that you have the ability to work with brings in a whole new set of people that think and interact.

"Go in wide-eyed and skeptical at the same time. You have to always have both sides of that. Like a child-like fascination with everything, but with one eyebrow raised to watch the bullshit meter. If you don't love both those sides, then this is not the industry for you."

Make unwanted advances known: "I was once removed from a piece of business because a client representative physically came on to me," says Rice. "I complained and ended up being taken off the account. That made me angry because I liked the account, but I was in no position to control my destiny at that point. That happens a lot in this business. That doesn't mean you should put up with it.

"It happens conversely, too. Clients go after young men. If it happens, go and complain to your supervisor and make it well known. Visibility is the best defense. If it's covered up at your agency—if that's their attitude toward young women or men—you should probably get the hell out."

Be prepared for change: "There's a lot of movement within the field," says Rice. "You really have to be prepared to have many different careers if you want to last in this business. Situations change, people change, partners change, clients change, and agencies you work at will change. If you stay someplace long enough it may become two or three different agencies along the way. Knox Reeves certainly did.

"People don't stay for large chunks of time anymore at an agency, and that can be good or that can be bad. You just have to be open to the fact that things are going to change. And you have to grow in a positive way from situations that you perceive are negative, because they're always going to be there. You just have to pull back and say, 'Well now, things have changed, and it's time to re-think this or that and move on.' And then you move on from your point of view, position, whatever."

POSTSCRIPT 1:

THOUGHTS FROM A CLASS

Throughout the chapter, we heard about the attitude you must take to create breakthrough work—no matter what kind of product or service you're selling.

Since attitude plays such a big role in your early years, let's spend a little more time on this subject. Here are the thoughts that Rice presented to a graduate class she taught at Syracuse.

Rice opened the three-day seminar with the following words: "You have probably spent a lot of time poring over years of advertising and design awards books like D&AD, *CA*, *Graphis*, *Print*, and One Show. And if you haven't, shame on you.

"On those pages, you'll find the best collection of what's hot and very little of what's not, and it may have already occurred to you that as you're paging through those books, you're seeing great work for clients like Levi's or Apple Computer, that it's going to be a long time before you'll ever get a chance to work on great products like those.

"They're probably spending about a zillion dollars on ads for television. 'How long will I have to wait before I can do great stuff like that? How long before I can get anyone to notice me?'

"'I want to work on a great account at my agency. I want to work at a good agency. I want my first job. I want to change jobs.'

"'My creative director just doesn't get it. I've got great stuff in me now, I just don't know how to get it out. Because I have such small accounts. My accounts are dogs, and I want to show what I can do.'

"The problem is not your accounts. The problem is your attitude.

"Many of the people whom you admire, who are doing those big accounts now, started just that way. And now we're going to do an assignment together. This is what we're going to do.

"I asked you to bring in the Yellow Pages from your hotel room. We're going to go through here, pick out a client, and find out about that place. By tomorrow morning you are going to come back in and you're going to have picked the client, you're going to have called them up, and we're going to fill in a positioning statement. We're going to decide whom they're trying to reach and what you want to tell them about your client's business. Whether it is true or not, it's going to be set in stone by the end of class tomorrow.

"And then we're going to talk about how to do some ads around it. And then we're going to come in with some sketches, and that's as far as we're going to go."

Rice concluded the seminar with these comments: "This exercise was to just develop an attitude that no matter what it is, it can be exciting. We picked tiny little insignificant things. Some people picked brick manufacturers. A place that made American flags. A place that taught square dance. I did the assignment the night before I came, and we picked a tattoo parlor (see portfolio section). The fact is, you can approach almost everything you do this way.

"No matter what it is, you can do something exciting.

"And that was the whole basis for the three days. That's what we talked about: The fact that you don't have to wait; that you can do terrific work on what you have right now; that you can start making yourself visible with what you have at your fingertips."

Postscript 2:

LAYOFFS AND YOUR LIFE

In the advertising industry, highly talented, productive people can still find themselves losing their jobs for a number of reasons. As you may recall it even happened to Roy Grace (Chapter 9) and Steve Hayden (Chapter 3) early in their careers.

In fact, it could happen to anyone in the industry at any point. And it's becoming more prevalent every day. In addition, the industry is filled with job-hopping.

So what does this mean to you in structuring your career? As a former agency owner who then moved back into the role of being an employee, Nancy Rice has been forced to grapple with the tenuousness of having an agency position.

Here's what she has to say:

"One thing I'd say that I've thought about a lot over the past few years is that I was really lucky with my first job in the industry. I had a long period of time there, which I didn't think was a long period, but it was—11-and-a-half years. My God! And the next two positions I had were as an owner, so I almost didn't think of them as different jobs.

"I think in my early career I was really quite naïve about what people learned when they experienced different agencies. I think I arrogantly looked down on it. I thought that you're supposed to get a job at one place and stay forever. And, unless you move on because you're building another agency, movement must be something really bad.

"Then when I became an employee again, I thought, 'Man, I'm moving around a lot.' And then I thought, 'Wow, why didn't I ever think of doing that before?'

"I learned so much that I would have never learned if I had never set foot inside great agencies like DDB or Ogilvy or BBDO. You should never forget that you have much to learn wherever you go.

"It keeps you fresh to look on the variety as a really neat learning experience, as scary as it is.

"Layoffs have become a way of life in the past few years, and we'd never had it in the industry before as open as it is. I've seen some amazing people, huge award winners, laid off and out on the street. And they just have to say, 'Wow, it's time to re-think this and try something different.'

"It's going to happen. Almost everyone is going to experience it in his or her career at some point for whatever reason.

"You just have to be prepared for it. Stuff is going to happen. The people who hired you are going to leave. Accounts are going to leave. Presidents of agencies are going to leave. People are going to pass away. Agencies are going to merge or split. It happens, and you have to be ready.

"Change, though, doesn't mean you have to be paranoid. You just have to know that at some point you are going to be affected. It just happens, and a lot of times it happens for the absolute right reasons, and you just have to be open to the next opportunity. You've got to be honest with yourself why something didn't work out. And then you go, 'Well, it's time to move on.'

"The good news is that in some cities small and mid-sized firms are actually hiring a lot of people, giving people shots and trying them out. That surely was the way it was when I entered the business. I entered in an agency that was about to be downsized. And it was the young kids coming out of school that were good and eager, and were getting some of the jobs.

"The opportunities are there; it's just taking longer.

"I've seen students get an amazing position and lose it within the year as part of cuts, and they go, 'Oh my god, it's so bogus.' And then right away they find something else and they're doing much better. They haven't stopped producing one iota. They're doing really good work. Good people will continue to do good work.

"People entering the field have to be smarter, better, and more eager. I don't think anything's changed about having to love this field. I don't think anything's changed about having to totally love your craft. You have to love starting from nothing and creating something wonderful. A lot of times you have to be your own Tom Sawyer and talk yourself into a positive attitude.

"But that's a pretty good attitude for life, too."

A motorcycle it ain't.

What is it?

It's a Vespa. A motorscooter.

The difference between a Vespa motorscooter and a motorcycle is that your neighbors won't move out of the neighborhood when you drive home on a Vespa.

The Vespa is a piece of transportation that makes the kind of sense nobody can argue with.

The Vespa is quiet. It has an oversize muffler. You can drive it at night without making anybody mad.

It'll give you between 125 and 150 miles to a gallon. Depending on how you drive. And using regular gas.

It's one of the most reliable pieces of machinery ever made. The Vespa engine has only three moving parts. There's not much that can break. (People have driven Vespas over 100,000 miles without major repairs.) And it's so simple to work on, a complete tune-up costs six dollars.

It's air-cooled. There's no radiator. So there's no water to boil, no anti-freeze to buy.

The transmission is so well built that it's guaranteed for life.* It's direct drive. No chains to break, no driveshafts to grease.

Vespa has unitized body construction. The whole thing is made from one piece. It isn't bolted together. It can't rattle apart.

Of course, we don't want to give you the impression that it's all sense, but no go.

Just for kicks, a guy in Austin, Minn., entered his Vespa in a professional motorcycle ice race. He had never competed in anything be-fore. But he ran away from everything in sight. The next year motorscooters were banned.

But then, as we said before, a motorcycle it ain't.

Vescony, Inc., 949 Commonwealth Avenue, Boston, Massachusetts. Overseas delivery available.
*Providing regular maintenance is performed in accordance with schedule outlined in the warranty. Warranty provides for replacement or repair (at importers' option) of all transmission parts at no cost for either parts or labor. ©1964 Vescony, Inc.

Ed McCabe

"For a business that thrives on imagination, there's amazingly little of it in advertising."

Throughout this book, we've met creative people who've thrived because of their imaginations. In this chapter, we'll see how far you can go with just imagination—and some of the roadblocks that can come up along the way.

Ed McCabe, writer, sportsman, adventurer, frustrated artist, and advertising legend, has won virtually every advertising award possible. In some years, he won more awards than entire agencies—even the creative ones. He was the youngest person ever inducted into the Copywriter's Hall of Fame.

McCabe's lack of formal training may have contributed to his success. "People tried to teach me the rules, and I learned them all over a long and arduous period of time. And I learned all the writing styles, all the methods," says McCabe. "But I've never been a technique person. I try to identify the substance and put it in my work. I have an innate instinct for boiling things down to the most simple and naive way of presenting an idea."

When McCabe talks about the clients he's worked with, he talks in the first person. "We wanted our product to.... They understood what we were doing.... Our objective was to..." It shows his strong affinity for his clients' goals, and it may partly explain why many of his campaigns have had great longevity.

THE MAKING OF AN ADVERTISING LEGEND

Live by your instincts. McCabe learned to follow this simple philosophy early in life. At the age of eight, after the death of his father, he got his first job, working in a Chicago newsstand. At 15, bored and with a history of juvenile delinquency, he dropped out of school. He had been attending a tough public high school on Chicago's north side and felt he was only being taught how to survive. "And I already knew that," he says.

These events forced him to rely on his instincts. "I had to make quick decisions. Friend or foe."

They'll Hire Anybody

McCabe was first exposed to the profession shortly after leaving school.

Needing a job, he went to an employment agency, and the recruiter sent him on many interviews. But no one was interested.

The recruiter tried everything. She even sent him to Spiegel Catalog to take an aptitude test for a copywriter position (the results said he'd make a better auto mechanic than copywriter, establishing McCabe's skepticism about testing right from the start). Finally, one day, the recruiter said, "I've got it. I'll send you to an ad agency. They'll hire anybody."

She advised McCabe to lie about having a high school diploma and sent him to interview at McCann Erickson for a job in the mailroom. McCabe got the job and earned a modest salary. But he kept his eyes and ears open.

He took in everything and decided that the creative people have the most fun. He observed that the women were attractive, that the men were nice looking, that they all drove nice cars and seemed to have a lot of money. McCabe was impressed.

After a few months, McCabe asked to transfer to the art department. There, he worked emptying water pots and cleaning brushes.

The bullpen for the traffic department was nearby, which gave him an opportunity to get acquainted with the people in that area as well. He began to learn how the work flowed through the agency.

He also learned who worked on what account and how the work progressed.

He noticed that one copywriter was perpetually behind in his assignments because he was having an affair with a woman in the art department. McCabe saw another opportunity. He went to the writer with a proposition: "I know you'd like to see your friend at lunch, but I also know you've got six ads overdue and a bunch of little trade ads to do. I'd like to try my hand, so why don't you let me help? What do you have to lose?"

The copywriter took advantage of this offer and gave him some assignments. His first ad was for International Harvester. A few months later the agency entered it in a competition, and it won a merit award from the Advertising Club of Chicago.

McCabe continued to work on the copywriter's projects, and after about a year, he went to the copy chief with the portfolio he'd developed and asked to become a full-time writer. The copy chief refused to accept that anyone without a college degree—let alone without a high school diploma—could write ads.

"I think it was an act of self-preservation," says McCabe. Since upper management had never sanctioned McCabe's writing activities and the copy chief had refused to grant him a promotion, he quit.

His next job was with Automatic Electric, a manufacturing subsidiary of General Telephone. The first ad he wrote there also won an award.

Says McCabe, "I didn't know the rules, so I didn't get caught up in either playing by them or trying to break them." This gave him an edge in creating unusual—but appropriate—ads.

After two years at the telephone company, McCabe was attracted to the unique work being done at Doyle Dane Bernbach. He decided to pursue a career writing consumer ads. So he quit his job. "I always quit before getting another job," says McCabe. "I'm a dangerous kind of guy. I love to do things the hard way."

Once interested in advertising, McCabe read everything he could find on the field. He studied the people who were successful in the 1930s and '40s, people like James Webb Young, Raymond Rubicam, Claude Hopkins, and Albert Lasker.

He observed that the greatest ads were simple, honest, and very obvious.

He admired work like "A Hog Can Cross the Country Without Changing Trains—But YOU Can't!" for the Chesapeake & Ohio Railway Company.

McCabe also read Strunk and White's *Elements of Style* and the Harvard Classics. In addition, he'd been writing Broadway-style shows, short stories, and poetry. In spite of his lack of formal education, he was clearly a writer.

But because there was a recession, he couldn't find a job. After more than seven months of unemployment, he decided to try his luck in New York. He went there with his girlfriend. She was working as an assistant advertising manager of a bank in Chicago and wanted to learn copywriting. So McCabe helped her develop a portfolio. Says McCabe, "She comes to New York and gets a job as a copywriter at Macy's. The first day. Me, I can't get elected. I ended up as a cashier in Schrafft's."

For the most part, McCabe's portfolio consisted of trade and industrial ads. Says McCabe, "There were not a lot of broad-minded people in advertising who could see how someone could make the transition to consumer." McCabe believes that this still is the case today because "people need to classify and categorize." Just like Steve Hayden (Chapter 3), his lack of consumer experience held him back.

McCabe finally took a job at an industrial agency, where he was asked to write 70-page technical brochures for clients like GE. Topics included thermionic integrated micro modules. His goal was to convert what the engineers told him into English. Again, like Hayden, McCabe believes this experience helped him later on in his career.

Still determined to do consumer advertising, McCabe continued applying to Doyle Dane Bernbach, as well as to other agencies.

Around that time, Benton & Bowles introduced a campaign for Western Union that excited McCabe. It consisted of a picture of a telegram with the headline saying, "Ignore it." Then, on the telegram, it said, "Ignore a telegram? You can't." McCabe recalls, "It was very powerful and epitomized everything I believed about good advertising."

So McCabe sent them a telegram that said, "Ignore a telegram? You can't. That's why I'm sending this. I'm a copywriter and I need a job." Benton & Bowles called him for an interview. They kept him in a room for more than 45 minutes until he accepted a job. They kept bringing in new people to try to convince him to take the job. "Little did they know," he says. "They thought that DDB would hire me in a minute if they let me walk."

What took him so long to accept the job? While waiting in the reception area, McCabe began to have second thoughts about the agency because he saw some of their work that wasn't so terrific. Once on board, however, McCabe began working on television ads for Maxwell House Coffee and Gaines Dog Food.

His first assignment was for Instant Maxwell House Coffee featuring an American theme using Norman Rockwell paintings. "It never ran," says McCabe. "But everybody loved it around the agency because it was unusual without trying to be unusual."

In another campaign, he had male celebrities like Edward G. Robinson and Vincent Price talking about cooking and coffee. "I was interested in cooking and thought that it would be interesting and unusual to use men as spokesmen for coffee. If I was going to use celebrities, I wanted to do it differently."

At that time, Benton & Bowles was a hotbed of talent. McCabe worked with such creatives as Amil Gargano and Roy Grace. But aspects of Benton & Bowles, such as big-agency politics and the feeling that he wasn't living up to his potential there, disturbed McCabe. The last straw, however, came during a client meeting.

McCabe presented a print ad he'd written and tried to sell it to the client on the basis of its uniqueness. The client responded with a puzzled look and asked why uniqueness was so important. At that moment, after more than two years of employment there, McCabe decided there was absolutely no future for him at that agency. Says McCabe, "I couldn't work for any place that put up with a client that stupid."

McCabe still aspired to DDB, where he thought clients would be less conservative and stodgy, but they still wouldn't hire him. So he moved to yet another agency, and his career continued to grow. He won quite a few awards for work on accounts like Elgin Watches and Chun King.

McCabe lasted at that agency for only six months. He quit because he disliked their management style. "I worked on projects and found out that three other guys were working on the same project," says McCabe. "I don't mind competition, but I don't like underhanded competition. Bosses would be selling their own stuff and using your work as a foil to feed their own egos. There's a lot of that in certain places in this business."

Again McCabe applied to DDB. Again, no luck.

So this time he took a job at Young & Rubicam, but he only lasted there for eight months.

McCabe quit because he thought his Christmas bonus was too big. "I tried to give it back because I thought if they gave that kind of money to someone who had only worked there for six months—and had done as little as I had—they probably gave other undeserving people all kinds of money. I inherently believe that you should get rewarded for a job well done and not for simply occupying a seat. I told them so, and they laughed at me.

"I decided to move on because, philosophically, I was a misfit."

Shortly before McCabe quit, a copywriter working under him said he was applying for a job at Carl Ally. This copywriter was only making $16,000 and the job paid $2,000 more. He applied, but wasn't hired. Since McCabe knew Amil Gargano from Benton & Bowles, he called him up and asked for the job. He had to cut his salary in half, but he took it.

While at Carl Ally, McCabe worked on consumer products (Salada Tea, Vespa Motor Scooters, Citizens for Clean Air) and won four major gold medals the first year. They tripled his salary.

"That's where I really made a big name for myself," says McCabe. Why was he able to make a bigger name for himself here than at his previous jobs? Two key reasons. The management of the agency supported him, and he worked directly with the clients.

McCabe stayed at Ally for three years. Then he received a long-awaited call from Bill Bernbach offering him a job. Finally. He met with their key people.

But when word got out that Bernbach was thinking of hiring him, DDB's middle management protested. Ten of them said that they were hoping to be considered for the position that been had offered to McCabe. They weren't happy.

"I got wind of it and told Bernbach it would be very bad for his agency to hire me," he says. "He agreed, and we were friends from then on."

But this offer gave McCabe the fire to seek more. "It was my year," he says. "I felt I was very valuable to Carl Ally, Inc., and I wanted more stock than I had."

He asked for a certain percentage, and they offered him half of what he wanted. Says McCabe, "I just couldn't see myself spending the rest of my life settling for half of what I wanted. I decided that the only way to get what I wanted was to work on my own."

Then Sam Scali called McCabe and asked him to recommend a copywriter because he and some others were thinking of starting an agency. "I called Scali back and said, 'Yeah, I have your man.' He said, 'Who?' I said, 'Me.' So we negotiated for about five months. I told Carl I was leaving and announced that we were opening an agency."

Scali, McCabe, Sloves went into business in 1967—without clients or prospects. Their first client was Volvo, which happened to have been with Carl Ally.

McCabe had done some work on Volvo, and they called asking if the new agency would be interested in pitching the account. McCabe said yes, they got the account, and the agency was under way. Scali, McCabe, Sloves quickly became one of the top creative agencies.

In 1978, the agency principals sold Scali, McCabe, Sloves to Ogilvy & Mather. Part of the agreement was that Ogilvy people were barred from the premises. "We wanted to protect what we'd built," says McCabe. "They were good about it—as long as it worked. We ran it the same way we had always run it."

But eventually the focus shifted. As a division of a larger organization, pressure grew to maximize profits. McCabe felt that this was a mistake. He felt the goal should be to be the best agency—then the profits would come.

Suddenly, McCabe was taking the kind of clients he'd always wanted to escape—big companies who weren't all that interested in great advertising. Says McCabe, "As soon as you put profit ahead of principle, you're in trouble."

Consequently, in 1986, McCabe decided to take a few years off. He drove in a car race in Africa (he wrote a terrific article about it for *Esquire*), worked in a presidential election, wrote a book, and went to art school.

In 1990, he was drawn back to advertising and joined Beber Silverstein & Partners. Says McCabe, "I thought it would be nice to be in Miami half the year but after seven months I realized that was a mistake. I really need to run my own show."

So, in 1991, McCabe started McCabe & Company in New York—an independent agency. It was funded with investment support from Abbott Mead Vickers UK, who would also loan him people and resources when needed.

He quickly attracted a roster of clients that included Coleman Natural Beef, the School of Visual Arts, Maxell, Rally's hamburgers, and others.

He grew the company to about $50 million in billings at one point. "But clients would die or we'd lose them, and we had trouble replacing them," says McCabe, "so we hit a peak, but it was a constant struggle to stay there."

McCabe's business plan was based on landing a large account and staffing his agency with industry heavyweights. "I didn't want to start completely from scratch with juniors," he says.

This resulted in a very large overhead. "It might have been a bad idea at the time, because we never closed the giant one, so it didn't work profitably or rewardingly."

He had to make a choice: close the agency or rebuild it with cheaper talent, which he didn't want to do. Says McCabe, "You don't bring people in, make them commit their lives, and then dump 'em because your thinking was wrong."

He decided to close the agency in 2001 and then hung around New York for a few years. But growing tired of the city, he then decided to split his time between Miami and the Caribbean.

"After 45 years in New York, it's enough," he says. "Miami is a great place to live. And it's convenient to everywhere in the world." He particularly enjoys the weather, its art community, and proximity to the ocean.

Today, McCabe spends his time working on a book, teaching, and consulting with businesses on long-term strategic marketing and advertising planning projects.

He works for approximately one company a year. "It's an exhausting and time-consuming process," he says. "It's more than enough."

That's not all he does. "I boat, I fish, I write, I swear at the elements. I'm not having a bad time. And, if I ever get this book finished, it'll be an even better time."

Not bad for a high school droput.

MCCABE'S PORTFOLIO: CAMPAIGNS WITH LONGEVITY

—— PERDUE ——

Perdue was the first branded chicken.

Scali, McCabe, Slove's assignment was to explain why it was better and worth more money than regular supermarket chicken.

The solution was found in Perdue himself. "Frank Perdue was a fanatic about quality," says McCabe. "He was tough. He was insensitive and difficult, but it was all motivated by a dedication to quality."

McCabe didn't rely on research. He simply showed the man behind the product. "With chicken you buy in a butcher shop or grocery store, you don't know where it comes from," says McCabe.

By using Perdue as a spokesman, McCabe humanized the product. To reinforce the image of quality, he included a money back guarantee.

Says McCabe, "Six months after it was launched a copywriter asked me, 'Okay, you got Frank Perdue doing the advertising and you're winning awards. What are you going to do next?'

"I told him, 'That will still be running when you have blue hair.' More than 30 years later, the campaign is still running with Frank Perdue's son as the spokesman.

—— COLEMAN NATURAL BEEF ——

McCabe got this account because the client had been at Perdue and knew that McCabe understood the product category. Also, it was in a category that McCabe believed in—natural, healthy foods.

Says McCabe, "I was enthusiastic about it, which I think is critical."

He also had a great deal of information about consumers and their potential acceptance of the product. For instance, McCabe knew how much consumers would pay for it. However, he claims he couldn't have done it without further market research. He discovered some data that no one could have known, information from which he built the entire campaign.

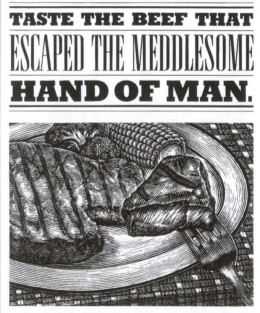

TASTE THE BEEF THAT ESCAPED THE MEDDLESOME HAND OF MAN.

Once upon a time, all beef tasted pure and natural like the Coleman Natural brand. But that was a long time ago, back before science and technology reared their heads.

That was back when beef was untouched by humans who, being human, don't know how to leave well enough alone.

Today, most beef cattle are raised with man's unflinching eye turned more toward profit than palatability. From birth,

many are shot with hormones to speed their growth. It is common practice to give cattle regular doses of antibiotics to ward off disease.

There is no clinical proof that eating this kind of beef is bad for you. But plain common sense should tell you that, at the very least, it ain't natural.

Now we know "natural" is the most overused and near meaningless word in advertising lingo today.

But when it comes to the Coleman family and the beef we raise, "natural" isn't a word, it's a mission. We Colemans have been involved in the rearing of natural beef since 1875. That's a long-term commitment.

In recent years, we've grown into a totally integrated beef producer that controls every aspect of product quality from conception to consumption, enforcing rigorous standards every step of the way.

No Coleman cattle are given hormone or steroid implants ever.

No Coleman cattle are treated with antibiotics, either by injection or through feeding, ever.

All foods are regularly tested for chemical residues and rejected if any traces are found.

All Coleman beef cuts are trimmed of fat to tighter standards than conventional beef. Some cuts are as much as 40% lower in fat.

One of the results of this total dedication: Coleman has surged to become the largest selling brand of beef in America's natural food stores, where customers are fanatically finicky about the wholesomeness of the food they eat.

Another result is the taste of the beef itself. Coleman beef is lean without any loss of tenderness, never stringy. It's juicy without tasting fatty.

In fact, it's so clean, unadulterated and honest-tasting that once you've tried it, there will be no going back to anything less.

Especially if your family is eating less beef than it used to. When it's Coleman, less is more.

For more information write to: Coleman Natural Meats, Inc., 5140 Race Court, Denver, Colorado 80216.

WHERE TO BUY COLEMAN NATURAL BEEF

A & P • Big D • Big Y • Bread & Circus • Demoulas • FINAST • Foodmart • Hannaford Brothers • Purity Supreme • Roche Brothers • Shaws • Star Markets • Stop & Shop • Victory

MAN HASN'T MESSED WITH IT.

One of the great revelations? He discovered that, while fat and cholesterol were issues, health-concerned consumers were really more concerned about food additives. They could control their fat and cholesterol intake through diet, but they couldn't control their food additive intake if it were in everything they ate.

McCabe built the campaign in a week using the first research indications.

Then he waited four more weeks for the full research to back up the direction he'd taken.

Says McCabe, "If someone would ask me how much time it takes to make an ad, I'd answer, 'Five minutes.' But I may need six months to do the thinking that leads up to it.

I mean, I could do a Marlboro poster in 30 seconds, but beforehand somebody spent two or three years of thinking about developing the campaign. That's what's important."

—— GOEBEL BEER ——

Early on, McCabe learned the importance of emotional appeal over intellectual argument. He was working on the Goebel Beer account.

Recalls McCabe, "They had a horrible reputation in the Detroit market. Their beer had degenerated and become a joke."

To regain their foothold, the company launched a new beer. "It was fabulous," says McCabe. "It was the first draft beer in a bottle." McCabe created a campaign that made fun of the old product to convince everyone that this beer was better.

Yet the sales didn't meet expectations.

One day, on the way to see the client, McCabe was

One of the best things about new Goebel Beer is that it doesn't taste anything like old Goebel Beer.

talking to the cab driver and the subject of beer came up. "I asked him what kind of beer he drank," recalls McCabe. "He said, 'Bud.'

"I asked him if he ever tried Goebel. He said, 'Yeah, that's a great beer too.' And he factually and rationally played back every point presented in the campaign. Everything. You couldn't have asked for better research.

"So I asked, 'Then how come you drink Bud?' 'Cause I like Bud,' he answered.

"So intellectual doesn't do it. The job was to make him like the new beer more than he liked Bud. I don't know if that was possible."

VOLVO

"Sometimes you have to develop the campaign based on where the market is going; not on where it is," says McCabe.

When he first did the Volvo campaign, automobile advertising addressed styling and price. No one talked about safety and durability.

"Research indicated that was the wrong way to go," says McCabe.

The decision to position Volvo was based on instinct. "This is the artistry of advertising that most people still don't understand."

MAXELL

Maxell is more a visually oriented campaign. Says McCabe, "It's the one with the now-famous image of a guy being blown away in a chair." McCabe first handled this account while at Scali, McCabe, Sloves, and in 1991, his new agency took over the advertising. The trick of the campaign was to keep developing new ways of expressing the concept of being blown away by the sound quality. Says McCabe, "Any single image wears out, but the concept doesn't."

MAXELL RELEASES A NEW HIGHER PERFORMANCE TAPE.

Since its introduction a few weeks ago, Maxell's new XLII-S has been blowing away critical listeners.

It has also had a major impact on listening critics.

In a recent analysis of 27 tapes conducted by *CD Review* magazine, they named Maxell XLII-S first choice in the Type II high bias category, placing it, in the words of their reviewer, "Head, shoulders and torso above the rest."

"Bass response that doesn't stop, staggering dynamics, real music," is how *CD Review* described the listening experience. But don't take *their* word for it. Don't take *our* word for it. Pick up a Maxell XLII-S cassette and try recording your most challenging CD. One you thought was uncapturable by any cassette tape.

See if you don't find your ears picking up things you never noticed before. Like plaster dust.

maxell
XLII-S 100

TAKE YOUR MUSIC TO THE MAX.

—— PLYMOUTH ——

Here's another highlight from Ed McCabe's portfolio. But what were some of the other highlights of his career? McCabe counts helping to build Scali, MaCabe, Sloves into an agency with a billion dollars in billings, getting in the Copywriters Hall of Fame (this campaign is an example of the work that justified that), and meeting people like Bill Bernbach, David Ogilvy, and Rosser Reeves as among his personal triumphs (look for more on Ogilvy and Reeves later in this chapter). Says McCabe, "On the frivolous side, one year I had a headline in the *New York Times* that said 'McCabe Wins Four Gold Medals, Doyle Dane Finishes Second with Three.' That was fun."

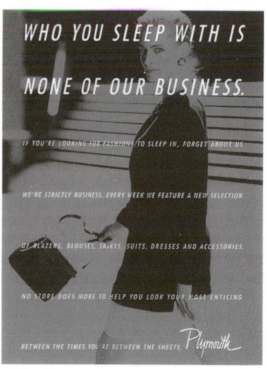

WHO YOU SLEEP WITH IS NONE OF OUR BUSINESS.

IF YOU'RE LOOKING FOR FASHIONS TO SLEEP IN, FORGET ABOUT US.

WE'RE STRICTLY BUSINESS. EVERY WEEK WE FEATURE A NEW SELECTION

OF BLAZERS, BLOUSES, SKIRTS, SUITS, DRESSES AND ACCESSORIES.

NO STORE DOES MORE TO HELP YOU LOOK YOUR MOST ENTICING

BETWEEN THE TIMES YOU'RE BETWEEN THE SHEETS. *Plymouth*

You can't eat atmosphere.

Horn & Hardart. It's not fancy. But it's good.

This poster has become a classic.

"There has always been this natural desire to grand-stand," he says. "People naturally want to do a TV commercial over a print ad. And they want to do a consumer ad more than a trade ad.

"And they'd rather do a trade ad than a matchbook cover or a brochure.

"About 15 years ago I saw an article by some big creative type I'd never heard of who was bragging that he had commercials on eight different Superbowls, as if that had anything to do with anything.

"It's grandstanding. It's showing off.

"But if your objective is to do supreme quality work, it doesn't matter. It will be discovered and seen."

McCabe believes this is a change from the past. "People used to be boxed in and typecast when I started. If you had brochures in your book, you were a brochure writer. I don't think that's true anymore.

"I really think we've actually progressed beyond that. If you're good at something, you're also going to be good at something else."

—— Scali, McCabe, Sloves ——

According to McCabe, employees of SMS joked that the agency was like a marine boot camp or a prison camp. "I never wanted any of my people to suffer the humiliation I did when I worked at a big agency, walked into a client meeting, got shat all over, and no one supported me," says McCabe.

"There was not one piece of work anybody ever took to a client when I was in the agency that I wouldn't fight for. But it had to be good enough to be worth fighting for. If I believed in it, I would go all the way with it."

How he fought for an ad or a campaign—which he defines as making a principled stand, not as bickering—depended on the client. "My peculiar and particular strength was that I got along well with so-called giants and tyrants," says McCabe, "because we tended to speak the same language, not that I'm saying I was either a giant or a tyrant. I just felt more comfortable dealing with those mercurial people, the Charles Revsons, the Frank Perdues, who ultimately made tough, hard decisions, and you could fight with them.

"It's very hard to make a principled stand in front of a committee, because you may sway one or two and there's still three others working against it. But if you make a principled stand with one person who is the decision maker, your odds of carrying the day are better."

TWO OUT OF THREE AIN'T BAD.

SAM SCALI
Inducted into the Art Director's
Hall of Fame, 1984

ED McCABE
Inducted into the Copy Hall of Fame,
1974

MARVIN SLOVES

All of us at Scali, McCabe, Sloves would like to congratulate Sam Scali on his induction into the Art Director's Hall of Fame.

We're very proud.

We're also proud of the fact that Sam is not alone. He joins his partner, Ed McCabe, who entered the Copy Hall of Fame in 1974.

And that makes Scali, McCabe, Sloves something very rare indeed: an advertising agency with two founding partners in the Hall of Fame.

Both of these men are advertising legends for good reason. Together, they have created some of the most renowned advertising of all time.

If you're interested in talking to a great art director or a great copywriter about your advertising, Sam and Ed aren't hard to find. They still come to work every day.

Or, if you'd like to talk to the person who does most of the talking for Sam and Ed, call Marvin.

There is, unfortunately, no such thing as a Management Hall of Fame.

But Marvin Sloves is a great reason for creating one.

SCALI, McCABE, SLOVES, INC.

800 Third Avenue, New York, N.Y. 10022 (212) 421-2050 Offices in: Houston, Melbourne, Montreal, Toronto, London, Düsseldorf, Mexico City
© 1984, Scali, McCabe, Sloves, Inc.

McCabe recognizes that it's these CEOs who are in a position to make decisions based on long-term thinking. "None of the people in the other jobs who are jockeying for position want to take the responsibility for a failure," says McCabe. "And really good thinking often appears risky. No risk, no gain."

AN AD LEGEND'S WORDS OF WISDOM

How does McCabe know he has a great ad? Through the pressure in his stomach. Says McCabe, "If I don't get that, I won't even give it the intellectual time.

"I look for something uncategorizable. As soon as you categorize, you make it the same. It has to be something new, something that I've never seen or felt before."

He hates advertising rules for the same reasons. Says McCabe, "As soon as you make rules, you've eliminated the whole concept of creativity. There are no 'no's' in advertising. There are understood tradeoffs."

"Of course, I read all the books," says McCabe. "Then I decided what I thought had merit and what didn't have merit. The problem is there are a lot of people who don't think. They just follow."

During the course of his career, McCabe has probably trained more people who have gone on to form their own successful agencies than anyone else in the industry. If you're ready to think, here are some ideas from McCabe to inspire you.

Know thyself: "Don't apply for a job in advertising until you know enough about yourself, what you believe and who you admire," says McCabe. "Then use some judgment in your approach. Do a little bit of homework." He says if you do a mass mailing of your resumé, there's almost a 100 percent chance he wouldn't hire you. Says McCabe, "It already shows a lack of judgment."

Do your homework: "I think one of the unfortunate things today is that nobody has time for homework, which is to say they don't have time to ever be good at anything," says McCabe. "Until you know what was and why and who you don't believe and disagree with, how do you know what you do believe in?"

McCabe also believes people should take more time to learn about the industry after they graduate from school. "People used to come out of school and go to agencies where they could learn most of what they wanted to know and do. Now I think they go to a place that offers them the most money, which is already putting a roadblock in front of their learning curve."

Always be paid a little less than you're worth: "Then you're valuable," says McCabe. "And you'll be appreciated. If you're paid a little more than you're worth, you'll be the first to be cut when layoffs happen."

Know everything else: "You can't do anything until you know everything," says McCabe. "I execute under the gun, but I never conceptualize under the gun. It took five or six months to research Perdue and eight months to research Coleman. It depends on the complexity of the product."

McCabe believes that's why speculative presentations are not a good and true test of an ad agency's skills. No one can possibly have enough information about the product or the market to effectively guide the creative. You need the research to direct you to a sound strategy.

Learn different styles: McCabe believes that beginners should read the advertising annuals, but that most people are doing it in a very superficial and shortsighted way. He particularly objects to writers and art directors who pull out the award books every time they have to create an ad. "It's not a tool to use on the job," he says. "That's just starting out where someone else already is. Here's the way it should be done: You should spend one night a week reviewing awards books, so they become background information in your head. And when you have it all, then you sit down and do your own thing. Then it comes naturally."

Study international advertising: "You have better students overseas," says McCabe. "They do their homework. They're more interested in learning, and we are more convinced that we know everything. It's our greatest weakness.

"I see great advertising in Brazil, Singapore, and South Africa. I still see some very good advertising in England and Germany. Probably the percentages of good work from those countries is close to the same as here. But what I do see that's good is really very, very good."

Demonstrate how you think: "I want to see something indicative of the person," says McCabe, "his or her ability to be unexpected—yet sound. I'm not looking for off-the-wall ideas that make no sense. The answer should always grow out of the problem; and all problems are unique.

"I'm more impressed by someone who's done his or her homework than by someone with glib ads that aren't based on reality." McCabe realizes, however, that ads in a spec book may be a little off-base. Says McCabe, "No spec book is ever going to be as brilliant as work coming from people with the full facts in their hand."

Abandon the black book: Portfolios—and even how you approach an agency—should be unique the same way ad campaigns are unique. Says McCabe, "The answer should grow out of the problem." Unlike Ted Bell, he thinks the first step is getting rid of the black portfolio.

"People are trying to convince me they are different, creative, and brilliant," he says, "but they've all got the same ads in the same black book."

He has been looking at books for 45 years, and most don't hold his attention for more than the first 10 seconds. "The black portfolio inspires the first yawn.

Then I open it, and if I'm not absolutely blown away by the first ad, there's no reason in continuing because they've missed the whole point."

Build an image: "I'm not interested in day-after recall. I'm interested in a ten-year recall," says McCabe. He does that by maintaining a consistent image that builds brand recognition over time. "The ad is only one of the mediums you can use to build the image," he says. "When I get involved with a client, I try to get involved in all aspects of their image. We look at the uniforms that employees wear, the design of the building, the graphics on the correspondence. Everything."

Make your own product assignments: "The selection process of picking assignments shows part of a beginner's creativity," says McCabe. "I think people should work on something they are knowledgeable about." When choosing products, stay away from the things everybody else selects—like insect repellants, No Doz, and Master Locks. "If I see another one of those, I'm going to jump out the window," says McCabe. "People tend to gravitate toward the easy products because there's an obvious story to tell."

Think simple: "I wasn't educated," says McCabe. "I was off the street, so I had an ability to talk straight to people without a lot of embroidery." That authenticity is what makes good advertising.

Aim to pass the "doorman test": Not only does McCabe want his work to win awards, he wants it to create responses from real people. "It has to work on both levels," says McCabe. For instance, he knew that the Perdue campaign was a hit when the doorman of his building said, "I wish you hadn't done that campaign 'cause my wife keeps saying, 'Why can't you be more like him!'" The doorman's comments were a confirmation of the principles of the man in the campaign, which far transcends advertising. It has to do with making a national icon.

Be yourself: "I've hired more oddballs than anyone else in the business," says McCabe. He's hired a guy who drove a cab and whose pitch was he knew what makes people tick. He's hired a fallen priest and a short-order cook. He feels anybody can learn to write copy. What he looks for is people who are able to cut through the boredom and humdrum of life and have a quirky way of looking at things. "You can teach a monkey to write the body copy for an ad," says McCabe. "But I can't teach anybody to think. Writing has to be in touch with humanity. There has to be a humanness to it, something that reaches people."

Speak honestly: Once, at Carl Ally, McCabe was interviewing a young art director and, as part of his questioning, asked which agency he thought was producing the best work. Instead of trying to be flattering and naming Carl Ally, the art director mentioned a different agency. This impressed and shocked McCabe so much that the agency hired the art director. Who was this art director? Mike Tesch, who went on to create some of the greatest campaigns at that agency.

Take on all types of projects: Some creative people have an attitude about the projects they're willing to work on. For instance, they think doing a matchbook cover is beneath them. "That never works for me," says McCabe. "Can you see Michaelangelo saying, 'I don't do ceilings.' I see that as juvenile idiocy." In fact, one of McCabe's favorite projects was the copy for a matchbook at Scali, McCabe, Sloves. On the cover, the headline said, "Maybe you wouldn't smoke so much if you were happy with your job." Inside was information about a correspondence school.

Look for clients with potential: McCabe is careful about choosing clients. "I look for products and companies that have the potential to explode in the future," says McCabe. "At Scali, McCabe, Sloves, we took a lot of little clients and five years later everybody said, 'Where did you get all those big clients?' We made 'em big!" Back in 1986, SMS had a lot of accounts billing in the $40 to $60 million range. "We looked around and we were a giant agency," he says. "But only once in its entire history did we get an account that was more than $3 or $4 million in billing. We built every one, except for one, Hertz. All of the others were tiny, tiny accounts when we got them."

Keep your eye on your true audience: "You know why so much advertising is bad?" asks McCabe. "Because most agencies are corporations doing ads for corporations. But that's not what it's all about. We're in a business of communicating with people. Corporations can't do that." He also thinks that copywriters and art directors are now being trained to make portfolios, not to be advertising people. "One is slick and glib and superficial," he says, "and one is a deep understanding of business realities that you must have in order to create great advertising on an ongoing basis. I think there is too much premium on awards and not enough on business thinking."

Be wary of immediate acceptance: "If something is liked immediately, you should be very suspicious of it," says McCabe. "As I said, advertising is about the future. Beethoven wrote a concerto, and the violinist came in and said it couldn't be played. Beethoven answered, 'Oh yes, of course, it's meant for a later age.' That has a lot to do with advertising."

Work backwards: "There are many people in this world who look at something and see it for exactly what it is," says McCabe. "I don't know how to do that. I start with a 20- or 25-year vision. And then I work backwards and figure out what I need to do today to get on the course to make that vision happen. Once you know where it could be, then you know where you're going." He adds that most people don't know where they're going. "That comes from taking the time to understand everything, from being able to form a credible and exciting picture of the potential. Once you know all that, it's easy. But I don't think many people are doing that today."

POSTSCRIPT 1:

ADVERTISING IS DEAD; LONG LIVE ADVERTISING

In the first edition of this book in 1994, Ed McCabe talked about the advent of integrated marketing communications (IMC)—before it officially had a name.

Since he's now pretty much retired, he doesn't feel comfortable talking about the realities of ad agencies today. However, he was willing to provide an historical perspective to help us understand how agencies evolved. Here's what he had to say:

"Advertising agencies have obviously changed a lot. All you have to do is look at their holding companies and see all of the other kinds of companies they have.

"There was a time when advertising agencies were semi-masters of all of their functions.

"One of the things agencies did was devalue their own product by giving it away in speculative presentations, which I've spent my career in fighting for a multitude of reasons. It leads to the shortest and most superficial thinking. A very intelligent friend of mine in London once said to me, "There are two kinds of advertising, Ed. There's advertising advertising, and then there's pitch advertising. You're no good at pitch advertising." And it's true. Pitch advertising gets the client. Advertising advertising builds their business.

"Clients who come in and say, 'We want to see you in a month with your ideas and thinking for our company' just make me want to puke or laugh. It's a joke.

"It just boggles my mind that they don't look at agencies that trot in with these wonderfully deep thoughts after a month and see it for what it is. It's show biz at its worst.

"Clients have got to look at who's capable of delivering the big idea that can make the company a lot of money and put them in the right position down the line. I don't think there are people on client committees hiring ad agencies that have a clue of what that's all about. They're mostly not advertising or marketing people; they're something else on their way to somewhere else.

"Another thing is the Jacoby factor. When he [Bob Jacoby] made all that money selling Ted Bates, there was a client backlash, and advertising became a generic business where clients began regarding agencies as impersonal suppliers. It's just advertising, and anybody could do it, so go get the best price. And the advertising industry played right into their hands by wheeling and dealing and negotiating.

"Because clients are in this mode where they believe that it's generic, can review it every couple of years, change agencies, and it doesn't matter, very few agencies can keep a client long enough to do a good job for them.

"Clients go shopping for agencies based on which are the newest and the hottest, which have nothing to do with who's the best.

"At one time, there were good agencies and bad agencies. The bad ad agencies did the bad advertising, and the good ad agencies did the good advertising.

"That no longer plays. Now there are agencies that are sometimes capable of being very good and also equally capable of being very bad. What's happened is all these well-trained creative people got spread around to a lot of different agencies and, occasionally, they peep out and you see something. But the managements of these agencies are not necessarily dedicated to that thing.

"They're much more dedicated to the bottom line.

"Many of these agencies are part of public groups, so there's more pressure on the profit picture than there is on the creative picture. And once you have a going concern, making money, delivering earnings, it's very hard to step back and say, 'Well, I'm going to change all this.' You can only do it when you start.

"But it's become very difficult to start an agency based on just good work and to get any meaningful clients and make the company work.

"First of all, you can't get the huge clients. And if you can get some small clients, you can do some good work. You can do good work, but you're going to starve a long time.

"I hope that nothing I've said trashes the industry, because that's not my intention. In fact, I see a lot of good things happening. I have seen a lot of terrific work; I mean, really terrific stuff. I'm seeing a lot of good strategic thinking that was missing for quite a few years. I think the Mini Cooper advertising is very good (See Chapter 1). And its promotion is as good as their advertising.

"I bought one of those cars, and I get quarterly mailings with really cool stuff, and they're on the case. They understand one thing, which is probably the single biggest thing about any advertising, but particularly true in cars: No one buys a car without talking to other people about their plans and desires and feelings.

"And they go around trying to get input. So if you've got current owners saying the right things about your product, that's more than half the battle. It's engineering word-of-mouth advertising."

POSTSCRIPT 2:

ADVERTISING LEGENDS

While Ed McCabe is an advertising legend in his own right, he had the chance to meet many of the other industry legends, people like Bill Bernbach, David Ogilvy and his brother-in-law, Rosser Reeves, who was the head of Ted Bates Advertising and the author of *Reality in Advertising*, which explained the concept of the unique selling proposition.

While we already covered Bernbach, here's what he had to say about others:

"Rosser Reeves was largely correct about a unique selling proposition.

"The fundamentals that he talked about in his book, *Reality in Advertising*, are (still) absolutely valid. I would have changed the word "unique" to "relevant" but, fundamentally, I think what he was saying was right.

"But he was in a very sticky and peculiar position. He was caught in a position of having to justify some pretty old executional thinking, so it strained a lot of people's credibility. If they (the Ted Bates Agency) had been doing award-winning creative, everybody would have embraced his book and said it is the Bible.

"As for Ogilvy, he built a great agency. He was a master at hiring the right people to manage the company. It was always one of the most well run agencies. He brought management sophistication to the advertising agency business. His account management teams were awesome. And the managers of his various offices were really great people and good at what they did.

"He found some oddballs there too. They weren't all by the book, but boy did they know how to run an operation.

"They did some unique and surprising stuff in the early years. Even today, one of the standout campaigns for me in the world is IBM. And that's Ogilvy (see Steve Hayden in Chapter 3).

"And what always impressed me about him in personal talks was that he was the most practical and pragmatic guy I'd ever met—without all the lecturing and posturing that his books are so full of.

"He was very down-to-earth. Which is sort of the opposite of what you'd expect. I admired that in him and found it unfortunate that more of that didn't come out publicly.

"But David was not one of my favorites. I felt he did a disservice to the creative community by making idiot rules and making it sound as though creative people were shooting from the hip and had to be controlled. There were isolated instances of it, but it wasn't rampant.

"What he did was pander to the lowest common decision-making denominator, which were the MBA brand-manager types, and he wrote some books that gave them a high level of comfort—these people speak the same language kind of thing—which became a very successful new business sales tool for his agency.

"Good for him. Not so good, ultimately, for the industry."

Susan Hoffman

"Today, an Ogilvy-style ad wouldn't make a difference, would it?"

"It's different today" says Susan Hoffman, Executive Creative Director/Partner for Wieden+Kennedy. "The younger market doesn't want things in a box or formulaic."

Hoffman is clearly someone who has broken free of the formulas used for years to create advertising to truly make a difference. She is best known for her work on Nike, but her clients have also included Miller High Life, Miller Genuine Draft, Microsoft, Google, Coca-Cola, Powerade, and Target. She has won many of the industry's most prestigious awards for her work. In 2003 alone, she received One Show Pencils, Andy Awards, and D&AD, as well as a Cannes Gold Lion. But while her work is highly regarded, she has kept a very low profile throughout her career.

"I am not shy with people," she says. "But I am very shy with a public image."

In this chapter, we'll focus on how to self-teach the craft of advertising. Throughout this book, we've met many art directors who grew up with classical art skills and found advertising to be an avenue to channel their training. But while Hoffman was "good" at art, she didn't discover art as a career possibility until college—and that was because she didn't like the liberal arts. "I didn't go to a good college my first year, and when I transferred to a big university the only art course available was "commercial art." She recalls, "That's when I keyed into advertising."

Hoffman studied advertising at several colleges, but never graduated. After a stint as a ski bum, she started her art direction career at a small publishing company and then worked at a variety of agencies before joining Wieden+Kennedy two years after they opened. She is still with them today. Among her accomplishments at WK, she helped them open their Amsterdam and London offices.

A DIFFERENT, NON-TRADITIONAL CAREER PATH

What drives someone to study advertising? How about a dislike of other academic subjects? "I was never very good in school," Hoffman says.

"I enrolled in a junior college, which was a joke," she recalls. Hoffman hated the junior college. "I was kicked out, but they changed their mind when I told them the housemother was an alcoholic." She then transferred to the University of Arizona, because it had a reputation as being a party school. She stayed there a couple of years and took advertising classes.

"Looking back," she says, "these schools were not very good, but it was the beginning of the advertising spark." But she never graduated.

"I never liked school and did whatever I could to get out of it, which I'd never recommend nowadays."

She then became a ski bum and lived in Vail for a few years before moving to Seattle to try to get into advertising. "At the time, my mom told me I wasn't smart enough to be in advertising," she says. "My mom feels badly about saying that today."

Not only was she smart enough, but she set out to teach herself the craft. "I didn't go to a specialized school, my education wasn't great, and I didn't take many credits in advertising because I had so many other requirements along with my major, such as English and history. But of the few classes I did take, I realized I loved advertising, and I just felt that I could figure this thing out."

To learn, she took unglamorous jobs. For instance, she designed coupons and school notebooks for a company called Peanut Butter Publishing. And, she took night classes at two local ad schools: The Commercial Art Center and The School of Visual Concepts.

Finally, she landed a position with Alaska Northwest Publishing Company. She considers this to be her first real job, producing mechanicals for *Alaska Magazine*, *The Milepost*, and other magazines as well as designing book covers on Eskimos and other Alaska-themed subjects. Her employer's ad agency considered the publishing company to be a small account and gave it very little attention.

This gave her an opportunity to create some ads, including four-color, full-page executions for the magazine. "I thought they were great," she says of her first ads. "But looking back, they were pretty bad."

For inspiration, Hoffman relied on *Communication Arts* magazine. "It was my bible," she says. "I just studied that stuff. I worked really, really hard. And I really loved it." Hoffman enjoyed the artistic part of the business. It gave her opportunities for personal expression. She put together a book using samples from the publishing company—mostly production work—and some school assignments.

Landing a Job in Portland

With two years of experience at the publishing company, she left Seattle for Portland to seek a job in an ad agency. She applied at the now defunct Pihas, Schmidt and Westerdahl, a firm that provided advertising, PR, and government relations services. Small for the overall industry, they were average in size for the area, and they needed a senior art director. Hoffman's portfolio, however, was not at that level. "I was always told that when you go in to an agency, don't get an assistant or a mail job," she says, employing the opposite strategy of Burrell. "Get the job you want. Otherwise, you won't move up."

Hoffman was determined to get the job. "I look back on my book, and it was horrible, but maybe it wasn't so bad for this particular agency. They said they liked the work, but that they were looking for a senior art director and didn't think I had enough experience," she says. "I wrote a letter to the creative director—I bet it took me a day—and I explained myself, why I thought I was right for the job. I must say, I think that letter got me the job because it showed that I really, really, really wanted the job. I wish I had kept this letter."

At the agency, Hoffman worked on the advertising for a range of local businesses, including a real estate company, Oregon Portland Cement, and Cox Cable. She found the job gave the real assignments she needed in order to learn about advertising. "I wasn't very good, but the job gave me things that I needed at that time. I could start producing work and get better," she says. "But my book was still not the best."

A couple of years down the road, Hoffman received a phone call from a creative director at a slightly larger agency called William Cain. A writer she had been working with had gone over to that agency for an interview, and the two creative directors there had liked the art direction and wanted to meet her. When they called her, her reaction was that she wasn't looking for a job. He said, "That's okay. We've seen your book, we like it, and we'd like to talk to you."

So Hoffman went, met with them, and ended up dying for a job. The two creative directors were Dan Wieden and David Kennedy. Three months later, they called and offered her a job.

The Cain Mutiny

At this agency, Hoffman worked on Louisiana Pacific, ADP, and a few of other accounts. She also worked on a tiny account named Nike. About a year-and-a-half into the job, she noticed that Dan Wieden and David Kennedy were continually whispering to each other and holding meetings. She wondered what was going on. Then, one Wednesday at the end of March, she showed up to work, and the place was empty. She wondered, "Where is everybody?" She learned that they—as well as an account executive, someone from finance, and a print production person—had resigned from the agency to start Wieden+Kennedy. (They launched the next day on April 1.) "It was interesting," she says. "Most of William Cain's agency had left, and he goes golfing the next day. I'm like, 'Whoa! What would possess this man to go golfing? He doesn't have an agency left.'"

To make matters worse, Hoffman then got word that the owner, Bill Cain, was going to fire her because he knew that she didn't respect him and that she wasn't planning on staying. So she moved out of the agency that day, a Friday. But, over the weekend, her friend Bobby talked her into going back. "You're making it too easy," her friend said. "You need to get fired, otherwise you won't get any benefits. Don't walk away and make it easy for him."

Hoffman realized her friend was right. She went back to her immaculately clean office to get fired. "Bill came in," recalls Hoffman, "and said, 'I'm surprised to see you.' I said, 'Why?' He said, 'Because I thought maybe you'd quit.' I said, 'Why would I do that? I'm starting anew.'

"To make a long story short, he left my office, and I had to go and tell him I knew that I was getting fired and that he might as well sign my check because I had decided to leave. But before I walked out, I let him know why Dan and David had left, why I was leaving, and walked out the door."

Unable to find another full-time agency job in Portland, Hoffman freelanced. "I'd never do that again," she says. "I'm a people person, and freelancing was too lonely for me. It freaked me out. Every time there was a problem, I was on my own. We have problems here at Wieden+Kennedy, but we also have a lot of support when needed."

Hoffman knew she wanted to get back into an agency and started applying for jobs in Seattle. She chose that city because it was close enough to be able to commute back and forth to Portland to be with her partner. Hoffman applied for quite a few jobs, and her insecurities started taking over. "I didn't think I could get a job in a bigger market," she says. "It was scary."

At this point, her portfolio consisted of some good basic ads but nothing earth shattering. But, to her surprise, she got three job offers on the same day. "This helped my self-esteem a lot," she recalls. "I guess my book was okay."

She took an offer from Chiat/Day/Livingston. "It wasn't a hard decision," she says. "They were certainly doing the best work." She also had another reason for taking the job: she had discovered why Dan and David weren't planning on hiring her, even though she'd freelanced for them. It was because she had no experience with big accounts.

"At William Cain I had worked only on local print assignments, and Dan and David were looking for people with television and national experience." Hoffman learned this news from an account person. "She was quite honest with me," says Hoffman. "And it helped me make the decision to take the Chiat job."

At the time, Chiat/Day/Livingston was a big agency. "It was doing very well," she says. The agency had Alaska Airlines, Holland America, and Pacific Northwest Bell, among other accounts. "Seattle was a big ad center back then." This was a big change for her. "I had been working on a lot of little stuff," she says. "Even Nike at the time was teeny."

The agency and accounts were a lot bigger, and the job gave her a chance to continue developing her skills and work on national ads. "It was the first time I had worked with a studio," she says. "I learned how to make an ad look better. And, I started working with some larger clients. It was the next step up." And, she started creating ads for Alaska Airlines. "I hadn't done ads of that size and caliber before," she says. This experience paid off with an award from *CA* for an Alaska Airlines billboard (see portfolio section).

Hoffman stayed at Livingston for two-and-a-half years. "I actually thought I was only going to stay for about six months," she says. "I went up there temporarily. I just put some clothes in my car and found a place to live." She waited for an opening at either Borders, Perrin & Norrander or WK. "Weirdly, they both called the same week."

Anti-Advertising at Work

Her decision was easy: WK. She began working on Nike again as well as on all of the other accounts. "We got the Honda scooter account a couple of years later," she recalls. "And that became a big part of our business." She says the agency had an "anti-advertising" philosophy back then. "Dan believes that people need freedom—he allowed people to explore new ideas in their own way and not be put in tight little boxes." This gave her the chance to be more experimental with her art direction. "Become less formulaic," she says. "I believe freedom allows for really different, inventive work."

Nearly seven years after joining the agency, Hoffman and Jim Riswold were promoted to creative directors. "It was strange," she says. "Dan and David were the creative directors. I knew they needed help. We certainly had enough people for an additional creative director team. But it felt like I was being put out to pasture, because I still wanted to do the work. That's the fun part. Both Jim and I had the same concerns: would we ever be good again as an art director or a writer? The more you practice your skills, the better you get. When you stop doing that, you stop being in tune to all the latest things."

She believes that her family background helped in her transition to management. "My father had a construction company. He said, 'Creatives have not been taught how to manage.' He was exactly right. I think I have more management skills because my family was involved with business. Not that my dad was the best teacher in the world, but I learned things that other people in advertising don't know."

A Two-Pronged Job

Hoffman feels that being a creative director is a two-pronged job: it's managing people and it's inspiring them to do great work. "Some people are great at one or the other; I'm not sure most people are great at both."

Says Hoffman: "It can be tricky. The three things I hear the most about creative directors are they keep the best assignments, they want their team to copy their style, and they don't give good direction.

"I don't expect people to copy my style. I don't have preconceived ideas on a project. Rather, I really like to see new ideas even if they're scary or wrong. And then I see if we can make them work."

Hoffman Goes Dutch

With success as a creative director, Hoffman was asked to help open the agency's Amsterdam office in 1992. "We went because Nike needed to expand internationally. We were doing the European work from Portland," she says. "We kept hearing, 'You don't understand our market.' We were like, 'Well, you don't understand good advertising.' But they were right. We didn't understand the market.

"It was quite clear once we got over there. European's choices of sports were different from ours, and their point on the learning curve was hugely different. I was amazed. I went, 'Oh, now I get what Nike's saying.' We were so naïve."

To start the agency, WK sent over seven people who had worked together on the Nike account in Portland. Just like in Portland, they opened the office on April 1. "We all got over there wondering, 'God, do you think we'll be any good?' But it turned out to be great," she says.

"I think our success was because we had all worked together and we hired a lot of Europeans. We tried to do two things with the teams in Amsterdam: make sure there was a good mix of Americans and Europeans and that they knew sports. So if it's running in Germany, we needed a runner on the team and a German if possible. This seemed to work, and now that office is larger than the one in Portland."

Her experience in Amsterdam also changed her thoughts about art direction and design. "Design in Europe is different. It's quite strong, very simple. And, it's more of a craft," she says.

"I went from doing ads to doing things that looked more editorial. I compare our ads to a magazine. A magazine is half ads and half editorial, and I try and get our ads to look and sound more like editorial. Instead of the standard headline/visual/body copy, if an ad is emotional and informative people will be more interested in the message."

Do You Make These Mistakes in English?

After two years in Amsterdam and four years back in Portland, Hoffman was also asked to help open the agency's U.K. office. "I went over there naïvely thinking it would be similar to Amsterdam, but I was wrong," she says. "It was very hard for me.

"In the end, I loved living in London. But, I didn't like the job. It wasn't good for my career." She believes a couple of things contributed: they didn't send over a group like they did in Amsterdam. "That was mistake one—it was only myself," she says. "And WK didn't understand the London market."

"I made a huge mistake thinking, 'Well, this is Britain. We all speak English. We'll have a lot in common.' But there's a different way of communicating. Americans are a lot more direct. That was difficult for the Brits."

Trying to instill the agency philosophy also got Hoffman into trouble with her staff. "In Portland, we believe in chaos," she says. "When things are a little more chaotic, they're more inventive and more surprising. That just goes against the British system. When I was in a meeting and said, 'We need more chaos,' I was met with people who said, 'No, we don't want chaos.' I realized that they had a different belief system."

Plus, Hoffman found the approach to advertising to be different. "We started in a very 'un-addy' city—Portland," she says. "To go to a real advertising mecca was difficult for me. While I take this business seriously, it's not the end all be all.

"It's cutthroat in London. A lot of emphasis on awards and PR. It was a bigger game than I was used to. And, in the end, it wasn't successful for me." But the experience taught her to become a better listener. "I was the type who said, 'This is how we do it.' That was a huge mistake," she says. "It should have been, 'Let's talk this through and together figure out the best solution.' It's important to explore the issues and listen."

Home

But her career survived, and she is back in Portland. So how does she stay motivated? "I really like to work," she answers. "I'm ADD, and I've always needed to work. I've been very lucky. I've been able to work on some of the best brands. I've been able to travel the world. I've been able to meet amazing people. I now have a really, really rich background because of this place."

A MORE INVENTIVE PORTFOLIO

—— ALASKA AIRLINES ——

This was Hoffman's first piece to make it into a *CA* Advertising Annual. "Winning awards always matters," she says. "I'd be lying if I said it didn't. But try and stay humble.

"When I left Seattle a week before I started at Wieden+Kennedy, there was a local awards show. All of WK was there, and they had won every award in the book. I had this little Alaska Airlines outdoor board that had also won, and because I saw how many awards they had won I over-revved. 'Well, here's mine.' And, I learned something real quick about egos: you need to be humble. I wasn't very humble, and I learned a big lesson.

"It's not that I don't want awards, but I'm careful that they're not the end all to be all."

—— NIKE ——

Wieden+Kennedy is known for finding an emotional way to sell a product, and this groundbreaking commercial is a great example of that approach.

"Somebody wrote a magazine article about how this wasn't advertising," says Hoffman. "We said, 'Great!' It leaves the consumer thinking more about your brand as opposed to dismissing it. We've been lucky to have a client like Nike that really appreciates more truthful, insightful advertising. I think consumers remember this type of advertising."

Initially, the concept for the commercial wasn't internally embraced. "We went to Dan and David with the idea of using the Beatles song "Revolution" and showed them a director's reel we liked.'

"They looked at us and said, 'Huh? Tell us again how you think we're even going to get that song.' They really said, 'Sorry, girls. Not a good idea.'

"But by the end of the day, they called us back and said, 'We've listened to everyone's idea, and as ridiculous as it is to think we can get a Beatles' song, we're fascinated by the idea.'

"We then had somebody in broadcast production put a ripamatic together to show to the client instead of a story-board. The reason we were able to sell this concept to Nike was because of the rip. It got them really excited and wouldn't have worked the same as a storyboard."

Getting the Beatles song was easier than Dan Wieden and David Kennedy first thought. "We later on got sued," says Hoffman, "and thank God we had somebody at Nike do all of the negotiations, because the press reported that we had stolen the song, which we hadn't. At the time it was really scary. We were like, 'Oh my God, I hope the Nike lawyer did this all right.' And he had."

Hoffman believes that the spot was powerful because it was so unusual at the time. "It was easier to be different back then," she says. "We were more filmic and less addy, but now it's not new."

For another example of this approach, Hoffman points to a spot that Jim Riswold created to advertise the Honda Scooter. It featured the song "Walk on the Wild Side" and an on-camera appearance by Lou Reed.

"It was the real turning point for the agency," she recalls. "It probably broke every ad rule imaginable. And it ended up being a talked-about, important piece for the agency. It was so new and fresh."

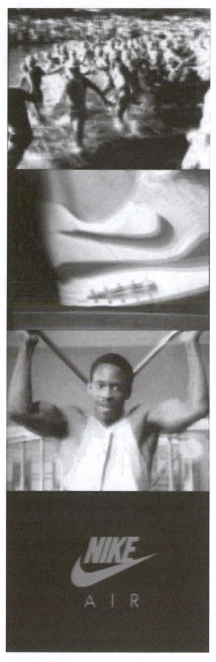

The ad also demonstrates the difference between working at Wieden+Kennedy and at many other agencies. "When you work at big agencies, you work on a lot of established campaigns. As a creative, you have to follow a format, a voice, and that's difficult. It becomes more of a job," she observes. "I understand why brands have to do that, but we've been lucky and haven't had those constraints."

Girl: If you let me play…
         If you let me play sports.
         I will like myself more…
         I will have more self-confidence
         If you let me play sports

Girl: If you let me play…
         I will be 50 percent less likely
         to get breast cancer.
         I will suffer less depression.
         If you let me play sports.

Girl: I will be more likely to leave
         a man who beats me…
         I will be less likely to get
         pregnant before I want to…

Girl: I will learn what it means to
         be strong… (to be strong)
         If you let me play sports…
         (play sports…)

If you let me play sports…
(play sports…)
If you let me play sports…

Hoffman was the creative director on this groundbreaking spot (written by Janet Champ and art directed Rachel Nelson). It was in response to Title 9, which mandated that girls have the same access to school sports as boys.

"It was a really interesting time for us," she says. "There was a long time that women weren't given opportunities in different areas, one of them being sports. Nike wanted to make a statement about it. The spot was just trying to get people aware that women need sports just as much as men."

This spot also underscores Hoffman's goal of going beyond typical advertising. "Nike, God bless them, was always at the forefront of trying to make sure their communications have an importance to the consumer."

This commercial also signaled a changed at Nike. "It was very obvious that Nike was a male-oriented company in the early days. But when these men started having children, many of them had girls, and I think that was very influential in changing the brand to be more inclusive of women."

—— MILLER HIGH LIFE ——

Unlike other agencies, there's more than one creative director assigned to a project at WK. This campaign is a good example of that approach.

"We work a little differently here," says Hoffman. "We always have a writer and an art director oversee every piece of business as a team."

309

At most agencies, just one creative director oversees a piece of business. "We always have two," she notes.

"We do that primarily to balance writing and art direction. At other agencies, if it's a strong writer overseeing a group, the writing may be strong but the art direction may suffer. That's not to say writers can't provide input on art direction. And art directors can't comment on writing."

—— NIKE ——

Here's another ad that demonstrates Hoffman's philosophy that advertising should not look like typical advertising.

"I really believe that it's a stronger way to communicate," she says. "It's funny. I had a conversation with somebody the other day and I asked, 'Is there a book out that tells clients that they have to be a less obvious and boring?'

"People want to play it safe. But safe is boring. The architecture in Paris is stunning from the old to the new, because they didn't play it safe. They were very inventive."

In creating advertising, Hoffman takes her work seriously, but also tries to have fun and put herself into her work.

"When you get too serious," she warns, "the process becomes heavy, and it starts affecting the work. That's something Dan and David saw really early in their careers. And that's why they wanted to create a place where people could truly be experimental and have a voice."

SUGGESTIONS ON HOW TO CREATE
A GREAT CAREER

Hoffman admits that WK does hire beginners. "We do hire juniors out of school," she says. "Not a lot. Sometimes I wish we hired more because young talent is a good way to keep a company fresh.

"That way we have an opportunity to educate and train juniors to understand the WK style."

So what does she want in a book? It depends—both on your discipline and experience level. "You can come out of many schools, if you're looking for a job as a writer," she says. "But we usually hire art directors who come out of one of the specialized advertising schools. Art direction is a skill you need a specific education."

Besides juniors, Hoffman also considers slightly more experienced art directors who come out of ad schools. "It depends on their portfolio," she says. "If someone shows strong print in their book, no matter if it's local, national, or international, if it's well art directed and well concepted, it doesn't matter if they had a formal advertising education." However, she expects even more experience if she is looking for a team to do television.

But what does it take to be considered?

For beginners, Hoffman suggests you emphasize inventiveness and uniqueness over polish. "It doesn't matter to us how put together a book is," says Hoffman. "If we see a really different, interesting voice or we see unusual art direction, these are the kinds of books we look for.

"We've hired people with little scrapbooks. There was one writer who had stapled 8.5 x 11" pieces of paper together, and he hand drew his ads and his headlines. It was inventive, and the voice was strong. We hired him, and he turned out to be a great writer. When it comes to a senior team, however, we can't hire them with just a little scrapbook. They need to have a more proper portfolio."

To help you assemble a more inventive portfolio—or to help in your development as a creative professional at any agency—here is some additional advice:

Don't start at the top: While WK hires beginners, would Hoffman recommend people starting in a great agency? "I'd say no," she says.

"I started at a lesser known agency so I could learn the business and put a great book together. The intimidation factor isn't as scary at a smaller place. And, I think you can be more experimental."

She also recognizes that she would not have been hired as a junior at a great agency. In fact, she wouldn't have even hired herself.

"When I started out, I had a crummy portfolio. But I was determined to teach myself to get better. And I was able to do that at a smaller firm.

" I wouldn't have been able to do that if I had walked into a WK."

Work hard: "If I've done anything right," says Hoffman, "it's that I've worked really hard. You have to be persistent, you have to really want something, and you have to work hard at it.

"With persistence, you'll go places you can't even imagine. I knew I wasn't qualified for the senior position at Pihas. I was barely qualified for a junior position. I just really, really wanted the job." And, of course, she got it.

Learn what the agency needs: Hoffman looks in part for people who think beyond the page. "Nike calls it impact media. We look for people who really want to try something different."

She realizes that most agencies are more traditional. "When people show me their books, I make it clear that I am not interested in regular ads. Show me something new. But not all agencies would agree with this, and it can get slightly confusing," notes Hoffman. "You just have to decide which way you're going to go—a creative agency or a more traditional one."

Follow your heart: When Hoffman was getting into advertising, her friends told her she needed to move to New York. But she refused, because she wanted to stay near her partner.

"I really struggled with that," she says. "I wanted this career, but I didn't want to move to New York." She again went against the obvious choice when she received offers from both WK and Borders. "Borders at that time was bigger," she says. "Friends suggested I go to Borders, but I really liked working with Dan and David.

"At that time, Wieden was teeny. Nike was only a million-dollar account, and I didn't expect a lot of growth from them. Nobody did." But she followed her gut, and it turned out to be the right choice.

Know what's new: "When new people come into the business, they get excited about doing their first ad," warns Hoffman. "If it is something that was done ten years ago, then it's not good. They think it's a good ad, because it's their first ad. A great first ad today has to be a great ad.

"It's tricky. I did some really crummy ads at the beginning of my career, but at the time they were okay, because there wasn't very much competition.

"But now there's just so much. You have to be careful."

Stand out from the wallpaper: Hoffman believes that brands are not only in competition with their direct competitors, but they're also in competition with all other products and services being advertised.

To beat all of this competition, she suggests that you find new ways to talk to people. "Don't just think about traditional ads," says Hoffman. "Sure, you have to learn to do an ad. You have to start there. But when everything's the same, it becomes wallpaper. The consumer isn't interested.

"It's our responsibility to change that and figure out new approaches—something that the consumer will say, 'Wow, I've never heard or seen it that way.' They've got to react to it."

Protect good taste: When Hoffman was installing a driveway at her house, she was told a certain material was cheaper than the one she wanted to use.

"And if I made a choice to have it cheaper, it wouldn't look as good," she says.

"My kids were like, 'Oh, Mom, you're so particular.' But I am. There never would have been a shopping mall if I had my choice. You have to protect good taste." That's also how she approaches her creative work.

Think beyond traditional ad disciplines: "The younger generation is very inventive and shouldn't necessarily think only in ad terms," says Hoffman.

"It's important to bring this kind of thinking to your work—the descriptions of writer or art director may be confining. Take this inventiveness and apply it to the business. Or not. But do more than just ads. Produce an album, experiment with graffiti, invent a new product, shoot a film or write a book."

She also looks for this inventiveness outside of the agency. For instance, she recently noticed a newspaper article about an 18-year-old who had started a record label in Portland. "His studio is his bedroom in his parents' house. I have to think, 'That's great.' I don't think the guy is a millionaire or anything yet, but it's so inventive. Challenge the status quo."

Then hire inventive people to execute your ideas: Hoffman reminds us that it's not just people who create the idea who should be inventive, it should also be the people who you hire to help you execute the idea. "We make sure that we hire as many inventive people as we can," she says.

"Spike Jonze is a great example of this. We haven't used him for a while because he's now producing movies, but he's a great example of someone who made our commercials more inventive, fun, and unexpected."

Find the emotional core: "Our philosophy at WK is to find the core of what the brand is about emotionally and then expose this to the consumer," says Hoffman. "That's different than selling 'things.' Making people feel something in your advertising is a stronger way to reach them.

"Again compare it to the ads and the editorial in a magazine. If an ad is editorial, it offers insights and information that is relevant to the consumer. It's interesting information people want to hear, instead of being told something."

Read ad magazines: Looking at advertising magazines is helpful for beginners— up to a point. "People coming into the business have to get a base from these magazines, but then you need to be inspired in other ways. There's one thing I don't do anymore: I don't have advertising magazines or annuals in my office," she says.

Then put away *CA*: Hoffman believes ad magazines eventually become more of a hindrance to creativity.

"You've seen enough ads, try and do something new. The magazines in my office aren't about advertising. They're fashion and design with unusual or challenging photography/illustration. And we often use these kinds of magazines when we are looking for illustrators or photographers. They feel less commercial.

"My challenge to people who show their books is to throw out all of the rules and find a new way to get the consumer's attention while still keeping it relevant."

Don't let awards drive your career: "WK has always had this great saying that you're only as good as your last ad," says Hoffman. "And it's true.

"You're only as good as your last ad. So if you get an award, you can enjoy it for about a week or a day, and then on to the next thing."

Stay in it: Even though she's a creative director, Hoffman remains an active art director. "If you stop doing creative, you stop being able to do it," she says. "Technology is changing so rapidly. If you don't stay in the thing, you get a bit rusty. I keep my hands in it as much as I can, but I also have to balance it with not taking an opportunity away from a team."

How does Hoffman choose which projects to take? "If people are too busy and it seems like something appropriate for myself and a writer to do, we'll do it," she says. "I also try to make sure if I work on a project as a creative director/art director that I keep it totally fair. I don't go for my idea, and it seems to work okay. When I was in Amsterdam, I had to work long-distance as a creative director with people in Portland and be an art director with people there.

"I had to make sure I played fair. People can tell if you don't."

Try to make people look: "If you need an ointment because your joints are hurting, you'll probably pay attention to ointment ads," says Hoffman. "If you're looking for a car, you'll probably pay attention to car ads. But say it in a new way, and it will get a greater response.

"Sagmeister, a famous designer, has a saying: 'Made you look.' I think that's a really interesting way to evaluate work. If an ad makes you look, even if you don't need the product, you'll remember it."

Build relationships with your client: "Since advertising is so subjective, it is better to have a good relationship and an open dialogue with the client. Get them to trust you and make them a part of the process. This way you will have an easier time selling the work.

Most agencies rely on account service to sell the work. Change that. The creatives came up with the work. Only they really know why they did the work, and it's a lot easier for them to hear client comments first hand.

This doesn't mean that account service isn't part of the process. They need to be part of your team. Get them on board, then everyone can help sell the work.

"Our best relationships and our best accounts are the ones with teamwork between the agency and the client. When you have that kind of camaraderie, you can have open dialogue which often sells the right work in."

Surround yourself with youth…: "When I was 30, I said, 'Well, it's not an older person's business.' Now I'm over 50, and I now realize that was a stupid comment. Older creatives can inspire and help younger people grow.

"But you have to stay young in your thinking," says Hoffman. "I have kids who are now 12 and 14. That certainly keeps me in tune to a younger market.

"And because I work with so many younger people, I would say that I probably act a lot younger than my friends who aren't in this business. I'm not saying I'm immature or anything, but if you're not involved with youth every day, you're just an observer."

…And, listen to the younger people: "You have to be careful when you're over 50," warns Hoffman, especially when you work on accounts that tend to target younger audiences. "Sure, you've got your own opinions, but when it comes to things like music, they know more about what their market will like. It's not all about Bruce Springsteen or the Beatles. It's about garage bands, etc. Music that feels unrehearsed, that's what kids like.

"There was a big debate at our agency about some music for some TV spots. The music was so raw and so unpolished that it scared some people. But even though it was not considered proper, it was what appealed to a younger audience. We have to be careful that we're not talking to ourselves and that we are relevant to the younger market."

Include your family: "When I first debated if I should have kids, I thought no— because I wanted my career," she says. "But kids are more important than my career. I'm not selfish, I just didn't think I could handle both. Well, you can. It's a constant balance. One of the things I've always tried to do is to make sure to include my kids in my job. For example, they've been on shoots, they play basketball and video games at the agency, etc.

"As long as it's not disruptive to my job or other people. My older son Edge— he's 14—took over an office at WK. I said, 'What are you doing?' He said, 'I'm moving into this office. I am so excited. I've always wanted to work at WK.' At the time there were extra offices and it wasn't disruptive, so I said why not. Most of their friends don't have working moms, so it's important that they feel a part of my working world. This way they understand that moms can work or stay at home."

POSTSCRIPT 1:

RESOLVING CONFLICTS

Earlier in this chapter, Hoffman talked about the potential power struggle among team members when a creative director works on a project. But there could also be a power struggle within a team. Here is a strategy for resolving potential conflicts:

"Advertising is a subjective business. There's not a right or a wrong answer. Imagine if we went to an art gallery together. I'm not going to pick your favorite picture; you won't pick mine. So I have this rule that I learned early on: If there's something I love and the writer doesn't—or vice-versa—we still present it to the creative director. If someone feels so strongly about an idea, if nothing else it may spark a constructive conversation that may lead to a good solution.

"There might be something that becomes a bigger idea, or maybe you realize why it wasn't a good idea after all.

"Always try to make sure the writer/art director team presents to both creative directors at the same time. If they go separately, they're going to get two different points of view. If everyone is together, the group can debate together and come out with one point of view.

"That's how you get better work. Even though it doesn't happen all of the time, it's a good rule to stick by.

"If this doesn't happen and the team goes to my partner and then they come to me and say, 'Well so-and-so saw it and just wanted this change blah blah blah,' then I'll have to call my partner if I don't like it and say, 'I don't agree with you.' And, then it gets complicated for the team.

"It's like anything—nobody thinks the same, so you should just keep your heads together, challenge a team together, and not confuse them."

Postscript 2:

The Nike Brand

Nike is considered one of the top brands in the world. But what is the brand? And how did it get to be so strong? Perhaps Hoffman's experience could shed some light:

"When I talk about brand, I try to define it in very simple terms. I believe there should be a strong point of view about the core message and everything should relate back to it. The work can be different, but it needs to apply back to the core message. For Nike, it's performance sport.

"When they started doing sunglasses, I wondered how that fit the brand. But if you think about it, you need good equipment—shoes, glasses, hat, or gloves—whether you are a runner or a skier.

"On the other hand, Nike lost their focus when they had a jewelry line. That was years ago, and it was a total mistake. Some guy had designed all this jewelry, and Nike got all excited. But if you define the brand as 'performance sport,' whether it's in their communication or in their product, it's clear what works and what doesn't: jewelry doesn't, sunglasses do.

"If you look at the Nike work, there's not one typeface; there's not a style.

"The brand is 'performance sports,' but it's interpreted in many different ways. Plus, it's continually being reinvented.

"There was an interesting study about nine years ago. Nike doesn't typically do research, which is terrific, but they hired a group to analyze their brand and to tell them what the consumer felt about the brand. These guys said that they were absolutely amazed when they looked at the brand. They had never seen a brand that had so many different voices and that the consumer—at any level—could relate and understand the Nike brand. Some people related to the basketball voice, and other people related to the golf voice. And through the years Nike touched so many different consumers with these different voices that this research company calls Nike the 'living brand.'

"When I heard this, I thought about all the people at WK who had worked on the Nike brand. There have been lots of writers and art directors who brought their own voice to the brand. And this is why I think the brand is so interesting. This is a huge reflection on Dan and David, their style of working, and their style of management. Dan complains about management until the cows come home. It's like management abused him somewhere along his career path. He thinks that too much management and organization really stilts people. There is something to say about that. I think the freedom they allowed shows why Nike is a living brand.

"Nike is the greatest piece of business I have ever worked on. We grew up together, and we were rebellious together. By that, I don't mean mean-spirited. I mean trying new things. That is still front-and-center with Nike, and it's still important to us. And they also make sure that they are always replenishing the pot with youth by hiring and growing younger people.

"The other thing that's great about Nike is that they truly have a product that's necessary. We all need to work out in some capacity. Anyone who doesn't believe that is wrong. It's a necessary thing. They have made working out synonymous with their name. That's why I think that the advertising on Nike is interesting and emotional. There's a love of sport. There's a need of sport. This is really, really nice for us."

F

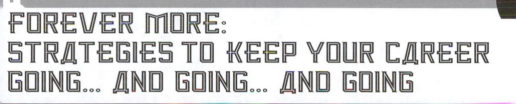

FOREVER MORE:
STRATEGIES TO KEEP YOUR CAREER
GOING... AND GOING... AND GOING

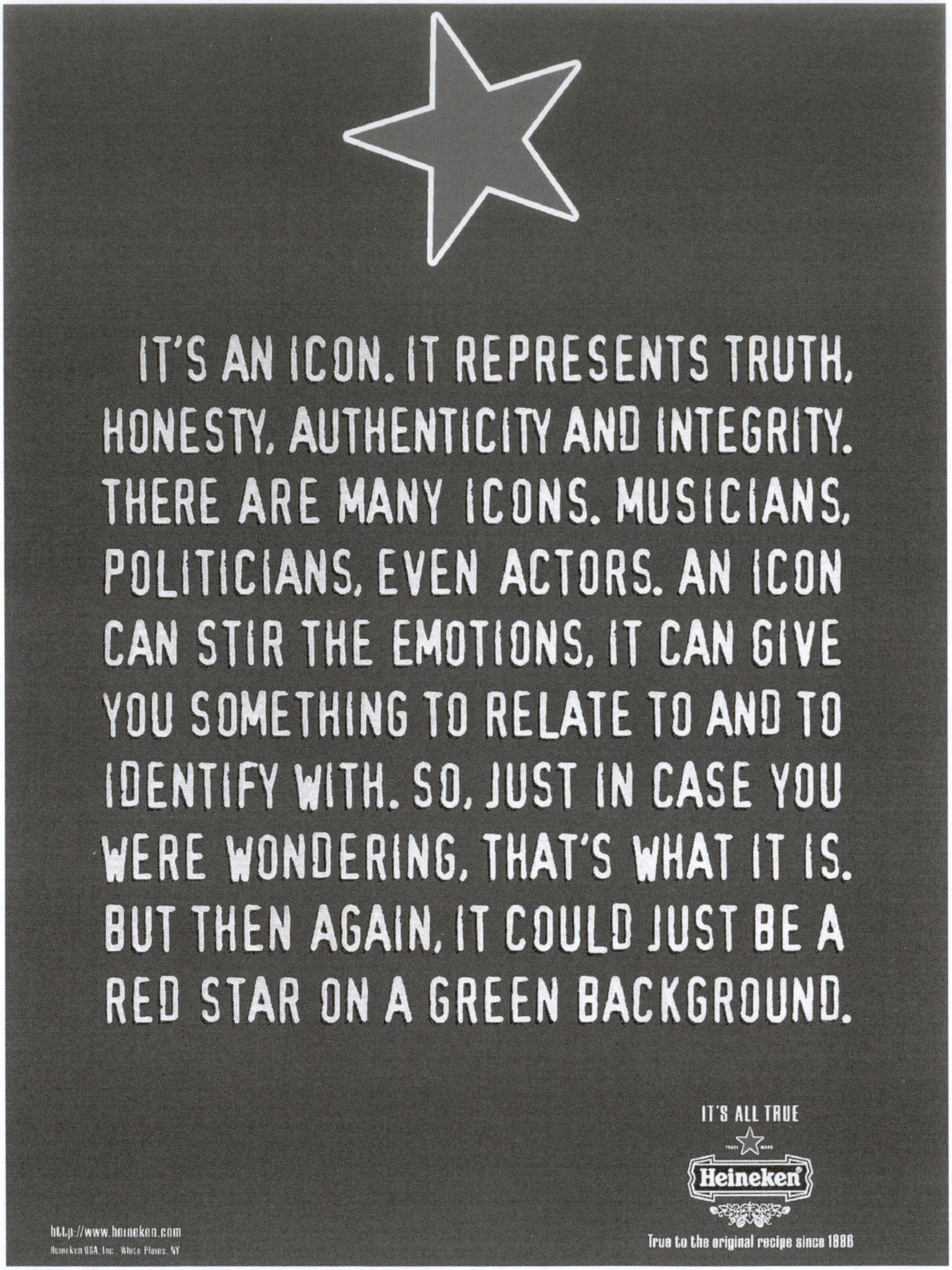

IT'S AN ICON. IT REPRESENTS TRUTH, HONESTY, AUTHENTICITY AND INTEGRITY. THERE ARE MANY ICONS. MUSICIANS, POLITICIANS, EVEN ACTORS. AN ICON CAN STIR THE EMOTIONS, IT CAN GIVE YOU SOMETHING TO RELATE TO AND TO IDENTIFY WITH. SO, JUST IN CASE YOU WERE WONDERING, THAT'S WHAT IT IS. BUT THEN AGAIN, IT COULD JUST BE A RED STAR ON A GREEN BACKGROUND.

IT'S ALL TRUE

Heineken

http://www.heineken.com
Heineken USA, Inc. White Plains, NY

True to the original recipe since 1886

Linda Kaplan Thaler

"Being hip in marketing is often the kiss of death."

Linda Kaplan Thaler is CEO and Chief Creative Officer of the Kaplan Thaler Group, the second fastest growing shop among the top 50 agencies in the country. She has played a role in developing some of the most memorable advertising ever created—advertising that has become part of the American pop culture—including "Kodak Moments," the jingle "I Don't Wanna Grow up, I'm a Toys 'R' Us Kid," the Clairol Herbal Essence shower experience, and the AFLAC duck.

Her approach can be described as humorous, touching, and topical.

Kaplan Thaler also wrote and composed for theatrical and television shows; has acted in a touring comedy troupe and in off-off Broadway shows; and she co-created the theme song for an Emmy-nominated children's television special.

And, she is the co-author of *Bang*, a book that explains how you get marketing ideas noticed and adopted with very little time or money.

In this chapter, we will focus on how to create advertising that gets noticed—and quickly absorbed in our overloaded, over-messaged culture. (Of course, more of her valuable advice can be found in her book.)

Her many awards include the YWCA's "Academy of Women Achievers," *Advertising Age*'s "100 Best & Brightest Women," Women in Communications 2000 Matrix Award for Advertising, Crain's "100 Most Influential Women in Business," Advertising Women in New York Woman of the Year 2001, and the Maxwell Dane Award for Humanitarian Excellence.

She has also been featured in the *Wall Street Journal* Creative Leaders campaign, which honors the best creative talent in the business. To date, she has won 13 Clio Awards.

She is married to composer Fred Thaler and has two children. A book about her oldest child, who was a National Elementary School US Chess Champion, was published by Little Brown. It's called *Opening Moves*.

Now let's look at her "opening moves."

A CAREER BUILT ON CREATING A BANG

What is more important in becoming a great creative: nature or nurture?

We may never know for sure, but we do know that environment played a big role in Linda Kaplan Thaler's creative development. She grew up in the Bronx and graduated from the Bronx High School of Science.

"The Bronx was devoid of culture of any sort, so you had to make your own entertainment and create your own fun," she recalls. "That's why it produced a large number of comedians, designers, and other creative people."

But Kaplan Thaler fondly recalls her childhood neighborhood. "Nobody was rich and nobody was poor—no 'Jones' down the block that had it better than you—so you never felt you were in need of anything."

Her mother was a writer, and her father an electrical engineer. "I got some of my imaginative DNA from her side and my analytical DNA from his side," she says. "It made me a pretty competitive person." But the '50s and '60s were not a liberated time for women. "The expectation was that I would become a school-teacher and get married by 21. It didn't happen." (She did get married—but at 36.)

Her relationship with her older brother also played a part. "He was absolutely brilliant in math. The only way I could compete was to go into creative fields." She took up the piano and started singing and writing poems and lyrics.

By the time she was 13, Kaplan Thaler was writing limericks and funny pieces of music on the guitar for her friends to record and play. "It wasn't like we were going to the theater, museums, or concerts," she says. "I don't think I stepped foot in Manhattan until I was 20. So I had to go internally to create my own life."

Her creative drive continued in college. "I never wanted to be class president," she says, "but I always wanted to write the skit or song that got the class president elected." A Phi Beta Kappa, she earned a BA in psychology, magna cum laude, from CCNY.

Then, in 1974, after obtaining a master's degree in music, she started performing in off-off-Broadway shows and touring. "I toured in 'Stop the World' as an actress, and I was in a road company of 'Hair,' but got kicked out because I didn't want to take my clothes off," she recalls.

"I was also in a stand-up comedy group called the Ed Sullivan Memorial Revue, which played at Catch a Rising Star and the Improv. I wrote some music for some awful off-Broadway productions and just did all sorts of odds-and-ends type of work, including teaching music. Of course, I did not make any money from any of it."

Little did she know, but all of this was preparing her for a career in advertising.

"One of the first lessons you learn in improvisation—which is why it is so important—is the 'yes but' theory of communication," she observes.

"If you understand that most decisions and ideas are not linear but are actually very chaotic streams of consciousness, you recognize that it is important to hear bad ideas.

"Very often people throw out an idea that is so bad that when it's flipped around, it's great. So if you get a bad idea, just laugh and say, 'yes, but.'

"For instance, if someone says, 'I think all of the people in the ad should have purple ties.' You go, 'Yes, but what if they just wore purple altogether?' Then one thing leads to another. But if someone is afraid to give you a bad idea or doesn't feel validated, he or she is going to shut down, and you've cut your chances in half of getting a good idea."

Kaplan Thaler also realized that while she enjoyed performing in comedy groups, she liked writing more.

Starting a Bang with Ad Jingles

Two years later, while she was teaching music in grade schools, music theory and history at City College, and private piano lessons, one of her students asked her to write some jingles. "He had a company called Brain Reserve with a woman named Faith Popcorn, who studies trends," she recalls.

"He said, 'Write ten of them for LifeSavers, and I'll pay you $150.' So with one of my closest friends, Laurie Garnier—we were both in this off-Broadway show at the time—I wrote some music and lyrics and had lots of fun doing it. I thought, 'Well, there's big money to be made in advertising.' Then the father of another piano student suggested I try to get a job at an ad agency."

Her father also encouraged this pursuit. "It was his attempt to get me to make a living," she says laughing. "He went into toy manufacturing and worked for a division of CBS After School, called CBS Toys. They developed Skittle Pool and Skittle Bingo and had Don Adams do these hilarious commercials, which were written by a man named Manning Rubin at Grey Advertising.

"Because one of the clients was my dad, Manning Rubin offered to see me, and he showed me how to put a book together. I came back a week later with jingles and ads with headlines and stick-figure illustrations and enjoyed it. He offered me a job working on Korvettes."

Through cold calling, she also got a chance to meet Bernie Owett, then the co-executive creative director at J. Walter Thompson. "He was one of the few people who bothered to call me back," she recalls. "I was nervous as hell."

But she got through the interview, and later got a phone call offering her a job as a junior copywriter on Kodak. "I then had the choice between working on Korvettes and Kodak. And Manning Rubin at Grey said I should work on Kodak, because it'll be much better for my career to work on an icon brand. And Korvettes eventually went bankrupt and out of business."

While she had written jingles, her first real agency job was at JWT. "I fell into it in a backwards kind of way," she recalls. "I was not schooled in advertising. I really started in the business because I wanted to write jingles.

"I also found copywriting to be easier than teaching." Not only was it easier, but she was good at it. She quickly found success. Within a year, she had sold her first television commercial, a spot for Kodak that had Dick Van Dyke as the spokesperson. Not long after that, she was working on Toys 'R' Us (see portfolio section).

She also helped positioned the Kodak disc camera as easy to use and contributed to a series of spots designed to tug at the heartstrings by showing touching occurrences in people's lives.

"Until then, we had never used that phrase in their advertising, but soon everyone started calling the poignant incidents in their lives 'Kodak moments,'" she says, "and now it's part of the American vernacular."

In the mid-1980s, Kaplan Thaler became Creative Director on Burger King.

"This account was teaching me the importance of focusing on the retail experience." She eventually rose to the position of Senior VP/Group Creative Director at JWT. In this position, she ran Burger King, Kodak, Northwest Airlines, Pepsi, and other top accounts. And, it's when she first worked on Clairol.

"I was asked to create some commercials for Nice 'n Easy," she recalls. "It was an entry-level product for women who were just starting to color their hair, and it promised that it wouldn't be noticed."

The approach was not working, and the product was not selling well.

Kaplan Thaler wanted to take a different approach and use humor in the new set of commercials. She suggested Julia Louis-Dreyfus for the commercial. Louis-Dreyfus was in *Seinfeld*, but the show was not yet a big hit.

The executives rejected this idea, but Kaplan Thaler persisted. She went to the head of Bristol-Myers Squibb with the idea, and the spots were produced. "They were an instant hit," she says. "And sales went to an all-time high. The commercials made it seem okay—and fun—to color your hair, even if others noticed."

Then after 17 years at JWT, she was ready for new challenges.

In 1994, she moved over to Wells Rich Greene BDDP (WRG) to become their Executive Creative Director. The legendary agency—started in 1966 by the legendary Mary Wells (who you can read about in *A Big Life in Advertising*)—had sold to BDDP for $160 million in 1990.

The agency was already in decline by the time Kaplan Thaler arrived. However, with her creative team, she had the chance to pitch the Heineken business. "I never had a beer until then," she recalls. "But because I did not know a lot about beer, I was able to move away from typical beer advertising." Her team developed an unusual but effective approach that convinced the client to give WRG the account (see the portfolio section).

Her improvisational training contributed to her ability to help win the pitch.

Why? Because she was able to read the client's body language to understand his unarticulated vision. "Although he was talking about the barley and hops, the way that he was raising the beer in the air made me think that maybe he wanted an iconic brand," says Kaplan Thaler. "Recognizing that was ultimately tantamount to winning the business."

But the overall slide of WRG continued. Kaplan Thaler felt it was time to move on.

In September 1997, just one year shy of WRG finally shutting its doors, she opened The Kaplan Thaler Group, Ltd. (KTG) with several partners. With a total of five employees, they set up shop in her kids' former playroom on the top floor of her house. She became Chief Executive Officer and Chief Creative Officer. One of their first clients was Clairol.

They positioned the agency as an advertising/entertainment company. She also served as executive producer of a 1998 Christmas Eve TV special for the American Red Cross. A first in the group's history, the show was entitled "Real Life Miracles" and was broadcast on CBS. It featured such stars as Garth Brooks, Trishia Yearwood, and Ray Romano.

To help with financing of the quickly growing agency, McManus, a private company, purchased KTG in 1999. This holding company, through a series of mergers, became part of Bcom3 in 2000. Then in 2002, Publicis bought Bcom3 and NW Ayer, America's first advertising agency, was merged into KTG. That was also the year KTG first got ranked as one of America's fastest growing agencies.

Today, KTG has billings of over $520 million and has worked for such clients as Clairol Herbal Essence as well as other Procter & Gamble (P&G) hair care brands (they bought Clairol in 2002), P&G's Dawn and Swiffer, AFLAC Insurance, Pilot Pen, Toys 'R' Us, Continental Airlines, the American Red Cross, Coldwell Banker, Panasonic Personal Care Products, Zoloft, Celebrex, Blimpie Subs & Salads, Burger King, General Motors' Pontiac division, Villeroy and Boch, Ruby Tuesday, Lane Bryant Capital One, United Jewish Appeal, and others.

The growth of her agency and the success of her creative ideas inspired Kaplan Thaler to write *Bang*. She and co-author, Robin Koval, general manager of KTG, worked on the book during nights and weekends.

"We started by trying to figure out why, even as a young agency, so many of our ideas and commercials for Toys 'R' Us, Kodak, Northwest, Bell Atlantic, and others got incorporated into the culture so quickly," says Kaplan Thaler. "Robin said it was like the Big Bang.

"In physics, you start with a cauldron of some very hot substances. In our case, that would be ideas. And, suddenly, an explosion takes place. And you create a whole universe from it.

"So a Big-Bang idea has the ability to break through and explode into the marketplace almost instantaneously.

"It's not a slow burn. It's something that happens very, very quickly, and I think in today's climate we're so inundated with messages that we must create Big Bangs to get noticed."

Let's look at a few.

KAPLAN THALER MOMENTS: A LOOK AT HER PORTFOLIO

—— AFLAC ——

In 1999, KTG was asked to pitch against the incumbent agency. "The product, supplemental insurance, is very complicated to explain and there are many facets of it," notes Kaplan Thaler.

"So we asked the CEO, Dan Amos, who is a wonderful and brilliant man, what exactly he wanted to communicate in 30 seconds. And, like the best of clients, he said, 'I just want to get across one thing, and that is to get people to remember the name of the company. If they can remember the name, then they'll ask about it at work, and our sales people can tell them about it.'

"In other words, AFLAC needed what is called a "doorknob warmer," something that would make people more receptive to the insurance salespeople when they called. Better name recognition would enable the salespeople to explain the insurance and the fact that people can get it through their workplaces."

Until that time, people couldn't remember the company's name, and if they did remember it, it didn't mean much to people, even though it was a Fortune 200 company.

"We were even having trouble remembering the brand we were pitching," she recalls. "We kept saying 'AFLAC, AFLAC,' and one of the people here said it sounded like a duck. He kept saying, 'AFLAC, AFLAC.' And his partner agreed.

"So they created a commercial where two people, just like us, who were pitching it, couldn't remember the name of the company—and the duck kept answering."

The results: 55 percent increase in sales. "Their name recognition went up to about 91 percent," says Kaplan Thaler. "They are almost as well known as Coca-Cola.

"It's just an amazing story of taking a very, very simple idea and going with it."

Yogi: Not too close. What do you think, I got that insurance.

Man: What insurance is that, Yogi?

Duck: AFLAC

Yogi: The one you really need to have. If you don't have it, that's why you need it.

Man: Need what?

Duck: AFLAC

Yogi: Well, if you get hurt and miss work, it won't hurt to miss work. And they give you cash, which is just as good as money.

Anncr: AFLAC. Ask about it at work.

—— BILL CLINTON: THE MAN FROM HOPE ——

Working on the Clinton 1992 presidential campaign advertising committee was a career highlight. "I was told that he didn't have a chance of winning; I can't believe you're doing this," she says. "But he enthralled me. He's a brilliant, passionate man, and I saw a side of him that was caring—and with a deep concern for the American people. His heart was in the job."

She was also proud to develop some of his advertising. "I was most proud of creating a biographical commercial that was going to run in September or October before the election. It showed his roots in Hope, Arkansas, his years as governor, and his hopes and dreams for America," she remembered. "It was done in a very 'Kodak' kind of way—emotional and with slow motion. My husband wrote a touching piece of music to underscore his life. And Clinton narrated the spot."

Kaplan Thaler believes that Clinton was making a promise to the American people with this commercial of something that he himself had accomplished.

"It was a real Horatio Alger story," she says. "I think the latent content of the spot said, 'If I can do this, you can do this too. I can make the economy better. I can make your life better, because I was able to do it for myself.

"He apparently cried when he saw it. And I like to think that, in some small way, I helped get him elected."

—— Heineken ——

When WRG was invited to pitch Heineken, a large number of microbreweries were being launched. Heineken had been brewed the same way for over 100 years.

"It was really the 'true' beer," she notes. "So we made commercials that had to do with truth and true conversations.

"We went to bars, actually overheard conversations, and made them into advertising. We did one with Mary Matlin and James Carvell fighting on election night. And, we had people on the street trying to get directions to the US Open, because no one ever knows how to get there. So we had a lot of fun making them."

They started with a teaser print ad. "We put a red star on a green background and pasted them all over the place," says Kaplan Thaler. "It just aroused a lot of curiosity, and then we thought that it would be funny to put down some of the overheard comments.

"We had lines like, 'No, it's not a Nike ad,' 'No, it's not the Chinese flag,' and 'To a dog, this would be a black star on gray,' because dogs are colorblind. Then a couple of weeks later, we broke the fact that it was for Heineken. It got people re-energized on the brand."

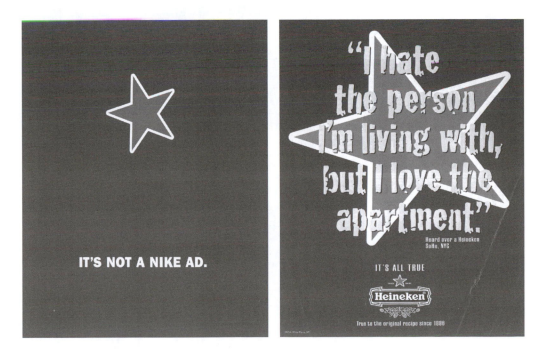

—— Continental Airlines ——

After emerging from bankruptcy, Continental became one of the top airlines to fly out of New York–Newark. "It mainly caters to business travelers," Kaplan Thaler notes.

"So we created a campaign that basically said, 'Work Hard, Fly Right'— that there are some very simple things you need, such as making sure the airplane takes off and lands on time and that you get your luggage back.

"Those are the things that business travelers want to know about—not some dreamy shot of the airplane going off into a sunset. And the campaign showed that we really understand their concerns."

KTG also created this eye-catching print work to explain all the routes they fly. "This campaign has been wonderfully successful in turning around the airline's image."

Peter Jacobs, 1982

Peter Jacobs, Now

TOYS 'R' US
www.toysrus.com

Toys 'R' Us

As a junior copywriter at JWT in 1981, Kaplan Thaler wrote the song "I Don't Wanna Grow Up, I'm a Toys 'R' Us Kid" for a commercial based on a line that James Patterson, then Executive Creative Director (now a best-selling author), and Deyna Vesey, then her art director, created. "People grew up with that song," she recalls.

Twenty years later, KTG had the opportunity to recreate the commercial. "We took the original kids and paired them with the people they are today. We dressed them in the same clothes and put them in the same type of environment.

"We called it, 'Then and Now.'

"It was really charming. And I think it was a testament to the legs of the campaign and the song to withstand two decades of consumers watching it."

—— PILOT PEN ——

Here's an example of creating a "big bang" on a very small media budget. "They usually only do their advertising during the back to school time in September.

"So with a limited budget, we had to create advertising that would not only get noticed when it was on the air, but would create its own PR frenzy.

"For the first spot, we had two guys on a train. You don't see them from the waist down, and one guy looks at the other's waist and goes, 'That's some instrument you have.'

"It was obviously very suggestive and filled with double entendres, as we reveal that he was talking about a Pilot Pen. And, boy, did it get noticed! It was featured in a big article in the advertising section of the *New York Times*."

After the Enron debacle, KTG did it again.

"We did a 15-second spot where the viewer heard a funeral death march and saw a guy furiously erasing page after page, as the announcer comes on and says, 'What could one Fortune 500 Company have done when they could no longer shred their documents? Pilot Pen introduces the first erasable gel ink pen.'

"It was shot on videotape and cost basically nothing—and it got listed in the *Wall Street Journal* as one of the best-remembered commercials.

"It was just amazing. And it just ran a couple of times."

KODAK

Early in her career, Kaplan Thaler created a series of very emotional commercials for Kodak. "Up to that point, we didn't see any advertising that ever called anything a 'Kodak moment.'

"Then people started calling the special moments in their lives 'Kodak moments.'"

It's an example of a Big-Bang idea that permeated the culture. And to have people discover and incorporate the brand into their everyday lives is certainly the end-all and be-all.

To create these spots, Linda turned to herself for inspiration.

"What could be simpler than drawing from your own experiences and emotions?" she asks.

For instance, in 1985, she was on deadline for a new commercial, and her father's 65th birthday was approaching. Wanting to find a worthy gift, she wrote a song called "Dear Old Dad," took her old home movies, and cut them into a commercial with the song as the soundtrack. She then sat her father down to watch an old movie, and on came the 120-second spot that opened with a note that said: "To Dad, on his 65th birthday. Love, Linda." "I made my dad cry," recalls Kaplan Thaler, "as well as dads all over the country."

—— CLAIROL ——

The Clairol Herbal Essences campaign not only helped the brand become the second leading shampoo on the market, it has also helped Clairol become a worldwide icon. And, it continues to amuse and provoke.

"It's challenging to stay fresh," says Kaplan Thaler. "We have to stick with our core idea of having an organic experience, but we also have to keep evolving.

"You always have to do something unexpected. Where could somebody have an organic experience? How can they have the organic experience? Are there other ways of expressing an organic experience?

"Sometimes we pepper it with celebrities. We had Richard Simmons and Dr. Ruth for a couple of years. I don't think anybody ever thought that Dr. Ruth would end up in a shampoo commercial. But that's how you stay fresh and fun."

HOW TO CREATE A BANG WITH YOUR BOOK

"No one should ever think that something is unattainable," says Kaplan Thaler. "I didn't have experience in advertising when I got my job at JWT. And, I had the crudest book that you could imagine. It was put together with stick figures."

Even today, people with unpolished portfolios can still get a creative job.

"We recently hired a team," she says. "One of them had gone to the School of Visual Arts. He was in his early 30s and wanted to change jobs. I knew him through a friend of a friend and was basically going to be polite by looking at his book. But we ended up hiring him because he's a terrific writer.

"For his partner, we hired somebody who had been a waiter in Atlanta, believe it or not. He had studied advertising, but never had a job in the industry. He sent us his raw book, and it was terrific. We paired him up with the other young man. They've been here a year, and they must have sold at least a half a dozen commercials already. So if you have talent, you will get hired by somebody."

But how do you get noticed, so you can get hired as a writer or an art director? "Throw away the rules," advises Kaplan Thaler. "Forget industry standards and create unexpected ideas, so they can't be ignored."

If you can do this and want to help your career to move faster, here's some additional unconventional advice from Linda Kaplan Thaler:

Treat your clients like an audience: "I call everybody that I talk to client-wise when selling an idea the 'audience,' and I think that theatrical skills in selling are extremely important," she says.

"As my partner Robin Koval says, 'At any given point a client would rather be at the movies than watching a business presentation.' So we just try to keep people delighted, and our track record with this approach has been really excellent."

Entertain, entertain, entertain: How does she keep clients engaged during presentations? "We're a society that's addicted to entertainment. You get into a cab and you hear somebody telling you a joke about why you should wear your seatbelt. Even the war in Iraq was theatrically staged for the viewing audience. It was like watching the ultimate reality show.

"So we try to entertain our clients.

"For the Panasonic pitch, our strategy was that shaving sucks and that men really hate it. So I wrote a song was called, 'Shaving Sucks.' And I performed it with a bevy of bountiful men behind me.

"For Coldwell Banker, we created a campaign where people do the tango, so we danced it at the meetings.

"This is even the goal when we present something as dry as a reel of competitive advertising. One of our editors came up with the 'sameness' video.

"It's called 'Genericorp,' and we make fun of what everybody else is doing by saying that your goal should be to do exactly the same.

"Of course it's tongue-in-cheek, it's hilarious, and it works in getting our point across."

Keep it simple: Kaplan Thaler believes that a Big-Bang idea is extremely simple.

"We often try to solve problems in very difficult and intricate ways, but the fact of the matter is that problems usually have very, very simple answers.

"As the CEO of Proctor & Gamble said, 'When you have more than two moving parts, things can get complicated.' A brand should stand for one thing."

Become a parent: "I think having children and teaching school was a fabulous— no pun intended—breeding ground for learning how to manage a company and managing clients," she says.

"We are, in fact, all children. We all need to be stroked, and we all need to be heard and validated. A child says, 'Mommy I know it's snowing outside, and I want to wear my sandals.' If you say no, you haven't validated his or her feelings, and the child will shut down and feel pushed into a corner. You'll get a tantrum with yelling and screaming.

"Rather, you learn to say something like, 'I love your sandals. I love them so much, why don't we wear them in the house. And then when we go outside, we can wear your blue boots. I love the color blue. What's your favorite color?' This way, you have validated your child's feelings. And you have also steered him or her in a direction that is safer and better.

"Most women learn this very quickly when they become mothers. And, you need to learn to do the same with employees, co-workers, and clients."

Learn to concentrate: "I think also what happens when you have a family is that you learn to focus better when you're at work because you know you don't have the luxury of a two-hour lunch break.

"Because most of us here have families, we have learned to get our work done in a pretty timely fashion."

How? She sets very short deadlines.

"The intense pressure of having to make a decision in a short period of time forces me to really focus, and then I get a million ideas."

Stay focused on the goal: Kaplan Thaler learned this from the Clinton presidential campaign. "The message was the economy, and whenever we came up with an idea that veered even one centimeter off the economy, we were told to stay on track.

"We had a lot of fascinating things that we wanted to talk about: the rising cost of drugs and schools. But at the end of the day, we had a very limited time.

"Stephanopoulos and Carville kept saying to us, 'Stay on the premise—it's the economy, stupid. Just keep talking about the economy.'

"It was a great lesson for me in making sure that we don't veer too far off course. When we get a competitive commercial from a rival brand, it's very tempting to want to get into the ring and fight with them. But you've got to stay true to your brand.

"Fuji tried to get Kodak into the ring countless times, but Kodak stayed with the higher platform of being America's storyteller, and they would not get into a fight on color and sharpness and all that. It was smart of them to do that."

Study improvisational theater: Kaplan Thaler believes improvisational theater teaches people to listen and to act intuitively.

"As a society, we don't rely on our intuitive instincts at all any more," she says. "We go by verbal cues rather than what we actually see.

"You know, you sense stuff when you meet someone. If you instantly don't like this person, you will try to talk yourself out of it.

"But there's usually a reason you don't like this person. There's some very subliminal little visual cue or something you see in the eyes.

"By following our instincts, we've won pitches because we have been able to sense what the client really wants to communicate, and the client might not even know what they want to communicate on a manifest level."

Follow your gut, but do your homework: "You need to do your research and your homework," says Kaplan Thaler, "but I always tell people to write down their first instincts and thoughts, because they may end up coming back to it later."

Become emotional: How does Kaplan Thaler know that an idea will connect with consumers? Simple: she bases her judgment on her own emotional reaction.

"If an idea makes you laugh, it probably will make others laugh," she says. "And if it makes you cry, it probably will make others cry.

"The truth is that we all share 99.99 percent of the same genes."

Stick to the basics: "Trends come and go too quickly for use in an expensive, ongoing advertising campaign," she observes. "And being trendy could be alienating. Those who aren't in the know will turn their backs on your message, limiting the number of people who will connect with it."

Evaluate every moment: How does Kaplan Thaler balance work and family?

She assesses every request for her time.

"If I'm supposed to go out of town for this meeting, I ask myself: 'Do I have to go? What would happen if I don't go? Must I be on this shoot? What would happen if I didn't go to the shoot?'

"My husband is also very helpful in that regard, because when I say that I think I need to go, he'll question it," she says. "Then I'll think about it, and there's a lot of stuff that I thought I had to do that I really don't have to do.

"I very rarely go to client dinners. I don't really want to. And they don't really care. I don't go to a lot of shoots.

"I don't do stuff for political reasons, because politics have changed in the business, and the clients that we want are the clients who are interested in the work. They also want to get home to their families. They don't want to play golf with me.

"I don't play golf, which is another reason not to play golf with me."

Forget the vision: While it may sound counterintuitive, Kaplan Thaler suggests that you don't plan out your career.

"At the end of the day, you don't need to have a vision about your future.

"No one has time for it anymore. And what's the point of having one? It's limiting. It's easy to create because there's nothing in the future that's going to negate your vision.

"It's harder to deal with the present, and your present will dictate your future.

"I know you're supposed to have these big five-year plans, but we went into this business not knowing what we were going to do. We just knew that we were going to hire really smart people to do it. And then people create the company.

"We got somebody who's a good writer, so the agency wrote a book.

"We got someone here who likes to do direct, so we produced an agency film that won a film award."

POSTSCRIPT:

WHY NOT-FOR-PROFIT IS GOOD FOR YOU

With notable exceptions like Susan Gillette, the conventional wisdom is to stay away from including work for not-for-profits in your beginning portfolio. But throughout her career, Linda Kaplan Thaler has donated her time and talents to charitable groups and political campaigns, including the American Red Cross, the Girl Scouts of America, the United Jewish Appeal, the Clinton/Gore presidential campaign in 1992, and the Bill Bradley 2000 presidential campaign.

She has some key insights into what it means to work for these organizations. Here are some of her comments on the subject:

"I believe you could never go wrong doing good. A lot of not-for-profit work, like the stuff we do for the United Jewish Appeal, helps enormously in raising money for people. They raise a lot of money for everybody around the world—not just Jews.

"My husband writes the music for these films and I usually write the lyrics, and they've been very successful in helping raise money and the spirit of goodwill. For many years, I've also worked on the American Red Cross, and after 9/11, they used our theme line 'Together, we can save a life.' We were very proud to have been a part of that cause. And we wrote a wonderful film, 'Don't Turn Away,' that ran in movie theatres to raise money for Rawandan refugees.

"We also did a great campaign for the Girl Scouts, which asked parents to keep their daughters involved with math and science because that's where most of the jobs will be in the future.

"In the commercial, a little girl asked her daddy, 'Why is the sky blue?' He answered, 'Oh, to match your pretty eyes.' She then said, 'No.' And she gave a complicated, mathematical answer about the refraction of the rays and the curvature of the earth. The spot ended with the line, 'It's her future. Do the math.' It was a very simple idea: the juxtaposition of a highly intricate explanation from the mouth of a five-year-old, when the stereotype of a five-year-old girl is that an uncomplex answer will suit her. We're very proud of it. The commercial was disruptive to watch and certainly very funny. And, it won some nice awards.

"At the end of the day, you want to be able to look in the mirror and say, 'I've done something good for the world.' And, you kind of want to do that every day of your life, so I feel you should always have part of your creative juices dipped into the spirit of goodwill. I think it keeps people honest and whole.

"Some people say that not-for-profits are an easy target, because it's easier to get people emotional about causes. But if you're putting together a portfolio, I would urge beginners to include a piece for a not-for-profit, just so long as it's not the only piece."

Tom Burrell

"Anybody who's getting into advertising today needs to understand that the mass market is dead."

In this chapter, we're going to explore ways to create effective communications in a post-mass market era. Thomas Burrell, founder and former chairman of the renowned marketing communications firm that bears his name, was one of the first to bring big agency experiences and sophisticated tactics to segmented marketing. He founded his agency in 1971 and has provided such clients as Coca-Cola, McDonald's, Sears, Verizon, Toyota, and Procter & Gamble with marketing campaigns targeted to the African-American and urban youth markets. The firm also has provided general market advertising for Verizon and other brands. But simply through rotation, the general market sees—and is affected by—much of what Burrell does for the African-American and urban youth markets. "It gets blurry," says Burrell. "Much of what we do crosses over."

Prior to forming his agency, Burrell worked for general market advertising powerhouses—Needham, Harper & Steers; Foote, Cone & Belding; and Leo Burnett, U.S.A., among others. He started his advertising career with the now defunct Wade Advertising and earned his undergraduate degree from Roosevelt University in Chicago.

Burrell retired in the summer of 2004 and, today, continues to live in Chicago—he claims to love the city—and is active in numerous community organizations outside of his work. "My involvement has nothing to do with what I do for a living. As a citizen, I'm involved. I volunteer."

Burrell helps community organizations all over the country, including the Urban League and such trade organizations as the American Advertising Federation (AAF). "We have a Tom Burrell chapter of the AAF at Howard University in Washington, D.C.," says Burrell. "We set up scholarship funds. I'm also in the process of starting a foundation." His philosophy? "I just strive to be helpful to a lot of different organizations."

THE TEST OF AN INDUSTRY LEADER

How do you know you have talent? Sometimes, it means painful years of struggling. And sometimes it is as simple as taking an aptitude test in school.

A product of Chicago's South Side, Burrell wandered through his first two years of high school not knowing what he wanted to do with his life. "As a matter of fact, I was at a school that was not conducive to making any decision," he says. Yet he became a highly influential industry leader—all because of the results of an aptitude test. A look at his life after he took the test—as well as slightly before it—can be highly instructive to anyone interested in a career in advertising.

Knowing that he wanted to make something of his life, he engineered a transfer to a better school and started hanging out with students who wanted to be doctors, lawyers, and engineers. He also enrolled in a course called Careers, a class with the sole purpose of helping kids determine what they ought to pursue, and he took a test to measure his areas of interest and aptitude. The results? He scored highly in two areas: "artistic" and "persuasive."

Burrell had no idea what to make of these results. So he took them to his teacher. She suggested he become an advertising copywriter because it required both abilities. "Whether I believed it or not, I now had something to tell people," he says. "And not only was it something definite, it was something unique. Something that made me special. My friends didn't know what an advertising copywriter was either. So the lunchroom conversation now focused on me."

"No secretaries, no mailroom people, no receptionists. Nobody."

Eventually, he had to back up his claim by becoming more knowledgeable about what he was telling people. So he started studying ads and trying to figure out how they were written. And when he graduated from high school, he went to college as an English major and advertising minor, enabling him to take copywriting courses.

"At this time [1960], there were no black people working in Chicago advertising agencies in any capacity," says Burrell, "no secretaries, no mailroom people, no receptionists. Nobody."

Burrell remembers his copywriting instructor at his college asking him, "What do you think you're doing? Nobody's hiring black people in the advertising business. What are you going to do with it?" Burrell's reply? "Well, I'm going to do it."

To help himself along, Burrell found a job in a related area. "I not only worked for free, I worked for a struggling company whose owner was strapped for cash himself," he says. "On a couple of occasions, I wound up loaning him 50 cents." But the job gave him much-needed experience.

Through a network of friends, Burrell learned that Wade Advertising, then the third largest advertising agency in Chicago, was looking to hire a black youth to work in the mailroom. Says Burrell, "That was revolutionary." He interviewed for the position and found he wasn't what they wanted. "I was too old," he says. "They were looking for an 18-year-old who was going to night school. I was 22 and going to day school. And they wanted a marketing major. I was majoring in English with a minor in advertising."

Burrell believes they set up that criteria because they were hoping to take a longer time to move that person into a professional area. Says Burrell, "An 18-year-old in night school would have given them maybe eight years." And they wanted someone studying marketing so they could move that person to an account services position. "But I was the only guy looking for that job because, for the most part, black kids didn't know anything about advertising and the agency business," he says. "So they didn't find any other candidates."

Wade hired him. Burrell promised he'd switch to night school. "I lied," he now admits. "I convinced my mailroom supervisor to allow me to take my lunch break at various times during the week. So I continued to go to day school and continued to go pretty much full-time." Within six months, he graduated. "They thought I would take a year or two," he says.

"Doesn't he look ridiculous pushing that wagon around?"

When working, Burrell always conducted himself as if he was above the mailroom job. "I wanted people to look at me and say, 'Doesn't he look ridiculous pushing that wagon around?' That was a visual message I wanted to convey. I wanted them to realize that they were holding me back by having me do that work. I wore white shirts and ties. I was neat even while I was changing towels in the men's washroom or working with that messy mimeograph machine [this was before Xerox]."

Even though he wanted to communicate that he was being held back, he found many opportunities to use his job to help him along. "One of the great things about being in the mailroom is that it gives you a chance to find out what's going on. I was collating memos and running the mimeograph machine, so I'd make copies for myself. I had quite a file. I also got a chance to see everybody. I got into the habit of going past secretaries and putting the memos right in the executives' offices."

While collecting the agency material, Burrell also started working on some projects of his own. He was aware that the creative director was having some problems with Alka-Seltzer. So he conducted research, going house to house in his free time.

And once his research was completed, he pushed the mail wagon to the creative director's office and asked if he could have a minute. He told the creative director about the research he had done. He emphasized that he had some ideas that would be helpful.

What was the problem? Alka-Seltzer was an all-purpose medicine—for upset stomachs, headaches, hangovers. But at that time, specialized remedies were coming out. "You have a stomachache, you take something for the stomach. You have a headache? Why take Alka-Seltzer, when you can take a headache remedy? Alka-Seltzer was like an old patent medicine."

Unfortunately, Burrell doesn't remember the creative solution he presented. "I was so focused on getting the job," he explains. "But my ideas came out of my research. And frankly, these ideas did not become part of the solution. They were just for talking. The important thing was that I demonstrated that I was thinking and talking about the problem in an intelligent way."

Burrell then made his pitch. He explained that it didn't make any sense for him to be in the mailroom when he could be helping solve problems. They talked, and within three weeks, Burrell was transferred to the creative department as a copy trainee.

As mentioned, the strategy never changed. Burrell's first Alka-Seltzer commercial involved a family at the monkey cage of a zoo. The father wasn't feeling well, and the chimp was mimicking how he felt. Then the father took Alka-Seltzer and was a totally different person. And reflecting the change, the monkey acted totally different toward him.

At the start of the creative revolution, Wade lost the Alka-Seltzer account—and ultimately went out of business. "Wade was doing work for this account for 34 years and basically doing the same stuff," says Burrell. "They got complacent, and here come these hotshots, and they get the Alka-Seltzer business and then, quickly, the rest of Miles' business. Since Wade allowed Miles to constitute about 85 percent of their total billings, when that account went, they went."

Burrell sees two lessons in this. First, you shouldn't let one client dominate your business. Second, always make sure you don't become complacent. Instead, you must continually test the work and see if it is still fresh. Wade's work did not adapt to the changing marketplace.

"I became a cake and frosting guy."

While at Wade, Burrell enrolled in the initial course of the Institute for Advanced Advertising Studies, an intensive one-year program set up by the American Association of Advertising Agencies in conjunction with Northwestern University. This exposed him to other agency people, and helped him get an offer from Leo

Burnett. "I went there in '64 and worked on Pillsbury cake and frosting mixes," he says. "I became a cake and frosting guy."

Unlike his later jobs, Burrell found that Burnett did not provide the greatest learning experience for him. "Part of that was due to my own immaturity," he says, "and my failure to really take advantage of the situation." He claims he spent too much time shooting darts. "There was not enough pressure put on me." Consequently, he believes in putting pressure on his employees. He sets deadlines and gives employees as much work as they can handle. "I make sure they understand I'm counting on them to do it," he says.

Burrell also found the competition at Burnett to be discouraging. "The person supervising your work was competing with you," he says. "If I give you an assignment and say I'm going to work on it too, that changes your level of motivation quite a bit. You may say, 'What's the use.' Or, 'I'll try, but if I don't come up with it, I know he's going to have the answer.' So you give it a shot, and it doesn't work. That stunts the growth of the junior people."

What's more, Burrell found it very hard to get his work approved because of Burnett's creative review process. "I was a copywriter," Burrell explains, "and there was a copy supervisor, an associate creative director, the creative director, a group creative director, and, finally, the creative review board. Most of my work got past the copy supervisor level, but very little got past the associate creative director." This lack of approval didn't change his views of advertising, though he did become a bit disillusioned.

"Even in those days, I looked at Burnett not as one agency, but as five agencies," he says. The creatives were assigned to groups depending on the kind of work they did. The group that handled the cigarette brands and beer ads was hot and dramatic. There was the group that created all the little critters like the Jolly Green Giant and Charlie the Tuna. There was the hard-sell demonstration group; they had products like Secret, Lilt, and Ponds. And there was the cereal group, which largely used little people, but also functioned as the "warm fuzzy" soup group. Burrell was in the Pillsbury group. He felt he was in the wrong group. "The group I was in at Burnett did not fit for me," he says. "You have to figure out what fits for you."

"I was already too late."

After Burnett, Burrell left the country to travel. He wound up in Paris and stayed there for a while. "I was basically looking to fulfill an earlier dream of just hanging out in Europe," he says. "I was getting older, and I figured I might as well do it."

As it turned out, he found himself hanging out with 18-year-olds. "It was ridiculous," he says. "I was already too late." So he decided to find a copywriting job in Paris or in Belgium, but there was an obvious language and cultural problem, so nothing happened. In London, however, he wound up getting a couple of job offers.

He took one at Foote, Cone & Belding's London office to work on the British Overseas Airways Corporation (BOAC) account, now known as British Airways. This gave him quite an education. He learned how the industry differed between the United States and Europe. "An art director was paid paltry wages," Burrell says. "But they really loved words over there. And word play. They were selling the comfort of the seat, and one line I wrote said, 'On BOAC, your seat will have an awful lot against you.' They loved that kind of stuff."

"There may not be many jobs, but I only need one."

Burrell soon grew tired of the British wage scale and came back to Chicago in what was the middle of a recession. He was warned not to return. His friends said there were few jobs to be found. His response, "There may not be many jobs, but I only need one."

Within a week, Burrell was at Needham, Harper & Steers (NHS) working on Betty Crocker cake and frosting. "That was the best agency experience of my career," he says. "I learned about marketing strategy and strategy-based advertising, and I learned the importance of basing your advertising concepts on a unique set of ideas."

Burrell found that he was working for people who made sure the advertising was kept "on track." They wouldn't approve anything if it did not follow the direction they gave. (For more thoughts on "tracking," see McElligott's comments in Chapter 7.)

He was also forced to discover the unique characteristics that sold products. "I listened to cakes to see if they sounded moister," he says. "I was cutting them with spoons, with forks, with knives, with paper. I was looking for that extra 'little thing.' Is my frosting thicker? Sweeter? Richer?"

His boss, who was not a creative genius but a marketing strategist, mandated Burrell's intense relationship with Betty Crocker. His boss expected him to find that extra advantage.

For instance, on a special assignment for Schick shavers, Burrell remembers his boss looking for a way to demonstrate the product's superiority. "I stopped by his office and he was shaving a bar of soap, looking for slight variations between razors. He was shaving wood—and the furniture. I had visions of him at home after work, taking his shaver to all kinds of stuff to figure out how to demonstrate that it was better than any other razor. That was his way of thinking. He drove us nuts."

Eccentric or not, Burrell credits this person as being one of his mentors. "The interesting thing is that people in this business would sneer at him because he was so uncreative," says Burrell. "But he had the focus I needed."

This focus has helped Burrell run his own business. "I now have to evaluate other people's creative. And I have to do it on behalf of clients who have some very delicate, subtle messages that they want to get across. If I had not gotten any further than just creating, then I would not be able to evaluate the work as thoroughly as I do now."

"We were unique."

In 1971, after four years at NHS, Burrell started his own agency, then known as Burrell-McBain, with an idea to specialize in reaching African-American consumers. A number of agencies targeting African-Americans had opened before Burrell's, but they did not consist entirely of people with extensive general market advertising expertise. "We were unique because we had the combination of the special insight that comes with being black," says Burrell, "and the kind of experience in general market advertising that brought a high level of sophistication and expertise."

Despite their level of experience, they did not have any prospects for business when they opened. Burrell's partner was committed to opening on a certain date even without a client. He felt if they waited until they got business, they could wait for a long time.

Nevertheless, it took them six months before they got their first piece of business—some public relations work for the Edison Theater Company on a freelance basis. They wanted to attract blacks to a nightclub for a Dixieland band. Says Burrell, "I can't tell you how far away Dixieland music is from black people and their interests. But we said we'd get them in."

They played it by ear, because they needed the $1,000 a month they were to be paid. To fill the seats, they convinced their friends to come to the Happy Medium to hear the band. "It was incredible," says Burrell. "They fired us fairly quickly. They felt we didn't know what we were doing."

Eventually their agency started attracting clients, including McDonald's in 1972. Burrell bought out his partner in 1974 and re-christened his agency Burrell Advertising.

Positive Realism

A hallmark of his agency's early advertising style was to convey a positive lifestyle. "We called it positive realism," says Burrell. "It's actually an exaggeration of realism. We look at ordinary, real-life events and portray them in a positive way. This was not true of everything we did, of course."

Burrell started this back in the early '70s when he opened the agency. "Black people rarely saw themselves portrayed in a realistic, positive way. We were accustomed to seeing ourselves in the mass media as either exaggerated, acceptable exceptions to the rule, or as welfare recipients, criminals, and the downtrodden. The mass media was missing the whole group of blacks who lived normal lives and had emotional, poignant kinds of events happening to them. They have romances; they get married; they go away to the service; they come back; they miss their families; they have grandmothers; they love. We tried to present those images at a time when people very rarely saw them. And it was relatively easy to do because you could take the most commonplace occurrence in the black community, put it on film, and people would say, 'Wow,' because it hadn't been communicated before."

With the growth of "below-the-line" services, Burrell later opened public relations and sales promotion divisions. Then, with the growth of truly integrated marketing communications, the divisions were eventually merged into one operation. Says Burrell, "We're no longer referred to as the Burrell Communications Group."

"Sidewalk art or postors or skywriting or…"

Now, when his agency is given an assignment, they explore the problem, review the objectives, and then determine the best way to reach the consumer. "It's our job to figure out the whole gestalt of the product and the consumer we're trying to reach," he says. "Somebody at some level has to say what is going on with this consumer—he's out in the street all the time, he's not watching television, he is watching television, he doesn't read, he does read, he goes to clubs, what have you."

This analysis is what determines Burrell's choice of media. "We may determine that the best medium is the sole of his shoes or the sole of someone else's shoes or that it's sidewalk art or posters or skywriting or an event or a game or a 30-second commercial. We may decide that it's a short film that gets shown in a nightclub or a radio program that we run on Saturday night at one in the morning, when media time is cheap and kids are listening. It could be a program and not just a commercial. That's what we did for Truth, the American Legacy Foundation account that we have for anti-smoking. So, it's really keeping an open mind and trying to figure out the best way to sell something and not be married to one discipline."

After they figure out the best way to sell a product or service is when Burrell calls in his agency's PR, promotions, and/or advertising specialists.

The 51 Percent Solution

In 1999, Burrell sold 49 percent of his agency to Publicis. "It helps us talk about our strength and our access to their resources," he says. "It also helps us get to clients who are on their roster." Burrell, however, sees pros and cons of an outside owner. "Of course, there are some advantages to being independent. In our case, we've got what we call the 51 percent solution," he says. "I think we have the best of both worlds."

In addition, he does not see corporate ownership affecting employees. "Most agencies, whether they are wholly or partially owned, tend to work independently," he says. "It's in the holding company's best interest to keep it that way, because it lets the agencies serve competing products and services." And as a plus for employees, Burrell says, "I think that in some cases, you can offer employees more opportunities and more benefits when you're part of a bigger operation."

As he prepares to turn it over to a new generation of leadership, he says the agency is finally the way he envisioned it. He positions its core competency as the ability to reach the primary trend initiators of cultural ideas—the urban youth market and the African-American consumer market. He believes reaching these segments is key for marketers because they influence all of the other segments. "If you pick the right segment, then you will have a domino effect towards other segments because of the emulative pattern that takes place in our society," he says.

Core Influencers or Cultural Catalysts

Burrell believes that if a marketer reaches the right segment, then the message spills over to youth culture all around the world. "If you talk to the African-American youth market, then you are really talking to what we call core influencers or cultural catalysts," he says. After influencing other youth, he believes it reaches up into older segments. "You see that happening fairly frequently with language and style," he says. "While Katie Couric is interviewing somebody, she's talking about someone 'dissing' someone else. Or you hear John Madden say, 'Give him the ball, dawg' during a football game. He's taking what has come from the urban youth culture and applying it to the athletic culture. President Nixon during his day was talking about rapping with students over this Vietnam thing."

For another example, Burrell points to the wide-scale power of hip-hop, which he defines as primarily rap. "The hip-hop culture is the dominant influence on youth," he says. "The evidence of that is the fact that right now about 80 percent of all hip-hop music is consumed by white kids. And you certainly see that reflected even in the suburbs, where not only are they buying the music, but they're taking on all the accoutrements of that culture, such as wearing the baggy clothes."

Today, he's very mindful of his physical health. To keep up his energy level, he's a stickler for fitness. But there's also another secret to his energy. "The more things you do that you enjoy, the more things you can do," he says. "Because you just do them. If you had a job you didn't like and you kept looking at the clock, you'd find that five minutes seem like a half hour. But if you're doing what you like that's a whole different story. And I love what I'm doing."

A VERY INFLUENTIAL PORTFOLIO

—— McDONALD'S ——

Here are some examples of "positive realism," the creative approach Burrell used to build his agency. Here, we see common occurrences that were rarely shown in the media, with positive images although slightly exaggerated in the presentation.

"Everything comes out of observing what's going on around you," he says. "Most good writers do that, whether they're writing advertising, comedy, or fiction. The best work comes out of reality—out of some truth—even if you exaggerate it or extend it."

People appreciated seeing these stories and images, which contributed to achieving what Burrell thinks is a primary objective of advertising—to make people feel good about the product. "The influence that advertising has doesn't always happen on a conscious level," he says.

—— Coca-Cola ——

Burrell's objective with this older spot was to enhance the brand's image by showing it as hip and humorous. "It had nothing to do with talking about the brown stuff in the bottle," he says. Just like the previous example, the idea came out of the realities of life. "This is a Laurel and Hardy situation. You have Charles Barkley, who's the bad, naughty guy of basketball, and Scottie Pippen, who's the good guy. It was an extension of that reality. We took it, lightened it up, and made it fun."

The result: "You wind up liking both people more than you did before. It helps humanize them because they show they aren't just superstars. They're vulnerable. They're good sports. They're capable of laughing and having a good time with each other. Even though they compete with each other, they're friends." And, of course, it sold a lot of Coca-Cola.

did somebody say ⓜ ?

[FOOD FOR THOUGHT]

BE AMAZED AT THE ACCOMPLISHMENTS AFRICAN AMERICANS HAVE MADE IN THE FIELDS
OF MEDICINE, TECHNOLOGY, SPORTS, EDUCATION AND ENTERTAINMENT. MCDONALD'S®
IS PROUD TO PRESERVE THIS HERITAGE. IF YOU'RE HUNGRY FOR KNOWLEDGE, COME TO
MCDONALD'S AND PURCHASE YOUR COPIES OF LITTLE KNOWN BLACK HISTORY FACTS.
AT PARTICIPATING MCDONALD'S. WHILE SUPPLIES LAST.

——— McDONALD'S ———

For Burrell, good advertising is based on a sound marketing strategy. He doesn't believe that an ad can be effective just because it's creative. "Those are two separate things," he says. "It has to be effective and creative. It has to be focused on achieving an objective."

While the client usually provides the objective, Burrell reminds us that many times the agency is charged with identifying it. Either way, the agency then needs to find a creative strategy that will achieve that objective. "A beginner needs to understand the importance of strategy and how you get to that," he says. "What are we going to focus on as the reason for the consumer to buy our product?" Is it cheaper, tastier, quicker, easier, better quality, or something else? What is the basis of sale?"

Then Burrell develops the "concept," which he defines as "the idea that delivers on the strategy." This includes the considerations about the execution. "What is the best form, style, structure, or presentation that will deliver the concept," he asks. "Some people may call this the gimmick." Burrell's process concludes with the production and, finally, post-production results and analysis.

"I've certainly worked with people who don't subscribe to that," says Burrell. "They're successful ad people who believe that it's all execution. Do a great execution and, hey, people will pay attention. But I want people to do more than pay attention. I want people to develop a specific attitude towards the product."

Fruitopia

The urban youth market, according to Burrell, is an unconventional segment because it's not just about young people who live in cities. "It has to do with an attitude—an urban attitude, if you will—which is something that much of the youth in all communities have embraced," says Burrell. "This is a guy in his 60s talking, but I think the attitude is 'cool,' which is interesting because that word has been around for a while. But I think that 'cool' is how I would describe it."

COCA-COLA

"Nobody is sitting around waiting for you to impart product information," says Burrell. "And with TIVO, video games, and all the other options people have, the competition for communication is so much greater today that your communications have to be arresting and engage consumers. That's first and foremost. And the way to engage consumers in today's environment is by entertaining them."

Burrell believes this is partly why humor has taken on a much greater role in marketing communications. "People are also looking for enjoyment," he says. "With all that's happening in their lives, they need release. If you can put your product in that kind of context, then you're going to be successful."

A perfect example of that is this Coke commercial featuring humor, music, and an interesting visual style.

Burrell also recognizes that there are some things that just don't readily lend themselves to humor. "Certainly if you're selling a funeral chain or something else that has a certain amount of inherent solemnity to it, then it gets to be more challenging. But, even with insurance, technology, automobiles, and other serious purchases, communications have become more humorous."

ADIDAS

To create a successful piece of marketing communications, Burrell believes that you have to understand both the brand personality and the mood and the temper of the consumer that the brand is trying to reach.

"The trick is coupling the brand's personality with that mood," he says. "If you strictly stick to the brand personality and disregard the consumer's mood, then you're not going to engage him or her. On the other hand, if you try to engage the consumer with a story about the product that is out of whack with his or her perception of it, then you are also not going to reach them."

His advice: Stretch the brand personality as much as you can, but don't lose it. "There have been instances where people in this business have disregarded the brand personality and have failed. And there have been instances, of course, where people have disregarded the consumer's mood and feelings and just concentrated on perpetuating the brand personality and have failed," he says. "The challenge is to take those two disparate entities and pull them together so that they meet."

SOME POSITIVE ADVICE FROM TOM BURRELL

To create any type of good advertising that will be seen beyond a job interview, a person must obviously first break in. "It's harder today," says Burrell. "Beginners have to realize that. One of the sad facts about this business is that most of the training programs have gone to hell. Today's advertising people aren't going to live forever. My fear is that this business is going to be in deep trouble because we're not doing anything to develop new talent."

The economy of the past few years has compounded the problem. "Companies have a much harder time today justifying training programs," says Burrell. "And they have a much harder time justifying bringing people in who they have to overly direct or supervise. This means that in order to make it in this business, you're going to have to bring a lot more to the table right from the start. It also means that if you're committed to going into this business, you may have to take a circuitous route instead of going directly into the area that you ultimately want."

In other words, you may need to find a creative way to get the training you need—not only in the position you want, but also areas that are allied or related to that position. To help develop your skills, Burrell has the following ideas and suggestions.

Target small agencies: "Small companies can't afford multiple teams working on an assignment. They need help, so you're more likely to have your ideas used," says Burrell. "If you start at a gargantuan agency, getting your ideas heard is more difficult."

Make up products: "One of the best conceptual thinkers I have ever worked with here came up with new products. And he developed unique selling propositions and very fresh, new ways to sell them," says Burrell. "He was hired on the basis of that speculative stuff. I never asked to see his produced work because I knew that was done for somebody else."

Show your conceptual abilities: "I'm looking for the ability to take a product or service and not only find the advantages, but dramatize those differences in a way that is innovative and fresh," says Burrell, "including the look, the sound, and the feel of the communication."

Be a Renaissance person: "I liken education to getting a really nice looking, expensive book-bag, especially if you are talking about marketing and communications courses," says Burrell. "But it's not the bag. It's what you put in the bag that's important. The best thing you can put in your bag is a broad general knowledge about a lot of different kinds of things: be open to the world, be a cultural anthropologist by avocation, understand society, trends, and how people think, how society works, how social change takes place, be what Mark Twain calls a "noticer" and take in what's going on around you, have a grasp of history, and be a real student of life. That's the stuff that really gives you the material that you need to come up with creative ideas."

Maintain a life outside advertising: This is partly how you stay a Renaissance person. "You have to know what's going on and be aware of what's happening," says Burrell. "If you don't have a life outside, you don't have anything to bring to the job."

Know your audience in detail: "There used to be a magazine rack," says Burrell, "now there are magazine stores. There's a proliferation of different kinds of magazines for many different population sub-segments. You even need a whole section just for women's magazines. You've got one for older women, for fashionable women, for young mothers, for women who run, for women into fitness, there's even one for women who run long distances. That's the way marketing is going. The world is getting complex and competitive, so you've got to figure out what piece of the pie you want. That means when you're preparing to communicate something about your product or service, you'd better know who you're talking to in specific terms. Talking to women or talking to men—or even to subsets of talking to black women or white men—is not enough."

Define your target audience: "When putting together a portfolio, write down a description of the sub-segment you want to talk to," says Burrell. "You might even want to share it—what the product and the strategy are—with whoever is reviewing your portfolio."

Expand your thinking—and your styles: "The way the business has evolved, it is very important to stop thinking along the narrow lines of advertising. Substitute the term 'marketing communications' instead. It's more comprehensive," says Burrell. "And as your career progresses, you have to become more eclectic. Experience different kinds of clients with different kinds of problems, different corporate cultures, different attitudes toward advertising. Do image stuff. Do product-oriented advertising. Be flexible."

Don't wait for inspiration: Burrell feels that creative people whose careers excel are self-starters and know how to generate ideas on demand. "Don't expect dart shooting and sitting around waiting for an idea to come. That could take a day—or three weeks," says Burrell. "When it's time to do it, just get up and do it."

Determine the product's character: "Every product and service has a personality and some kind of emotional gestalt to it. For many of our clients, the product or service's brand character is based on a history of how people perceive it," says Burrell. "We have to understand the product's personality, and the advertising should be within that context. When people drink a soft drink, they're not just drinking a sweet liquid. The product is an extension of them. I don't think you can build this personality. You have to find it."

Use logic: Burrell seldom found traditional brainstorming techniques helpful in developing his concepts. Instead, he used deductive reasoning. For instance, when he was asked to advertise a sandwich where the cold lettuce and tomato were packaged on one side and the hot hamburger was packaged on the other, he came up with the concept of the package being a combination stove and refrigerator. "It tasted good because you got all that hot, cold, crispy, and juicy all together," he says. "That was its advantage. And that's a very clear, unique selling proposition. To dramatize that, we transformed this package—through the magic of television— into a little range on top with the meat and a little refrigerator on the bottom with the tomato and lettuce. And we asked, 'Wouldn't it be great if we could have a sandwich that's hot on the one side and cool on the other? Now you do.' We produced three commercials based on that concept. They were very successful. And they logically followed from the strategy."

Create an emotional connection: "Advertising's role is to do more than just inform people," says Burrell. "Its role is to give people a feeling about the product or service. And the best way to do that is by striking some emotional chords that build a bond between the audience and the product or service." Although he recognizes that there are some products that lack an emotional appeal—for instance, paper clips—he emphasizes that in a competitive environment, establishing an emotional connection is a requirement. "The product has to inspire fear, humor, love, romance, aspirations—something," he says.

Broadcast your plans: "If you have any pride at all, telling other people your plans will help you achieve them," says Burrell. "Once you commit to doing it, you follow through. I do that all the time. When I want to make sure that I'm going to get something done, I go out and tell other people that I'm going to do it. Then I'm expected to do it. Since I want to make sure I have a reputation for doing what I say I'm going to do, I do it." Not only does this force you to stay committed, it enables other people to help you do it. "That's how I got into the advertising business," says Burrell. "I told people I was going to do that. Somebody remembered and called me up and told me that a job was available."

Appreciate pressure: "At Burrell, your future depends on your work being good because our growth as a company depends on it as well. If you don't make it, then we're going to be in deep trouble. I know that's pressure. But people learn they are vital, they are necessary; they are critical. It forces them to use more of themselves," says Burrell. "Most of us use so little of ourselves. I try to push people to their potential."

Keep a lookout for creative talent: Creative talent is everywhere—but it's hard to find. If you move into a position where you are responsible for hiring creative people, you may discover talent in unconventional places. Burrell hired Anna Morris as a part-time bookkeeper in 1974. But her creative answers on her application hinted at a wealth of ability. Eventually, she became Burrell's executive vice president/chief creative officer. Then she left the industry to produce television shows, which she did for a number of years. "Look for people who look at the world differently than most people," says Burrell. "Make sure that you're not passing over the people who could be the real contributors of ideas and innovations."

Postscript 1:

BRANDING IN THE AGE OF SEGMENTED MARKETING

Throughout this book, you're hearing how advertisers have stopped talking to the mass market and have started targeting various market segments. Now here are some issues to keep in mind from one of the originators of segmented marketing.

"The way you handle integrated marketing communications is a big issue within the industry, and we've been dealing with it from the beginning. The people who are having a hard time are those who were into mass marketing. They've been taught that all you need to do is broadcast a commercial. But we're not into mass marketing.

"In my early days there was some concern about our selling a product to the black consumer market. Marketers were concerned about how general market audiences might react. Testing found that not only did whites like the advertising we did for the black consumer market, but that they recognized that the ads were for the black market.

"This was more than 30 years ago. Now you have advertising that is designed for seniors, youth, Hispanics, blacks, working women, women who are homemakers. People understand and accept that certain ads address particular segments. The confusion factor is overrated.

"When you focus on segmented marketing, it is incumbent upon you to use all of the marketing communications tools you can in order to get maximum efficiency. And you have to make enough noise to be heard above all the noise that's being made by other communications.

"Ideally, clients tell us their problem and objectives and then we come back with the solutions. Those solutions may involve advertising, public relations, sales promotions, or some combination.

"In creating a segmented campaign, you have to think about consistency in message and branding. You don't want to say in one message that, hey, this thing is big and, in another message, that this thing is small. That's what creates confusion. And keeping a consistent brand image means looking for the common denominators. Sometimes they come in the form of a 'look.' Sometimes they come in the form of a central theme that works across the board. But if you're going to talk to various segments of the market, you can't be contradictory. You have to strategically decide what's important about the product and build on that generality with more specifics that relate directly to the segment you're targeting.

"There's also an overestimation of how people think about advertising campaigns. The client is sitting here developing an overall strategy and campaign, looking for consistency. While the consumer is interested in what you're saying; nobody looks at television and says, 'Oh, wait a minute. That's not part of the campaign.' A campaign is not part of the lexicon of the consumer."

POSTSCRIPT 2:

SOME DEFINITIONS TO HELP YOU FIND WHERE YOU FIT

Marketing communications is breaking apart into more and more specialties. At the same time, the field has come together with an integrated approach. So where do you fit? And where do all creative people "play?" To help you decide, here are some thoughts from Burrell.

"I think people tend to have different strengths. But the key today for a writer and an art director is understanding how it all fits together and then showing that you can think in many different ways. I think that's where you'll find the real opportunity, and that's fairly different than the way it usually works.

"After you get the understanding of the brand character and the needs of the consumer, sit down and figure out what is the very best way to get this product into the hands of the consumer. Without thinking about any kind of restrictions, what is the best way to do it?

"Once you figure this out, then you can start thinking about the various specialties and define them. For instance, advertising is publicity through paid media and generally done for long-term returns. To complicate matters, I would rather classify retail and image advertising as intrinsic versus extrinsic advertising. Extrinsic advertising promotes an image of the product beyond its intrinsic properties, while intrinsic advertising focuses on product attributes.

"The next area, public relations, is generally—but not always—publicity through unpaid media. And sales promotion is the catchall for various marketing tools not formally classified as advertising, publicity, or personal selling.

"Now, to help you decide where you could fit as a specialist, art directors are generally thinkers and conceptualizers who want to solve problems beyond simply the design aspect. A graphics person, on the other hand, may not care as much about the other aspects of marketing.

"On the writing side, both copywriters in advertising and public relations specialists need a certain level of creativity. But with copywriting, what you write down is totally out of your head. And with public relations, you are basically a reporter. It's the difference between writing fiction and nonfiction. If you have a tendency to go toward the fictional, then you're more likely to be an advertising copywriter. If you want to report, then you're more likely to be in public relations.

"As for sales promotion, I know people who were advertising copywriters and art directors who went into this area because they like its short-term aspect.

"This is radical, but I think that when considering where you fit, you need to establish yourself as an idea person first, with certain specializations.

"I would have much more interest in someone who shows a breadth of ability in terms of how advertising ideas get applied. I would rather see a portfolio with a combination of print ads, posters that might be used for street marketing purposes, a unique creative idea where the message is on the back of somebody's pants, the sole of their shoes, or the bill of a baseball cap. The breadth of applications shows that the person has an understanding of the reality of marketing communications in the 21st century."

Rich Silverstein

"He was that bad and he turned out good?"

That's what Rich Silverstein thinks people would say if they saw his early work.

Today, he is Co-founder and Co-chairman/Creative Director of one of the most respected agencies in the country, Goodby Silverstein & Partners (GS&P). Their clients include Hewlett-Packard, Anheuser Busch, the California Milk Processors Board (Got Milk?), Saturn, Comcast, and Motorola. *Advertising Age* named them agency of the year three times (and counting). He and Jeff Goodby were also selected three times as *Adweek*'s Creative Director of the Year.

They consistently win the top national and international advertising awards. Silverstein was inducted into the New York Art Directors Club in 2002. And, in 2004, he and Jeff Goodby were inducted into the One Club Creative Hall of Fame.

GS&P is recognized for using clever, offbeat humor. Their creative output is intelligent, well designed, journalistic, and timeless.

"We strive to create solutions that are brilliantly created and brutally simplistic," says Silverstein. "To me, that is really good advertising."

But while GS&P's solutions are simple, they also have great depth.

"What I don't like is the patina on advertising, the surface level that is all varnish," he says. "I like to be able to scratch through the varnish and get paint, more paint, more paint, and the primer. I like it when there are levels to advertising, so you can watch it over and over again because there's something to see that doesn't wear out."

In this chapter, we'll gain insights into how to create this type of advertising.

THE DESIGNER WHO WAS CURSED TO LIVE
IN AN ADVERTISING BODY

Does a person find a career or does the career actually find the person?

Rich Silverstein felt connected to art and design even before he knew the name for it. He grew up in a middle-class area of northern Westchester County, New York, called Yorktown Heights. It's only about 45 miles from New York City, but it could have been a million miles away in terms of attitude. "The place was just cow pastures and apple orchards," says Silverstein.

"Art wasn't something that people talked about," he says. "There was no one saying, 'You're going to be a designer or an art director.' He claims that art instruction didn't exist in junior high and his high school art classes weren't sophisticated. But he was drawn to art—a connection to something he'd never felt before. "I even connected to the *Time* magazine art page," he says. This made him feel "odd."

"I didn't know what I was doing, but I made the most of art classes," he says. He also excelled at "alternative" sports—lacrosse, soccer, and track—rather than the traditional sports of baseball, football, or basketball. "It was because I looked at the world a little odd," he says. "I liked things that were a little different and strange."

He struggled with his academic subjects and, today, understands that he's dyslexic. "I get words backwards," he says. "I can read everything, but I have to take my time. High school was pretty tough, because I didn't understand why I was having a hard time. Later on, it was probably a benefit because, while this may sound strange, it's a more creative way of looking at the world."

He decided to attend the Parsons School of Design in New York City and had drawings of nature, mostly leaves and sticks as well as a couple of oil paintings in his admissions portfolio. "The work was really primitive," he recalls. "I did them to get into school and then I found out that they take everybody. You give them money and they take you."

In New York City, he discovered he was not alone. "There was a whole school of people who were odd," Silverstein says. "It changed my world." The city became his "classroom." "Walking around, going to the Museum of Modern Art, watching films, I was soaking all of that up," he says.

He also benefited from an internship while attending school. "The secretary of the graphic design department recommended that I meet Dick Hess," says Silverstein. "I called him and said, 'I want to sharpen your pencils.' It took me two months of badgering him before he gave me a job."

Hess excelled as a graphic designer, art director, writer, and illustrator. He produced logos, album covers, annual reports, and magazines, including cover illustrations for *Time* and *National Lampoon* and the art direction for the United Nation's then-acclaimed *Vista* magazine. "I admired him so much that I had him write a letter declaring my status as a conscientious objector to the Vietnam War," recalls Silverstein. "I thought so much of the guy that I figured my draft board would think much of him, too."

Silverstein served as an apprentice. "I still believe that's the way it should be. I got his lunch, shoveled gravel on his roof, and produced the mechanicals. I had a healthy sense of insecurity, so I wanted to learn everything I could without sticking my neck out. And it was amazing, because I learned a heck of a lot."

While he feels he gained more from his internship than from the classroom, there were a couple of instructors who also influenced him.

One gave him a chance to design the cover to the course catalog for Parsons. And an industrial design teacher had him help hang a famous photography exhibit, "Harlem on My Mind," at the Metropolitan Museum of Art. One instructor, however, was more influential than the rest, because this person was more critical of his work. "But the harshest critic for me is myself. I'm driven by feelings that I'm not good enough. I've been proving something to my father for my whole life. He passed away, unfortunately, but I'm still trying to prove something to him."

The secretary to the design department head also influenced Silverstein's career direction. "She said that I would become an art director. She must have seen something in me, because I was a lousy designer. My mind had the ideas, but my hand couldn't draw them," he says. This prediction was a revelation, because while he had attended school for three years, no one had ever mentioned this position. "I didn't know there was such a job."

After Parsons, with a portfolio of student assignments and his work with Hess, Silverstein moved to San Francisco. "I wanted to run away from my family," he says. "Three thousand miles from New York to California is about as far away as you can go in America. I got married, packed up my Volkswagen Beetle, drove west, and interviewed with every designer in San Francisco."

At the time, the design work coming out of San Francisco was some of the best in the country. "I didn't happen to know that," says Silverstein. "I just lucked out." After two weeks of interviewing, Dean Smith, a designer famous for the Channel 7 circle logo and the signage in Yosemite park, hired him.

Silverstein found the experience frustrating. "I was in a firm of designers," he says. "I didn't realize that my hands couldn't do what my mind was thinking. But I've always had a very strong work ethic, which they appreciated."

Drawn to editorial design through his work with Hess and seeing the work of Push Pin Studios, Silverstein then got a job at *San Francisco* magazine as art director and paste-up person. "The everything," he says. "It was just me."

Shortly thereafter, he moved over as a junior designer/art director at a then-new magazine called *Rolling Stone*. "I didn't do much, but I soaked up that place," he says. Annie Leibovitz and Hunter Thompson were there. Jann Wenner was the editor. "Just being around that intensity was amazing. I didn't go to *Rolling Stone* because of Bob Dylan and The Rolling Stones. I didn't take drugs. I was a goody-goody."

Silverstein's passion was design and one thing he learned at *Rolling Stone* was how to work faster.

"The tension of a deadline," he says. "We went to press every two weeks."

But even with his passion for editorial design, he returned to working at design firms. "In a period of a year-and-a-half, I must have worked at every firm in San Francisco," says Silverstein. "I was cutting and pasting and making magazines. These ads were sent to me—they were all slick and beautiful—and I was putting them in the magazines. I went, 'Maybe advertising would be interesting.' It was as simple as that."

He applied for a job at the San Francisco office of Bozell and Jacobs. "It was a small agency," he says. "And I convinced the man who ran it to give me a trial. He was very skeptical, because I was a designer. But I said, 'If you don't like what I'm doing, fire me.' I did that a couple of times in my career. I think it's a smart thing to do because if you can't pull your weight, then you should move on."

During his trial, he worked on Hewlett-Packard. "It was really dry, engineering-oriented," he says. "I saw all the other people doing this interesting work with wine and whatever." Ironically, today, he's working on HP again. "But it's a whole new world."

He then had a stint at J. Walter Thompson and, later, at Foote, Cone & Belding with Mike Koelker (see Chapter 11). "I cared so much about Levi's that the client asked for me to be removed from the account," he says. "I wanted it to be great. Maybe my intensity scared her or I did something. I don't know. I was devastated at the time, but it was probably a good learning experience."

He then got a call from a former creative director at Bozell and Jacobs who had moved on to Ogilvy & Mather/San Francisco, which was being run by Hal Riney.

"Never burn your bridges," says Silverstein. "If you do a good job somewhere and someone moves on, they'll remember you. That's how you move forward."

His former boss advised him to edit his portfolio to his ten best samples and told him to send it to Hal Riney and Jerry Andelin. "I can't say the work was good, but I put in what I thought was my best," says Silverstein. The resulting book had a mixture of design and advertising samples. "It was probably distinctive. And I think that helped me."

"It's a good book."

During his interview with Riney, he saw a note on his portfolio that said, "It's a good book." Riney asked, "Do you see that?" When Silverstein then went, "Oh" in response, Riney said, "Hey, read that as a compliment." "I guess that Jerry didn't usually do that," says Silverstein. "I went, 'Whoa,' and I got hired."

Ogilvy & Mather changed Silverstein's life. "I was finally at a place where craftsmanship mattered and was demanded," he says. "I remember people saying, 'You'd better not go there, it's too hard.' It was fantastic. I blossomed from the moment I got there."

For his first assignment, he was partnered with a writer named Jeff Goodby to work on Billy Ball for the Oakland A's baseball team. "I wasn't a baseball fanatic, but Jeff was," he recalls. "I worked on it like I was an art director for a magazine. I hired a design firm to help me. And Jeff complemented me. He was clearly different from me, like black and white or Yin/Yang. It really works."

It was a golden time at Ogilvy & Mather/San Francisco under Riney's leadership. "He had an amazing amount of talented people," says Silverstein. "And you were always competing with everyone, but there was definitely room to make great work."

Silverstein and Goodby worked on the Billy Ball account from soup to nuts. "While we were on the set for a TV commercial, we were also creating print ads," says Silverstein. "People today complain that they can't do the print ads, because they're working on the TV. But you've got to do both. When it's your account, you do the little jobs, the medium jobs, and the big jobs. You make it run; you go sell it; you do everything."

Andy Berlin and Silverstein started freelancing for a company called Amazin' Software. "Electronic games were just coming out," says Silverstein. "We renamed the company Electronic Arts. When it got to be too busy, we brought in Jeff. Jeff and I had this perfect world at Ogilvy and could do anything we wanted, but Andy convinced us to start an agency. We were earning enough to cover our salary. And since my partners were journalists and I was a magazine art director, we saw the world the same way."

Riney's reaction: "He said we'd do fine, which was a great compliment.

"For us to go off on our own was a big deal. But Hal liked Jeff and me and for some reason was very supportive.

"In fact, he liked us so much that he became our second client. He paid us a monthly retainer to do projects for him. Life will be a lot better for you if you don't burn your bridges. People with respect don't leave on bad terms."

The partners didn't have a plan for growing the agency, but they gained one little client after another. "We were able to eke it out," says Silverstein. "We never wanted to be a boutique, but as any small company, we took anything we could get. A newspaper. A winery. We got the Oakland Invaders in the United States Football League, which didn't stick around too long, and a local radio station, KGO radio. Those were not big accounts, but we tried to do good work and we started winning local awards." Their strategy for winning accounts: "We convinced people that we were smart and cared."

The partners didn't want to be known for running a local agency and tried finding clients from all over the country. "We just wanted to live in San Francisco," says Silverstein. But their first big break, ironically, was in San Francisco—the $10 million Royal Viking Cruise Line account. They had to pitch against Riney. "We beat our father. Hal was asked if he'd work on it. And he answered honestly that he wouldn't be on it day-to-day.

"The three of us said we would. We probably got it for that reason, because we had no track record. But they hired the right agency. We did some really good work for them and gave them an identity and a voice."

From there, Goodby, Berlin & Silverstein started growing, developing a range of very, very small accounts to very large accounts, says Silverstein. "We didn't want to have one client overwhelm the agency."

But none of the partners had ever been a creative director before. "I learned that you have to be clear when giving feedback," says Silverstein. "Of course, you want people to like you, but you'll get nowhere and end up doing bad work by watching what you say so they will like you. You have to be very honest and direct about what is working and what is not." He admits that this could be a little intimidating for people who are new to the agency. But people who know him aren't afraid. "They always know where they stand with me."

This honesty also extends to how they treat their clients. "We got clients because we were honest with them," says Silverstein. "We say it the way it is.

"Nobody plays golf with the client. There's not a lot of wining and dining. It's all about the work."

The partners also discovered a little bit of the obsessiveness in their DNA. "My wife and I are so relentless about perfection that we made the contractor we'd hired for our house buy a little level and put it on the light switches," says Silverstein. This aesthetic translates into his work. "I believe that if something was supposed to look like it was beautifully varnished, it should be varnished. If it's supposed to look like natural wood, use natural wood."

"We are relentless."

As part of their obsessive drive for perfection, the agency never stops trying to improve on their executions. "We work on a project until the moment that it actually ships," says Silverstein. "If you give up on it a week or a day early, you're not making it better. We are relentless. At any stage, if you don't like it or if it doesn't work, a creative director has to say it and fix it. Give us a day and we're tweaking."

Silverstein believes this drive separates the good agencies from the bad ones. "The places where I worked that didn't do it weren't very good," he says. "But at Ogilvy & Mather, I found a place that believed that God was in the details. Jeff and I felt comfortable in that kind of environment."

Goodby, Berlin & Silverstein was also one of the first agencies to bring the British discipline of account planning to the United States. "About five years after we formed, Andy Berlin started focusing more on what we could become and less about the day-to-day work," says Silverstein. "Somehow he got hooked up with Boase Massimi Pollitt in England, which had the best planning in the world and we thought they were the best agency in the whole world. They were going to help us bring in planning, and we hired a young planner from there, Jon Steel. He was just one of many they had there, but he was willing to come to San Francisco. He became famous for being the best planner in America."

BMP also took an interest in their agency and bought 37 percent of it to give them some operating cash. Then when BMP was fighting a hostile takeover bid, Omnicom bought them. "By doing that, Omnicom now owned a third of us," says Silverstein. "So a fish eats a fish eats a fish." Since the head of Omnicom didn't see a future with West coast agencies, he offered to let the partners buy themselves back. "He didn't know who the heck we were," says Silverstein. "He said it was no big deal. 'If you don't, I'll just keep you.' But it was a little too hard to buy us back at the time. And they ended up realizing what they had and bought the rest of us. So we're owned by Omnicom."

Did their ownership of the agency change operations? No, claims Silverstein. "We have to return a profit to them and we keep the rest for the company," he says. "But it was a calming factor to be bought. In the young days of starting a company, it helped Jeff, Andy, and me become self-sufficient." Shortly thereafter, Andy Berlin left the agency and it was renamed Goodby Silverstein & Partners.

To manage all of their accounts, Goodby and Silverstein decided to divide and conquer. "Jeff touches half the clients," says Silverstein. "And I touch half of the clients."

The company went from three people to over 300 people and now has more than $800 million in capitalized billings. "We have grown to a level and intensity where I don't work day-to-day on all of my accounts," says Silverstein. "I lend my hand on things and see all of the rough cuts for my accounts, but we now have a team of senior creative directors in place. For the first time in history, projects that

Jeff oversees actually run on TV before I see them. And he doesn't see all of the work that I oversee."

In addition, GSP now has offices throughout the country, particularly to service the Saturn account. "We've toyed with having a presence in Asia and Europe for HP," he says. "Instead, we've decided to bring the creatives from those places to America. We've made a United Nations in San Francisco. The creative department will always be here."

Why does Silverstein want to keep the creatives in San Francisco? "For people to bump into each other and talk," he says. "Exchanging and exploring ideas is a good thing. There was something to the round table for the writers of the *New Yorker*. There was something about Matisse and Picasso seeing what each other was doing, even though they were competing with each other. There's something about artists who are willing to critique each other. If you close doors and have people compete out of fear, you might get something, but it's not as much fun as having open doors and sharing."

Even though he has cut back on day-to-day oversight of his accounts, Silverstein remains a working creative. But he doesn't design on a computer. Rather, he figures out the solution in his head or creates a pencil sketch. He then selects the typography and the photography style and sits with a digital artist to produce it. "There are some designers who are so computer savvy that the design is overwhelmed by what can done with the technology," he says. "I still have my drafting board from art school, all chewed up. I have three Exacto blades next to my desk. I'm not an old fart, but I'm more tactile about cutting and pasting and Xeroxing."

Silverstein likens himself to a conductor who directs a pianist. "I tell him when I want him to stop and start and his fingers are hitting the keys," he says. "It works really well." This enables him to work faster. "I'm very focused. No time to waste. I produce more work in three or four hours than most people produce in a day."

Keeping a Balance

Silverstein is dedicated to keeping a balance between his work and home life. He arrives at work at 8:30 and leaves at 5:00 or earlier. He doesn't work nights or weekends unless it is for a new business pitch.

"I look at it like I'm punching the clock," he says. "I look forward to my lifestyle. I go home, I play with my cat on the floor, we have dinner, I go to a movie— advertising stops the moment I walk out the door."

Outside of advertising, his passion is cycling. He serves on the board of the USA Cycling Development Foundation, a group that sponsors Americans to race in Europe in hopes of training the next Lance Armstrong.

He is also on the board of directors of Specialized Bicycles. He goes to the Tour de France every year, knows the team, and has even ridden with Lance Armstrong. He also cycles to work three days a week. "When I get to the Golden Gate Bridge, it's unbelievable," he says. "The aesthetic of cycling and a bike is right up there. Everything on a bike is beautiful and is there for a reason."

He also loves cars, attended racecar school, and raced a couple of years. "I got to the point where I scared myself," he says, "but I am totally, totally fascinated by sports cars, Formula 1 racing, and bicycle racing."

Along with his wife, Carla Emil, he also collects photography. "We have a very good collection of the history of photography," he says. And, he is the father of two grown children. One studied design at Rhode Island School of Design and is now an industrial designer. The other studied at Boston University and then worked at GSP, until she quit to open a yoga studio.

"I am so lucky," he says about being able to follow his passions both inside and outside of work. "I got to design the typography for the Williams BMW Formula 1 Team. You can't get any better than that. To me, Frank Williams is like a God in auto racing. You have Williams, Ferrari, and McClaren. I got to go to Indianapolis with a giant ruler to measure the side pods of the track. It was a dream come true."

A LOOK AT A BRUTALLY SIMPLE, BEAUTIFULLY EXECUTED PORTFOLIO

 Silverstein doesn't know too many advertising art directors who get involved with logos. "But it's part of my DNA," he says. "I start with the logo and then work from there. If there's an ugly logo, I'm the first one who wants to clean it up."

He believes that logos are the foundation for any ad. "It's the proof," he says. "The logo is the brand. A logo has to have strength, to be elegant, and to mean something."

When GSP got the assignment to re-launch the HP brand, the CEO said the only rule is to not change the logo. And the first thing Silverstein did was change the logo. "I removed things," he says. "I made it more elegant by removing Hewlett and Packard as ty- pography, updated the color to a more modern blue, gave it a little bit of a shadow, and then we came up with the 'Invent' theme line.

"We needed to compete with IBM and Apple," he says. "And HP hadn't made the leap into a more modern world. It took a day to do that logo—smart thinking in a day—which is now all over the world. It doesn't take long to come up with the solution, but design firms will take your money and spend a year on it."

 For Unum, a 125-year-old insurance company out of Portland, Maine, GSP brought back a more classical logo. "Their logo, a lighthouse, had gone through so many iterations it had become a modern, stick figure-like, geometric form which had no emotion," says Silverstein. "The first thing we did was to get someone to create an engraving of the Portland lighthouse. That lighthouse has integrity. I modernized the logo by making it old and made it relevant with our line, 'We see farther.' Then we did the advertising."

"We also brought back the Porsche crest. Their logo was just typography, but they had this great symbol," says Silverstein. "So I always start from the sense of graphic design."

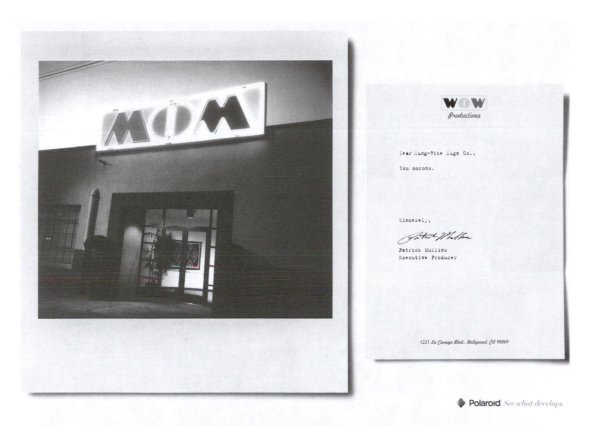

——— Polaroid ———

Before digital cameras, the use of a Polaroid camera created a fun, magical experience. But it had lost its way and GSP had to show its relevance. The idea was captured in the line "See What Develops." "This was literally, 'That's what happens when you watch the technology work in front of you,'" says Silverstein. "Most print ads are passive. You just sit there and look at them. We tried to make these print ads as engaging as the experience of using the camera. We wanted people involved in them. Our solution was to make them like little unfolding movies or storyboards with the camera as the star of each one."

─── ISUZU ───

Isuzu was one of the first manufacturers of SUVs and this campaign was created before there was a lot of SUV advertising. "Our goal was to create an aura around SUVs. This was at a time when people didn't have them, so it was quite unique and fun," says Silverstein. "I think the key to any print advertising is that you shouldn't scream "ad"—or even scream at all—but, rather, you should be respectful of the publications and be consistent with the aesthetic of the magazines. I think the Isuzu photography and typography show that respect. It sets the mood in an intelligent way. The photograph tells a story. If I could make everything work like a piece of editorial, I would."

Take the wheel and we defy you not to smile. 400 horses. Zero to sixty in just over four heartbeats. Eighteen inch wheels. A new wider stance. It's the new Nine Eleven Turbo. Some very serious amusement. Call 1-800-PORSCHE and prepare to agree: Porsche. There is no substitute.

Like your own portable amusement park.

Porsche

GSP was probably the first agency to have two car accounts at one time, Isuzu and Porsche. "That was a big deal," says Silverstein. "We said they didn't compete with each other, and they didn't. They got totally different thinking." GSP landed Isuzu when they were small. "Because they had respect for us and were not in this high-performance market and Porsche wasn't in the SUV market, they allowed us to have both. But we had to pitch for both." For Porsche, they developed a visual language for the brand, which continues to be used in their advertising. "This is amazing, because we don't have Porsche anymore," he says. "But we connected the car to the road, which is an equal part of the experience, because with Porsche, you feel every bump."

—— THE *NEW YORKER* ——

GSP landed the *New Yorker* account a year before Tina Brown took over, and needed to show relevancy of this magazine. "A lot of young people were not reading it and a lot of media buyers are very young," says Silverstein. "The rub was that the *New Yorker* was just too hard to get through, because the stories were too long. But if you took the time to read it, you'd never be disappointed. So we showed that any paragraph from the *New Yorker* is riveting. We literally hand-ripped out a paragraph from the magazine—artfully, of course—scanned it, and found a photograph to go a long with it. There is elegance to the layout that doesn't try to outdo the magazine, which is brilliantly written. But I also tried to make it seem simplistic, so people would get to it."

—— HP ——

Silverstein has been able to go from design into advertising and, with HP, then influence the overall direction of a giant company like Paul Rand and Charles Eames did for IBM. As part of his work, he gave a speech to all 60 of HP's industrial designers. "They were from all over the world," says Silverstein. "They've always made great products, but they were never known like Apple or a Nike for an aesthetic. They've hired a chief of design who wants to have one, so they're on the right track. And I showed the advertising we're doing to them. It was wonderful to come from the other end: show graphic design in advertising to industrial designers to be holistic to the design aesthetic of a company and to influence its overall spirit. It was one of the things I wanted to achieve in life."

—— California Milk Processing Board ——

"This logo was never intended to become famous," recalls Silverstein. "The young art directors here even wanted to hide it in the print ads and didn't want it used in the voiceover of the commercials." Silverstein created the logo in about ten minutes. "We just took a piece of typography—a typeface that hadn't been used before, but felt friendly when it was condensed and set in lower case—and it became a way of speaking, a voice. We had to convince the client that you could read it and we had to play with the spacing a little bit for use on billboards."

The logo was developed for a campaign produced by the California Milk Processing Board and was based on the insight that people don't think about milk until they run out. It was intended to remind people to buy enough milk.

Then their client sold the rights to the logo to the National Dairy Board, which produces the milk moustache campaign. "We never did that version." And this campaign creates a mixed message between the logo and the image. People with a milk moustache imply that they already have milk, so why should you remind them with a question mark in the logo? This shows why you should follow Silverstein's advice to start with the logo when creating a campaign, rather than creating a campaign and then pasting on the logo.

——— Beaver Creek ———

For this campaign, Silverstein wanted to harken back to his design roots to capture a period when European travel and train posters were important. "It seemed like the thing to do because the client wanted Beaver Creek to be more of a European destination in Colorado," he says.

——— ADOBE ———

Ironically, while Silverstein doesn't design on a computer, he creates the advertising for the software that enables designers to work on one. "Adobe makes an amazing product that changed the course of advertising and design," he says. "They came up with PhotoShop and Adobe typography—a way of setting type—and the world is never going back. It's a staggering piece of software. And people take for granted that you can open a picture or a document on a computer. But, the reason you can is because of this software called Acrobat. So our job is to tell people about the company behind the products."

—— ROYAL VIKING CRUISE LINE ——

Silverstein believes that there are no rules to creating a campaign, except that it has to fit the client's personality and product. "The layout here is very complicated," he says, "but since you are paying so much for a cruise, I wanted the ad to feel like it was worth the money. I grew up with Oxford Rules in design school. *Rolling Stone* always liked them, and we put the destinations within them. No one had done that before and it set the framework for every ad. The typography and photography all added to the ambience of the experience. This is one way of creating a solution. Another way is to be amazingly simplistic, such as showing a cookie with a bite out of it for the 'Got Milk?' campaign. You can't get any simpler than that and any more complicated than this."

She's not your child.

But if you give her a ride home with your kids,

she might as well be.

Carpooling. On the wings of Goodyear.

MORE MOMS AND DADS TRUST THEIR CARPOOLS TO US. GOODYEAR.COM

GOODYEAR

—— GOODYEAR ——

Paying attention to all of the details is what helped make this campaign successful. They again started by going back to the original logo of this 100-year-old company and cleaning it up. The partners then developed a tagline based on the logo: "on the wings of Goodyear." Says Silverstein, "This remarkably warm safety line really felt right." Finally, they focused on the storytelling. "Instead of screaming 'retail,' we wanted it to be a piece of editorial." And they tried to make the tire as attractive as possible. "A tire is really important to your life. You take them for granted—they just go around and around—but they can save your life and that's poignant. With this one, the driver is responsible for the safety of the little girl, so it's like you're carpooling on the wings of Goodyear."

—— MOUNT TAMALPAIS ——

Silverstein serves on the board of directors of the Golden Gate National Parks—all of the 24 parks that ring the Bay area. "It was originally named the Golden Gate National Recreation Area," he says. "I thought that nobody cared about a recreation area. So by an act of myself, I renamed it and the Parks Department said 'okay.' We got Michael Schwab to be the illustrator and designer, I'm the art director, and we create images for the parks. We needed some symbols to connect all of these little jewels. This one is for a park that happens to share a water district with the state park, which is why there are four different names at the bottom of it. Before this campaign, the public took these parks for granted because they had no idea that they're as important as Yosemite or the Grand Canyon. It's been a real success."

SOME BRUTALLY SIMPLE ADVICE
TO HELP YOUR ADVERTISING CAREER

Silverstein reports that the process of getting hired at his agency can be very long. "We make sure the personalities are right for the company," he says. "It could take up to nine interviews to get the job. That's true for every level, including beginners."

For beginners, GS&P mainly hires graduates of ad schools like the Art Center, Portfolio Center, and the Miami Ad School. "I've never been a fan of them, although we hire a lot of people from them," he says. "For students who have already gone to college, it's like going to a graduate school. But I don't know if you learn enough if you go directly from high school to an advertising school."

He likes to hire people with design and journalism backgrounds. "We have three design-oriented art directors working with the writer/creative director on HP and Jeff still takes a journalistic approach," he says. "But it's been a long time since somebody came with a journalistic background from, say, Penn State to get a job here. Not that they couldn't, but we don't see them. And we hire people who don't know anything about design or journalism; they're just great advertising people. The agency is a mix of people."

GS&P has a full-time recruiter who looks at every portfolio, so Silverstein hasn't reviewed a student book in a long time. "We get a lot of books," he says. "But by the time I see one, we're considering flying the person here for an interview. I don't see a lot of the crap that our recruiter has to see. It seems that, with student books, everyone has the same, almost ridiculous assignments. If you're really good, you stand out. But if you're just okay, you become part of this almost invisible world."

If you make the cut, Goodby and Silverstein try to personally hire every creative person. "It's not 100 percent," he says, "but it's pretty close. There are two things that help get you the job: the quality of your book and how well you present yourself. I have to see you present your book so I can ask the questions. In advertising, duh, you have to be able to present yourself."

As for the resume? "Put it in the garbage," he says "I don't care about it. I've never said that we've got to talk to a person because of the resume. That book is you. Just let me see the book."

If you're on your way to producing a good, original portfolio that you can defend, here's some additional advice from Silverstein:

Get an apprenticeship: "I've found that young people today have no patience for being an apprentice," says Silverstein. "They want to go directly from college to making commercials. But I think that people should pay their dues because it means more. It matters in the history of your life. I feel good to tell people that I apprenticed at Dick Hess Design because I'm proud of that. It's not like the master taught me everything, but I just soaked up what was going on there. Then I went to the next place and the next place."

Become an outsider: "It's our job to look at the world and play it back," says Silverstein. "The people who do that—people like Larry David, Woody Allen, Jerry Seinfeld, the Coen brothers—have always been outsiders looking in."

Learn to tweak: "Companies that have leaders like a Steven Jobs probably tweak, but most big companies have not been taught to tweak," says Silverstein. "Everyone makes mistakes. What makes a bad creative director is the fear of mistakes or saying the wrong thing. You shouldn't have fear. If you realize it's not right, you fix it. Sometimes you may work really hard on something and think it's great, but come in the morning, look at it or show it to someone, and throw it away. You have to be willing to start again. Maybe it really wasn't such a good idea. And a rough cut is probably the scariest thing. It's like you're on trial. Perhaps it isn't as good as you want it to be or you really like it and you're worried they won't. But when I see a rough cut, I usually don't say, 'That's fantastic.' I usually look for the problems. I know it's painful, but I figure that if you're going to get it right, I have to tell you what's wrong with it first."

Show an understanding of the client's problem: "If you can convey that you understand client needs, you will build trust with them," says Silverstein. "But don't go in assuming you know everything. You have to be a good listener and hear what they're saying. Then you have to figure out who they are and what they need. This is what will enable you to have an informed point of view."

Build trust one project after another: The trust you build with the client will help you create great work, but you don't get it automatically. "You have to prove to them that that you are going to work hard to solve their problem," says Silverstein. "But trust is not something you can keep forever. Once you build it for one project, you have to rebuild it for the next one. It's never like, 'You guys are great; do whatever you want.' It's always, 'What are you going to do for me today?' And trust is only there until you screw up. Then you have to start over and work to rebuild it. Even in a new business pitch, you may win their trust just as much as, 'Hey, let's give them the job.' But then you have to start all over again to win their trust when you work on the real assignment."

Win back unhappy clients: GS&P does not lightly resign accounts. "We've given up two or three," says Silverstein. "But we're really conservative and we try very hard to keep clients. It's so hard to get them. You can always work something out. There's a famous quote by Jay Chiat, 'The minute you win a piece of business, you start to lose it.' I think he means that it's hard to keep a client happy. It could be for one of many reasons. The worst is when a new marketing director joins the client and wants to put his or her own stamp on things, so they throw away everything you've just worked on. But they could also be unhappy, because the people who hired you aren't there anymore and they question your loyalty to the new people; they feel that you haven't done anything for them lately, or the product is not selling. Maybe the product's not very good, but you can't say that. For whatever reason, it's like you have to win the account—and trust—again."

Appreciate what you do on the weekend: Silverstein believes in pursuing passions outside of the industry. "Go to at least one movie a week, read, spend time with your children if you have them," he says. "Don't think advertising is the center of the world. To me, if it's just advertising, it's just not interesting. Do many other things besides advertising so that you can become more well rounded."

Go for your passions: In addition to pursuing your passions on the weekend, try to incorporate them into your work. "It comes across," says Silverstein. "They see how passionate you are and so they trust you. For me, it comes across with Porsche and with the bicycles. It came across with an HP/Porsche spot and an HP/F-1 spot I got to do." And since every assignment can't be for a product you're passionate about, Silverstein suggests that you look for something within the problem that you can be passionate about. "I just get excited about the next problem," he says. "It's a puzzle. And I get to work on it."

Work as a team: Silverstein believes that a great partner is worth everything. "I don't think Jeff or I would be successful without each other," he says. "We're very different in personalities, but we balance each other. We've hired teams. They come out of school and they're comfortable with each other. Or they've worked together in their first jobs, they feel comfortable with each other, and they go and market themselves to us as a team. And it's worked out."

Give your partner space: "For a successful team, you have to respect for each other, to understand the personality of the other one, and give each other room," says Silverstein. "Jeff is different than me, but we've found a way where I give him space and he gives me space. That takes time."

Be willing to confront your partner: Silverstein recognizes that there will be conflicts. "Just get it out," he suggests. "It's so classic: 'I got a problem. You did this. I don't feel good about it.' And the other one goes, 'Oh, I didn't realize it,' or, 'Yeah, I did that.' Then you talk it through and it's over. Confrontation, which nobody wants, is the best thing to do. Just make sure it's done respectfully and professionally."

Move on from bad partnerships: Silverstein has seen some partnerships go sour. "It's human nature," he says. "Somebody thinks they're getting more attention than the other one. Someone thinks they're better than the other one. I have tried to patch up some partnerships. It's like being a marriage counselor with a husband and wife. But, generally, move on. There are bigger problems than teams staying together."

Freelance, but keep it quiet: As mentioned earlier, Berlin and Silverstein started freelancing together at O&M. "Who isn't freelancing?" asks Silverstein. "It is a fact of life. I can't stop it. But I don't want to know about it. It's like 'don't ask/don't tell' in the Army. Freelancing might be healthy for the person doing it, but it's not healthy for the person running the company. If you're not earning your pay, I'm going to know. You have to make it seamless."

Aim to make you next project your best project: "To keep going forward, you have to look at each project as a challenge that you have to solve and that it's going to be your best project," says Silverstein. "I don't consciously go, 'I've never done anything good, so I've got to make this one good.' I just look at the next project as a great opportunity. But it's just an opportunity. If you don't do a good job on it, you've just missed a chance to do your best work. I have found that, for some reason, people who do not feel good enough about their work tend to work harder than other people. The reason I bicycle at the intensity I do is to prove something each day."

Learn to sound secure: "Nobody teaches you how to be in the boardroom," says Silverstein. "That's a whole learned experience. I was deathly afraid to talk in front of people. I kept thinking that I had nothing to offer or that I was going to say something stupid. Now I'm really comfortable. I realized that everybody in the world is insecure. By the very fact that you tell people what you really think and how you arrived at you're thinking, they go, 'Oh, you really got it.' It's a question of having confidence in your ideas and beliefs. Timid people sound timid. If I've got a hundred million dollars to spend, why should I entrust a person who's timid? My feelings of not being good enough are personal. It's between my stomach, my heart, and me. People don't see these feelings."

Be a little humble: "You have to pay your dues," says Silverstein. "If you're talented, you can move up fast, but if you come with arrogance, you'll get knocked down pretty quickly in our company. It's not what you've done; it's how you're working with the people here. You've got to be talented, but you've also got to be a nice person and get along with others. We might see a really nice book and think the guy's a jerk. We might find someone who's got a great book, but the personality isn't one where we're going to get anything out of them. We want both sides. Do we like the person? Is this person interesting? Do we want to sit on an airplane and talk to this person for seven hours? These are things we want answered in an interview."

Accept that not everyone will like you: "There are people who aren't going to like you and you can't make them like you. You just have to move on," says Silverstein, reflecting on his experience being asked off the Levi's account. "We juggle around instantly if a client doesn't like someone on the team. In some cases, it's the individual's fault. In some cases, it's not his or her fault. But it doesn't matter. We want to change the dynamics. Sometimes a really bad account becomes a really good account with new people and a new way of looking at it."

Keep and protect your client's brand: Silverstein believes that a brand is a company's most important asset. "Clients don't usually come to us unless they need help," he says. "So we're doctors of brands. We fix them and bring them back to health. But a brand doesn't come out of the ether; a brand doesn't work unless it's relevant to the public. Bringing a brand back to health is going back to something that was good about it when it started and making it relevant today. In the 1990s, everyone wanted an instant brand in the e-commerce world. But you don't just come up with a brand. Most brands are built over time. The only time we were successful was with e-Trade, where we made a brand in six months, but it took a tremendous amount of media."

Relax: "I found out when I stopped worrying about coming up with a good idea, it came to me," says Silverstein. "It may sound like Zen, but the less you worry, the more you think. If I have a problem I'm thinking about, I just wander through a bookstore. Creativity should be fun and not a noose around your neck. Believe me, I've been there. You become paralyzed when you think, 'What am I going to do? The meeting's tomorrow, and I've got to present this work.' Free yourself to just enjoy thinking. If you relax, the ideas will come. If you worry and worry and work it too hard, you'll just be nervous and a mess. I can talk real big now, but that didn't happen to me until I was 30. My mind calmed down and I got more self-assured. And then it just all started to come to me. I don't even know why. But now I just don't get in the position of having something due in the morning that's just not right by the end of the day. It just comes in my head. Somehow deadlines come and go and I meet them."

Exercise: Exercise, according to Silverstein, is an amazing tool for creativity. "I look forward to getting up in the morning and going to work on the bike. My mind becomes clear. And I look forward to riding home. My mind becomes clear again. Ideas just come to me. I am able to think. So cycling—exercising—is just a way to relax and solve problems. I ride my bicycle home and ideas hit me. I ride to work, and ideas hit me."

Never let up: "It takes a lot of effort to be remain good," says Silverstein. "It doesn't get easier. We can probably solve problems quicker, but the clients need care and feeding and people in your office need care and feeding."

Stay young: "You have to respect the past, but move forward," says Silverstein. "When I shaved off my moustache, it was a very big deal because I had it 30 years. It's funny. There were no young people in my office with moustaches. I'm now wearing my shirts out. It's hilarious because so is Goodby. I'm in my 50s and I stay young physically by cycling and emotionally by being around young people and seeing what's out there."

Clients, spend time with prospective agencies: "The pitch process these days is crazy," says Silverstein. "If clients were smarter about how to pick an agency, they'd spend some time with the people who were going to work on the account, have dinner with them, talk and see if they liked them. It's that simple."

POSTSCRIPT 1:

HOW TO PLAN FOR THE BETTER USE OF PLANNING

Throughout this book, we have heard a lot about the role of research and planning. But what does the partner from the agency responsible for introducing planning to America think about it?

"I have a mixed feeling about planning. It's only as good as the planners and the creative and account people working with them. There's bad in every discipline. There are a lot of architects who remodel homes, and then there are architects like Frank Gehry who create a whole new aesthetic. There are really bad art directors and really good art directors. There are some really good planners and really bad planners. That's just the law of averages. Planning is wonderful if you've got a brilliant planner and a pain in the neck if you've got someone who doesn't really understand creative and is an over-thinker.

"Planners like to say they come up with the briefs, and we all then work on them. But it has never really worked that way.

"What works is the coming together of the planner thinking one thing, the creative team thinking another thing, the account person thinking a third thing. It's not like 'Got Milk?' came because a planner said, 'When you don't have milk.' It came from a collection of people sitting around going, 'You know, milk does a body good. That's been done, and who believes it? What's the truth with milk?' And then someone says, 'When I cut up my strawberries for my cereal, and I start to go get the milk,' and we go, 'Okay, there's something there.'

"Planning at its best is an intuitive look at consumers, hearing what they're saying, and feeding it back to us. Planners try to understand how consumers use or would use a product. They whittle down a complicated problem to a simple insight such as, 'When you don't have milk, it matters more and you'll start to think about milk.' Very, very, very few planners have ever come to me with such a simple comment.

"The first thing a planner does is go and find out what people are thinking about a given thing. That's a pure, fun research problem. It's wonderful when you get to find out what consumers think about an area, a product, or a category before you start the advertising.

"Secondly, planners go back to probe what consumers think about the ideas. But this is a problem to me. Creativity cannot be judged in that setting. *Star Wars* would never have been bought. It's tough asking consumers what they think about something they've never seen before. It's like asking them to become movie producers. That's not their job and they don't understand film. The only time this type of research helps is when you can take something to a client that he or she might think is outrageous and you can say, 'But consumers understand this without us even shooting it.' That's fantastic.

"There's no reason that anyone can't think like a planner. You need to be able to do that to be a good creative or account person. It's just that in an ad agency, having someone dedicated to planning makes life a lot easier. They don't have their ego tied up in the commercial. They don't have to deal as much with the business problems of the client. They have a little more freedom to think about the problem in its purest form."

POSTSCRIPT 2:

A DESIGNER'S TAKE ON THE
UGLINESS OF ADVERTISING

Traditionally, art directors have looked down on designers for not being able to solve problems and designers have looked down on art directors as people who create crass and ugly advertising. But Silverstein approaches advertising with a designer's sensibility. Here is what he has to say about this great divide and how it has shaped his philosophy behind creating various forms of advertising:

"I have a healthy dislike for advertising, which probably comes from beginning as a designer. I think that it's shallow and cheap and ugly and stupid. I don't like the stupid punk jokes, butt jokes, and poop jokes. It's tiresome. It's the lowest common denominator and it doesn't treat consumers with respect.

"Overall, I believe that advertising is bad, with some wonderful spots of brilliance.

"At its best, advertising can be part of popular culture. It's a force that is no different than books or movies. It can touch, move, and educate people. It can give something back in some strange way. That's how I approach it.

"I treat consumers with great respect. They have intelligence. I can still watch *Seinfeld*, the *Larry Sanders Show*, and *I Love Lucy* episodes because the humor is timeless. They're very intelligent. If they can treat a touchy subject with intelligence, it's funny. There's a little bit more depth. And it's nice when we put that timeless humor into advertising as well.

"I hope that our agency has proven that art direction and design can go hand in hand. Why can't you take a great idea and also make it aesthetically attractive? But you need to put both together. I think it's very hard for designers to create ads. And I think that a lot of art directors don't have a clue about the aesthetics of design. An art director thinks and conceives and solves problems.

"For TV, I try to make little films. Even if it happens to be 30 seconds or 60 seconds, treat it like it's a piece of film, a movie, with fine acting and storytelling. Don't treat it like it's a commercial.

"As for radio, good luck. Everyone I know who really listens to radio listens almost exclusively to national public broadcasting. My son listens to that when he designs and my wife listens to it only in the car, and I only listen to classical music on the radio. So I think we find stations that are not in your face with advertising.

"Since no one seems to get famous with radio and it seems to be the cheap advertising medium, people don't take the time to do it right. And the resulting commercials are derogatory to our senses. They seem to just scream.

"It could be better.

"I believe that the best of radio works in your head like the great shows from the beginning of this medium. The spots are intelligent and fit the specific environment.

"And with outdoor advertising, I used to think that it was a blight on society and had no place in the world. But I think things have changed. I now enjoy it.

"Some cities are more interesting with outdoor, the way it takes over a building side. It all becomes part of the look of that city and I think that's a very powerful statement.

"But it should be arresting and respectful to the audience.

"Treat it with brutal simplicity and attractiveness.

"I don't believe a photograph has to be ugly. People have said that I just want things to be pretty. But I want them to be aesthetically attractive. I think fashion outdoor works great in cities, like when the Gap used Annie Leibovitz—not recently—and had great portrait photography, and I've seen Nike do some nice things.

"Bus shelters are like large print ads and they glow.

"So I've actually changed my mind and feel that you can do some nice outdoor advertising."

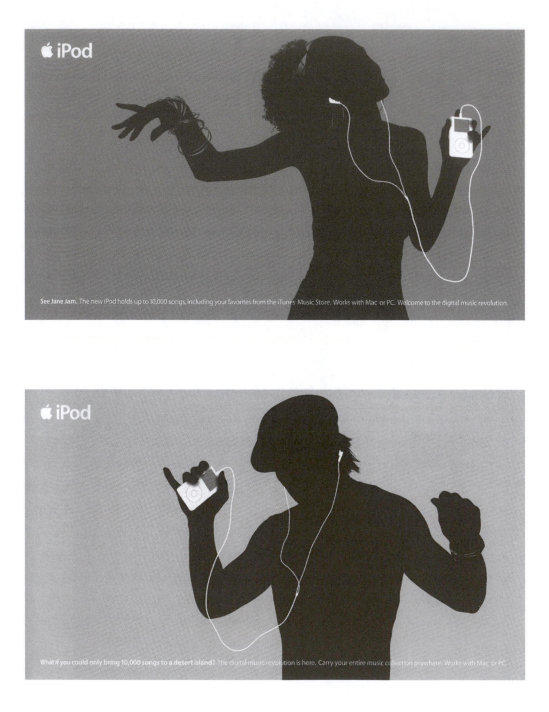

Lee Clow

"My portfolio is my credentials. It shows what I've been able to do in this business. So developing it is where I place my focus."

That may seem an unexpected comment from a man who has worked at one agency for most of his adult life and is generally considered one of the most illustrious art directors practicing today.

Whether you plan to parlay your portfolio into a new position or stay in the same agency, Lee Clow, Chairman and Chief Creative Officer of TBWA/Chiat/Day, emphasizes the importance of continually improving it. He believes focusing on your portfolio produces the best solutions for you—and your clients.

Throughout his career, Clow has demonstrated that this approach works.

He has won numerous advertising awards, including a Cannes Film Festival Gold Lion. His work has helped launch the Macintosh for Apple, as well as produce outstanding results for Porshe, Nissan, Nike, Adidas, Absolut, Yamaha, Pioneer, Taco Bell, Reebok, and Pizza Hut. And under his creative leadership, TBWA/Chiat/Day is considered to be one of the best and most innovative agencies in the country.

A California native, Clow grew up on the beach with a surfboard, the sun, the surf, and a transistor radio playing Beach Boys tunes. That was Clow's youth, and it may have helped him learn to ride the waves of a volatile business.

He also feels lucky to be able to use his talents in such a rewarding and exciting way. And he feels lucky to have found a partner, whom he describes as his anchor. His wife of 35 years understands his intensity and passion for his work and encourages him to pursue it. He has two stepdaughters, now married, four grandchildren, and many dogs.

FROM SURFBOARDS TO ART BOARDS

Although most of the people featured in this book communicated their early passion for creative work, that sense of drive isn't always a necessary ingredient for successfully beginning a career. Instead of the focused passion for communications that he'd later show, Lee's early years were spent enjoying the sun and surf.

His career goals were secondary. But this doesn't mean he magically developed an interest in art later in life. In fact, this interest dates back to first grade.

Clow was one of those kids who could paint a train and make the smoke rise in the right direction from the smoke stack. He was lucky enough to have a teacher who told his mother of his artistic talents—and a mother who encouraged him, rather than insisting he be a lawyer or a doctor.

By the seventh grade, he was sure that he wanted to be a commercial artist. But he wasn't sure what that meant. By the time he went to Santa Monica Junior College, his interests had broadened to include graphic design and advertising art direction. But he doesn't pretend to have been a dedicated art student. In fact, he was actually more dedicated to his surfing. "I thought someday I'd be a commercial artist, but not now," he says. "I was working in a bowling alley at night, so I could surf during the day. Those were my priorities."

He had learned about Art Center College of Design, but never had a burning desire to attend. Nor did his parents have the resources to support him as a full-time student in an expensive school.

So, he worked to pay for art classes and enjoyed the beach.

From Draft Board to Drafting Table

Attending college in the '60s had benefits beyond an education. Full-time students were exempt from the military draft. So, like many people at that time, Clow enrolled in junior college as much to avoid fighting in Vietnam as to keep his artistic juices flowing. But because of his lack of academic enthusiasm, he let his credits drop below the "safety zone," and the draft board snatched him up.

Ironically, being drafted was good for his career. The Army realized Clow's artistic talents and placed him in a peaceful position as draftsman/illustrator. "I thought it was kind of charming of the Army to offer me such a position before telling me to grab a rifle and fight," recalls Clow. He was assigned to White Sands Missile Range where he worked on a variety of design projects.

Without surfing to distract him, he became more committed to developing a career. He started investigating options and discovered Long Beach State College had a very good design curriculum and an excellent art department.

When he was discharged, he enrolled there. But Clow wasn't motivated enough to stick around for graduation—or for the portfolio development classes. "I still wasn't focused on what type of career to pursue," he recalls. "So I had a varied portfolio of everything from illustration to lettering to advertising design projects."

He considered becoming an illustrator, but after doing a few illustration assignments, he was frustrated. Says Clow, "I found it to be very one-dimensional and uninteresting to execute someone else's idea."

A West Coast Career Path

He found a job in a Santa Monica design studio doing mostly production. This gave him the opportunity to associate with trained graphic designers.

One designer, who had graduated from Art Center College, talked to Clow about developing an advertising portfolio. He suggested Clow needed more focus. His work wasn't showing that he knew how to apply his talents.

He had also heard he should go to New York to break into advertising. But his affinity for the California sun and beaches would not allow him to sacrifice the West Coast environment for the concrete caverns of New York. He wanted to stay near the ocean while pursuing a career.

Working at the design studio gave him a chance to study *Communication Arts* magazine, as well as numerous awards annuals. He became absorbed in the difference between illustration, graphic design, and advertising. "I realized that graphic design and illustration were terribly one-dimensional career paths. What I really loved were the ideas," he says.

Advertising art direction, both television and print, went beyond type, graphic design, and illustration to the development of a total message. In addition, advertising during the '60s was making many breakthroughs in communicating messages. That's what made it exciting to Clow, so he decided to funnel his enthusiasm into building an advertising portfolio.

Adding to his enthusiasm was another associate who was then working for Young & Rubicam and had become disenchanted with advertising. He shared experiences that gave Clow insight into how insane the business could be.

In a Pickle

One such story involved the McDonald's account. His friend, who had been working on the account, was in a meeting where the group was examining a dye transfer. All of a sudden he found himself in the middle of a heated argument.

They were going crazy because McDonald's always put three pickles on a hamburger and the model only had two pickles. They would have to retouch the photograph for the print ad. The account people were tearing their hair out because the deadline would be missed and the account would be in jeopardy.

His friend, finding himself in this incredibly high-stress situation over a pickle, thought, "I can't deal with this. These people are about to have a heart attack over how many pickles should be on a hamburger. It's absurd. I gotta get out of this business."

He moved to the design firm where his life was simpler and warned Clow about advertising's craziness.

Clow felt a little intimidated, but the warning also challenged him.

Building His First Portfolio

This associate also offered advice on what to include in a portfolio—and what to exclude. Clow included some four-color jobs only because they demonstrated he'd actually had them produced. Yet, he wasn't too excited about the work.

His friend explained that a portfolio should represent the best work, whether it's produced or not. He advised Clow to create his own assignments.

"This is when I learned your portfolio is probably the most important piece of communication you'll work on throughout your entire career," he says. "It shows your level of quality, taste, judgment, and ability." That led him to become incredibly critical of the content.

To create a strong network, Clow then joined L.A.'s junior advertising club.

Although most of the organization's members were account people, they took on *pro bono* projects, offering Clow the opportunity to produce creative work, as well as meet other people in the business. "When creatives work for free, clients can't be too critical of the quality of your thinking or execution," he says. "So it was a very good opportunity to learn what works."

Clow soon found a job at a small ad agency, and quickly moved on to N. W. Ayer's L.A. office. "At first, I felt intimidated," he says. "The large agency was filled with well-educated people wearing suits and ties." But Clow soon learned there are fewer talented people in the business than he expected.

To Lee, it seemed people were motivated more by fear and defensiveness than smart thinking. "I found that lots of people were more worried about keeping their clients happy rather than finding the smartest answer to the problem. They were less the caliber of managers, executives, or administrators than I expected," he says. "So I wasn't as in over my head as I thought I might be."

Gradually, he gained confidence. He realized that many creatives just job-hopped, still doing the same caliber of work. He understood that could stifle his career. Instead, he polished his portfolio.

His goal? Chiat/Day! He wanted to work there more than anywhere else.

He called on Hy Yablonca, who was the creative director there, and customized his résumé for the interview. The meeting was scheduled for noon, during his lunch break, but when he arrived, he was informed that Yablonca had just left for lunch. Clow decided to wait it out—for an hour and fifteen minutes.

When Yablonca stepped off the elevator, Clow caught a flash of embarrassment on the creative director's face. Clow believes the embarrassment over missing their meeting may have been why Yablonca took an inordinate amount of time going through his portfolio. Even so, the interview concluded with, "I just hired a guy. I wish I had met you last week. Now, we don't have anything."

That was all Clow needed to hear. He was encouraged to continue sending samples to remind Yablonca that he was still available.

Finally, Yablonca hired him as an art director, a move he still wonders about.

He's still not sure whether he was hired so he'd stop sending his monthly mailings or because they really wanted him.

"I often wonder if my life would have been different if Yablonca had remembered that first meeting and not felt a little guilty. He might have shuttled me in and out in ten minutes in order to make his lunch date," he says. "Jay Chiat said that I only had one piece in my portfolio that he liked—and that was a menu design."

On the Bus at Chiat/Day

Clow swallowed a cut in pay to join the agency. But working there wasn't about money. It was about learning and opportunity. Chiat/Day was the "graduate school" of the advertising business—a great agency that cared about great advertising.

It was an agency where everyone was expected to get up in the morning thinking up wonderful ads for their clients. With every assignment Clow thought, "I want this to be as good as anything that's ever been done in advertising." He worked as diligently as he could to create the work that matched the best in the business—which, at the time, came from New York.

Being a perfectionist is frustrating. "Nothing was good enough," he recalls. "I saw every wart and flaw." That insecurity, plus an intense commitment to create the best work in the business, caused his work to keep getting better and better. It wasn't long before he'd earned the title of Group Art Director/Group Creative Director, and then Creative Director of the entire Los Angeles office.

"About halfway through my stay at Chiat/Day, I realized I am going to stay on this bus until it gets to the end of the line," says Clow. "So I was not going to try to parlay my portfolio into a new job or higher salary someplace else.

"But my portfolio is still important to me from an emotional standpoint. It always needs to be the focus."

Next Stop: Apple

Then came Apple. Steve Jobs, the president, was very intense, and his standards were high. "Jobs was a cross between Leonardo DaVinci and John MacEnroe," Clow says. "He was truly a genius, one of the most brilliant people I've ever worked for, but he was incredibly demanding. And, at 25 years old, that was obnoxious.

It was difficult to live up to his vision of what personal computers would mean. Jobs knew computers were going to change the world."

Jobs loved communication and realized the value of a consistent message. He put together one of the most complete internal design groups ever assembled. The Apple Design Group did everything—from trade shows and sales meetings to manuals and packaging. He insisted that Chiat/Day work with Apple's designers to evolve a consistent look and tone of voice.

That brought the agency outside the realm of traditional advertising. And soon they were involved with all aspects of communicating Apple's message—from the manuals and brochures to dealer posters or a tee-shirt design. Everything had to be as great as the TV commercials.

"After meeting with Jobs, Steve Hayden and I felt like masochists," recalls Clow, "but we kept going back to try to satisfy his demands. We had a client who wanted great advertising. We'd be damned if we'd fail to deliver it for him.

"But the process of coming up with breakthrough ideas was grueling. We even had arguments about how much leading should be in the type."

Blending Jobs's genius with Chiat/Day's creative talents brought about a consistent style and tone and helped position Apple as an industry leader.

It also helped Chiat/Day recognize how to best help their clients.

The Chiat/Day Way

To win business, Chiat/Day tries to understand the client and then pitch the business in an appropriate, smart, charming, and clever way. Clow recalls doing just that to get Nike's Los Angeles Olympics assignment.

The agency had made their presentation. As a follow up, the agency built a brick wall out of about thirty bricks and painted an athlete, Michael Cooper, bending over backwards across the wall. Then they sent a brick, individually wrapped and numbered, to each member of Nike's marketing department.

Each package had a note instructing the recipient to take the brick to the marketing director's office, where they were to reassemble the wall.

Nike said they'd let the agency know of their decision the following Tuesday. But no one called. So on Wednesday Guy Day called Nike. He was told the marketing director was in a meeting and couldn't be interrupted, so Day left a message. But still no one called. By Thursday, the folks at the agency were starting to think the worst. More messages went unreturned.

Finally, on Friday morning, the Olympic runner Mary Decker showed up in their lobby with a big bottle of tequila. She said the marketing director had suggested she come over and have a drink with the agency, because they would be working for Nike.

The marketing director decided the brick wall merited more than just a phone call as a response. He had to come up with something special. But Mary Decker was out of town, so he decided to stall everyone until she returned.

That pitch was characteristic of the agency's desire to involve their clients.

The Chiat/Day creative development process also requires client participation. It allows the agency to learn who the client is and what its message is in order to come to an agreement about direction. But learning to incorporate the client company's personality into the advertising and create original new business pitches was just the beginning.

Chiat/Day's entire culture was designed to generate uninhibited creativity.

They have open offices. Employees are grouped by account team rather than by function or department. And everybody's office space is the same as everybody else's—from Clow to the traffic manager.

The message: They're all there for the same reason—to make great ads.

This culture helped establish Chiat/Day as one of the best and most innovative agencies in the world. *AdAge* named them Agency of the Decade in 1990. Then in 1995, Chiat/Day was acquired by Omnicom and merged with TBWA. Advertising trade magazines reported financial troubles at Chiat/Day, but Clow has another take on it: "It was an opportunity to be a global agency," he says. "And it's worked out really great for us."

Today, as Chairman and Chief Creative Officer of a worldwide network with 8,700 employees, 221 offices, and a presence in 72 countries, Clow finds himself working harder than ever.

"Size is the enemy of idea companies," says Clow, "because idea companies are very free flowing and have a kind of constant energy. When you become big, just the effects of size and number of people makes it a little bit more difficult to maintain a fiery, high-energy creative environment."

Another unhappy reason making it more challenging to continue to maintain this atmosphere—Jay Chiat, architect of Chiat/Day's culture, passed away in 2002.

"Jay was constantly challenging, shaking things up, and expecting people to do something better than they did yesterday," says Clow. "Do something new. Do something different. Jay was never satisfied with what had been done. He never yielded to the pressure of giving the client what he wanted just to make him happy." One agency slogan read, "Good Enough Isn't."

"When Jay passed away, everybody felt the soul of the agency would be gone if we forgot what he taught us," says Clow. "But we can keep it alive.

"As we've merged with TBWA, all of the good, creative offices welcomed the spirit, the cultural infusion. It's only the weak, less talented offices that threaten it dramatically."

So how does Clow maintain TBWA/Chiat/Day's unique culture—known for its unrelenting pursuit of perfection? He does it by demanding that the work be as good as it can be and be making its employees feel the same sense of responsibility that they had back when there were only a dozen staffers.

A Very Rare Commodity

He is also looking to find the right leaders—people who can consistently improve upon the agency's high creative standards—to staff his offices. "There are plenty of managers," says Clow, "but people who can lead, who can challenge other people to be great, are a very rare commodity.

"Finding enough leaders to go around a worldwide organization is probably the hardest challenge."

For Clow to consider someone a leader, that individual must first have talent and passion. On top of that, he or she must have the ability to inspire others to do what he or she wants them to do by setting an example and by nurturing, coaxing, and encouraging them to dig down, strive, and not settle for the status quo.

"There are lots of people that can do good work," notes Clow, "but they end up being trapped in the 'only do it for themselves, selfish, it's all about me' kind of model. That person is of value, but not near the value of somebody who can not only do great work, but inspire other people to do great work as well."

In making this assessment, Clow found that many people in this industry don't have these leadership skills. "Every talented writer and art director thinks that now that he's done three great ads he deserves to be promoted to creative director," says Clow. " But some of them just don't have the tools; they don't know how to lead; they don't know how to inspire other people."

The reason for Clow's focus on finding the right leaders is simple: "Whoever has the best people wins," says Clow. "Creative talent plus leadership is a very rare commodity. Whoever can corner the market on it is going to be way ahead of the game. Unfortunately, a lot of other companies are after the same thing."

Staying Passionate

Of course, the striving that Clow expects in others can be clearly found in himself. He stays passionate about the industry by thinking that there's one more great campaign, one more great ad, he could create.

"I stay very focused on the work," he says. "It's the kiss of death when you stop doing the work. There are people who get away with it, but they're basically a waste of everybody's time. Either you contribute to the challenge and the work, or you're just part of the overhead—the bureaucracy. I don't think that 'management' can make things happen."

When he's not contributing to the work, he's playing tennis and working on his house, which he built. But his greatest passion is still reserved for advertising.

He believes that most people succeed in doing what they really love to do—and can get incredibly passionate about.

"Every day I consider myself incredibly lucky," he says, "to have found a way to channel my love for art into something I can be so passionate and intense about.

"It's wonderful to be able to do something I find emotionally rewarding and make an incredibly good living at it.

"It's a great business for imaginative people. Ideas and media are just the texture of our society. It's always fun and always different."

CLOW'S CREDENTIALS: A LOOK AT HIS PORTFOLIO

—— YAMAHA ——

Like all companies, Yamaha needed advertising that was distinctive and relevant. They invited Chiat/Day to pitch the account. The agency enthusiastically plunged into developing the pitch and felt their presentation went well.

But the client said, "Thank you very much," and hired the competition.

Several months later, Yamaha asked for a capabilities plan to see how the agency would run their business. After the presentation, Yamaha gave the go-ahead to start producing the work they had seen the previous year.

This ad demonstrates how Chiat/Day brought distinctiveness and relevance to Yamaha advertising. Black leather, bandanas, and studded belts wouldn't work for

Yamaha. Instead, with children, warm colors, and a light message, their ads would be distinctive in the world of cycling. For relevance, the message concentrated on engineering excellence and pointed out features and benefits.

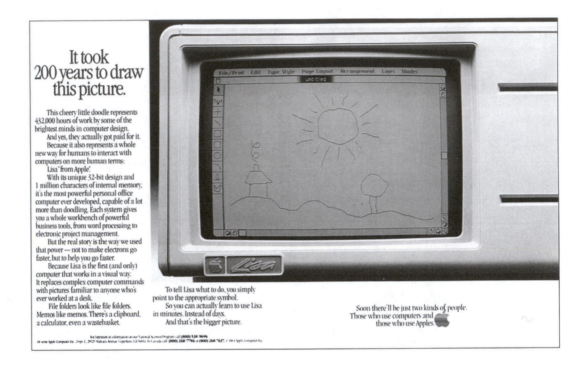

Apple

Clow's task was to develop very simple, approachable advertising for Apple computers—advertising that would make people feel comfortable with the product. But Clow is often told, "You were introducing personal computers for the first time—who couldn't do that?"

Clow responds by saying, "It's never as easy as it looks on the surface. Creating great ads for Apple was hard work. It took great people working very hard to find a simple, obvious, great solution. It was one of the most incredible experiences of my career. And it was all worth it."

—— NISSAN PATHFINDER ——

For a long time after it ran, the president of Nissan talked about the work sessions that developed this campaign to advertise the Pathfinder, a four-wheel drive, all-terrain vehicle.

In the work sessions, it was suggested that Nissan have a man and woman start out in Chicago and drive the vehicle all the way through Central America into Brazil and on to Rio de Janeiro. Then each was to change into their tuxedo and gown and go dancing.

During the work sessions, the client and creatives talked through the logistics and decided on the number of spots.

With a limited crew, the agency documented the couple's trip across the continents. The agency planned to air the spots on *Monday Night Football*. Even though the budget wasn't very big, they ended up creating a big impression.

"If we had met with the president and announced we were going to have a couple drive from Chicago to Rio, and he had no part in the development, he might have rejected the idea. And the president's discomfort would be understandable. If anything went wrong, they'd waste a lot of money.

"But he was part of the decision—and he is still proud of that piece of advertising," says Clow. That's why he believes involving the client in developing the idea is key.

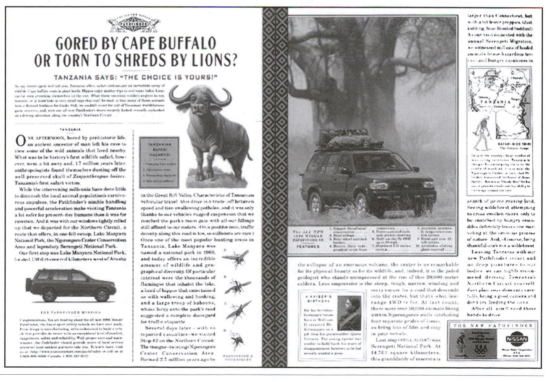

—— NIKE ——

Clow believes the job of the agency is to understand the personality of the company. "You become the spokesman for these companies, and you have to accurately and faithfully translate their culture, spirit, and point of view to the consumer."

"Nike is a great example," says Clow. "It's a company with soul and passion. And the spirit of their advertising is not born out of their agency—it's from them."

Although Nike does most of its work with Wieden+Kennedy in Portland (See Chapter 14), they came to Chiat/Day in L.A. when they wanted something special and different for the 1984 Olympics in Los Angeles.

They disdained the commercialism of paying millions of dollars to be the "official shoe" of the Olympics and wanted to do something special to salute the athletes.

To stay true to the brand and personality, Clow had to learn who Nike really was. "Portland is a very pure part of the world. They think billboards are visual pollution," he says. "But Nike was coming to celebrate the Olympics in the home of outdoor advertising—because in L.A., people live in their cars. Billboards line the freeways. It's *the* medium. If Nike was to be comfortable using billboards, the advertising had to be incredibly pure and simple."

Along with billboards, Chiat/Day found walls and murals to paint all over the city. The ads featured different athletes—a tribute to their dedication and focus. Post-production research showed people thought the ads communicated Nike's dedication and passion for quality athletic shoes without even using words. In the end, research also showed that 48 percent of the public thought Nike was the official shoe of the Olympics. Only 28 percent could name the actual Olympic shoe sponsor.

—— Energizer ——

When Clow was warned early in his career about the craziness of advertising, it wasn't an unfounded observation.

Energizer is an example, but Clow's attitude is light-hearted. "It seems silly, but there was an incredible amount of pressure and energy spent on deciding what the bunny should do next.

"A bunch of adults sitting around discussing what the bunny should or shouldn't do—it's very entertaining," laughs Clow.

—— APPLE ——

When Apple returned to TBWA/Chiat/Day, it was almost out of business (see Chapter 3). "Apple was in a real mess," says Clow. "The leadership over the years had gotten worse and worse. The idea for what the brand stood for, what they were trying to do, was very confused." When he returned to Apple, Steve Jobs called and asked Clow to help save the company.

The first thing they did was to identify the values of this brand and what Apple represents. They recognized that creative people, the idea people, love to use Apple, whether it's for doing graphic design, advertising design, film editing, whatever.

"So we decided to celebrate the creative spirit," recalls Clow. "'Think different' became this mantra that celebrated Pablo Picasso and Frank Lloyd Wright as well as Gandhi and Thomas Edison, anyone who had great ideas. Of course, Apple was that 'think different' kind of company that changed the world with their technology."

The call to "Think Different" went beyond advertising. Jobs used the line to change Apple back to a company that offered fewer products but did them better. And, of course this inspired new products.

"If we would have just done Gandhi and Picasso posters and kept making the same computers, it probably wouldn't have worked," says Clow. "Steve invented the new iMac, in which product designer Jonathan Ives really revolutionized tech-

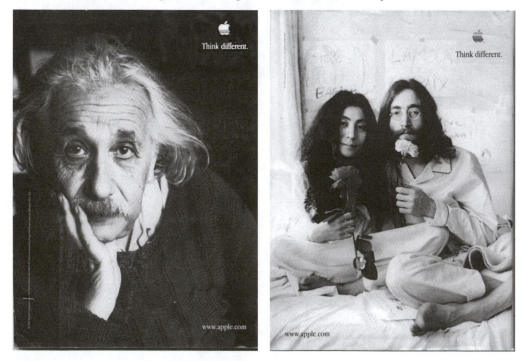

nology design. And he continues to do it with PowerBooks and the iPod, which is an amazing breakthrough."

Today, the Apple brand is healthy and, with the Apple store, it can sell kind of anything it wants to invent or design that has to do with technology. "It's the whole enchilada, which the other computer companies don't do," says Clow.

"It has a very special niche in the world to do great technology. It does software and hardware and operating systems.

"Re-launching the Apple brand was pretty exciting for someone in his mid-50s to do," says Clow. "It was a great opportunity and challenge, and we did it pretty well. I'm proud of it. The brand stands for a lot of good stuff again. Getting great challenges in terms of brands who need good advertising, that's what keeps me excited."

——— NISSAN SHIFT CAMPAIGN ———

When Nissan formed a joint alliance with Renault as part of its three-year revitalization plan, Carlos Ghosn from Renault took over the brand and became its Chief Operating Officer. He then stepped up the car design and challenged TBWA/Chiat/Day to figure out how to orchestrate and organize his brand around the world.

The goal: to get customers to "rethink the Nissan brand because we're going to do some great stuff," says Clow.

Tell better stories. Stories as epic and grand as where they were created. Inside the Pathfinder you'll find three rows of seating for seven and 270-hp that can turn an ordinary outing into the stuff of legends. For more, including why Strategic Vision named us Best Full-Line Manufacturer on its 2005 Total Quality Index," visit **NissanUSA.com.**

The Nissan Pathfinder

SHIFT_adventure

"Renault and Carlos have done it in the product area, and our advertising kind of challenges people to take a look at Nissan in a new light."

The result was a campaign called "Shift," which was run around the world. "I'm proud of it. We've got the Z-back, which was one of my passions for years," says Clow. "We just launched that and some other really great product designs." And Clow should be proud of the sales results as well, because it's helping Nissan regain sales around the world.

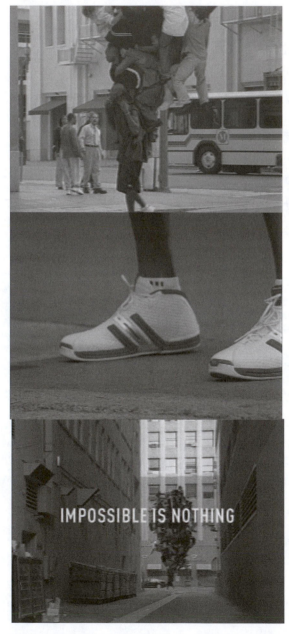

ADIDAS

Here's another example of working on a worldwide basis to restage a brand. "Right now we're working on Adidas all around the world, trying to re-stage that brand. Getting that brand positioned properly is a very great challenge.

"It's the authentic sports brand in the world, but kids who've grown up in the last 20 years think Nike is the original sports brand." This effort is designed to help change that perception.

ABSOLUT

Absolut is one of the most famous brands in the world because of long-term, consistent advertising. "Absolut is one of those brands that found a way to talk to people and has been smart enough to be very consistent for many, many years and at the same time bringing fresh thinking to it every year," says Clow.

"The campaign was already going when we joined them (Absolut was a long-time TBWA client). We've developed Web components and mini-movie components and different celebrations of the brand, always in the same campaign structure."

This integrated approach is not new to Clow. "I think our responsibility has always been to orchestrate all of the media components of a brand when we have the opportunity to do it," he says. "We design and create as much of the marketing communication mix as the clients give us permission to. We do promotions. We do Web design. We do package design and store design."

Clow also points out that the stronger brands, such as Nike and Apple, embrace an integrated approach to marketing. "Everything about Apple is orchestrated to be Apple. The stores feel like the ads feel like the manuals that come with your product feel like the packaging," says Clow. "It's not a new idea. It's whether it can be articulated by mega-agencies on all of the levels because PR is as valuable as package design as is an ad."

ADVICE FOR BUILDING YOUR PORTFOLIO

"In advertising, you always worry about the quality of your portfolio because those who want to be great at this business never think that they are," says Clow.

"That insecurity drives most good creative people. It's never good enough. It's never done. It could always be better."

To help you make it better, Clow believes you need to become a student of human emotions—and the communication of those emotions. To do this, he says television is a good resource. "It's is the most powerful medium on the planet.

"Sure, there's lots of garbage being broadcast, but if you look at all the books written in a year, how many of them are quality literary works? The percentages are probably the same. Be selective with television, in the same way you are with the printed word, and you open doors to new ideas.

"I was part of the first generation of television-watching kids. And I believe you can't help but have a much bigger and sometimes altered view of the world with that medium in your house every day. The time that most kids spend watching television gives them a broader view than kids growing up in previous generations without television—or the intellectual snobs who say, 'I won't own a television.'

"Television gave me an incredible understanding of communication. Whether it's Yogi Bear, PBS, or sports, it can help us understand how to communicate emotion. Just watching an important event or an exciting achievement in sports shows how much emotion you can pack into a few moments.

"When you see people feel intense emotions, whether it's patriotism inspired by the national anthem, or sympathy when hearing the plight of a family on *60 Minutes*, you realize the power of television. It's that excitement that hooked me. It's more than being able to paint a train and make the smoke go in the right direction. It's having millions of people hear, feel, and react to something."

Once you've studied how to communicate emotions, advertising requires that you convey them in a very short time frame. Combine emotional power with simplicity, and you get a whole different understanding of the business. "Then, you're not just a graphic designer, writer, or illustrator anymore," Clow says. To help you go beyond those job titles, here's some more of Clow's advice:

Show only the best: Your portfolio work is your credentials. Period. Nothing should be in there that you don't think is the best you can do.

Even once you're out of school and settled in your job, your portfolio should be the focus—and should be kept up-to-date. "It has to demonstrate what you think is good communication.

"It is the most important product of your career.

"It's the best of all your efforts."

Value all information: Clow believes you need to be attuned to the world.

"To be a communicator—particularly in advertising where you talk to millions of people—means being aware of many things."

The "real world" experience you gain from living, interacting with the public, or in a liberal arts education, is critical input.

Good creative people store information to draw on when creating advertising.

It's not the degree; it's the degree of quality work that counts: Education never held Clow back. And, he doesn't believe education is any substitute for a great portfolio. "Wherever—and however—you develop your talents is unimportant.

"Whether you have a degree from Art Center, Long Beach State, or Santa Monica City College is irrelevant. If your portfolio does not demonstrate an understanding of communication, you're not going to get a job. Even without a degree, if you have a portfolio that demonstrates talent, you'll find work."

Use spec or published—as long as it's the best: "If you put your work on a desk in front of somebody and ask him or her to judge it, then it should be the best work you've ever done—whether they're scribbles or tight comps, they should be your best solutions.

"If you aren't there to explain why you've included a sample, the interviewer will think that's what you think great design or writing is. Then, if the interviewer asks to see your work that has been produced—presenting it helps explain your experience level. Have published work with you as a tool."

Always focus on relevance and distinctiveness: "Good ads are made up of two things," says Clow, "a relevant message for the audience and the means to make the audience pay attention to it.

"You've got to figure out what the essence of the product is.

"Why should the consumer test drive the car or buy the six-pack? You have to find the reason why consumers should give your product their time.

"Then, because of the zillions of messages out there, you've got to find the freshest, most distinctive, most articulate way to communicate that message.

"A relevant benefit, stated in a mundane way, is invisible. It goes right past people. Conversely, you can produce the most outrageous commercial in history and if it doesn't say anything that people care about, it's a waste of money."

Find an agency where you can swim, not sink: Chiat/Day seldom hires people right out of school. "Beginners need a few years of real-world experience," warns Clow, "before we can throw them into the deep end of our swimming pool.

"If we threw someone in right out of college, I don't think they'd have the strokes down. They'd probably sink to the bottom. If they get a few years of experience at another agency, they can learn the ins and outs of the advertising business. They need to learn about account executives, clients, and budgets."

Regard your first job as an internship: "An education doesn't make you a doctor—or an art director. For a year or two, you need to learn what the advertising business is all about.

"The best way to do that is to be hired by an agency, so you can follow the 'doctors' around. When you get your first job in the business, don't be concerned with salary because you're really continuing your education.

"Look for an agency that has a real shingle on their door and makes real advertising for real clients, because you've only been in school making fake advertising for pretend clients.

"Then only change jobs when you think you've learned as much as you possibly can. Your focus should be to improve your talents as a communicator and to make your portfolio more complete and real."

Keep in mind, a bad agency can be a good experience: "You can learn a lot working at a bad agency—if you keep your focus."

Clow's early jobs taught him what he didn't want to do. "I didn't want to work for an agency that was totally subservient to the client—an agency that didn't have enough integrity to believe their job was to sell great advertising. Sometimes that means taking a stand, rather than just giving them what they want."

To make matters worse, advocating the better concept is often perceived as being contradictory to the way agencies do business. "It was very frustrating to have a passion for great ideas and recognize the obstacle wasn't the client, but the agency who did not want to make the client uncomfortable!"

Diversify your talents: After getting a feel for the business, look for opportunities to diversify your talents. "Look for agencies where you can work on television if you need that experience," says Clow. "Or look for agencies that have different types of accounts. You want to round out your experience."

Look to the best: Steve Hayden regards Clow as one of his mentors. Clow feels Jay Chiat greatly influenced his career.

"When I came to Chiat/Day, Jay Chiat opened doors for me and gave me opportunities," he says. "But I've always looked to the people who were doing the best work—in whatever category they worked at—as being the ultimate challenge.

"Whether it was George Louis, Bill Bernbach, Roy Grace, or Walt Disney, whoever was doing great things influenced me.

"Ultimately, Jay Chiat felt my work was up to the standards of the company he had formed. Doing ads that satisfied Jay Chiat made me what I am today."

Self-promotion should be arresting: Clow receives a myriad of self-promotion pieces from aspiring creatives, but it's difficult to have much impact because there are so many. Understand the audience. Then, if you find exactly the right message to cut through the clutter, it works.

The most exotic self-promotion stunt Clow recalls was designed by an Art Center graduate. "I had met her at a Christmas party where she gave me something to hold. As I left, some LAPD officers, who happened to be friends of the aspiring creative, said they'd heard I'd been trafficking in stolen items and mentioned the package. They really had me going for a minute, but when they said they'd take me in if I didn't look at her portfolio right then, I caught on." Clow looked at her portfolio.

Don't mistake a passion for profits as a passion for advertising: Clow reminds us that many people in the advertising business don't care about making ads.

They care about getting accounts, keeping clients happy, and making money. Great advertising is very low on their list of priorities.

"I think I was lucky to have learned to recognize those qualities quickly. Chiat/Day was the only place that seemed moved by the excitement of advertising.

"They had passion," recalls Clow. "They didn't start an agency to get accounts and make money, but to do advertising."

Give 100 percent in everything, because practice makes professional: Beginners seldom get the glamorous accounts. Clow sympathizes with that fact, but he urges them to "realize that every assignment gives you an opportunity to create the next great ad for your portfolio.

"Don't think, 'This is only a trade ad, I want to do national television.' You're in training for a couple of years. Even with a dreary assignment, give it 100 percent. Your efforts will demonstrate intensity and passion, so ultimately you'll get bigger responsibilities."

He also suggests getting your hands on briefs for projects that weren't assigned to you and then trying to solve the problem your own way.

Draw from the personality of the company, not from yourself or your agency: Distinctiveness should come from the personality of the product or company, not the personality of the creative person or the agency.

Nike, Apple, and Nissan are all examples of how the personality of the company comes into play in creating a great ad. The advertising must be true to their personality, their tone of voice, and who they are, warns Clow.

Dress appropriately: Chiat/Day is well known for its "California style." Says Clow, "I grew up in California. I love the warm climate and the casual dress that goes with it. One of my heroes is a guy who started a surfboard shop, invented the Hobie Cat, and wore shorts to his board of directors meetings.

"We have comfortable and unusual facilities here in Venice, so I don't feel awkward wearing my shorts into the office, even if a client happens to drop in for an unscheduled meeting.

"But, when I go to Nissan or American Express, I don't wear shorts. I put on my coat and tie. My goal is not to be in people's faces."

Maintain your integrity: "Some people say creatives burn out after a point. Their work is no longer fresh. I think it's because they sell out," says Clow.

"They lose touch with their craft and try to become 'good business people.' They rationalize that they're contributing to the agency's best interest by keeping clients happy, but the only reason you're in an agency is to make great ads."

Go beyond traditional advertising—to all forms of communication: "I've always wished that we could lose the word 'advertising.' It seems incredibly limited," says Clow.

"I love all facets of communication that contribute to a company's position and value in the marketplace.

"Sometimes public relations is the tool; sometimes it's direct mail. Sometimes traditional television and magazine advertising works best.

"We do our best when we think of ourselves as communicators for our clients."

Develop promotions out of the soul of the product: Clow has a problem with most promotional marketing. "Promotions are usually just some giveaway deal concocted by some guys who can get a bunch of stuff that they can use as prizes instead of developing truly synergistic promotional ideas that complement the brand."

But Clow agrees that promotions, when done right, are definitely part of a brand. "Usually all these things are done in silos by different marketing groups with almost a provincial attitude, not wanting to do what somebody else is doing.

"It's why most brands are such a hodge-podge out there."

To overcome this, Clow expects his core teams to conceptualize in all of the ideas for a brand. "I like the lead creative teams to think in all media and not isolate it off to specialists.

"You might need a specialist to ultimately execute a direct mail campaign or a promotion, but I think the conceptualizing should be the responsibility of the core team.

"The idea that one guy just does TV commercials and doesn't have to think about the rest of it is bullshit. They have to think about all the components of a brand, and maybe what's on the Web can do more for the brand than the TV commercial."

Look for new communication avenues: "A communicator's job is to figure out the fresh, new ways to get the message across," says Clow.

"Apple introduced the Macintosh with a 60-second Super Bowl commercial. That had never been done before, but it's not a breakthrough approach anymore.

"As a matter of fact, I'm not sure the Super Bowl is even the medium it used to be because now it's so cluttered."

Postscript:

GETTING CLIENTS TO BUY INTO CREATIVE WORK

TBWA/Chiat/Day is known for producing risky, breakthrough advertising.

According to Clow, that reputation is the result of their ability to strike a balance between creative advertising and effective advertising.

"In the early days, we were a bit arrogant. Too often we thought, 'We do creative work. If you don't like it, tough.' That's a very immature, creative-boutique mentality.

"We realized that you have to strike an honest balance between wanting to do great advertising and thinking that you're an artist working for clients.

"TBWA/Chiat/Day went through a maturing process. We learned a long time ago that you can stay small and petulant and tell clients to go away if they don't like the work, or you can do special advertising that clients are as proud of as you are.

"But if an idea doesn't intimidate or scare a client a little bit, then probably it isn't good—it isn't breakthrough."

Here's how Chiat/Day gets clients to buy into those great ideas.

"The early stages of the process are when we learn our clients' opinions and gauge their comfort level. We call them strategic and creative work sessions.

"We ask our clients to spend a lot of time in the development phase of advertising. In the strategic sessions, we often come up with insights that may be different from the way they see things. We talk about it.

"After we begin to share an understanding of the approach, we start developing the advertising. In creative work sessions, we brainstorm and show a number of ideas in very rough form. We're looking for something special.

"There may be really bold ideas that are a little intimidating, but the client is assured they can really be great.

"They respond with reservations like, 'I'm really not comfortable with the spot,' and 'It's focusing on the negative side of the problem rather than the solution,' or 'I'm worried we're not showing enough of the product.'

"At other agencies, if a creative does something daring and the client gets nervous, the defense mechanisms kick in. The creative department is pressured to come up with ads that will please the client.

"The creative is told, 'You've had your shot at the solution. Now figure out what the client wants and give it to him.' The result is that the client gets advertising that's very safe and comfortable. Because when the client is happy, the account is safe. But the creative people are frustrated. You should never give in to the pressures of just being a good agency and just giving the client what he wants.

"Here, if a client doesn't like an ad, instead of putting pressure on the creative department, we try to figure out why the client didn't like it. Then we figure out what solution is still distinctive, unique, and special.

"We have to find out what the client wants, then figure out what the client needs. Then try to make the client want what is needed. In stages, they come to accept what advertising will work best for them.

"It's like being an architect. If the architect does only what the client wants, the client can end up with fairly mundane architecture. On the other hand, other people passively put their faith in the architect's talents or the architect takes total control of the project. In those cases, the architect is the only one comfortable in the house.

"In these cases, if an architect goes away for three months, comes back with a solution, and asks the clients to sign off on it, the clients may look at each other and say, 'We hate Spanish. We don't want to live in a Spanish house.'

"A successful client/agency relationship strikes a balance by understanding the people who are going to 'live in the house' and then 'building them a house' that they'll enjoy living in.

"It's building and developing the advertising together that allows clients to embrace fresh, daring ideas. They've made some contribution to the development of it. They are a part of it. That's always the best mechanism. The higher up in the company you can get to work with a client, the better—as opposed to being stuck down in some middle advertising level of the company.

"I think the turn out of 2000, all of the hype about technology, and dot-coms crashing down has put a damper on people being brave about marketing. The uncertainty of the marketplace, the lack of confidence in companies, and the concerns about what's going on in the world has been pretty much a wet blanket on everything. But I believe it will revive again.

"At some point, people will decide—and it will be the smartest companies first—that they have to go out and do some brave, aggressive stuff to make their brand vital and active in the marketplace. It goes in cycles where things get soft and conservative, then somebody does something really brave that shakes things up, and then other people decide they have to do that too.

"The good clients will always want to be stimulated and pushed by their agency and challenged with good ideas. Steve Jobs, for instance, has been very courageous and aggressive during all of this stuff. He doesn't shrink from a good idea.

"But if you look at advertising across the board, the reality is that 80, 90 percent of it is crap. That's because most clients do not have vision and passion and take a comfortable, middle-of-the-road path that doesn't scare anybody.

"You can't make a client who doesn't believe in advertising a believer. It's too hard. You have to start with somebody who has a basic belief that advertising is a very powerful, potent force. There will be 10 percent who are brave and courageous, and, in the boldest of times, 15 percent of the advertisers do brave stuff. Most advertisers aren't really that brave.

"We try and hire clients who do in fact come in and believe that advertising is very important to their brand. Then we try and stretch them a little bit further to do something that's even more daring than they thought they were going to do.

"There are culture-changing ideas that brands can grab a hold of, and that's what they want their agency to do. Then there's always a debate whether the idea is too brave or too scary. I don't think you can tell clients who don't believe to believe. I think you just have to find the more passionate and courageous people and make them your clients, and then try and challenge them a little bit further than they maybe wanted to go."

AFTERTHOUGHTS

How to Create Great Advertising

By Patrick Hanlon

This essay served as the preface for the first edition of
How to Succeed in Advertising When All You Have Is Talent.

Someone once said that advertising is the toy department of the business world.

Someone else said that advertising is the most fun you can have with your clothes on.

It's also one of the few professions where you can make as much as a doctor or lawyer and come to work in blue jeans.

But only if you are great.

To be great, you must start by writing 100 headlines.

Do 100 layouts.

Then do 100 more.

Many people have the talent to become great, but only a few have the energy.

Great advertising requires energy. You'll find that most people want to be home by five o'clock. They want to go to the bars. They want to do their laundry.

Forget it. Advertising is much better than having a social life.

Advertising is a competitive business. You must always, *always* work harder than your competition.

One writer in this book was a high school dropout. Another started out as a secretary. Other writers and art directors have been lumberjacks, ministers' sons, surfers, and the sons and daughters of people already in the business (you met a few of these people in the book). Advertising is one of the few professions that will accept anyone who can work hard, think smart, and do great work.

What more could you ask?

When Patrick Hanlon wrote this, he was Senior Vice President, Creative Director at Hal Riney & Partners/Heartland. He later went on to a senior creative position at Young & Rubicam in New York. Today he is the Founder and CEO of Thinktopia, Inc., and the author of Primal Branding, *published by Simon & Schuster/Free Press. The essay is still a good way to look at the industry.*

The Freelance Life

By Lynn Dangel

Cabbie Wisdom

Perhaps the most insightful commentary on the life of the freelancer was offered to me by a cab driver in Los Angeles.

We had just left the airport and were traveling to my hotel. I enjoy striking up conversations with local people wherever I travel, and this man was colorful and passionate about life. He asked what I did for a living, and I told him that I was a freelance writer and creative director, in town for a film shoot. He seemed surprised.

"And you're here freelancing?"

"Yes."

"And your client is paying you for this?"

"Yes."

"Well, then," he replied, with some confusion, "clearly, freelancing in Chicago means something very different than freelancing in Los Angeles."

"Really?" I asked. "What does it mean in Los Angeles?"

"Well, here, if people tell you that they're freelancing, what that really means is that they're unemployed."

"No kidding?" I say.

"No kidding. The only thing worse than freelancing is consulting."

"What does 'consulting' mean in Los Angeles?" I ask, now totally intrigued.

"If somebody tells you that he's a consultant, well, what that really means is he's been unemployed for a very long time."

What Price Freedom? The Cost of Living in the Freelance World.

In a strange way, my cab driver was absolutely right.

When you choose a freelance career, there is no job security. You are basically unemployed. In addition to turning out stellar creative work, you now have the additional job of actually getting work. And you need to get it on a regular basis. For this reason, I don't recommend freelancing for beginners in advertising. Nor do I recommend it for the weak-hearted.

In my years of working with a range of clients at several great agencies, I developed a broad range of experience and a broad base of personal contacts. To succeed in the freelance arena, you'll need both of these.

A successful freelancer must be able to turn around smart, stunning creative work, often overnight, without the advantage of long-term client rapport. While some beginners may have the ability to generate this level of creative work at lightning-speed, most need a few years to develop their chops.

In my ten years as a successful freelancer, virtually all of my work has come through personal referrals. These are people whom I have known and with whom I've worked through my many years as a senior player with FCB, O&M, JWT, McCann Erickson, Hal Riney, and Y&R. These are the people who were in the trenches with me when we worked side by side within an agency and, as a result, they now know that they can count on me in a tough situation.

Also, as a freelancer, I often need to reassess the strategic direction that a client has taken. The ability to quickly analyze a marketing objective and translate that into a creative direction is a skill that takes years to develop.

SOME BENEFITS OF WORKING IN THE FREELANCE WORLD

So, why would anybody sign up for a career that is, in essence, perpetual unemployment? After all, most people kind of like job security.

My belief is that, in this day and age, there is no real job security in advertising. The days of agencies standing loyally by their creative teams—the days of the lifer—are over. Look within any agency. While you may find one or two teams who have been on board for ten years or more, they're the exception.

In leaving my staff job to work freelance, I felt that I was trading the illusion of job security for the things that I most enjoy. I truly enjoy hands-on creative work. I like diversity. I like to collaborate with smart, talented people. And I like interesting projects. As a freelancer, I get the chance to work on a broad range of clients and accounts. In the past few years, my freelance client roster has included an awesome group of blue chip clients from American Express and AT&T to Bell South and Saturn. I've worked on credit cards, cars, blue jeans, beverages, underwear, the Olympics, the rodeo, fashion, Internet start-ups, and airlines.

Usually, agencies hire freelance talent when their own teams aren't able to solve the problem. This means that, as a freelancer, you're often brought in at the most senior levels. While this demands a high level of performance, it also tends to do away with the bureaucracy that typically comes with big, blue chip accounts. By the time an agency brings in a senior freelancer, its middle-management has already tried to solve the problem and failed. At this point, I'm usually working with a small group of senior-level decision makers or, sometimes, one key individual. I've found that this structure has helped me to turn around top-drawer creative work quickly and effortlessly. I spend less time in meetings and more time actually doing the work. It's wonderful.

The other great joy of freelancing is, of course, the freedom. I have generated award-winning campaigns from beautiful beaches, lodges, parks, and courtyards around the world. As I write this, I'm overlooking a group of oak and elm trees behind our house. Of course, I still must travel to agencies and clients on occasion. And I still need to be on-site for big meetings and production. However, most days, the hands-on work is something that I do from home. I can create a campaign while I'm making soup in my kitchen. I see it as the ultimate win/win situation. If the campaign doesn't move forward, the soup is still good.

The other great seduction of freelancing is the absolute freedom that comes with the down times. As a freelancer, you work like mad for six weeks, then you're off for three. Of course, this is only a benefit to the strong of heart and the financially settled. For some people, six weeks without work is not liberating at all, just downright frightening. However, if you're lucky enough to know that work is out there (and I've been lucky enough to have this for ten years now), then you have the luxury of regular three-week, four-week, and six-week vacations. During these stretches, your time is absolutely your own. Again, it's a double-edged sword, and I've yet to talk with a freelancer who, after week six, didn't start wondering if the phone would ever ring again. Nonetheless, if you've got the temperament for it, it's a great life.

Wishing You a Long and Happy Career

A healthy career, like any good relationship, takes a number of twists and turns over time. It changes as we do.

In my career, I deeply value my early years on staff with major agencies. I worked all the time. I learned a lot. I made great friends. I traveled the world. I was given a wealth of experience. However, I also worked incredibly long hours, and over the years, I began to feel that my work life was taking too much from my personal life. The decision to work freelance gave me both the personal time that I wanted, while working in the industry that I loved.

If you're a creative person, creativity is your lifeblood. The only unknown is what, in fact, you will ultimately apply your creativity to.

After years of being creative for some of the world's leading companies, I went on to ultimately find a way of working that has proven to be richly rewarding for me.

I invite you to create your way as well.

Over the past 20 years, Lynn has earned a reputation as a respected brand strategist, writer, and creative director.

She has received many major awards in the advertising industry including Cannes, Andy, Addy, Communication Arts, *Ads, Archive, Houston International Film Festival, Chicago International Film Festival, and the Art Director's Club of New York. She has also served as a judge in many of these and other creative competitions.*

Her ideas have contributed to a number of major brands including American Express, Bell South, DuPont, Sears, Saturn, AT&T, Motorola, Oscar Mayer, Spiegel, Citicorp, Wrangler, Lipton, and several major churches and charities throughout the United States.

As a creative director, Lynn's global experience includes overseeing advertising across Europe, Asia, North America, and South America. As a writer, her international assignments have taken her to China, Kenya, Thailand, Brazil, Guatemala, Honduras, Albania, Sweden, and Switzerland.

When she's not working, Lynn enjoys holistic medicine, cooking, her family, and her friends.

The Ultimate in Creative Marketing: Looking for a New Job

By Wendy Lalli

Everyone who has ever been through outplacement or read a how-to book on job hunting is all too aware of this truism: "Finding a job" is not only a "job," it's the ultimate exercise in self-marketing. And even those who are successful at advertising the products and services of others can find it an extremely daunting task to do the same thing for themselves. So, for veterans and newcomers alike, here's a list of marketing principles to keep in mind when trying to market that all important product—yourself.

Know Your Product

As a career coach the first question I ask people is "What do you want to do?" The second is "Why?" It's amazing how many people struggle to answer these queries. In all too many cases, the job they think they're searching for is *not* something they really *like* to do!

Another important question is "What are you really *good* at?" This may or may not be what you think you'd like to do. Before you can begin selling yourself to a potential employer, you should be crystal clear about just what you have to offer and why your "product" is superior to that of the competition. How does your previous experience—or spec work—demonstrate your superior ability to work for them? Be specific. Be honest. Be convincing.

Know Your Audience

Today, finding out about a potential employer is as easy as signing on to the Internet. Visit and thoroughly explore the company's website, read their annual report, research articles written about them during the last year. In addtion, there are also a host of research sites you can use to get objective insight about the company's financials, industry standing, and prospects for future success. If possible, talk to someone who works there to get a sense of the culture and day-to-day work ethic of the company.

When you write your resume and cover letter, try to use the same words they do in describing themselves and their mission. Define your experience in the same terms as the job requirements. In short, speak their language. Address their needs. Create a sense of relationship between you—the product—and them, your target market.

Research the Competition

Of course, you can't actually read the resumes others have submitted for the same position, but you can get a sense of what the general marketplace expects in terms of experience and salary for the job at hand. To get a realistic perspective of the required skills and salary parameters, go online to www.salary.com or www.talentzoo.com to check out the job definitions and salary ranges for specific positions within your geographical area. (After all, if the other people interviewing are asking $10,000 less than you are, they have 10,000 more chances of getting the job than you do!)

Develop a Unique Selling Proposition (USP)

What's the special benefit you offer an employer that makes you the strongest possible candidate? Perhaps it's insider product knowledge from years on the client side. Or a strong track record for innovative creative that wins awards at every turn. How about your ability to manage difficult clients and grow accounts no one else can? State your USP in the summary of qualifications that opens your resume, using terms that reflect the employer's most pressing need.

Use Synergy to Strengthen Your Message

Your cover letter, resume, portfolio, and interview presentation should all mutually reflect and enhance the selling power of each other. For example, if you mention something in your letter or resume, be prepared to cover it in depth during the interview. Also, maintaining a visual relationship between your stationary, resume, and business card is more professional than using different color paper stock for each piece.

Zig When Everyone Else Zags

If every other candidate is coming in with a CD-ROM to show their work, consider offering a CD-ROM as a leave behind and conduct the face-to-face interview as a new business pitch complete with presentation boards. Just make sure your "zigging" is appropriate to your product and target audience. For instance, in the example given above, showing your work on boards would not only offer a change from those just leaving a CD but also be an excellent demonstration of your oral presentation skills.

Integrate Your Marketing Efforts with PR

Public relations—getting newspapers, magazines, the broadcast media, and other "objective" third parties to mention your product in a favorable light—has always been a cost-effective way to advertise. The same applies to a job search—in spades! The job hunter's version of PR is networking. Getting friends, friends of friends, and friends of friends' friends to recommend you is absolutely vital to any successful job search campaign. So much so, that fully 65 percent of all jobs are gotten this way!

Ask for the Business

When you leave an interview make sure the employer, just like a potential client, knows you value the opportunity to work for them. Make it clear you want the job and ask about the next steps involved in closing the deal. Don't be pushy about it, of course. But let the interviewer know you're enthused, excited, and looking forward to the next encounter and, hopefully, an offer.

Wendy Lalli is a career coach who began her writing career as a junior copywriter at Marsteller, Inc., in New York, winning "Best Print Ad of the Year" for a McGraw-Hill campaign the first time out of the box. Less than ten years later, she was offered a partnership in a boutique agency, where she developed campaigns for products ranging from checking accounts to computer games and won 18 awards in three years.

Ten more years down the road found her pursing a new path in the marketing communications industry as a recruiter for art directors, copywriters, and production managers. Using her writing talent to create workbooks on resume writing, portfolio development, and other job search skills, she was instrumental in helping hundreds of job hunters enjoy more success when they interviewed.

Currently, she coaches private clients, does public relations and marketing campaigns for several firms, and is the career advice columnist for the Star *and the* Daily Southtown. *She also writes about career issues for the* Chicago Tribune, *the Business Marketing Association's magazine, the* Marketer, *and other leading publications.*

Bill Bernbach Is Dead

By Tom Monahan

This essay first appeared in Communication Arts *magazine in 1992 and then served as the afterword of the first edition of this book.*

I have to start by saying that I have more respect and admiration for Bill Bernbach than for anyone else in the business world.

He made the advertising industry respectable. He gave creative people status.

Tens of millions of Americans, and billions of people around the world, most of whom never heard of this ad industry Goliath, are indebted to Bill Bernbach for showing respect for them as readers and viewers and for cleaning up the media.

Bill Bernbach is Babe Ruth, Elvis, and Albert Einstein. He is Henry Ford, Picasso, and Neil Armstrong. No one has ever done, nor will likely ever do, as much for this industry I've chosen as my profession. Thank you, Mr. Bernbach. And rest in peace.

Bill Bernbach is dead.

He died many years ago. But there are too many people in our industry who, in the name of respect, won't let him pass.

I read, with great dismay, a piece in *Adweek* recently that had many of our industry's leaders ragging on the "'80s excess" and preaching a return to "traditional values" a la Bernbach. (It's kind of funny how a rebel of 30 years ago represents tradition today.)

Creative bashing has become quite fashionable. A popular way for veterans of our industry to endear themselves to the sentiments of risk-averse client types is to disassociate themselves from the "creative excess" of today's "boutique" creatives, and look to the tradition of the '60s as a time "when advertising tried harder," to quote the title of a book that romanticized that great era of 30 years ago.

Yes, the '60s can teach us a lot about advertising. But, it's not 1965 anymore. It's a different world we live in. And if we try to hold onto the past too tightly, we're going to miss the present.

"Think small" was a great, great ad. It, more than any other ad, is why I'm in this crazy business.

But, "Think small" might not work today. We'll never know. Just like we'll never know whether my boyhood idol Bob Cousy could play in the NBA of the '90s.

I returned to the home I grew up in recently. The hill in the back yard used to appear so high and so steep. We used to slide down that hill in the winter like it was Mt. Everest. Today that exact same topographic formation is barely a bump on the back lawn. But it used to be so huge. What's changed?

In *Communication Arts*, Steve Henry once wrote that having the same old players judge award shows could be causing us to perpetuate the same old standards. I couldn't agree more

In another recent issue of *Communication Arts* [August 1992] Marty Cook asked us to open our eyes and minds to the new, young talent who seem to be making a stir, and try not to judge them with our established rules. I will add my voice to this plea.

1992 is a different time than 1965. And we can't change that. Technology has made us different. Environmental consciousness has made us different. MTV has made us different. ("You don't look at rock 'n' roll, you listen to rock 'n' roll," says a voice in the back of my head. "Sorry," a more honest, aware voice says, "today, you look at rock 'n' roll, too.")

One of the great ironies of this whole "new wave creative" bashing is that a lot of the people who are criticizing the experimenters of today, and who "don't get" what these new, weird kids are trying to do, kind of forget that 30 years ago they were the experimenters whom their establishment "didn't get."

"There's a return to traditional values," the demographers have been telling us the past few years. Fine, but that doesn't mean we can turn back the clock.

Ed Sullivan just won't play today. "And now for your entertainment pleasure... Topo Gigio..." Yeah, right.

I love what the '60s did for advertising. I love what the '60s did for the world. But the times they have a changed. And those who try to preach a return to '60s Bernbachian values are just showing their age.

As for those who preach the Ogilvy values, well... sorry, but the man in the eye patch just doesn't cut it anymore. Not even close. When I hear the ranting and raving of that old man who lives in the castle in the vineyard in France... come on, who's out of touch, here?

The leaders of yesteryear were great for their time. Jerry Della Femina told us to ride the subway to get in touch. Today, one might say to watch MTV or Fox to feel the heartbeat of our culture.

Now, I'm not ready to flush everything the '60s stood for down the toilet. Some of the basic truisms still relate, but only in a '90s context.

Just like Jesse Owens' training methods might be as appropriate today as in 1936 when he was "the world's fastest human." Yet, sadly, even though his methods might still work, the great Mr. Owens couldn't place in most college track meets today. He might not even place in some high school meets.

It's a different world.

Jesse Owens is dead. Bill Bernbach is dead. And it's very dangerous to pretend otherwise.

This viewpoint might be just a tad controversial for some people. I'll add gasoline to the fire by saying, if you bristle at some of these thoughts, it only serves to prove how attached you might be to these 30-year-old ideals, and how out of touch you might be with where the world is at today And more importantly for our business, where the consumer's head is at.

I heard someone say recently that every generation thinks the music of its time was the best. My folks think swing was the best. I, of course, know that '60s rock is the best. My nephew, poor kid, thinks metal is tops.

(I wouldn't be showing my age, would I?)

When we ignore the values of youth, we start missing where our planet is heading.

The surest way for advertising to miss the future is to hold on to the present, or worse yet, the past.

Maybe the reason so many people in the business are looking back to the golden age of advertising is because there isn't a lot of true innovation today, creatively.

I might suggest that maybe there isn't much innovation, because too many of us are looking back.

To all the people in their 40s, 50s, and 60s in the ad business—remember how unhip your father was when you were growing up? Well, today, you're older than your father was back then.

Don't hold on to the past so desperately. Embrace the present. Be open to the future.

Sorry, but that's really all we have.

I love almost everything Bill Bernbach stood for. I also love bell bottoms, VW mini vans, and souped-up Pontiac GTOs. As long as they're kept in their proper perspective.

One important thing Bill Bernbach's professional life stood for was letting go of old concepts and reinventing. In a letter to the owners of Grey Advertising where he worked just before he started Doyle Dane Bernbach, Bernbach wrote that he was "worried... we're going to follow history instead of making it...." And, "We must develop our own philosophy and not have the advertising philosophy of others imposed upon us."

In another context he wrote, "For creative people, rules can be prison."

I suggest that the best way to truly keep Bill Bernbach's ideals alive is to let him rest in peace.

Amen.

Contributor's note: This piece originally appeared in a regular column I wrote for *Communication Arts*, and is reprinted here with permission. In the context of this very valuable book, this chapter serves as a punctuation.

Within these pages you get a glimpse into many great ad giants' minds. They represent many diverse styles, philosophies, opinions, ideals, convictions. In their own way, these leaders of our industry are their own Bernbachs. What they share with Bernbach and with each other is an unwavering respect for the power of creativity in advertising, or in life, for that matter.

They are followers of Bernbach. From the Bells and Graces who were so directly influenced by the great one, to the Clows and McElligotts who got the religion more indirectly.

And they are Bernbachian heretics, as well, all of them. Because you simply can't achieve any kind of greatness in the ad business unless you change the business, or add something to the business, or redirect the business, or reinvent the business, or simply break the rules of the business. Because that's what creativity is.

So, to the young people in the ad business, those whom this book is primarily designed to serve, know that Bill Bernbach is dead, know that the first violinist's chair is always open to a new tenant, and that there have been so, so many individuals who have sat in that chair at one time or another since Bernbach. Because that's the way creativity is. And that's the way the ad business is. Always looking for new ways to think and do. Always looking for new thinkers and doers.

Tom Monahan, Cofounder and Creative Director of award-winning advertising agency Leonard Monahan Lubards & Kelly, is now President and Head Creativity Coach of Before and After, Inc., a leader in the field of applied creativity in business. His clients include AT&T, VIACOM, ABC Sports, the Wall Street Journal, *McDonald's, Texas Instruments, Sears, and many others. Monahan is also the author of the book* The Do-It-Yourself Lobotomy *and is a regular contributor to* Communication Arts *magazine.*

Building a Successful Agency/Client Relationship:
What Every Beginning Creative Needs to Know

By Steve Nubie

When I was at the agency, I used to lay in bed at night and worry about clients. I never in a million years thought that when I got to the client side, I'd find myself in the situation of laying in bed and night and worrying about… the agencies. On both sides, I was concerned with improving the quality of the working relationship between "us" and "them."

After all, a client may hire an agency because of its reputation, but they keep the agency because it produces results through an effective working relationship. Believe me, there are plenty of agencies that get a foot in the door and shoot themselves in the foot not long afterward. If you think about it, there is nothing mystical or magical about how a client and an agency successfully work together. In fact, simple common sense and common courtesy are the typical benchmarks of good agency/client rapport.

Not surprisingly, they are also the benchmarks of any great partnership—whether it's between a man and a woman, two individuals starting a business, or two guys in a fishing boat.

But this doesn't just happen overnight. Trust must develop. The agency and client must learn to understand each other. And, they must appreciate the fact that they need each other. Certainly, you don't hire a supplier if you don't need one. But clearly defining that need may be the most crucial step in forming a successful agency/client relationship.

Take it back to a personal level. Think back to your first day of your first job. You were probably in your early teens—you didn't make a lot money—and the first thing you probably said to your boss was "What do you want me to do?" That is probably the clearest, best question you can ask. Why is that the last time many of us ever make that inquiry? You'd be amazed how often companies work together for years without ever addressing that simple question. They never stop and identify the needs and expectations regarding deliverables, timing, costs, desired results, and agreement to how the results will be measured. Yet these areas are typically at the root of most problems between an agency and the client.

If a client fails to define their needs and expectations or if the agency fails to meet them, the connection becomes strained. Both sides have to perform or partnership is not successful.

However, client expectations that take the form of mandates are also doomed to fail. It's true, because here's what happens: Every agency wants nothing more than for the client to be happy… to like them… to say nice things to them. It's human nature, so there is a palpable fear in the hallways when one of the clients is unhappy—for any reason. Memos appear on agency desks: "Tell the client what they want to hear." "Don't tell them anything that will get them mad." "I want 0 percent client dissatisfaction." I've seen those words in writing at every agency where I worked. So what does the agency say when confronted with this Sisyphean task? "Sure! No problem. We'll find a way." I've seen this pattern time again. The client expectations were unrealistic, and the agency didn't have the guts to tell them. In the end, dissatisfaction grows. The relationship deteriorates. And both parties suffer.

The best results are when agreements and decisions about expectations are negotiated using a clearly defined, effective process. It's simply an agreement on how we're going to work together, communicate, and manage decisions. They're called various things: Strategic Review Boards, Creative Review Committees, Creative Review Boards, Media Reviews, Business Reviews. In the end, they're simply meetings with a definite protocol and process that allows everyone to freely say what they feel is true and, most importantly, result in a decision.

A curious fact about marketing is that those decisions represent our real product. Marketing isn't about making widgets; it's about forming opinions and making decisions. You can't hold a decision up to the light and say, "Yep, looks pretty good. Just like the one we made last week." Each decision is unique, and that's why a process is so important. It's what ensures that expectations are met, needs are satisfied, and trust is built.

Trust is the most important element in any agency/client relationship. It's fair to say it's the most important element in any relationship, but with it comes a burden.

It means that the client will trust the agency to perform as promised—that they can give an agency an assignment, a budget, and a deadline and get results without constant supervision.

And, it means the agency can expect the client to stay true and consistent to their decisions and approvals, so the agency can spend their time, energy, and resources doing their job and trust that it will not be lost due to capricious change or indecision.

In the end, a small group of people determines the strength and quality of the relationship. It's the ability of the client and agency people who work together on a day-to-day basis to define expectations, encourage understanding, and develop trust that ultimately determines the success of their companies and their careers. The more those individuals interact with each other in a spirit of common courtesy and common sense, the more likely the agency/client relationship will evolve and grow with the business. This includes you. Building the agency/client relationship is your job, whether you want it or not.

Steve Nubie has the curious distinction of being one of the few creative people who have worked on both sides of the business, giving him a unique perspective on building effective agency/client relationships. He served as Department Director in Creative at McDonald's Corporation for ten years, retiring to become a consultant, writer, and teacher in 1999.

On the client side, he worked with such agencies as Leo Burnett, DDB Needham, McCann Erickson, Arnold Advertising, Fahlgren, Frankel, Del Rivero Messianu (DRM), Landor & Associates, Golin Harris, Burrell Communications Group, Burson Marstellar, CKS/Partners, Glennon, Kragie/Newell, Castor Advertising, Davis Ball & Colombato, Peck Sims Mueller, Stern Advertising, Moroch and Associates, Karsh & Hagen, Elgin Syferd, Bandy Carroll Hellige, Cossette (Montreal), and Heye & Partners (Frankfort).

Prior to working for McDonald's, he was a Creative Director/Vice President at Leo Burnett, working there for 11 years. He began his career as a copywriter for four years at J. Walter Thompson in Chicago. While on the agency side, he worked on Oscar Mayer, Gillette, Kellogg's, Schlitz, 7-UP, Jovan, Kraft, RCA, Wilson, Nestle, Procter & Gamble (various brands), Kimberly Clark, Philip Morris, Pillsbury, H. J. Heinz, and McDonald's. His comments should give you some help and direction in dealing with clients.

Radical Careering

By Sally Hogshead

The year 2002 was a low point for me personally. I struggled with tough questions about work and life. How could I control my career, instead of being controlled by it? Why was I suddenly making decisions based on fear, instead of possibility? When did work stop being fun, and start feeling like... work?

Maybe you've struggled with the same sort of questions, and if so, you know the answers aren't easy to find. I looked around, asked questions, read books, and sought advice from people I respected. But most people felt the same way I did: purposeless, discouraged, unfulfilled. Eventually, I figured out my own answers, and started reclaiming my job, my career, and my life.

Later that year, Creativity *magazine invited me to write their feature article. I wrote what I needed to read: an action plan for turbocharging momentum, attacking bigger possibilities, and getting excited about Monday mornings. I named it "Radical Careering."*

Within weeks, several hundred people from around the world wrote to me about the article, often describing their own personal struggles. Advertising Age *reprinted the article, and more people shared more inspiring stories. One guy emailed a marriage proposal (which my husband suggested I decline).*

A few months later I left my job as Creative Director at CP+B in L.A., and took a six-month sabbatical. I focused on two personal areas:

First, the birth of our daughter, Azalea.

And second, a book that was released in 2005. It's titled Radical Careering: 100 Truths to Jumpstart Your Job, Your Career, and Your Life.

(Incidentally, delivering a baby requires less pain medication than birthing a book.)

Is your career kicking you in the nuts? Kick back.

There are creatives who are thrilled with each of the dozens of spots they've produced this year, who just got a big fat raise, and are catapulting towards world domination. Both of them are kindly requested to skip to page 41. I'm talking to the rest of us.

This article is about radical careering. It's about refusing mediocrity. It's about doing everything possible, even reinventing your portfolio if necessary, to have a job you love. What it's definitely not about is maintaining the status quo or getting home in time to watch *Blind Date*.

So what exactly is radical careering? It's the relentless dedication to having exactly the job you want. No matter how daunting it might seem, or how discouraged you might feel. You always have the power to revolutionize your career. At any stage, at any agency, in any economy. And with that power comes a significant responsibility: being accountable for your own success. You have the portfolio you've earned.

Of course there are some outstanding exceptions to my observations below, so in the interest of avoiding caveats, feel free to consider yourself one of them.

Radical truth #1: Being in a crap job isn't your fault. Staying in a crap job is. I can already hear the chorus shouting that it's cruel to be making such grand statements about long-term goals during a time when so many people are just trying to survive in their jobs. But here's the thing. Being demoralized is not the same as being disempowered. Even if you're in a job that you loathe, you're not without options.

See where I'm going? Radical careering is about reclaiming your life.

Most of us build brands for a living, but have no idea where we ourselves are going. What exactly is your brand? Who are you as a creative person? Where do you ultimately want to be? Only when you figure it out can you construct the steps to get there. About 18 months ago I decided on an absurdly specific goal: to open a West Coast office for an internationally respected agency. I didn't tell anyone except my husband. A few weeks later, Alex Bogusky asked me to dinner to talk about opening the new CP+B office in L.A. Freaky karma, yeah, but not necessarily a coincidence.

Moving on. This next one's painful... get a leather strap to bite down on.

Radical truth #2: If your agency sucks, your ads will probably suck. Even a creative who's enormously talented and hard-working is still only a tiny fraction of the overall team. Coming up with great ideas is easy compared to selling them, and that takes a brilliant collection of account people, planners, and so on. Doing truly outstanding work requires that everyone, from the CFO to the client, prioritizes the creative over everything. Including in some cases the bottom line.

Of course, there's nothing wrong with being at an agency that's not creatively driven... unless you're committed to producing great creative. In which case, you and the company do not share the same goals. You're an artisan in a widget factory.

Radical truth #3: **Almost no one's having fun in advertising right now**. Creatives I talk to at every level, even at top shops, seem discouraged. The collective self-esteem is low. In a sense, I think this trend is heartening. If you're not having fun, it's not because you're doing anything wrong, that's just the weather report. Nothing personal. When the weather changes, your experience will probably change too.

Radical truth #4: Be ready to get laid off at any point. I'm not talking about being paranoid, just keeping your eye on long-term goals. The novelist Anna Quindlen wrote, "Think of life as a terminal illness because if you do you will live it with joy and passion as it ought to be lived." I find that incredibly inspiring. Your job is one stop on a journey, not a sofa to hang out on with a remote control and bag of chips. Figure out where you want to be next and then do something to move towards that every single day.

But back to that paranoid thing for a second. Signals that you may be asked to leave: If you're not included in meetings. If you're given only low-profile assignments. If you're pigeonholed on one medium (like radio or print) or genre (like humor or long copy). If you're not able to look back over the past six or twelve months and see progress. If there's a pink slip in your mailbox.

Radical truth #5: Agencies do not "turn themselves around." The quality of creative is part of a company's DNA. The culture, work ethic, day-to-day operations, even the physical office space, all of it defines the creative that the agency produces. A shiny new logo can't change it. A big speech can't change it. Philosophically, it's at the molecular level.

When I was at Fallon years ago, every computer started up with the same message: "To be the premier creative agency in the world with a short list of blue-chip clients." I still remember that mission statement by heart. The mailroom guy, the traffic managers, the receptionist, everyone was aligned around one purpose.

So. If a CD tries to hire you by saying "we're about to start doing award-winning work," I'm not saying you shouldn't accept the job. Just don't accept because they're about to start doing award-winning work.

Radical truth #6: Never let the size of your mortgage get bigger than the quality of your work. It's dangerously short-sighted to drive your career decisions by your cost of living. Money follows great work, not the other way around.

Radical truth #6B: You only get to sell-out once. Bide your time wisely. Do it in your 20s and you can make an extra $10,000. Do it in your 40s or 50s, and you can retire early.

Radical truth #7: Aspire to be the dumbest person in the room. Working with smart people is the mac daddy. The end-all and be-all. What to do if you're surrounded by myopic clients, apathetic co-workers, or wussy management? Find motivating people to partner with. Experiment with all kinds of styles. Read books by industry stars for insight. Get feedback on your work from people outside your office, even sending it to creatives whose work you respect. Constantly evolve your book. Then scram before you become a flabby midlevel drone.

Note to Human Resources: An agency's most crucial equity is its people. Not just for warm 'n' fuzzy reasons, but in terms of training investment and intellectual property and replacement expenses and morale and client consistency. Most people quit their jobs not because they hate their work, but because they either dislike their boss, or because they feel under-appreciated. On the flipside, most firings are not because of poor performance, but bad chemistry.

Radical truth #8: Stick your portfolio with a cattleprod. Never let your portfolio get lazy. When it's time to change jobs, your body of work counts a lot more than your batting average on the company softball team. Doing great work isn't just about collecting a glittery shelf of awards, it's about earning more control over your career, and more options for your life. It's currency, literally and figuratively. I've heard that every One Show pencil adds at least 20 grand to your price tag.

What to do if you're struggling to produce great work? Find under-the-radar assignments that people aren't really paying attention to. Develop cool projects for existing clients. Or, create as many opportunities as you can outside your job. Do a bunch of genius pieces and try to get them produced for cheap. Show spec in your book as long as you're honest about it. Constantly upgrade your thinking. Then parlay that into your next job ASAFP. A copywriter named Robin Fitzgerald used to work at Bozell in Omaha, and invented all kinds of work from scratch. Now she's here, and she's the most exceptional new talent I've ever seen.

Here's an analogy. Your career is like a tree. In order to pick the fruit, you need to continually add fertilizer. If all you do is pick fruit, eventually you'll go hungry.

Radical truth #9: Don't use cheesy analogies when writing an article. Okay, duly noted.

Radical truth #10: Friday afternoon beers won't boost morale. In a creative department, morale is directly linked to the quality of work people are currently producing. Lame work leads to insecurity, which leads to politics, which leads to serious distraction from doing great work.

Of course, the creative director is the one driving that process. A feeble CD won't have the courage to support brave ideas. A good CD will push your career by creating an environment in which you'll produce your best ideas. And a truly outstanding CD? He'll be able to keep you by offering you something you can't get anywhere else: the possibility of more of your best ideas.

Radical truth #11: You are not done paying your dues. Neither am I. We never will be. Mediocrity is tenacious; the second you stop fighting it, you become one of those lurking middle-aged cronies who brags about writing the Wesson tagline.

Chuck McBride, the North America Creative Director of TBWA\Chiat\Day, told me something ten years ago that's always stuck with me: "Doing great work is all about getting as many at-bats as you can." It's a statistical fact that the more assignments you have and the more options you create, the more likely you are to produce great work. If you're lucky, you draw up 100 ideas internally for every 20 that go to the client. You present 20 to the client for every 5 that get produced. You produce 5 decent ideas for every 1 that's great. If you're lucky.

Radical truth #12: This is the ideal time to accelerate your career. While the industry is stalling, crank the afterburners on. Use this time to become a smarter employee, build a stronger web of people to support you, and attack undiscovered projects.

My first job was as a baby writer at Wieden in Philadelphia. When they lost Subaru, the closing was announced before I'd even unpacked, and it seemed like my timing couldn't be worse. But Izzy DeBellis, now Creative Director at Berlin Cameron/Red Cell, said, "There's always opportunity in chaos." It was true in that situation, because I got assignments that I otherwise would have been too junior for, and it's true in chaotic times like these. When uncertainty overthrows the usual structure of hierarchy and bureaucracy, you can pounce on openings that normally wouldn't be possible.

Harry Cocciolo, Creative Director at Goodby Silverstein & Partners, recently commented, "Smart agencies and smart creatives don't waste time worrying about how hard the world is, they look at the landscape as an opportunity and they get back to work."

Radical truth #13: Jump, and a net will appear. This expression probably came from a fortune cookie somewhere, but I've repeated this to myself many a time. You can't be successful when you cling to obsolete situations out of fear. Only when you put yourself out there wholeheartedly can the best opportunities present themselves. Five years back, when Jean Robaire and I opened Robaire and Hogshead, we were about to sign the lease. I was nervous because the monthly payment was more than my mortgage. Jean told me something that I'll never forget: "Remember this feeling, because in order to be successful you'll have to get used to it. This is risk."

So when is it time to think about jumping? If you loathe the idea of going to work in the morning. If you're more focused on surviving than flourishing. If you've traded the goal of doing your best work for the goal of making the client happy. If you've lost faith in the people you work with. If you've lost respect for the company. If you've lost confidence in yourself. If you've stolen a closet full of office supplies and they're on to you.

Radical truth #14: It's never too late to reinvent your career. Or even re-start it, like my friend Stephen Curry did when he left his job as an ACD in Atlanta to become a junior writer for better work. Now that, my friends, is radical careering. It's not easy, and it might require a pay cut, but I've seen it work many times. I once watched a book go from pathetic to meteoric in literally three months, and the writer got hired immediately at Fallon.

Consider this. Statistically, 50 percent of creatives are below average. Making your book even a measly 10 percent better can take you from a B+ to an A+. You can do that.

Radical truth #15: Quality of work, quality of life, or quality of compensation. Pick one. Maybe two. Is your priority to do internationally award-winning work? Or to go home at 5 p.m.? Or to have a wheelbarrow of stock options? They're all valid choices, but no job gives you all three, at least not now. Being happy in your job is all about finding a company whose priorities are in line with yours.

Radical truth #16: That being said, nothing's more important than balance. Me, I struggle with this one every day. It's not easy being a mother and a creative director. But I'm learning. Advertising is an extreme sport; it requires so much focus on the next pitch, the next presentation, the next whatever, that it's essential to make sure short-term deadlines don't eclipse the bigger picture. A job that makes you fulfilled and proud is just one part of being a happy person. I hope that in some way, radical careering can help you create a career, and a life, that you love.

Good luck and godspeed. And when you kick back, I recommend steel-toed boots.

Further Reading

Read if you want to write.
Or even art direct.

That line sticks in my mind. I think I stole it. But it contains a truth—you should be well read if you want to succeed in the industry. It trains your gut. It increases your options. And it gives you more to talk about when your colleagues are gathered around the bar after a hard week at work.

But what should you read?

Everything. You should immerse yourself in popular culture. Read all kinds of books and magazines. Likewise, you should also see as many movies and plays as possible. And listen to all kinds of music. As Lee Clow pointed out, anytime you gain a deeper understanding of any form of communications, you become a better advertising creative.

You should also pay attention to all kinds of publications about advertising. You may later decide to ignore them (many are easy to ignore), but it always helps to know what is being said, who is saying it, and why he or she is saying it. To get started, you may wish to review these:

MAGAZINES

Advertising Age
711 Third Avenue
New York, NY 10017
www.adage.com

Adweek
BPI Communications
1515 Broadway Avenue
New York, NY 10036
www.adweek.com

CMYK Magazine
150 West 76th Street, #5B
New York, NY 10023
www.cmykmag.com

Communication Arts (CA)
Coyne & Blanchard, Inc.
410 Sherman Avenue
Palo Alto, CA 94306
www.commarts.com

Creativity
Crain Communications
711 Third Avenue
New York, NY 10017
www.adcritic.com

Luerzer's Archive
American Showcase
915 Broadway Avenue
New York, NY 10010
www.luerzersarchive.com

One. A Magazine
The One Club
21 East 26th Street, 5th Floor
New York, NY 10010
www.oneclub.org

US AD Review
Visual Reference Publications
302 Fifth Avenue
New York, NY 1001
www.usadreview.com

WEBSITES

New websites are being launched daily, but here are a few that should get you started:

- adbuzz.com
- adcritic.com
- adjab.com
- adrants.com
- adsoftheworld.com
- adverbox.com
- advertisingforpeanuts.blogspot.com
- agencycompile.com
- frederiksamuel.com/blog
- ihaveanidea.com
- printcritic.com
- talentzoo.com

ADVERTISING ANNUALS

There are many awards shows and awards annuals in advertising. Read as many of them as possible. At least the latest ones. The three annuals probably most often mentioned by the people featured in this book—and probably the easiest to find—are:

Communication Arts Advertising Annual (the December issue of their magazine)
Coyne & Blanchard, Inc.
410 Sherman Avenue
Palo Alto, CA 94306
www.commarts.com
(CA also publishes annuals in design, photography, illustration, and interactive.)

Art Directors Annual
The Art Directors Club
106 West 29th Street
New York, NY 10001
212-643-1440
www.adcglobal.org
The annual is published by RotoVision SA in Switzerland.

The One Show Annual
One Show Publishing
The One Club
21 East 26th Street, 5th Floor
New York, NY 10010
212-979-1900
www.oneclub.org

BOOKS

Aitchison, Jim, *Cutting Edge Advertising II: How to Create the World's Best Print for the 21st Century*, New Jersey: Prentice Hall, 2004.

————, *Cutting Edge Radio: How to Create the World's Best Radio Ads for the 21st Century*, New Jersey: Prentice Hall, 2003.

————, *Cutting Edge Commercials: How to Create the World's Best TV Ads for the 21st Century*, New Jersey: Prentice Hall, 2001.

Arden, Paul, *It's Not How Good You Are, It's How Good You Want To Be*, London: Phaidon, 2003.

Barletta, Martha, *Marketing to Women: How to Understand, Reach, and Increase Your Share of the World's Largest Market Segment 2nd Edition*, Chicago: Dearborn Trade Publishing, 2006.

Bendinger, Bruce, *The Copy Workshop Workbook 3rd Edition (Really New Edition),* Chicago: The Copy Workshop, 2002.

Berger, Warren, *Advertising Today*, London: Phaidon, 2004.

Bolles, Richard Nelson, *What Color is Your Parachute: A Practical Manual for Job Hunters and Career Changers*, Berkeley, CA: Ten Speed Press, published annually.

Caples, John (Revised by Fred Hahn), *Tested Advertising Methods 5th Edition*, Paramus, NJ: Prentice Hall, 1997.

Cialdini, Robert, *Influence 4th Edition*, Needham Heights, MA: Allyn & Bacon, 2001.

Crispin Porter + Bogusky (text by Warren Berger), *Hoopla*, New York: powerHouse Books, 2006.

Crow, David, *Visible Signs: An Introduction to Semiotics*, Switzerland: AVA Publishing SA, 2003.

The Designers and Art Directors of the United Kingdom, *The Copy Book: How 32 of the World's Best Advertising Writers Write Their Advertising*, Switzerland: RotoVision SA, 1995.

Dru, Jean-Marie, *Disruption: Overturning Conventions and Shaking Up the Marketplace,* New York: An Adweek Book – John Wiley and Sons, 1997.

Duffy, Joe, *Brand Apart: Insights on the Art of Creating a Distinctive Brand Voice*, New York: One Club Publishing, 2005.

Dzamic, Lazar, *No-Copy Advertising*, Switzerland: RotoVision SA, 2001.

Fisher, Roger, William Ury, and Bruce Patton, *Getting to Yes: Negotiating Agreement Without Giving In 2nd Edition*, New York: Penguin Books, 1991.

Fortini-Campbell, Lisa, *Hitting the Sweet Spot: How Consumer Insight Can Inspire Better Marketing and Advertising*, Chicago: The Copy Workshop, 2001.

Gladwell, Malcom, *Blink: The Power of Thinking Without Thinking,* New York: Little, Brown and Company, 2005.

————, *The Tipping Point: How Little Things Can Make a Big Difference*, New York: Little, Brown and Company, 2000.

Goldberg, Natalie, *Writing Down the Bones: Freeing the Writer Within*, Boston: Shambhala, 1986.

Gossage, Howard Luck, *The Book of Gossage*, Chicago: The Copy Workshop, 2006.

Hanlon, Patrick, *Primal Branding: Create Zealots for Your Brand, Your Company, and Your Future*, New York: Free Press, 2006.

Higgins, Denis, *The Art of Writing Advertising: Conversations with Masters of the Craft (David Ogilvy, William Bernbach, Leo Burnett, Rosser Reeves)*, New York: McGraw-Hill, 2003.

Hogshead, Sally, *Radical Careering: 100 Truths to Jumpstart Your Job, Your Career, and Your Life*, New York: Gotham Books, 2005.

Johnson, Michael, *Problem Solved: A Primer in Design and Communication*, London: Phaidon, 2002.

Kaplan, Morton H., *When You Speak, Do They Listen: A Sixty-Minute Guide to Public Speaking and Persuasive Presentations*, Chicago: Columbia College Chicago, 2005.

Kessler, Stephan, *Chiat/Day: The First Twenty Years*, New York: Rizzoli, 1990.

Kirchenbaum, Richard and Jonathon Bond, *Under the Radar: Talking to Today's Cynical Consumer*, New York: Adweek Books – John Wiley & Sons, 1998.

Klein, Naomi, *No Logo: Taking Aim at the Brand Bullies*, New York: Picador USA, 1999.

Lamott, Anne, *Bird by Bird: Some Instructions in Writing and Life*, New York: Pantheon, 1994.

Landau, Robin, *Advertising by Design: Creating Visual Communication with Graphic Impact,* New York: John Wiley & Sons, 2004.

———, *Designing Brand Experiences*, Clifton Park, NJ: Thomson Delmar Learning, 2006.

Levinson, Bob, *Bill Bernbach's Book*, New York: Villard Books, 1987.

Lidwell, William, Kristina Holden, and Jill Butler, *Universal Principles of Design: 100 Ways to Enhance Usability, Influence Perception, Increase Appeal, Make Better Design Decisions, and Teach Through Design*, Gloucester, MA: Rockport Publishers, 2003.

Lorin, Philippe, *5 Giants of Advertising*, New York: Assouline, 2001.

MacKenzie, Gordon, *Orbiting the Giant Hairball: A Corporate Fool's Guide to Surviving with Grace*, New York: Viking, 1996.

Mayer, Martin, *Madison Avenue U.S.A.*, Lincolnwood, IL: NTC Business Books, 1992.

———, *Whatever Happened to Madison Avenue?* New York: Little, Brown and Company, 1991.

Monahan, Tom, *The Do-It-Yourself Lobotomy: Open Your Mind to Greater Creative Thinking*, New York: Adweek Books – John Wiley & Sons, 2002.

Myerson, Jeremy, *Rewind: Forty Years of Design & Advertising*, London: Phaidon Press, 2002.

Oakner, Larry, *And Now a Few Laughs from Our Sponsor: The Best of Fifty Years of Radio Commercials*, New York: Adweek Books – John Wiley & Sons, 2002.

Ogilvy, David, *Confessions of an Advertising Man*, New York: Atheneum, 1985.

————, *Ogilvy on Advertising*, New York: Vintage Books, 1983.

————, *The Unpublished David Ogilvy*, edited by Joel Raphaelson, New York: Crown Publishers, Inc., 1986.

Paetro, Maxine, *How To Put Your Book Together and Get a Job in Advertising, 21ˢᵗ Century Edition*, Chicago: The Copy Workshop, 2002.

Peppers, Don, *Life's a Pitch: Then You Buy*, New York: Doubleday, 1995.

Peterson, Bryan L., *Design Basics for Creative Results*, Cincinnati, OH: HOW Design Books, 2003.

Pricken, Mario, *Creative Advertising: Ideas and Techniques from the World's Best Campaigns*, New York: Thames and Hudson, 2004.

Purvis, Scott C. and Philip Ward Burton, *Which Ad Pulled Best, 9ᵗʰ Edition,* New York: McGraw-Hill/Irwin, 2002. (Be sure to purchase the Answer Key along with the book.)

Reeves, Rosser. *Reality in Advertising*, New York: Alfred A. Knopf, 1961.

Richards, Stan, *The Peaceable Kingdom: Building a Company Without Factionism, Fiefdoms, Fear and Other Staples of Modern Business*, New York: Adweek Books – John Wiley & Sons, 2001.

Ries, Al and Jack Trout, *Positioning: The Battle for Your Mind, 20ᵗʰ Anniversary Edition*, New York: McGraw-Hill, 2001.

Roberts, Kevin, *Lovemarks: The Future Beyond Brands*, New York: powerHouse Books, 2004.

Roman, Kenneth and Jane Maas (with Martin Nisenholtz), *How to Advertise: Building Brands and Business in the New Marketing World*, New York: Thomas Dunne Books, 2003.

Schultz, Don and Heidi Schultz, *Brand Babble: Sense and Nonsense About Branding*, Mason, OH: Thomson South-Western, 2004.

Schultz, Don E., Stanley I. Tannenbaum, and Robert F. Lauterborn, *Integrated Marketing Communications: Putting It Together & Making It Work*, New York: McGraw-Hill, 1993.

Schmetterer, Bob, *Leap: A Revolution in Creative Business Strategy*, New York: Adweek Books – John Wiley & Sons, 2003.

Sharp, Bill, *How to be Black and Get a Job in the Advertising Agency Business Anyway*, Atlanta: Sharp Advertising, 1969.

Soloman, Robert, *The Art of Client Service*, Chicago: Dearborn, 2003.

Spence, Edward and Brett Van Heekeren, *Advertising Ethics*, Upper Saddle River, NJ: Pearson Education, 2005.

Steel, John, *Truth, Lies, and Advertising: The Art of Account Planning*, New York: Adweek Books – John Wiley & Sons, 1998.

Strunk, William, Jr. and E. B. White, *The Elements of Style Fourth Edition*, White Plains, NY: Longman, 2000.

Sullivan, Luke, *Hey, Whipple, Squeeze This: A Guide to Creating Great Ads Second Edition,* New York: Adweek Books – John Wiley & Sons, 2003.

Kaplan Thaler, Linda, Robin Koval, with Delia Marshall, *Bang: Getting Your Message Heard in a Noisy World*, New York: Currency Doubleday, 2003.

Twitchell, James, *Adcult USA: The Triumph of Advertising in American Culture*, New York: Columbia University Press, 1996.

————, *Twenty Ads that Shook the World*, New York: Three Rivers Press, 2000.

Underhill, Paco, *Why We Buy: The Science of Shopping*, New York, Simon & Schuster, 1999.

Vonk, Nancy and Janet Kestin, *Pick Me: Breaking Into Advertising and Staying There*, New York: Adweek Books – John Wiley & Sons, 2005.

Wells, Mary, *A Big Life (in Advertising)*, New York: Alfred A. Knopf, 2002.

Wells, William D., *Planning for ROI: Effective Advertising Strategy*, Englewood Cliffs, NJ: Prentice Hall, 1989.

Wilde, Judith and Richard Wilde, *Visual Literacy: A Conceptual Approach to Graphic Problem Solving*, New York: Watson-Guptill Publications, 1991.

Williams, Tim, *Take a Stand for Your Brand: Building a Great Agency from the Inside Out*, Chicago: The Copy Workshop, 2005.

Wunderman, Lester, *Being Direct: Making Advertising Pay*, New York: Random House, 1996.

Young, James Webb, *A Technique for Producing Ideas*, New York: McGraw-Hill, 2003.

Zinsser, William, *On Writing Well, 30th Anniversary: The Classic Guide to Writing Nonfiction*, New York: HarperCollins, 2006.

Acknowledgments

While it's been said that it takes a village to raise a child, it's also true of creating a book. In one way or another, each of the following people helped me realize my goal. I want to personally thank each one.

First of all, I want to thank Bruce Bendinger for seeing the possibilities in updating and expanding the original concept, Pat Aylward for helping me make this second edition even better than the first, and Lorelei Bendinger, Eugenia Velazquez, and the rest of the Copy Workshop team for their enthusiasm, support, and great sales and marketing ideas. And, since people are known to judge a book by its cover (at least initially), I want to thank Mark Ingraham for creating such an attractive "billboard" for my book; I truly believe it captures the spirit of the contents.

Of course, thanks to Ted Bell, Alex Bogusky, Tom Burrell, Lee Clow, Don Easdon, Amil Gargano, Susan Gillette, Roy Grace, Steve Hayden, Susan Hoffman, Mike Hughes, Linda Kaplan Thaler, Mike Koelker, Ed McCabe, Tom McElligott, Nancy Rice, Stan Richards, and Rich Silverstein for allowing me to share the story of their lives and a bit of their sage advice (this book would truly not have been possible without their willingness to inspire the next generation), Lynn Dangel, Patrick Hanlon, Sally Hogshead, Wendy Lalli, Tom Monahan, and Steve Nubie for donating their essays, and Maxine Paetro and Luke Sullivan for giving their time, support, and kind words.

I also wish to thank: Warick Carter, Steven Kopelke, Doreen Bartoni, Alton Miller, Margaret Sullivan, Tom Hamilton, and Herbert Allen of Columbia College Chicago for creating the supportive atmosphere that enabled me to complete this manuscript and to Steve Cartozian of Revalour for championing the call for innovation.

Plus, a big thanks to my co-author from the first edition, Emily Calvo, for agreeing to allow me to continue the franchise without her participation.

In addition, thanks to the following individuals for their help and support with either the first or second edition of *How to Succeed in Advertising When All You Have is Talent*: Shanita Akintonde, David Alabach, Richard Alexander, Sandra Allen, Joan Andrew, Michele Barker, Nina Bertoncini, Bob Boyer, Mary Brackin, Christy Calvo, Kevin Christophersen, Leslie Cole, Nancy Cuttito, Leigh Donaldson, Jeffrey Epstein, Kim Fouch, Phil Gayter, Dave Gordon, Matt Green, Janice Grube, Rich Hagle, Lynn Hazan, Evita Hoffmann, Hildy Hoppenstand, Jean Howe, Wayne

Johnson, Thomas Kemeny, Anne Knudsen, Elise Langan, Keri Lannigan, Jackie Lenigan, Heidi Lilli, Gerald Linda, Debbie MacKaman, Carol Madonna, Kim Maher, Jean Mamola, Fran Marzano, Kristen McCoy, Sherlene McCoy, Diane Mercier, John Moore, Richard Needham, Veronica Padilla, Wally Peterson, Alan Rado, Cindy Rowe, Nick Savastio, Kristin Scott, Jeanette Settino, Janice Sgrignoli, Karen Shaw, Bill Sharp, Jodie Skerritt; Nicholas Smith, Brian Sternthal, Bob Strassman, Phyllis Stroup, Mike Swidler, Mike Tardif, Gregory Thornton, Trig Van de Heider, Lynne Van der Sitt, Helen Vennard, Nerissa Villamaria, Sandy Wade, Margot Wallace, Mary Warlick, Karen Wenzel, Rebecca Willis, Cornell Wright, and Ellen Young.

Most of all, I wish to thank my wife, Rhonda, and my daughter, Jorie, for their support, encouragement, understanding, and acceptance of a large pile of notes in our home office.

About the Author

Laurence Minsky is one of Chicago's well-known creative professionals. He is a creative consultant and a professor in the Marketing Communication Department of the School of Media Arts at Columbia College Chicago.

His broad experience as a Creative Director/Writer includes work in brand and promotional advertising, interactive and guerrilla marketing, and new product development. He has worked full-time for such top agencies as Frankel and the Marketing Store Worldwide, freelanced for 141 Worldwide, Draft Worldwide, and more than 25 other agencies, and has created communication solutions for many blue chip clients, including Bay Valley Foods, Frito-Lay, Kraft, McDonald's (on an international, national, and regional level), Motorola, PETsMART, United Airlines, and the United States Postal Service.

The co-author of the first edition of *How to Succeed in Advertising When All You Have is Talent* and *25 Words or Less*, Minsky is also a frequent guest speaker at professional meetings and universities. He has been quoted in such leading print media as the *New York Times* and *Chicago Tribune* and interviewed on TV and radio talk shows across the country.

An award-winning creative, Minsky has also judged marketing communication award shows and is a member of the One Club for Art and Copy, the In-Store Marketing Institute, the Authors Guild, and the American Academy of Advertising. He holds a BA in psychology, *magna cum laude*, from Lawrence University in Appleton, Wisconsin. He lives with his wife, Rhonda, and his daughter, Jorie, in Evanston, Illinois.